Lecture Notes in Computer Science 8365

Commenced Publication in 1973
Founding and Former Series Editors:
Gerhard Goos, Juris Hartmanis, and Jan van Leeuwen

T0211868

Zhenfu Cao   Fangguo Zhang (Eds.)

Pairing-Based Cryptography – Pairing 2013

6th International Conference
Beijing, China, November 22-24, 2013
Revised Selected Papers

 Springer

Volume Editors

Zhenfu Cao
Shanghai Jiao Tong University
School of Electronic Information and Electrical Engineering
No. 800, Dongchuan Road, Shanghai 200240, China
E-mail: zfcao@cs.sjtu.edu.cn

Fangguo Zhang
Sun Yat-sen University
School of Information Science and Technology
No. 135, Xingang Xi Road, Guangzhou 510275, China
E-mail: isszhfg@mail.sysu.edu.cn

ISSN 0302-9743   e-ISSN 1611-3349
ISBN 978-3-319-04872-7   e-ISBN 978-3-319-04873-4
DOI 10.1007/978-3-319-04873-4
Springer Cham Heidelberg New York Dordrecht London

Library of Congress Control Number: 2014930884

CR Subject Classification (1998): E.3, K.6.5, D.4.6, E.4, F.2.0, I.1

LNCS Sublibrary: SL 4 – Security and Cryptology

Typesetting: Camera-ready by author, data conversion by Scientific Publishing Services, Chennai, India

Printed on acid-free paper

Springer is part of Springer Science+Business Media (www.springer.com)

Preface

The 6th International Conference on Pairing-Based Cryptography (Pairing 2013) was held in Beijing, China, during November 22–24, 2013. The conference was organized by the Information Security Center of Beijing University of Posts and Telecommunications (BUPT) and the Chinese Association for Cryptologic Research (CACR). The general chairs of the conference were Yixian Yang and Xuejia Lai, and secretarial support was provided by Min Lei from Beijing University of Posts and Telecommunications. We thank both Yixian Yang and Xuejia Lai for their constant efforts and for making this conference possible.

The goal of Pairing 2013 was to bring together leading researchers and practitioners from academia and industry, all concerned with problems related to pairing-based cryptography. We hope that this conference enhanced communication among specialists from various research areas and promoted creative interdisciplinary collaboration.

The conference received 59 submissions from 15 countries, out of which 14 papers from 10 countries were accepted for publication in these proceedings. At least three Program Committee (PC) members reviewed each submitted paper, while submissions co-authored by a PC member were submitted to the more stringent evaluation of five PC members. In addition to the PC members, many external reviewers joined the review process in their particular areas of expertise. We were fortunate to have this energetic team of experts, and are deeply grateful to all of them for their hard work, which included a very active discussion phase.

Furthermore, the conference featured three invited speakers: Pierrick Gaudry from LORIA, France, Francisco Rodriguez-Henriquez from CINVESTAV-IPN, Mexico, and Xu Maozhi from Peking University, China, whose lectures on cutting-edge research areas — "Computing Discrete Logarithms in Finite Fields of Small Characteristic," "Implementing Pairing-Based Protocols," and "Using Endomorphisms to Accelerate Scalar Multiplication," respectively — contributed in a significant part to the richness of the program. In addition, the program included tutorial talks by Robert H. Deng form Singapore Management University and Peter Schwabe from Radboud University Nijmegen, The Netherlands.

Finally, we thank all the authors who submitted papers to this conference, the Organizing Committee members, colleagues, and student helpers for their valuable time and effort, and all the conference attendees who made this event a truly intellectually stimulating one through their active participation.

November 2013
Zhenfu Cao
Fangguo Zhang

Organization

Honorary Chair

Dingyi Pei   Guangzhou University

General Chairs

Yixian Yang   Beijing University of Posts and
Telecommunications
Xuejia Lai   Shanghai Jiao Tong University

Technical Program Committee Co-chairs

Zhenfu Cao   Shanghai Jiao Tong University
Fangguo Zhang   Sun Yat-sen University

Organizing Committee

Qun Luo   Beijing University of Posts and
Telecommunications
Licheng Wang   Beijing University of Posts and
Telecommunications

Organizing Secretary

Min Lei   Beijing University of Posts and
Telecommunications

Technical Program Committee

Diego Aranha   University of Brasília, Brazil
Paulo S.L.M. Barreto   University of São Paulo, Brazil
Liqun Chen   Hewlett-Packard Laboratories, UK
Xiaofeng Chen   Xidian University, China
Jérémie Detrey   Inria, France
Xiaolei Dong   Shanghai Jiao Tong University, China
Sylvain Duquesne   Université Rennes, France
Junfeng Fan   K.U. Leuven, Belgium
Dario Fiore   MPI-SWS, Germany
Steven Galbraith   University of Auckland, New Zealand
Sorina Ionica   ENS Paris, France

Kwangjo Kim   KAIST, Korea
Tanja Lange   Technische Universiteit Eindhoven,
                              The Netherlands
Jin Li   Guangzhou Universtiy, China
Shengli Liu   Shanghai Jiao Tong University, China
Sarah Meiklejohn   University of California, USA
Atsuko Miyaji   JAIST, Japan
Takeshi Okamoto   University of Tsukuba, Japan
Haifeng Qian   East China Normal University, China
Jacob Schuldt   Royal Holloway, UK
Peter Schwabe   Academia Sinica, Taiwan
Michael Scott   Certivox Ltd., UK
Jun Shao   Zhejiang Gongshang University, China
Alice Silverberg   U.C. Irvine, USA
Tsuyoshi Takagi   Kyushu University, Japan
Katsuyuki Takashima   Mitsubishi Electric, Japan
Mehdi Tibouchi   NIT Secure Platform Laboratories, Japan
Damien Vergnaud   École Normale Supérieur, France
Baocang Wang   Xidian University, China
Lihua Wang   NICT, Japan
Jian Weng   Jinan University, China
Zhenfeng Zhang   Chinese Academy of Sciences, China
Chang-An Zhao   Sun Yat-sen University, China

External Reviewers

Razvan Barbulescu   Tao Jiang
Daniel J. Bernstein   Naoki Kanayama
Olivier Blazy   Yutaka Kawai
Angelo De Caro   Thorsten Kleinjung
Jie Chen   Liang Liu
Shan Chen   Francois Morain
Craig Costello   Michael Naehrig
Keita Emura   Takashi Nishide
Emmanuel Fouotsa   Baodong Qin
Yuichi Futa   Elizabeth Quaglia
Martin Gagne   Chunhua Su
Chaowen Guan   Satoru Tanaka
Aurore Guillevic   Christophe Tran
Shuai Han   Jianfeng Wang
Mitsuhiro Hattori   Hongfeng Wu
Kenichiro Hayasaka   Shota Yamada
Takuya Hayashi   Takanori Yasuda
Kai He
Zhengan Huang

Table of Contents

EAGL: An Elliptic Curve Arithmetic GPU-Based Library for Bilinear Pairing

Shi Pu and Jyh-Charn Liu

Department of Computer Science and Engineering, Texas A&M University,
TAMU 3112, College Station TX 77843-3112, USA
{shipu,liu}@cse.tamu.edu

Abstract. In this paper we present the *Elliptic curve Arithmetic GPU-based Library* (EAGL), a self-contained GPU library, to support parallel computing of bilinear pairings based on the *Compute Unified Device Architecture* (CUDA) programming model. It implements parallelized point arithmetic, arithmetic functions in the 1-2-4-12 tower of extension fields. EAGL takes full advantage of the parallel processing power of GPU, with no shared memory bank conflict and minimal synchronization and global memory accesses, to compute some most expensive computational steps, especially the conventional-Montgomery-based multi-precision multiplications. At the 128-bit security level, EAGL can perform 3350.9 *R-ate* pairings/sec on one GTX-680 controlled by one CPU thread. Extensive experiments suggest that performance tradeoffs between utilization of GPU pipeline vs. memory access latency are highly complex for parallelization of pairing computations. Overall, on-chip memory is the main performance bottleneck for pairing computations on the tested GPU device, and the lazy reduction in $\mathbb{F}_{q^2}$ gives the best performance. Increasing the size of on-chip memory, together with caching and memory prefetching modules are expected to offer substantial performance improvement for GPU-based pairing computations.

Keywords: Bilinear Pairing, Elliptic Curve Cryptography, CUDA.

1 Introduction

Bilinear pairings are useful for a broad range of secure applications, such as key agreement [29,65], identity-based encryption [19,63] and signature [50,59], short signature verification [17,34,43], privacy preserving verification [64], and secret handshake [24]. In addition to guaranteed security properties, computing throughput, and/or response time are also important consideration to bring pairings to real world applications. For instance, in the intelligent car system concept [53], vehicles within 110 meters needed to verify each other's BLS short signatures every 300ms for safety messages exchanges. Some of pairing-based protocols, e.g., secret handshake (SH), are well suited for decentralized Internet scale applications, provided that its computing needs can meet the performance requirements. In a recent study [51], the notion of privacy-preserving cloud service was proposed. A privacy-preserving cloud service provider (CSP) uses a

Z. Cao and F. Zhang (Eds.): Pairing 2013, LNCS 8365, pp. 1–19, 2014.

third-party SH server to authenticate requests from its customers. Both high throughput and low response time are required for the SH server to serve bursts of access requests in an emergency response situation.

Continual increase of the core count in the multi-core processor architecture will offer much needed computing resources for pairings [3,15,47,49]. In the meantime, the GPU architecture is also being deployed, e.g., the 256-GPU cluster [6], and the 960-GPU cluster *Jaguar* in the Oak Ridge National Lab, for large scale applications including cryptographic computations. Unlike many other applications that were effectively accelerated by the massive parallel processing power of GPU, some recent studies on GPU-based *elliptic curve cryptographic* (ECC) point multiplication [2,14,61] and pairings [35,66] reported inferior performances than their multi-core counterparts. Our paper is motivated to understand the relationship between computational structures of pairings and the *single instruction multi-thread* (SIMT) parallel execution model of GPU. Following the *Compute Unified Device Architecture* (CUDA) programming model, the *Elliptic curve Arithmetic GPU-based Library* (EAGL) parallelizes Miller's algorithm [54] for the *R-ate* pairing [40] at the 128-bit security level, and its correctness was validated by MIRACL [46]. Using EAGL as a benchmarking tool, we identify major performance bottlenecks among myriad design factors for pairings on the GTX-680 device, e.g., the GPU-based fast/slow memory configuration for intermediate results of pairings, GPU pipeline utilization, and proper use of the state-of-the-art pairing optimization techniques.

In terms of performance comparison, a single core of an Intel Core i7-4700MQ (2.4GHz) was able to run 2051 pairings/sec [47]. On the other hand, EAGL running on a GTX-680 can compute 1408 *R-ate* pairings in 420.19 ms (3350.9 pairings/sec as the amortized throughput), roughly 40% of the benchmark reported in [47] if [47] applied on all four cores of their CPU with a perfect acceleration model. With GPU as its co-processor for the pairing computation, CPU can instead perform other complex computation and business logic. To enable the research community to keep up with the technology evolution, and expand EAGL to support the new curve family [52], which is not included in the current release due to the extensive efforts required to rewrite its lazy-reduction-related parts for the cross verification of EAGL, EAGL is being released as an open source project. For security considerations of EAGL, we assume that the server that controls GPU cards is subject to malicious attacks, and therefore only *public* computations should be considered for the utilization of EAGL on the server site. For instance, in the health-care cloud scenario [51], the two inputs of a pairing operation on the server are a public key and an encrypted private key. Both inputs are public and hence can be computed on a server without privacy concern.

Main optimization techniques applied in EAGL include: (1) the type D sextic twist [57] of the Barreto-Naehrig (BN) curve over $\mathbb{F}_{q^2}$; (2) a low hamming weight BN curve [23]; (3) the denominator elimination [54], and optimization of the final exponentiation on BN curves [23,56]; (4) Karatsuba multiplication for multiplication in $\mathbb{F}_{q^{12}}$, Chung-Hasan SQR_3 [21] for squaring in $\mathbb{F}_{q^{12}}$; (5) the compressed squaring in the final exponentiation [58]; and for arithmetic of unitary elements in $\mathbb{F}_{q^{12}}$, we applied the fast squaring for elements in $\mathbb{F}_{q^4}$ [60] and Granger-Scott fast squaring [32] in $\mathbb{F}_{q^{12}}$; (6) the general lazy reduction scheme [3] in extension fields $\mathbb{F}_{q^2}$, $\mathbb{F}_{q^4}$ and $\mathbb{F}_{q^{12}}$, and we empirically applied lazy reduction in $\mathbb{F}_{q^2}$ to achieve the best performance.

1.1 Background Knowledge of GPU

In the CUDA programming model, one *host* CPU thread is used to control one *device* GPU, and a unit of task, named as the *kernel function*, is issued by the host to the GPU device. Our target platform GTX-680 is a GK-104 device ("K" means Kepler), which contains 8 *streaming multiprocessors* (SMX). Each SMX can concurrently run 32 *GPU threads* (known as a *warp*) per clock. Following the SIMT architecture, each GPU thread runs one instance of the kernel function. A warp may be preempted when it is stalled due to memory access delay, and the scheduler may switch the runtime context to another available warp. As such, multiple warps of threads are usually assigned to one SMX for better utilization of the pipeline of each SMX. These warps are called one *thread block*. Each SMX could access 64KB fast *shared memory*/L1 cache and 64K 32-bit *registers*. The shared memory of one SMX is organized into 32 64-bit *banks*. All SMXs share 2GB 256-bit wide slow *global memory*, cached R-ONLY *texture memory* and cached R-ONLY *constant memory*.

The rest of this paper is organized as follows. Section 2 introduces the related work. Section 3 briefly discusses Miller's algorithm and then presents our computing model with some preliminary benchmarks. Evaluation of the general lazy reduction scheme and tuning of memory parameters are presented in Section 4. The performance comparison with existing CPU/GPU-based solutions, our discussion and conclusion are in Section 5 and 6.

2 Related Work

Elliptic curves over finite fields can be divided into two types: *supersingular* (SS) curves, and ordinary (non-supersingular) curves. For their simplicity and ease of modular multiplication, SS curves have been proposed to construct pairing-based cryptographic protocols. For computational efficiency and security, SS curves have limitation on the potential values of the embedding degree k, and are usually applied in the finite field of small characteristic [7]. For example [1,23] set the characteristic as 3 when the embedding degree $k = 6$. Implementing characteristic 3-based computation on GPU leads to either higher memory cost, or more complicated logic and thus less suitable for parallelization [35]. Therefore, we only consider ordinary curves.

One major approach for reducing the computational cost of bilinear pairings is decreasing the length of Miller Loop in Miller's algorithm. [10] extended the Duursma-Lee method [25] to supersingular abelian varieties using the η_T pairing. The *Ate* pairing on hyperelliptic curves [31], the twisted *Ate* pairing [33,44] and its variation Ate_i pairing [67] on ordinary curves reduced the loop length to $r^{1/\varphi(k)}$ [33], where r is a large prime satisfying $r|\#E(\mathbb{F}_q)$. An *optimal Ate* pairing [62] was able to attain the loop length to its lower bound. The *R-ate* pairing [40] obtained even shorter loop length than [31] on certain pairing-friendly elliptic curves. Other efforts [5,18,54,55,56] worked on arithmetic optimization, such as denominator elimination, final exponentiation simplification, faster variants of Miller's algorithm under Jacobian [18] or Edwards co-ordinates [13], and efficient formulas for various curves with twists of degree 2, 3, 4 or 6 [22].

Another major acceleration approach is optimizing arithmetic operations in extension fields. [15] presented a software library of the optimal *Ate* pairing on a BN curve over a 254-bit prime field, and they could run one pairing operation in 2.33M cycles on a single core of an Intel Core i7 CPU (2.8GHz). To utilize optimized instructions sets, [49] represented one element in $\mathbb{F}_q$ as a vector of double-precision floating points (DPF), and computed modular arithmetic in the SIMT architecture. As such, it ran an instance of the optimal *Ate* pairing in 4.38M cycles on one core of an Intel Core 2 Quad Q9550 processor (2.83GHz). By introducing optimized cyclotomic subgroups and the generalized lazy reduction optimization technique, [3] ran one pairing operation in 1.562M cycles on AMD Phenom II and 1.688M cycles on a single core of an Intel Core i5 CPU. A recent work [47] showed that, by using the *mulx* instruction of the Haswell architecture, it could run one pairing operation in 1.17M cycles on a single core of an Intel i7-4700MQ CPU (2.4GHz). These implementations were at the 128-bit security level. Another recent work [4] presented that running one *Ate* pairing operation at the 192-bit security level needed 19M cycles on a single core of an Intel i5 CPU. In 2012, [52] proposed a subclass of BN curves that had better computational efficiency.

[2,14,61] pioneered implementation of elliptic curve point arithmetic on CUDA. [2] implemented point multiplication under the *Residue Number System* (RNS), and another work [20], also adopted RNS and implemented the *Ate* pairing on FGPA. [66] implemented the *Tate* pairing whose elliptic-curve group had composite order, and [35] the η_T pairing in characteristic 3 on CUDA. Both papers did not implement the parallel reduction function due to its complexity. In our *CI-2thread* and *CI-4thread* models, we implement both serial [48] and parallel versions of the reduction function and evaluate which version fits GTX-680 better. Moreover, both papers did not parallelize the final exponentiation (FE), which has almost the same cost as Miller Loop (ML) (see proof in Table 2 of [15]). EAGL supports both FE and ML, and also provides exponentiation of an element in $\mathbb{F}_{q^{12}}$ for applications that need to run additional exponentiation operations of the result of the pairing computation.

3   Computing Models of Miller's Algorithm

In this paper, the standard state-of-the-art optimization techniques are considered to target the 128-bit security level. This mainly involves computing the optimal *R-ate* pairing [40] on the low-hamming weight Barreto-Naehrig (BN) curves [11], towered extension [12], and the general lazy reduction scheme in [3].

In the form of $y^2 = x^3 + b$, BN curves [11] are ordinary elliptic curves defined over $\mathbb{F}_q$. Given the construction parameter u, the trace of Frobenius over $\mathbb{F}_q$ $t(u)$ = $6u^2 + 1$, the modulus $q(u) = 36u^4 + 36u^3 + 24u^2 + 6u + 1$, the prime order $n(u) = 36u^4 + 36u^3 + 18u^2 + 6u + 1$. In this paper, $u = -(2^{62} + 2^{55} + 1)$ and the embedding degree $k = 12$, and hence the pairing computation achieves the 128-bit security level [11]. Because the embedding degree k equals 12, ML and FE need to run arithmetic in the extension field $\mathbb{F}_{q^{12}}$, which is usually implemented as *a tower of extension fields* [54]. According to [12,26], k is in a format of $2^i 3^j$ with $i \geq 1, j \geq 0$. Following the conclusion in [12], and for the cross verification of our system with MIRACL [46], the tower of 1-2-4-12 is selected.

Let $\mathbb{F}_q$ be a finite field with the modulus q, $E/\mathbb{K}$ an elliptic curve E over a field $\mathbb{K}$, $E[r]$ the group of all r-torsion points of E, and $E(\mathbb{K})[r]$ the $\mathbb{K}$-rational group of r-torsion points of E over a field $\mathbb{K}$, π_q the q-power Frobenius endomorphism on $E(\mathbb{F}_q)$, the R-ate pairing is defined as a mapping $\mathbb{G}_2 \times \mathbb{G}_1 \to \mathbb{G}_T$, where $\mathbb{G}_1 = E(\mathbb{F}_q)[r]$, $\mathbb{G}_2 = E(\mathbb{F}_{q^k})[r] \bigcap Ker(\pi_q - [q])$ and $\mathbb{G}_T = \mathbb{F}^*_{q^k}/(\mathbb{F}^*_{q^k})^r$. The computation can also be represented as $Ra(Q,P) = (f \cdot (f \cdot l_{aQ,Q}(P))^q \cdot l_{\pi(aQ+Q),aQ}(P))^{(q^k-1)/r}$, where $P \in \mathbb{G}_1$, $Q \in \mathbb{G}_2$, $a = 6u + 2$, $f = f_{a,Q}(P)$ and $l_{aQ,Q}$ is the line function [54] through the points aQ and Q. The rational function $f_{i,P}$ is calculated based on the property $f_{i+j,P} = f_{i,P} \cdot f_{j,P} \cdot l_{iP,jP}$, where $l_{iP,jP}$ is the line function. Computing $f_{i+j,P}$ involves addition/subtraction/multiplication operations in $\mathbb{F}_{q^{12}}$. We refer readers to [40] for details of the R-ate pairing.

Table 1. Computing latencies of three arithmetic operations with INT32 or SPF operands on GTX-680

Instructions	INT32 A+B	SPF A+B	INT32 A×B	SPF A×B	INT32 A×B+C	SPF A×B+C
Latencies (ms)	0.0308	0.012	0.0326	0.011	0.0114	0.0117

Our first problem is whether we should follow [14] to utilize GPU's single-precision floating point (SPF) instructions for ECC arithmetic. The SPF implementation on GK104 is IEEE compliant, where each 32-bit SPF has a 23-bit significand. In [14], a 224-bit integer was converted to an array of 24 SPFs and each 10-bit segment of the original integer was stored by a 32-bit SPF. Although using 10-bit of the 23-bit significand can avoid the round-off problem, only 1/3 of the on-chip memory is utilized in this representation, which either reduces the degree of parallelism or triggers a large number of slow off-chip memory hits. As we will discuss in the last section, the primary performance bottleneck of the pairing computation on GTX-680 is the limited on-chip memory of GPU. And hence, any trade-offs related to on-chip resources need to be carefully evaluated. To understand the efficiency of integer arithmetic and SPF arithmetic on GTX-680, as shown in Table 1, we evaluate the computing latencies of an addition, a multiplication, and a multiplication with an addition (also known as fused M+A or FMA), with either INT32s or SPFs as their operands, where INT32 means 32-bit integers. Table 1 shows that, an addition or a multiplication with SPF operands, is roughly 3 times faster than its INT32 counterpart.

But for an FMA, the two versions have similar latencies, which is different from elder generation GPU devices used in [14]. In the end, an INT32 array is adopted to store a 256-bit variable due to the following reasons: first, as we will show later, the main operation of the multi-precision multiplication, which is the most expensive multi-precision arithmetic function for pairings, is the FMA operation; and an FMA with INT32s and that with SPFs have similar latencies. Second, one slow memory access is hundreds times more expensive than one SPF/INT32 arithmetic instruction on GPU. As such, the on-chip memory should be fully utilized to minimize the slow memory accesses. As a side note, we do not consider the representation in [49] because the throughput of DPF is 1/24 of that of SPF on GTX-680.

Previous studies on parallel pairings were mainly based on either the conventional *Montgomery* [48] or *Residue Number System-based* (RNS) *Montgomery*. The former aims to optimize $c = a \times b \mod q$ to a multiplication step $T = a \times b$ following by a reduction step $reduction(T)$. On the other hand, based on the *Chinese Remainder Theorem* (CRT), RNS decomposes a modulus M to n co-prime integers $(m_1, ..., m_n)$, then an arbitrary integer $X < M$ has a unique representation $x_i = X \mod m_i, 1 < i < n, M = \prod_{i=1}^{n} m_i$. The independency among computation in mod m_i makes RNS well suited for parallelization. However, RNS-based integers cannot be directly used in a prime field since M is not prime, unless two extra Base Extension (BE) steps [8] are inserted in the reduction step. As such, an $a[n] \times b[n] \mod q$ in RNS needs $2n^2 + 5n$ 32-bit multiplication (denoted by MUL) by using four threads [2], while its conventional-Montgomery-based counterpart needs $2n^2 + n$ MUL by using one thread. The other two extra overheads are from the synchronization for the complicated RNS-based comparison in a reduction or a modular subtraction, and potential branch divergences, where parallel threads need to sequentially run branches of computing logic in SIMT, in an RNS-based modular subtraction. Such synchronization overhead grows as more threads are set to compute one instance of the RNS-based arithmetic. As concluded in [20], their parallel RNS-based computing model worked better than a (serial) conventional-Montgomery-based model for a long addition sequence of modular multiplication $(a \times b + c \times d + ... \mod q)$. The length of such sequences is closely related to the extension field being used by the lazy reduction. We will discuss adoption of RNS for general lazy reduction policies [3] in the next section. In this section, we quantitatively evaluate the performance of the conventional-Montgomery-based computing models.

To evaluate parallel computing model candidates, we select $c = a \times b \mod q$ in the base field $\mathbb{F}_q$ as the representative code segment since it's the most expensive modular arithmetic function in $\mathbb{F}_q$. $c = a \times b \mod q$ is composed of (1) $T = a \times b$ and (2) $c = reduction(T)$. In terms of memory requirement for running a pairing on the selected BN curve, each of the modulus q, elements a, b and c needs one **uint32[8]** array ("**u**" means **unsigned**), and T one **uint32[16]** array. To parallelize the conventional-Montgomery-based $c = a \times b \mod q$, firstly we note that the step $T = a \times b$ consists of multiple independent sequences of FMA operations, mapping them to multiple threads is similar to mapping the computation

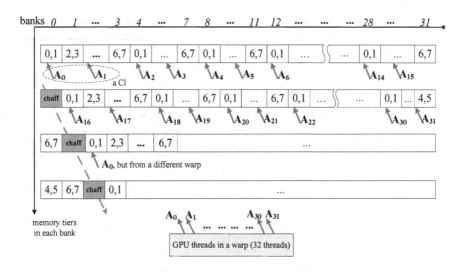

Fig. 1. Collision-free memory access of a 256-bit variable (*CI-2thread* model)

under different residues of RNS to multiple threads. Secondly, because the reduction step *reduction(T)* includes two multi-precision multiplications and one addition, parallelizing *reduction(T)* can re-use the parallelization method of $T = a \times b$. Next, we discuss four parallel model candidates for computing $a \times b$ mod q: *CI-1/2/4/8thread* models, where each *computing instance* (CI) is run by 1/2/4/8 cooperative thread(s). We focus on eliminating shared memory access conflicts, race conditions and workload balance among threads in the same CI.

Next, we consider the problem of optimal placement of an element of $\mathbb{F}_q$ in the shared memory of a GK104 GPU, which has 32 64-bit shared memory banks. An element of $\mathbb{F}_q$ is defined as `__shared__ uint32[8×BLK_CI_SIZE]`, where BLK_CI_SIZE is the number of CIs per block. In the *CI-2thread* model, each two threads access the same **uint32**$[8i + 0, 8i + 7], 0 \leq i < $ BLK_CI_SIZE. As such, threads {0,16}, {2,18}, ..., {12,28}, {14,30} are allowed to concurrently read the eight **uint32**[0]s, which is a typical access pattern in multi-precision arithmetic, but only 1/2 of the physical concurrency can be realized because threads 0 and 16 access different ties (a low-level GPU memory architecture) of bank 0 and thus they compete for the memory interface. This is also known as the "bank conflict". Because each SMX (in GK-104) has 32 LD/ST units, we only need to consider bank conflicts within a warp of threads.

Taking the *CI-2thread* model as an example, to remove such bank conflicts, as shown in Figure 1, we fill a strip of 64-bit *chaff spacers* in the front of every eighth **uint32**[8]. The chaff spacer in the 3rd row of Figure 1 is to simplify locating the start addresses. After inserting the chaff spacers, threads 0 and 16 read bank 0 and 1 respectively when they are reading the **uint32**[0]s associated with their CIs. As such, this type of bank conflict is removed. We also append spacers to ensure the address of each variable in the shared memory always starts from bank 0.

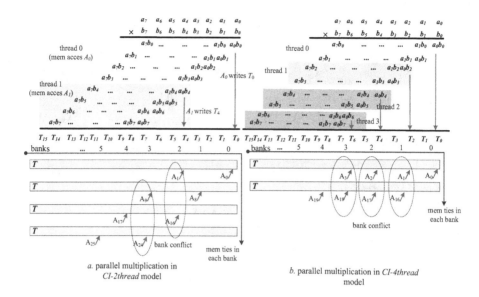

Fig. 2. Parallel multi-precision multiplication

$T[16] = a[8] \times b[8]$ can be considered as eight sequences of $T[x] = a[i] \times b[j] = 0 \sim 7], i \in [0, 7], x = i+j$ respectively. Considering the overflow effect in $a[i] \times b[j]$ and in the accumulation of $T[x]$, each sequence would be composed of FMA and addition operations $T[x] = $ (low 32-bit)$(a[i] \times b[j] = 0, 1,..., 7] + T[x] + carry)$, and $carry = $ (high 32-bit)$(a[i] \times b[j] = 0, 1,..., 7] + T[x] + carry)$ if $j > 0$. Therefore, the inter-dependency among sequences is the reading/writing (R/W) of $T[0\text{-}15]$. If each $T[0\text{-}15]$ array in the shared memory is partitioned into multiple segments with a constant size, each segment is mapped to one thread, and the constant offset i of each thread is large enough, then there is no race condition on R/W of $T[0\text{-}15]$. Considering that the bank width (of GK104 GPU) is 64-bit, which means $T[x]$ and $T[x+1]$ are in the same bank if x is even, the size of the segment should be at least one bank width. It also implies the infeasibility of the $CI\text{-}8thread$ model where two neighboring threads in one CI would simultaneously read and write the same bank respectively, and thus cause the inter-CI bank conflict. As a result, the parallel $T[16] = a[8] \times b[8]$ in the $CI\text{-}2/4thread$ models are designed as shown in Figure 2. It is evident that threads in the same CI, or across different CIs do not meet any bank conflict when computing $a[i] \times b[j] = 0 \sim 7]$ in the current execution order.

However, on GK104 GPUs, we observe a new type of the across-CI bank conflicts when threads sum the multiplication results and write back to T, as shown in Figure 2. Comparing with earlier GPU architectures, the bank width of GK104 grows from 32-bit to 64-bit, that is, $T[0\text{-}15]$ are stored denser in GK104 GPUs than in earlier generations of GPUs. As such, two segments of T with different start offsets and associated with different CIs may be placed on the same bank. We show one example in Figure 2, in the $CI\text{-}2thread$ model, threads

{0,1}, {8,9}, {16,17}, {24,25} for four CIs are writing results $T_0 = a_0 \times b_0$ and $T_4 = a_0 \times b_4$ back to the shared memory, the banks of T_0 and T_4 for the four CIs are {0,2}, {1,3}, {2,4}, {3,5}. In this example, threads 1 and 16 are competing for bank 2. To eliminate this type of bank conflict, 12 registers are used to temporarily save the multiplication results of $T_0 - T_{11}$ or $T_4 - T_{15}$ for each thread, and then a serial step is employed to accumulate results of two threads. NVIDIA profiling tool is used to validate our optimization schemes.

Theoretically, $a[n] \times b[n]$ ($n = 8$) in the CI-$2thread$ model costs $n^2/2$ MUL, which is the same as computing it in the RNS-based model with two threads for each instance. Taking into account the synchronization overhead for bank conflict elimination, the actual cost of $a[n] \times b[n]$ is slightly above $n^2/2$ MUL. On the other hand, elimination of this type of bank conflict is also necessary if an RNS-based $T[2n]$ is consecutively placed in the shared memory, and thus switching to RNS would not bring obvious extra gain for multi-precision multiplication. (An alternative, which saves an RNS-based $T[2n]$ as n separate variables in the shared memory, would avoid this bank conflict. But this option will grossly complicate the code structure of low level multi-precision arithmetic functions, especially the division function, and make the library difficult to expand to other precision numbers).

In [48], $reduction(T = a \times b)$ for multi-precision integers a, b, T was serially optimized as an iterative loop, where the dependency across iterations impeded the parallelization [35,66]. To parallelize the reduction function, the CI-$2thread$ model and the CI-$4thread$ model adopt the single-precision version in [48], which includes two parallelized multiplications (1) $m = (T \bmod R) \times q' \bmod R$, and (2) $m \times q$, and one parallel addition $T + mq$, where $R \times R^{-1} - q \times q' = 1$ and $R = 2^{256}$. Because the first multiplication only needs results in the low-256-bit half, it costs 56% of FMAs of a complete multi-precision multiplication. We skip the implementation detail of parallel $reduction(T)$ because it is similar to the parallel $T = a \times b$.

Next, we compare the combination of parallel multiplication $T = a \times b$ plus serial/parallel $reduction(T)$ (denoted by S-/P-$reduct$) in the CI-$1/2/4thread$ model on GTX-680. The degrees of parallelism of GPU in the CI-$1/2/4thread$ models are 160/352/738 GPU threads per block, equivalent to 160/176/184 CIs per block. Furthermore, when computing $T + m \times q$, the parallel version of $reduction(T)$ reads T from the global memory. Optimality of these configuration parameters will be discussed later. Table 2 lists the execution times of multiplication and $reduction(T)$ in these three models. In this experiment, 11938 times of multi-precision multiplication and 8312 times of reduction are executed, which

Table 2. Performance of 11938 multiplications + 8312 reductions in various thread counts per instance

models	$T = a \times b$	S-$reduct$	P-$reduct$	best mul+reduct	threads per SMX	throughput(/sec)
CI-$1thread$	57.87ms	39.95ms	N/A	97.82ms	160	13085.3
CI-$2thread$	39.40ms	36.71ms	48.73ms	76.11ms	352	18499.5
CI-$4thread$	28.58ms	51.64ms	83.59ms	80.22ms	738	18349.5

are simulations of these two functions in one complete *R-ate* pairing. The last column presents the amortized throughput.

Several conclusions can be drawn based on Table 2: (1) parallelization of $T = a \times b$ works, but the gain from parallelization shrinks as the thread count per instance increases. The reason is that increasing the thread count per instance also introduces more synchronization overhead for accumulating $T[i]$ in registers. (2) When the shared memory usage per CI is bisected into two threads, the increase of thread number per SMX is usually greater than doubling. Due to the limit of placing complete warps into each SMX, a large shared memory usage per thread usually results in poor utilization of the shared memory. As each thread consumes less shared memory, it is possible to put more complete warps into each SMX to make full use of the available shared memory. Therefore, as observed in the *CI-2thread* model, although the execution time is not reduced by half by using doubled threads per CI, it is still possible to have a higher throughput gain due to a higher resource utilization rate. (3) The serial reduction in the *CI-2thread* model is slightly faster than that in the *CI-1thread* model, possibly due to an outlier of the micro-architecture behavior. (4) In the *CI-2thread* model, the parallel reduction is much slower than its serial counterpart. The breakdown of execution time shows that computing $m = (T \bmod R) \times q' \bmod R$ and $m \times q$ took 43% execution time of the parallel reduction, the remaining time is spent in the addition $T + m \times q$ because the T in this addition is a copy stored in the global memory. Since computing addition operations is very cheap, $48.73 \text{ms} \times 43\% = 21 \text{ms}$ would be the true execution time of 8312 parallel reductions if all variables are in the shared memory. With the selected configuration parameters, the shared memory of GTX-680 cannot fit two 512-bit caches for the reduction, where one is used by $m \times q$ and the other stores the original value of T. As such, $T + mq$ stores its T in the slow memory because it only needs to read T once. According to Table 2, EAGL adopts the *CI-2thread* model for parallel multi-precision arithmetic functions.

4   Optimization for Extension Fields-Based Arithmetic

Applying the lazy reduction scheme to higher extension fields such as $\mathbb{F}_{q^6}$ and $\mathbb{F}_{q^{12}}$ was proposed in [3]. With this lazy reduction scheme, the number of reductions is reduced to 12 for a modular multiplication in $\mathbb{F}_{q^{12}}$. Lazy reductions usually reduce the execution time on CPU architectures, but this is not always the case for GPU architectures. Delaying reductions to the highest extension field ($\mathbb{F}_{q^{12}}$) requires doubling of the memory space for each variable in all arithmetic operations in lower extension fields. The first option to double the memory space for each CI is assigning it more shared memory, but this choice is at cost of decreased degree of parallelism. The alternative is to use the (much slower) global memory to meet the additional memory need, without changing the original shared memory usage per CI.

To assess the performance of these two options, we first select the modular multiplication in $\mathbb{F}_{q^4}$ as the code segment, and apply the general lazy reduction

Table 3. Performance of 1000 modular multiplications in the fourth extension field

optimization choices	execution time	threads per SMX	smem per CI	throughput (/sec)
lazy reduction in $\mathbb{F}_{q^2}$	265.4ms	352	256 Bytes	5313×10^3
lazy reduction in $\mathbb{F}_{q^4}$	301.8ms	352	256 Bytes	4662×10^3
prefetch+lazy reduction in $\mathbb{F}_{q^4}$	304.7ms	352	256 Bytes	4617×10^3
lazy reduction in $\mathbb{F}_{q^4}$	233.7ms	224	320 Bytes	3829×10^3
lazy reduction in $\mathbb{F}_{q^4}$	225.2ms	224	384 Bytes	3982×10^3

scheme to $\mathbb{F}_{q^2}$ and $\mathbb{F}_{q^4}$ respectively, following the algorithms and options for subtractions proposed in [3]. As listed in Table 3, in this experiment, we repeat 1000 modular multiplications in $\mathbb{F}_{q^4}$ with different shared memory usages per CI.

Execution times shown in rows 1 and 2 of Table 3 suggest that the performance of running less reductions is worse than that of the one needing more reductions, because of the slow global memory accesses. We further tested the software prefetching [39] from the global memory to L2 cache, but no noticeable performance gain was observed, because the *prefetching for next warp* policy at programming time is not guaranteed to make a positive hit at run time. Rows 2, 4, and 5 in Table 3 illustrate some marginal improvement of execution time, when more shared memory is allocated to each CI. The execution gain is only marginal because the temporary variable usage of EAGL is already optimized for spatial and temporal locality, so that little benefit can be further gained with additional shared memory. Increasing the shared memory size per CI leads to significant drop of throughput due to the reduced degree of parallelism. A quick complexity analysis on implementing the lazy reduction in $\mathbb{F}_{q^{12}}$ suggests a sharp increase of the size of temporary variables in the global memory as compared to the case of $\mathbb{F}_{q^4}$. The performance overhead is deemed to be too high for GK104 GPUs to be useful. In summary, despite the reduced computational complexities in $\mathbb{F}_{q^4}$ and $\mathbb{F}_{q^{12}}$, $\mathbb{F}_{q^2}$ is best suited for GK104 GPUs to achieve the best throughput in our tests.

As discussed in last section, the efficiency of RNS and conventional Montgomery systems for low-level multi-precision multiplication and reduction functions depends on which extension field the lazy reduction policy is used in. As aforementioned, running an RNS-based multi-precision multiplication with 2 threads, or the same operation in the *CI-2thread* model, have similar complexity ($n^2/2$ MUL plus the synchronization overhead). Although [20] mentioned that a serial RNS-based reduction costs $2n^2 + 3n$ MUL, this cost can be further reduced by parallelizing the base extension (BE). Details of advanced BE parallelization are beyond the scope of this paper. In brief, the two matrix multiplication operations, as the main part of BE, can be equally balanced on the two threads [9], and thus the cost of an RNS-based reduction would be $n^2 + 3n$ MUL, which is close to the case in the *CI-2thread* model. Therefore, given the same lazy reduction policy, the gains of the RNS-based model and our *CI-2thread* model from the lazy reduction are similar. Moreover, the RNS-based reduction needs extra memory for saving matrices in BE, which can produce more global memory accesses and thus slow down the pairing computation.

By summarizing the usage of temporary variables of EAGL's point and field arithmetic functions involved in the pairing computation, it is found that the most frequently accessed temporary variables are four elements in $\mathbb{F}_{q^2}$ per CI, a total of 256 bytes, while the overhead for chaff spacers and bank alignment is negligible. Next, we adjust the shared memory (smem) usage per CI from 192-byte to 384-byte, stepped by one element in $\mathbb{F}_{q^2}$ (64-byte), and observe the fluctuation of throughput of pairings. When the usage becomes 320-byte, we also implement a version with parallel $reduction(\text{T})$, where T of $T+mq$ can be accommodated in the shared memory. Results are shown in Table 4.

Table 4. Throughput fluctuation of pairings on a GTX-680

smem usage per CI (bytes)	192	256	320	320 (parallel reduction)	384
gpu thread per block	480	352	224	224	224
smem utilization	93.6%	91.7%	79.1%	79.1%	87.5%
throughput (pairings/sec)	2926	3350.9	2077	2564.6	2861

Table 4 first illustrates that the peak throughput occurs when each CI caches four elements in $\mathbb{F}_{q^2}$ in the shared memory. Secondly, it shows the trade-off between memory-accessing latency vs. pipeline utilization rate of each SMX. Less shared memory per CI means more visits to the global memory, and also more threads per block. Without a clear guidance for an optimal configuration rule, we gradually tune the shared memory usage per CI to find the peak point of throughput. When the shared memory usage per CI equals 320-byte, the shared memory usage utilization rate is fairly poor due to the limitation that only complete warps of threads should be assigned to each SMX. As the shared memory usage grows to 384-byte, the negative effect of worse pipeline utilization begins to negate the benefit of more fast memory hits. As such, trying even larger shared memory usages is unnecessary.

5   Discussion of GPU and CPU Based Pairing Computations

The performance of EAGL is obtained when its degree of parallelism is set at 8 SMX×352 threads = 1408. The computing latency of 1408 $R\text{-}ate$ pairings by using EAGL on a GTX680 is 420.19ms, and the amortized throughput is 3350.9 pairings/sec or 0.298sec/pairing. First, as illustrated in Table 5, we compare EAGL with other GPU-based implementations in the literature [35,66]. Here the throughput of the η_T pairing at the 128-bit security level is 254 pairings/sec, or 3.94ms/pairing, on one Tesla C2050 card [35]. Taking into account that GTX-680 has roughly three times more peak GFLOPS than M2050/C2050, EAGL is almost 4.4 times faster than [35]. We include the results of [66], which achieved 23.8ms/pairing, as reference in this study. However, it is difficult to make a quantified comparison between the two implementations due to the significant difference between the composite-order and the prime-order pairings.

Table 5. A comparison of execution times for GPU-based implementations

Implementations	Algorithm	Curve Type	Security	Exec time(ms)
EAGL on a GTX-680	R-ate,prime order	ordinary	128 bits	0.298
[66] on an M2050	$Tate$,composite order	ordinary	80 bits	23.8
[35] on a C2050	η_T pairing	supersingular	128 bits	3.94

Next, we compare EAGL with existing CPU-based pairing solutions [3,15,47,49], where all the performance results were based on a single CPU core by their authors. Our objectives are two-fold. The first is comparing the throughput of implementations on contemporary hardware. Furthermore, we aim to gain some understanding on the bottlenecks of different system architectures. We adopt a perfect acceleration model for CPU cases where the speedup is proportional to the number of available processor cores. The performance figures of studied cases are summarized in Table 6. One can see that EAGL on GTX-680 has about 40% of the throughput that could be achieved by [47] based on the perfect acceleration model for multi-core CPUs. We note that the GPU controller thread that runs on CPU has negligible performance cost. As such, the CPU host processor(s) can use GPU as a pairing co-processor, while the host process(s) can run other business logic such as database management, high-throughput networking or file I/O.

Table 6. Comparison of throughput, EAGL vs. CPU-base solutions

Implementations	Algorithm	Core Clk	Throughput
EAGL on a GTX-680	R-ate pairing	1006MHz	3350.9
[49] on Intel Q6600	Ate pairing	2.4GHz	4 x 669 (est.)
[15] on i7 860	Ate pairing	2.8GHz	4 x 1202 (est.)
[3] on i5	Ate pairing	2.8GHz	4 x 1661 (est.)
[47] on i7 4700MQ	Ate pairing	2.4GHz	4 x 2051 (est.)

Compilation results show that almost all shared memory is utilized and the register count per thread reaches the architectural upper bound. As such, EAGL fully utilizes on-chip resources of GTX-680. To identify whether the bottleneck is caused by the CI-$2thread$ model at the level of multi-precision arithmetic functions, we cross compare EAGL's acceleration rates on bilinear pairings and point multiplications. It was reported in [2] that MIRACL ran 14509 224-bit point multiplications/sec on 3.0GHz AMD Phenom II CPU. Based on the same type of curve, EAGL computes 47000 256-bit point multiplications/sec on a GTX-680 (3090GLOPS, peak). Comparing to the RNS-based implementation on GTX-295 (1788GLOPS, peak) [2], which computed 9827 224-bit point multiplications/sec, EAGL on a GTX-680 has 2.76 times higher throughput after normalizing the difference of peak GFLOPS. Although it is very difficult to compare the computing strength utilization rate across different generations of GPUs, a higher growth of throughput (2.76) than that of GFLOPS (1.72) at least proves that the CI-$2thread$ model is not worse than the RNS-based model on contemporary GPUs.

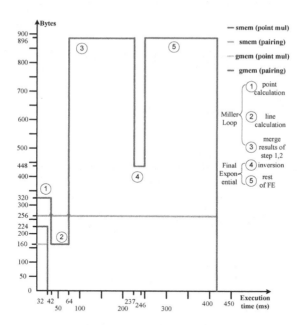

Fig. 3. The temporary variable usages of point multiplication and bilinear pairing in EAGL

Even comparing with [42] that was based on twisted curves and computed 22472 256-bit point multiplications/sec on a 2.6GHz AMD Opteron 252 single-core CPU, EAGL's acceleration rate on point multiplications is still 2.1-fold. It is interesting that EAGL shows different performance relationships on point multiplications and bilinear pairings vs. their CPU-based implementations. To gain some insights about the bottleneck, we first compare the temporary variable usages of EAGL-based point multiplications and bilinear pairings, as shown in Figure 3. The x co-ordinate in Figure 3 is the execution time, and the y co-ordinate is the size of temporary variables in the shared/global memory. Figure 3 illustrates that, in EAGL, most kernel functions of the pairing computation require much larger temporary variable usages than the point multiplication. As a result, the global memory is hit more frequently in the pairing computation.

Then, by assuming that the on-chip memory is unlimited, we analyze the optimal latency of 1408 pairings on a GTX-680. As we know, each pairing operation consists of 11938 multi-precision multiplications, 8312 reductions, plus over 20k inexpensive multi-precision add/sub operations (less than 15ms if residing in the shared memory). With unlimited on-chip memory, running one pairing operation almost equals to running 11938 multiplications and 8312 reductions in the shared memory and registers, which takes 76ms (in Table 2), plus 15ms for add/sub operations. This optimal latency is much less than the actual latency 420ms. Even though we do not have hardware level profiling tools available for precise measurement, we assert that the difference between the optimal latency and the actual latency is mainly resulted from swapping of variables between the shared and global memory spaces as follows. The NVIDIA profiling tool shows that each powering of arbitrary x in $\mathbb{F}_{q^{12}}$ in the FE takes 47ms, it further shows that one concurrent global memory copy of elements in $\mathbb{F}_{q^{12}}$ takes $35\mu s$, and one powering of x in $\mathbb{F}_{q^{12}}$ triggers nearly 500 times more global memory accesses than a copy in $\mathbb{F}_{q^{12}}$. Such a ratio indicates that global memory R/W in one powering of arbitrary x in $\mathbb{F}_{q^{12}}$ takes 17ms, equivalent to 35% of its execution time. And this estimation does not count in extra synchronization and branch divergent cost associated with global memory R/W, and overhead of global-memory-based multi-precision add/sub operations.

6   Conclusion

Our motivation of this project is to develop a usable GPU-based library for long term development, but also to gain some insights on the performance factors. The EAGL library is composed of parallelized point addition and doubling, add/mul/sqr/inv/powering arithmetic in the 1-2-4-12 tower of extension fields, and line functions calculation in Miller's algorithm. Its usage of temporary variables and its memory access model are optimized so that low-level bank conflicts and slow memory hits are minimized. Experiments show that EAGL provides 3350.9 R-ate pairings/sec (amortized) on one GTX-680 GPU. The source code of EAGL will be available soon on http://rtds.cse.tamu.edu/.

Computing performance is affected by computational complexity of the algorithm, programming techniques, and the computer architectures. All three factors need to be seamlessly integrated to achieve top performance. We explore critical factors that affect the performance of GPU-based bilinear pairings. On GPU, storage, placement and access of long operands in pairings, whose lengths range from 8 to 96 (32-bit) integers has the most significant performance impact. A significant number of optimization techniques for pairings focus on reducing the number of arithmetic steps, but this is usually at the cost of using more memory. Unlike the sophisticated prefetching and caching architecture on CPU-based platforms, GPU memory hierarchy is relatively simple. As such, this CPU-based optimization approach may not be also effective for GPU architectures, at least for the contemporary technology, due to the different characteristics with respect to large memory accesses on CPU/GPU. As GPU vendors advance the next generation of products to increase shared memory size (obviously) and add more sophisticated memory prefetching and pipelining architectures, the performance bottleneck of the memory hierarchy in GPU for pairings may be eased significantly.

References

1. Ahmadi, O., Hankerson, D., Menezes, A.: Software Implementation of arithmetic in $GF(3^m)$. In: Carlet, C., Sunar, B. (eds.) WAIFI 2007. LNCS, vol. 4547, pp. 85–102. Springer, Heidelberg (2007)
2. Antão, S., Bajard, J.C., Sousa, L.: RNS-based Elliptic Curve Point Multiplication for Massive Parallel Architectures. In the Computer Journal 55(5), 629–647 (2012)

3. Aranha, D.F., Karabina, K., Longa, P., Gebotys, C.H., López, J.: Faster explicit formulas for computing pairings over ordinary curves. In: Paterson, K.G. (ed.) EUROCRYPT 2011. LNCS, vol. 6632, pp. 48–68. Springer, Heidelberg (2011)
4. Aranha, D.F., Fuentes-Castañeda, L., Knapp, E., Menezes, A., Rodríguez-Henríquez, F.: Implementing pairings at the 192-bit security level. In: Abdalla, M., Lange, T. (eds.) Pairing 2012. LNCS, vol. 7708, pp. 177–195. Springer, Heidelberg (2013)
5. Arene, C., Lange, T., Naehrig, M., Ritzenthaler, C.: Faster Computation of the Tate Pairing. Journal of Number Theory 131(5), 842–857 (2011)
6. Babich, R., Clark, M.A., Joo, B., Shi, G., Brower, R.C., Gottlieb, S.: Scaling Lattice QCD beyond 100 GPUs. In: SC 2011 (2011)
7. Barbulescu, R., Gaudry, P., Joux, A., Thomé, E.: A Quasi-polynomial Algorithm for Discrete Logarithm in Finite Fields of Small Characteristic. In: IACR Cryptology ePrint Archive 2013:400
8. Bajard, J.C., Didier, L.S., Kornerup, P.: An RNS Montgomery Modular Multiplication Algorithm. IEEE Transaction on Computers 47(7), 766–776 (1998)
9. Bajard, J.C., Didier, L.S.: Modular Multiplication and Base Extensions in Residue Number Systems. In: IEEE Symposium on Computer Arithmetic, pp. 59–65 (2001)
10. Barreto, P.S.L.M., Galbraith, S., ÓhÉigeartaigh, C., Scott, M.: Efficient Pairing Computation on Supersingular Abelian Varieties. Designs, Codes and Cryptography 42(3), 239–271 (2007)
11. Barreto, P.S.L.M., Naehrig, M.: Pairing-Friendly Elliptic Curves of Prime Order. In: Preneel, B., Tavares, S. (eds.) SAC 2005. LNCS, vol. 3897, pp. 319–331. Springer, Heidelberg (2006)
12. Benger, N., Scott, M.: Constructing Tower Extensions of Finite Fields for Implementation of Pairing-Based Cryptography. Cryptology ePrint Archive (2009), http://eprint.iacr.org/2009/556.pdf
13. Bernstein, D.J., Lange, T.: Faster Addition and Doubling on Elliptic Curves. In: Kurosawa, K. (ed.) ASIACRYPT 2007. LNCS, vol. 4833, pp. 29–50. Springer, Heidelberg (2007)
14. Bernstein, D.J., Chen, T.-R., Cheng, C.-M., Lange, T., Yang, B.-Y.: ECM on Graphics Cards. In: Joux, A. (ed.) EUROCRYPT 2009. LNCS, vol. 5479, pp. 483–501. Springer, Heidelberg (2009)
15. Beuchat, J.-L., González-Díaz, J.E., Mitsunari, S., Okamoto, E., Rodríguez-Henríquez, F., Teruya, T.: High-speed software implementation of the optimal ate pairing over barreto–naehrig curves. In: Joye, M., Miyaji, A., Otsuka, A. (eds.) Pairing 2010. LNCS, vol. 6487, pp. 21–39. Springer, Heidelberg (2010)
16. Blake, I., Seroussi, G., Smart, N.: Elliptic Curves in Cryptography. Cambridge University Press (1999)
17. Boneh, D., Lynn, B., Shacham, H.: Short Signatures from the Weil Pairing. In: Boyd, C. (ed.) ASIACRYPT 2001. LNCS, vol. 2248, pp. 514–532. Springer, Heidelberg (2001)
18. Boxall, J., El Mrabet, N., Laguillaumie, F., Le, D.-P.: A variant of miller's formula and algorithm. In: Joye, M., Miyaji, A., Otsuka, A. (eds.) Pairing 2010. LNCS, vol. 6487, pp. 417–434. Springer, Heidelberg (2010)
19. De Caro, A., Iovino, V., Persiano, G.: Fully secure anonymous HIBE and secret-key anonymous IBE with short ciphertexts. In: Joye, M., Miyaji, A., Otsuka, A. (eds.) Pairing 2010. LNCS, vol. 6487, pp. 347–366. Springer, Heidelberg (2010)

20. Cheung, R.C.C., Duquesne, S., Fan, J., Guillermin, N., Verbauwhede, I., Yao, G.X.: FPGA implementation of pairings using residue number system and lazy reduction. In: Preneel, B., Takagi, T. (eds.) CHES 2011. LNCS, vol. 6917, pp. 421–441. Springer, Heidelberg (2011)

21. Chung, J., Hasan, M.A.: Asymmetric Squaring Formulae. In: ARITH 2007, pp. 113–122 (2007)

22. Costello, C., Lange, T., Naehrig, M.: Faster pairing computations on curves with high-degree twists. In: Nguyen, P.Q., Pointcheval, D. (eds.) PKC 2010. LNCS, vol. 6056, pp. 224–242. Springer, Heidelberg (2010)

23. Devegili, A.J., Scott, M., Dahab, R.: Implementing cryptographic pairings over barreto-naehrig curves. In: Takagi, T., Okamoto, T., Okamoto, E., Okamoto, T. (eds.) Pairing 2007. LNCS, vol. 4575, pp. 197–207. Springer, Heidelberg (2007)

24. Duan, P.: Oblivious Handshakes and Computing of Shared Secrets: Pairwise Privacy-preserving Protocols for Internet Applications. Ph.D. Dissertation, https://repositories.tdl.org/tdl-ir/handle/1969.1/ETD-TAMU-2011-05-9445

25. Duursma, I.M., Lee, H.-S.: Tate Pairing Implementation for Hyperelliptic Curves $y^2 = x^p - x + d$. In: Laih, C.-S. (ed.) ASIACRYPT 2003. LNCS, vol. 2894, pp. 111–123. Springer, Heidelberg (2003)

26. Freeman, D., Scott, M., Teske, E.: A Taxonomy of Pairing-friendly Elliptic Curves. Journal of Cryptology 23, 224–280 (2010)

27. Freeman, D.M.: Converting pairing-based cryptosystems from composite-order groups to prime-order groups. In: Gilbert, H. (ed.) EUROCRYPT 2010. LNCS, vol. 6110, pp. 44–61. Springer, Heidelberg (2010)

28. Frey, G., Rück, H.G.: A Remark Concerning m-divisibility and the Discrete Logarithm in the Divisor Class Group of Curves. Math. Comp. 62(206), 865–874 (1994)

29. Fiore, D., Gennaro, R., Smart, N.P.: Constructing certificateless encryption and ID-based encryption from ID-based key agreement. In: Joye, M., Miyaji, A., Otsuka, A. (eds.) Pairing 2010. LNCS, vol. 6487, pp. 167–186. Springer, Heidelberg (2010)

30. Galbraith, S.D., Lin, X., Scott, M.: Endomorphisms for faster elliptic curve cryptography on a large class of curves. In: Joux, A. (ed.) EUROCRYPT 2009. LNCS, vol. 5479, pp. 518–535. Springer, Heidelberg (2009)

31. Granger, R., Hess, F., Oyono, R., Thériault, N., Vercauteren, F.: Ate pairing on hyperelliptic curves. In: Naor, M. (ed.) EUROCRYPT 2007. LNCS, vol. 4515, pp. 430–447. Springer, Heidelberg (2007)

32. Granger, R., Scott, M.: Faster squaring in the cyclotomic subgroup of sixth degree extensions. In: Nguyen, P.Q., Pointcheval, D. (eds.) PKC 2010. LNCS, vol. 6056, pp. 209–223. Springer, Heidelberg (2010)

33. Hess, F., Smart, N.P., Vercauteren, F.: The Eta Pairing Revisited. IEEE Trans. on Inform. Theory 52, 4595–4602 (2006)

34. Huang, Q., Wong, D.S., Susilo, W.: A new construction of designated confirmer signature and its application to optimistic fair exchange. In: Joye, M., Miyaji, A., Otsuka, A. (eds.) Pairing 2010. LNCS, vol. 6487, pp. 41–61. Springer, Heidelberg (2010)

35. Katoh, Y., Huang, Y.J., Cheng, C.M., Takagi, T.: Efficient Implementation of the eta Pairing on GPU. Cryptology ePrint Archive, http://eprint.iacr.org/2011/540.pdf

36. Katz, J., Sahai, A., Waters, B.: Predicate encryption supporting disjunctions, polynomial equations, and inner products. In: Smart, N.P. (ed.) EUROCRYPT 2008. LNCS, vol. 4965, pp. 146–162. Springer, Heidelberg (2008)

37. Koblitz, N., Menezes, A.: Pairing-based cryptography at high security levels. In: Smart, N.P. (ed.) Cryptography and Coding 2005. LNCS, vol. 3796, pp. 13–36. Springer, Heidelberg (2005)
38. Koblitz, N.: A Security Weakness in Composite-Order Pairing-Based Protocols with Embedding Degree k > 2. Cryptology ePrint Archive, http://eprint.iacr.org/2010/227.ps
39. Lee, J., Lakshminarayana, N.B., Kim, H., Vuduc, R.: Many-Thread Aware Prefetching Mechanisms for GPGPU Applications. In: MICRO 2010, pp. 213-224 (2010)
40. Lee, E.J., Lee, H.S., Park, C.M.: Efficient and Generalized Pairing Computation on Abelian Varieties. IEEE Transactions on Information Theory 55(4), 1793–1803 (2009)
41. Lewko, A., Okamoto, T., Sahai, A., Takashima, K., Waters, B.: Fully secure functional encryption: Attribute-based encryption and (Hierarchical) inner product encryption. In: Gilbert, H. (ed.) EUROCRYPT 2010. LNCS, vol. 6110, pp. 62–91. Springer, Heidelberg (2010)
42. Longa, P., Gebotys, C.: Analysis of Efficient Techniques for Fast Elliptic Curve Cryptography on x86-64 based Processors. IACR Cryptology ePrint Archive, 335, 1–34 (2010)
43. Groth, J., Ostrovsky, R., Sahai, A.: Perfect non-interactive zero knowledge for NP. In: Vaudenay, S. (ed.) EUROCRYPT 2006. LNCS, vol. 4004, pp. 339–358. Springer, Heidelberg (2006)
44. Matsuda, S., Kanayama, N., Hess, F., Okamoto, E.: Optimised versions of the ate and twisted ate pairings. In: Galbraith, S.D. (ed.) Cryptography and Coding 2007. LNCS, vol. 4887, pp. 302–312. Springer, Heidelberg (2007)
45. Meiklejohn, S., Shacham, H., Freeman, D.M.: Limitations on transformations from composite-order to prime-order groups: The case of round-optimal blind signatures. In: Abe, M. (ed.) ASIACRYPT 2010. LNCS, vol. 6477, pp. 519–538. Springer, Heidelberg (2010)
46. MIRACL: Multiprecision Integer and Rational Arithmetic Cryptographic Library, http://www.certivox.com/miracl
47. Mitsunari, S.: A Fast Implementation of the Optimal Ate Pairing over BN curve on Intel Haswell Processor. In: IACR eprint archive 2013: 362
48. Montgomery, P.L.: Modular Multiplication without Trial Division. Mathematics of Computation 44(1985), 519–521 (1985)
49. Naehrig, M., Niederhagen, R., Schwabe, P.: New software speed records for cryptographic pairings. In: Abdalla, M., Barreto, P.S.L.M. (eds.) LATINCRYPT 2010. LNCS, vol. 6212, pp. 109–123. Springer, Heidelberg (2010)
50. Nakanishi, T., Hira, Y., Funabiki, N.: Forward-secure group signatures from pairings. In: Shacham, H., Waters, B. (eds.) Pairing 2009. LNCS, vol. 5671, pp. 171–186. Springer, Heidelberg (2009)
51. Pecarina, J., Pu, S., Liu, J.C.: SAPPHIRE: Anonymity for Enhanced Control and Private Collaboration in Healthcare Clouds. In: CloundCom 2012, pp. 99–106 (2012)
52. Pereira, G.C.C.F., Simplcio Jr., M.A., Naehrig, M., Barreto, P.S.L.M.: A Family of Implementation-Friendly BN Elliptic Curves. Journal of Systems and Software 84(8), 1319–1326 (2011)
53. Raya, M., Hubaux, J.P.: Securing Vehicular Ad Hoc Networks. Journal of Computer Security 15, 39–68 (2007)

54. Scott, M.: Implementing Cryptographic Pairings. In: Takagi, T., Okamoto, T., Okamoto, E., Okamoto, T. (eds.) Pairing 2007. LNCS, vol. 4575, pp. 177–196. Springer, Heidelberg (2007)
55. Scott, M.: Faster pairings using an elliptic curve with an efficient endomorphism. In: Maitra, S., Veni Madhavan, C.E., Venkatesan, R. (eds.) INDOCRYPT 2005. LNCS, vol. 3797, pp. 258–269. Springer, Heidelberg (2005)
56. Scott, M., Benger, N., Charlemagne, M., Dominguez Perez, L.J., Kachisa, E.J.: On the final exponentiation for calculating pairings on ordinary elliptic curves. In: Shacham, H., Waters, B. (eds.) Pairing 2009. LNCS, vol. 5671, pp. 78–88. Springer, Heidelberg (2009)
57. Scott, M.: A Note on Twists for Pairing Friendly Curves, ftp://ftp.computing.dcu.ie/pub/crypto/twists.pdf
58. Scott, M., Barreto, P.S.L.M.: Compressed pairings. In: Franklin, M. (ed.) CRYPTO 2004. LNCS, vol. 3152, pp. 140–156. Springer, Heidelberg (2004)
59. Smart, N.P., Warinschi, B.: Identity based group signatures from hierarchical identity-based encryption. In: Shacham, H., Waters, B. (eds.) Pairing 2009. LNCS, vol. 5671, pp. 150–170. Springer, Heidelberg (2009)
60. Stam, M., Lenstra, A.K.: Efficient Subgroup Exponentiation in Quadratic and Sixth Degree Extensions. In: Kaliski Jr., B.S., Koç, Ç.K., Paar, C. (eds.) CHES 2002. LNCS, vol. 2523, pp. 318–332. Springer, Heidelberg (2003)
61. Szerwinski, R., Güneysu, T.: Exploiting the Power of GPUs for Asymmetric Cryptography. In: Oswald, E., Rohatgi, P. (eds.) CHES 2008. LNCS, vol. 5154, pp. 79–99. Springer, Heidelberg (2008)
62. Vercauteren, F.: Optimal Pairings. IEEE Transaction of Information Theory 56(1), 455–461 (2010)
63. Wang, L., Wang, L., Mambo, M., Okamoto, E.: New identity-based proxy re-encryption schemes to prevent collusion attacks. In: Joye, M., Miyaji, A., Otsuka, A. (eds.) Pairing 2010. LNCS, vol. 6487, pp. 327–346. Springer, Heidelberg (2010)
64. Wei, L., Liu, J.: Shorter verifier-local revocation group signature with backward unlinkability. In: Joye, M., Miyaji, A., Otsuka, A. (eds.) Pairing 2010. LNCS, vol. 6487, pp. 136–146. Springer, Heidelberg (2010)
65. Yoneyama, K.: Strongly Secure Two-Pass Attribute-Based Authenticated Key Exchange. In: Joye, M., Miyaji, A., Otsuka, A. (eds.) Pairing 2010. LNCS, vol. 6487, pp. 147–166. Springer, Heidelberg (2010)
66. Zhang, Y., Xue, C.J., Wong, D.S., Mamoulis, N., Yiu, S.M.: Acceleration of Composite Order Bilinear Pairing on Graphics Hardware. Cryptology ePrint Archive, http://eprint.iacr.org/2011/196.pdf
67. Zhao, C.A., Zhang, F., Huang, J.: A Note on the Ate Pairing. International Journal of Information Security 6(7), 379–382 (2008)

Weakness of $\mathbb{F}_{3^{6 \cdot 509}}$
for Discrete Logarithm Cryptography

Gora Adj[1], Alfred Menezes[2], Thomaz Oliveira[1],
and Francisco Rodríguez-Henríquez[1]

[1] Computer Science Department, CINVESTAV-IPN
{gora.adj,thomaz.figueiredo}@gmail.com, francisco@cs.cinvestav.mx
[2] Department of Combinatorics & Optimization, University of Waterloo
ajmeneze@uwaterloo.ca

Abstract. In 2013, Joux, and then Barbulescu, Gaudry, Joux and Thomé, presented new algorithms for computing discrete logarithms in finite fields of small and medium characteristic. We show that these new algorithms render the finite field $\mathbb{F}_{3^{6 \cdot 509}} = \mathbb{F}_{3^{3054}}$ weak for discrete logarithm cryptography in the sense that discrete logarithms in this field can be computed significantly faster than with the previous fastest algorithms. Our concrete analysis shows that the supersingular elliptic curve over $\mathbb{F}_{3^{509}}$ with embedding degree 6 that had been considered for implementing pairing-based cryptosystems at the 128-bit security level in fact provides only a significantly lower level of security. Our work provides a convenient framework and tools for performing a concrete analysis of the new discrete logarithm algorithms and their variants.

1 Introduction

Let $\mathbb{F}_q$ denote a finite field of order q, and let $Q = q^n$. The discrete logarithm problem (DLP) in $\mathbb{F}_Q$ is that of determining, given a generator g of $\mathbb{F}_Q^*$ and an element $h \in \mathbb{F}_Q^*$, the integer $x \in [0, Q-2]$ satisfying $h = g^x$. The integer x is called the discrete logarithm of h to the base g and is denoted by $\log_g h$. In the remainder of the paper, we shall assume that the characteristic of $\mathbb{F}_q$ is 2 or 3.

The fastest general-purpose DLP solver is Coppersmith's 1984 index-calculus algorithm [18] with a running time[1] of $L_Q[\frac{1}{3}, (32/9)^{1/3}] \approx L_Q[\frac{1}{3}, 1.526]$, where as usual $L_Q[\alpha, c]$ with $0 < \alpha < 1$ and $c > 0$ denotes the expression

$$\exp\left((c + o(1))(\log Q)^\alpha (\log \log Q)^{1-\alpha}\right)$$

that is subexponential in $\log Q$. In 2006, Joux and Lercier [37] presented an algorithm with a running time of $L_Q[\frac{1}{3}, 3^{1/3}] \approx L_Q[\frac{1}{3}, 1.442]$ when q and n are balanced in the sense that

$$q = \exp\left(3^{-2/3} \cdot (\log Q)^{1/3} (\log \log Q)^{2/3}\right) \text{ and } n = 3^{2/3} \cdot \left(\frac{\log Q}{\log \log Q}\right)^{2/3}.$$

---

[1] All running times in this paper have been determined using *heuristic* arguments, and have not been rigorously proven.

Z. Cao and F. Zhang (Eds.): Pairing 2013, LNCS 8365, pp. 20–44, 2014.
© Springer International Publishing Switzerland 2014

In 2012, Joux [33] introduced a 'pinpointing' technique that improves the running time of the Joux-Lercier algorithm to $L_Q[\frac{1}{3}, 2/3^{2/3}] \approx L_Q[\frac{1}{3}, 0.961]$.

In February 2013, Joux [34] presented a new DLP algorithm with a running time of $L_Q[\frac{1}{4} + o(1), c]$ (for some undetermined c) when q and n are balanced in the sense that $q \approx m$ where $n = 2m$. Also in February 2013, Göloğlu, Granger, McGuire and Zumbrägel [27] proposed a variant of the Joux-Lercier algorithm that imposes a further divisibility condition on ℓ where $q = 2^\ell$. The running time of the Gögloğlu et al. algorithm is (i) $L_Q[\frac{1}{3}, 2/3^{2/3}] \approx L_Q[\frac{1}{3}, 0.961]$ when $n \approx 2^m d_1$, $d_1 \approx 2^m$, and $m \mid \ell$; and (ii) between $L_Q[\frac{1}{3}, (2/3)^{2/3}] \approx L_Q[\frac{1}{3}, 0.763]$ and $L_Q[\frac{1}{3}, 1/2^{1/3}] \approx L_Q[\frac{1}{3}, 0.794]$ when $n \approx 2^m d_1$, $2^m \gg d_1$, and $m \mid \ell$. The new algorithms were used to compute discrete logarithms in $\mathbb{F}_{2^{8 \cdot 3 \cdot 255}} = \mathbb{F}_{2^{6120}}$ in only 750 CPU hours [28], and in $\mathbb{F}_{2^{8 \cdot 3 \cdot 257}} = \mathbb{F}_{2^{6168}}$ in only 550 CPU hours [35]. The astoundingly small computational effort expended in these experiments depends crucially on the special nature of the fields $\mathbb{F}_{2^{6120}}$ and $\mathbb{F}_{2^{6168}}$ — namely that $\mathbb{F}_{2^{6120}}$ is a degree-255 extension of $\mathbb{F}_{2^{8 \cdot 3}}$ with $255 = 2^8 - 1$, and $\mathbb{F}_{2^{6168}}$ is a degree-257 extension of $\mathbb{F}_{2^{8 \cdot 3}}$ with $257 = 2^8 + 1$. Despite these remarkable achievements, the effectiveness of the new algorithms for computing discrete logarithms in general finite fields of small characteristic remains unclear.

In June 2013, Barbulescu, Gaudry, Joux and Thomé [7] presented a new DLP algorithm that, for many choices of field sizes, is asymptotically faster than all previous algorithms. Most impressively, in the case where $q \approx n$ and $n \leq q + 2$, the discrete logarithm problem in $\mathbb{F}_{q^{2n}} = \mathbb{F}_Q$ can be solved in *quasi-polynomial time*

$$(\log Q)^{O(\log \log Q)}. \tag{1}$$

Note that (1) is asymptotically smaller than $L_Q[\alpha, c]$ for any $\alpha > 0$ and $c > 0$. However, the practical relevance of the new algorithm has not yet been determined.

The aforementioned advances in DLP algorithms are potentially relevant to the security of pairing-based cryptosystems that use bilinear pairings derived from supersingular elliptic curves E or genus-2 hyperelliptic curves C defined over finite fields $\mathbb{F}_q$ of characteristic 2 or 3. Such a symmetric pairing, classified as a Type 1 pairing in [25], is a non-degenerate bilinear map $e : \mathbb{G} \times \mathbb{G} \to \mathbb{G}_T$ where $\mathbb{G}$ and $\mathbb{G}_T$ are groups of prime order N. Here, $\mathbb{G}$ is either a subgroup of $E(\mathbb{F}_q)$, the group of $\mathbb{F}_q$-rational points on E, or a subgroup of $\mathrm{Jac}_C(\mathbb{F}_q)$, the jacobian of C over $\mathbb{F}_q$, and $\mathbb{G}_T$ is the order-N subgroup of $\mathbb{F}_{q^k}^*$ where k is the embedding degree (the smallest positive integer such that $\#\mathbb{G} \mid (q^k - 1)$). A necessary condition for the security of pairing-based cryptosystems that employ the pairing e is the intractability of the discrete logarithm problem in $\mathbb{G}_T$. Hence, any advance in algorithms for solving the DLP in $\mathbb{F}_{q^k}$ can potentially impact the security of pairing-based cryptosystems.

Three symmetric pairings that have received a great deal of attention in the literature are: (i) the $k = 6$ pairings derived from supersingular elliptic curves $Y^2 = X^3 - X + 1$ and $Y^2 = X^3 - X - 1$ over $\mathbb{F}_{3^\ell}$; (ii) the $k = 4$ pairings derived from supersingular elliptic curves $Y^2 + Y = X^3 + X$ and $Y^2 + Y = X^3 + X + 1$ over $\mathbb{F}_{2^\ell}$; and (iii) the $k = 12$ pairing derived from supersingular genus-2 curves $Y^2 + Y = X^5 + X^3$ and $Y^2 + Y = X^5 + X^3 + 1$ over $\mathbb{F}_{2^\ell}$; in all cases, ℓ is chosen to be prime. These symmetric pairings were considered in some early papers [15,23,9,24] on pairing-based cryptography. Since then, many papers have reported on software and hardware implementation of these pairings; some examples are [8,29,43,3,30,13,16,20,12,4,1].

In all the papers cited in the previous paragraph, the pairing parameters were chosen under the assumption that Coppersmith's algorithm is the fastest method for finding discrete logarithms in $\mathbb{F}_{q^k}$. For example, to achieve the 128-bit security level, [3] chose $\ell = 1223$ for the $k = 4$ pairing and $\ell = 509$ for the $k = 6$ pairing, [16] chose $\ell = 439$ for the $k = 12$ pairing, and [4] chose $\ell = 367$ for the $k = 12$ pairing. These choices were made because Coppersmith's algorithm, as analyzed by Lenstra [39], has running time approximately 2^{128} for computing logarithms in $\mathbb{F}_{2^{4 \cdot 1223}}$, $\mathbb{F}_{3^{6 \cdot 509}}$, $\mathbb{F}_{2^{12 \cdot 439}}$, and $\mathbb{F}_{2^{12 \cdot 367}}$, respectively.

In 2012, Hayashi et al. [31] reported on their implementation of the Joux-Lercier algorithm for computing logarithms in $\mathbb{F}_{3^{6 \cdot 97}}$. Their work demonstrated that in practice the Joux-Lercier algorithm is considerably faster than Coppersmith's algorithm for DLP computations in $\mathbb{F}_{3^{6 \cdot 97}}$; note that the $k = 6$ pairing with $\ell = 97$ was considered in [9,24]. In contrast, the largest discrete logarithm computation reported using Coppersmith's algorithm (and its generalizations [2,36]) is the April 2013 computation by Barbulescu et al. [5] of logarithms in $\mathbb{F}_{2^{809}}$; note that 809 is prime and $3^{6 \cdot 97} \approx 2^{922}$. Shinohara et al. [44] estimated that $\mathbb{F}_{3^{6 \cdot 509}}$ offers only 111-bits of security against Joux-Lercier attacks, considerably less than the assumed 128-bits of security against Coppersmith attacks.

The purpose of this paper is to demonstrate that the new algorithms by Joux [34] and Barbulescu et al. [7] can be combined to solve the discrete logarithm problem in $\mathbb{F}_{3^{6 \cdot 509}}$ significantly faster than the Joux-Lercier algorithm. More precisely, we estimate that logarithms in this field can be computed in $2^{81.7}$ time with the new algorithms, where the unit of time is the (inexpensive) cost of a multiplication in $\mathbb{F}_{3^{12}}$. Moreover, the $2^{81.7}$ computation is effectively parallelizable, whereas the Joux-Lercier algorithm isn't because of the very large size of the linear system of equations that needs to be solved. While the $2^{81.7}$ computation is certainly a formidable challenge, it is already within the realm of feasibility for a very well-funded adversary. Thus, we conclude that $\mathbb{F}_{3^{6 \cdot 509}}$ does not offer adequate security for discrete logarithm cryptosystems and, in particular, the supersingular elliptic curve over $\mathbb{F}_{3^{509}}$ with embedding degree 6 is not suitable for implementing pairing-based cryptosystems.

We also analyze the efficacy of the new algorithms for computing discrete logarithms in $\mathbb{F}_{2^{12 \cdot 367}}$ and conclude that the supersingular genus-2 curve over $\mathbb{F}_{2^{367}}$ with embedding degree 12 should be considered weak and not employed in pairing-based cryptography.

The remainder of the paper is organized as follows. §2 collects some results on the number of smooth polynomials over a finite field. The new discrete logarithm algorithms are outlined in §3. Our estimates for discrete logarithm computations in $\mathbb{F}_{3^{6 \cdot 509}}$ and $\mathbb{F}_{2^{12 \cdot 367}}$ are presented in §4 and Appendix A, respectively. We draw our conclusions in §5.

2   Smooth Polynomials

2.1   Number of Smooth Polynomials

The number of monic polynomials of degree n over $\mathbb{F}_q$ is q^n. The number of monic irreducible polynomials of degree n over $\mathbb{F}_q$ is

$$I_q(n) = \frac{1}{n} \sum_{d|n} \mu(n/d)q^d, \tag{2}$$

where μ is the Möbius function. A polynomial in $\mathbb{F}_q[X]$ is said to be m-smooth if all its irreducible factors in $\mathbb{F}_q[X]$ have degree at most m. Define

$$F(u, z) = \prod_{\ell=1}^{m} \left(1 + \frac{uz^{\ell}}{1 - z^{\ell}}\right)^{I_q(\ell)}.$$

$F(u, z)$ is the generating function for m-smooth monic polynomials in $\mathbb{F}_q[X]$, where u marks the number of distinct irreducible factors, and z marks the degree of the polynomial. Thus, the number of monic m-smooth degree-n polynomials in $\mathbb{F}_q[X]$ that have exactly k distinct monic irreducible factors is

$$N_q(m, n, k) = [u^k z^n] F(u, z) \tag{3}$$

where $[\ ]$ denotes the coefficient operator, whereas the total number of monic m-smooth degree-n polynomials in $\mathbb{F}_q[X]$ is

$$N_q(m, n) = [z^n] F(1, z). \tag{4}$$

Furthermore, the average number of distinct monic irreducible factors among all monic m-smooth degree-n polynomials in $\mathbb{F}_q[X]$ is

$$A_q(m, n) = \frac{[z^n] \left(\frac{\partial F}{\partial u}\big|_{u=1}\right)}{N_q(m, n)}. \tag{5}$$

For any given q, m and n, $N_q(m, n)$ can be obtained by using a symbolic algebra package such as Maple [42] to compute the first $n + 1$ terms of the Taylor series expansion of $F(1, z)$ and then extracting the coefficient of z^n. Similarly, one can compute $N_q(m, n, k)$ and $A_q(m, n)$. For example, we used Maple 17 on a 3.2 GHz Intel Xeon CPU X5672 machine to compute $N_{3^{12}}(30, 254)$ in 3.2 seconds, $A_{3^{12}}(30, 254) = 14.963$ in 102.9 seconds, and $N_{3^{12}}(30, 254, 9)$ in 4305 seconds.

2.2   Smoothness Testing

A degree-d polynomial $f \in \mathbb{F}_q[X]$ can be tested for m-smoothness by computing

$$w(X) = f'(X) \cdot \prod_{i=\lceil m/2 \rceil}^{m} (X^{q^i} - X) \mod f(X) \tag{6}$$

and checking whether $w(X) = 0$ [18]. Here, f' denotes the formal derivative of f. If f indeed is m-smooth, then $w(X) = 0$. On the other hand, if f is not m-smooth then a necessary condition to have $w(X) = 0$ is that f be divisible by the square of an irreducible polynomial of degree $> m$. Since randomly selected polynomials f are unlikely to satisfy this condition, the vast majority of polynomials that pass the smoothness test are indeed m-smooth. The polynomials that are declared to be m-smooth are then factored using a general-purpose polynomial factorization algorithm, at which time the polynomials falsely declared to be m-smooth are identified.

Without loss of generality, we can assume that f is monic. Then the product of two polynomials of degree $< d$ can be multiplied modulo f in time $2d^2$, where the unit of time is an $\mathbb{F}_q$-multiplication. To compute $w(X)$, one first precomputes $X^q \bmod f$. This can be accomplished by repeated square-and-multiplication at a cost of at most $2||q||_2$ modular multiplications, where $||q||_2$ denotes the bitlength of q. Then, $X^{qi} \bmod f$ for $2 \le i \le d-1$ can be computed by repeated multiplication of $X^q \bmod f$ with itself at a cost of approximately d modular multiplications, and $X^{q^i} \bmod f$ for $2 \le i \le m$ can be computed by repeated exponentiation by q with each exponentiating having cost d^2 $\mathbb{F}_q$-multiplications. Finally, the product in (6) can be computed using $m/2$ modular multiplications at a cost of md^2 $\mathbb{F}_q$-multiplications. The total cost for testing m-smoothness of f is thus

$$S_q(m, d) = 2d^2(d + m + 2||q||_2) \quad \mathbb{F}_q\text{-multiplications.} \tag{7}$$

We will mostly be interested in the case $q = 3^{12}$. Then, $X^q \bmod f$ can be determined by first precomputing $X^3, X^6, \ldots, X^{3(d-1)} \bmod f$ by repeated multiplication by X. Thereafter, cubing a polynomial modulo f can be accomplished by cubing the coefficients of the polynomial, and then multiplying the precomputed polynomials by these cubes (and adding the results). In this way, we get a loose upper bound of $3d^2 + 11d^2 = 14d^2$ $\mathbb{F}_{3^{12}}$-multiplications of the cost to compute $X^{3^{12}} \bmod f$, and the total cost for testing m-smoothness of f becomes

$$S_{3^{12}}(m, d) = 2d^2(d + m + 7) \quad \mathbb{F}_{3^{12}}\text{-multiplications.} \tag{8}$$

3 New DLP Algorithm of Joux and Barbulescu et al.

The DLP algorithm we describe is due to Joux [34], with a descent step from the quasi-polynomial time algorithm (QPA) of Barbulescu et al. [7]. For lack of a better name, we will call this algorithm the "new DLP algorithm".

Let $\mathbb{F}_{q^{2n}}$ be a finite field where $n \le q+2$. The elements of $\mathbb{F}_{q^{2n}}$ are represented as polynomials of degree at most $n-1$ over $\mathbb{F}_{q^2}$. Let $N = q^{2n} - 1$. Let g be an element of order N in $\mathbb{F}_{q^{2n}}^*$, and let $h \in \mathbb{F}_{q^{2n}}^*$. We wish to compute $\log_g h$. The algorithm proceeds by first finding the logarithms of all degree-one (§3.2) and degree-two (§3.3) elements in $\mathbb{F}_{q^{2n}}$. Then, in the *descent stage*, $\log_g h$ is expressed as a linear combination of logarithms of degree-one and degree-two $\mathbb{F}_{q^{2n}}$ elements. The descent stage proceeds in several steps, each expressing the logarithm of a degree-D element as a linear combination of the logarithms of elements of degree

Table 1. Estimated costs of the main steps of the new DLP algorithm for computing discrete logarithms in $\mathbb{F}_{q^{2n}}$. A_N and M_{q^2} denote the costs of an addition modulo N and a multiplication in $\mathbb{F}_{q^2}$. The smoothness testing cost $S_{q^2}(m, D)$ is given in (7). See §3.5 for the definitions of t_1 and t_2. The Gröbner basis cost $G_{q^2}(m, D)$ is defined in §3.7.

Finding logarithms of linear polynomials (§3.2)	
Relation generation	$6q^2 \cdot S_{q^2}(1, 3)$
Linear algebra	$q^5 \cdot A_N$
Finding logarithms of irreducible quadratic polynomials (§3.3)	
Relation generation	$q^{16}/N_{q^2}(1, 6) \cdot S_{q^2}(1, 6)$
Linear algebra	$q^7 \cdot A_N$
Descent (Degree D to degree m)	
Continued-fraction (§3.4)	
$\{D = n - 1\} \ (q^{n-1}/N_{q^2}(m, (n - 1)/2))^2 \cdot S_{q^2}(m, (n - 1)/2)$	
Classical (§3.5)	
$q^{2(t_1 - D + t_2)}/(N_{q^2}(m, t_1 - D)N_{q^2}(m, t_2)) \cdot \min(S_{q^2}(m, t_1 - D), S_{q^2}(m, t_2))$	
QPA (§3.6)	
$q^{6D+2}/N_{q^2}(m, 3D) \cdot S_{q^2}(m, 3D) + q^5 \cdot A_N$	
Gröbner bases (§3.7)	
$G_{q^2}(m, D) + q^{6m-2D}/N_{q^2}(m, 3m - D) \cdot S_{q^2}(m, 3m - D)$	

$\leq m$ for some $m < D$. Four descent methods are used; these are described in §3.4–§3.7. The cost of each step is given in Table 1.

Notation. For $\gamma \in \mathbb{F}_{q^2}$, $\overline{\gamma}$ denotes the element γ^q. For $P \in \mathbb{F}_{q^2}[X]$, $\overline{P}$ denotes the polynomial obtained by raising each coefficient of P to the power q. The cost of an integer addition modulo N is denoted by A_N, and the cost of a multiplication in $\mathbb{F}_{q^2}$ is denoted by M_{q^2}. The projective general linear group of order 2 over $\mathbb{F}_q$ is denoted $\mathrm{PGL}_2(\mathbb{F}_q)$. $\mathcal{P}_q$ is a set of distinct representatives of the left cosets of $\mathrm{PGL}_2(\mathbb{F}_q)$ in $\mathrm{PGL}_2(\mathbb{F}_{q^2})$; note that $\#\mathcal{P}_q = q^3 + q$.

3.1 Setup

Select polynomials $h_0, h_1 \in \mathbb{F}_{q^2}[X]$ of degree at most 2 so that $h_1 X^q - h_0$ has an irreducible factor I_X of degree n in $\mathbb{F}_{q^2}[X]$; we will henceforth assume that $\max(\deg h_0, \deg h_1) = 2$. In order to avoid the "traps" discussed in [17], we further assume that each irreducible factor $J \in \mathbb{F}_{q^2}[X]$ of $(h_1 X^q - h_0)/I_X$ satisfies the following two conditions: (i) $\gcd(\deg J, n) = 1$; and (ii) $\deg J > m$ where m is the integer specified in the continued-fraction descent stage (§3.4). Note that $X^q \equiv h_0/h_1 \pmod{I_X}$. The field $\mathbb{F}_{q^{2n}}$ is represented as $\mathbb{F}_{q^{2n}} = \mathbb{F}_{q^2}[X]/(I_X)$ and the elements of $\mathbb{F}_{q^{2n}}$ can be represented as polynomials in $\mathbb{F}_{q^2}[X]$ of degree at most $n - 1$. Let g be a generator of $\mathbb{F}_{q^{2n}}^*$.

3.2 Finding Logarithms of Linear Polynomials

Let $\mathcal{B}_1 = \{X + a \mid a \in \mathbb{F}_{q^2}\}$, and note that $\#\mathcal{B}_1 = q^2$. To compute the logarithms of $\mathcal{B}_1$-elements, we first generate linear relations of these logarithms. Let

$a, b, c, d \in \mathbb{F}_{q^2}$ with $ad - bc \neq 0$. Substituting $Y \mapsto (aX + b)/(cX + d)$ into the systematic equation

$$Y^q - Y = \prod_{\alpha \in \mathbb{F}_q} (Y - \alpha), \tag{9}$$

and then multiplying by $(cX + d)^{q+1}$ yields

$$(\bar{a}h_0 + \bar{b}h_1)(cX + d) - (aX + b)(\bar{c}h_0 + \bar{d}h_1) \tag{10}$$
$$\equiv h_1 \cdot (cX + d) \cdot \prod_{\alpha \in \mathbb{F}_q} [(a - \alpha c)X + (b - \alpha d)] \pmod{I_X}.$$

Note that the left side of (10) is a polynomial of degree (at most) 3. If this polynomial is 1-smooth, then taking logarithms of both sides of (10) yields a linear relation of the logarithms of $\mathcal{B}_1$-elements[2] and the logarithm of h_1. As explained in [7], in order to avoid redundant relations one selects quadruples (a, b, c, d) from $\mathcal{P}_q$; here we are identifying a quadruple (a, b, c, d) with the matrix $\left(\begin{smallmatrix} a & b \\ c & d \end{smallmatrix}\right)$.

Now, the probability that the left side of (10) is 1-smooth is

$$\frac{N_{q^2}(1,3)}{q^6} = \binom{q^2 + 2}{3} / q^6 \approx \frac{1}{6}.$$

Thus, after approximately $6q^2$ trials one expects to obtain (slightly more than) q^2 relations. The cost of the relation generation stage is $6q^2 \cdot S_{q^2}(1,3)$. The logarithms can then be obtained by using Wiedemann's algorithm for solving sparse systems of linear equations [45]. The expected cost of the linear algebra is $q^5 \cdot A_N$ since each equation has approximately q nonzero terms.

Remark 1. (*running time of Wiedemann's algorithm*) Let B be the matrix obtained after the relation generation stage. Note that B is a matrix over $\mathbb{Z}_N$. However, the entries of B are coefficients of the discrete logarithms of linear polynomials that occur in the relations. Thus the vast majority of these entries are expected to be 0, 1, and -1, with the remaining entries (corresponding to repeated factors) being a number that is small in absolute value (e.g. ± 2). Wiedemann's algorithm treats B as a black box, and uses it only to perform matrix-vector multiplication with vectors over $\mathbb{Z}_N$. Since the nonzero entries of B are very small in absolute value, and since B has approximately q nonzero entries per row, the expected cost of each matrix-by-vector multiplication is $q^3 \cdot A_N$. Finally, since the block version of Wiedemann's algorithm [19] requires no more than q^2 such matrix-by-vector multiplications, the overall running time is $q^5 \cdot A_N$.

---

[2] It is understood that all polynomials of the right side of (10) and factors of the left side of (10) should be made monic. The same holds for (17) and (19).

3.3   Finding Logarithms of Irreducible Quadratic Polynomials

Let $u \in \mathbb{F}_{q^2}$, and let $Q(X) = X^2 + uX + v \in \mathbb{F}_{q^2}[X]$ be an irreducible quadratic. Define $\mathcal{B}_{2,u}$ to be the set of all irreducible quadratics of the form $X^2 + uX + w$ in $\mathbb{F}_{q^2}[X]$; one expects that $\#\mathcal{B}_{2,u} \approx (q^2 - 1)/2$. The logarithms of all elements in $\mathcal{B}_{2,u}$ are found simultaneously using one application of QPA descent (see §3.6). More precisely, one first collects relations of the form (17), where the left side of (17) factors as a product of linear polynomials (whose logarithms are known). The expected number of relations one can obtain is

$$\frac{N_{q^2}(1,6)}{q^{12}} \cdot (q^3 + q).$$

Provided that this number is significantly greater than $\#\mathcal{B}_{2,u}$, the matrix $\mathcal{H}(Q)$ is expected to have full (column) rank. One can then solve the resulting system of linear equations to obtain the logarithms of all irreducible translates $Q + w$ of Q. This step is repeated for each $u \in \mathbb{F}_{q^2}$. Hence, there are q^2 independent linear systems of equations to be solved.

For each $u \in \mathbb{F}_{q^2}$, the cost of relation generation is $q^{14}/N_{q^2}(1,6) \cdot S_{q^2}(1,6)$, while the linear algebra cost is $q^5 \cdot A_N$.

3.4   Continued-Fraction Descent

Recall that we wish to compute $\log_g h$, where $h \in \mathbb{F}_{q^{2n}} = \mathbb{F}_{q^2}[X]/(I_X)$. Note that $\deg h \leq n - 1$; we will henceforth assume that $\deg h = n - 1$. The descent stage begins by multiplying h by a random power of g. The extended Euclidean algorithm is used to express the resulting field element h' in the form $h' = w_1/w_2$ where $\deg w_1, \deg w_2 \approx n/2$ [14]; for simplicity, we shall assume that n is odd and $\deg w_1 = \deg w_2 = (n-1)/2$. This process is repeated until both w_1 and w_2 are m-smooth for some chosen $m < (n-1)/2$. This gives $\log_g h'$ as a linear combination of logarithms of polynomials of degree at most m. The expected cost of this continued-fraction descent step is approximately

$$\left(\frac{q^{n-1}}{N_{q^2}(m, (n-1)/2)} \right)^2 \cdot S_{q^2}(m, (n-1)/2). \tag{11}$$

The expected number of distinct irreducible factors of w_1 and w_2 is $2A_{q^2}(m, (n-1)/2)$. In the analysis, we shall assume that each of these irreducible factors has degree exactly m. The logarithm of each of these degree-m polynomials is then expressed as a linear combination of logarithms of smaller degree polynomials using one of the descent methods described in §3.5, §3.6 and §3.7.

3.5   Classical Descent

Let p be the characteristic of $\mathbb{F}_q$, and let $q = p^\ell$. Let $s \in [1, \ell]$, and let $R \in \mathbb{F}_{q^2}[X, Y]$. Then

$$R(X, X^{p^s})^{p^{\ell-s}} = R'(X^{p^{\ell-s}}, X^q) \equiv R'(X^{p^{\ell-s}}, \frac{h_0}{h_1}) \pmod{I_X},$$

where R' is obtained from R by raising all its coefficients to the power $p^{\ell-s}$. For the sake of simplicity, we will assume in this section that $h_1 = 1$ and so

$$R(X, X^{p^s})^{p^{\ell-s}} \equiv R'(X^{p^{\ell-s}}, h_0) \pmod{I_X}. \tag{12}$$

Let $Q \in \mathbb{F}_{q^2}[X]$ with $\deg Q = D$, and let $m < D$. In the Joux-Lercier descent method [37], as modified by Joux [34], one selects suitable parameters d_1, d_2 and searches for a polynomial $R \in \mathbb{F}_{q^2}[X, Y]$ such that (i) $\deg_X R \le d_1$ and $\deg_Y R \le d_2$; (ii) $Q \mid R_1$ where $R_1 = R(X, X^{p^s})$; and (iii) R_1/Q and R_2 are m-smooth where $R_2 = R'(X^{p^{\ell-s}}, h_0)$. Taking logarithms of both sides of (12) then gives an expression for $\log_g Q$ in terms of the logarithms of polynomials of degree at most m.

A family of polynomials R satisfying (i) and (ii) can be constructed by finding the null space of the $D \times (D+\delta)$ matrix whose columns are indexed by monomials $X^i Y^j$ for $D + \delta$ pairs $(i, j) \in [0, d_1] \times [0, d_2]$, and whose $X^i Y^j$-th column entries are the coefficients of the polynomial $X^i(X^{p^s})^j \bmod Q$. The components of the vectors in the null space of this matrix can be interpreted as the coefficients of polynomials $R \in \mathbb{F}_{q^2}[X, Y]$ satisfying (i) and (ii). The dimension of this null space is expected to be δ, and so the null space is expected to contain $(q^2)^{\delta-1}$ monic polynomials. Let $\deg R_1 = t_1$ and $\deg R_2 = t_2$. We have $t_1 \le d_1 + p^s d_2$ and $t_2 \le p^{\ell-s} d_1 + 2d_2$; the precise values of t_1 and t_2 depend on the (i, j) pairs chosen (see §4.5 for an example). In order to ensure that the null space includes a monic polynomial R such that both R_1/Q and R_2 are m-smooth, the parameters must be selected so that

$$q^{2\delta-2} \gg \frac{q^{2(t_1-D)}}{N_{q^2}(m, t_1 - D)} \cdot \frac{q^{2t_2}}{N_{q^2}(m, t_2)}. \tag{13}$$

Ignoring the time to compute the null space, the expected cost of finding a polynomial R satisfying (i)–(iii) is

$$\frac{q^{2(t_1-D)}}{N_{q^2}(m, t_1 - D)} \cdot \frac{q^{2t_2}}{N_{q^2}(m, t_2)} \cdot \min(S_{q^2}(m, t_1 - D), S_{q^2}(m, t_2)). \tag{14}$$

The expected number of distinct irreducible factors of R_1/Q and R_2 is $A_{q^2}(m, t_1 - D) + A_{q^2}(m, t_2)$. In the analysis, we shall assume that each of these irreducible factors has degree exactly m.

3.6   QPA Descent

The QPA descent method is so named because it was a crucial step in the Barbulescu et al. quasi-polynomial time algorithm for the DLP in finite fields of small characteristic [7].

Let $Q \in \mathbb{F}_{q^2}[X]$ with $\deg Q = D$, and let $m \in [\lceil D/2 \rceil, D-1]$. Let $(a, b, c, d) \in \mathcal{P}_q$, and recall that $\#\mathcal{P}_q = q^3 + q$. Substituting $Y \mapsto (aQ+b)/(cQ+d)$ into the systematic equation (9) and multiplying by $(cQ+d)^{q+1}$ yields

$$(aQ+b)^q(cQ+d) - (aQ+b)(cQ+d)^q = (cQ+d) \prod_{\alpha \in \mathbb{F}_q} [(a - \alpha c)Q + (b - \alpha d)]. \tag{15}$$

The left side of (15) can be written as

$$(\overline{a}\overline{Q}(X^q) + \overline{b})(cQ + d) - (aQ + b)(\overline{c}\overline{Q}(X^q) + \overline{d})$$
$$\equiv (\overline{a}\overline{Q}(\frac{h_0}{h_1}) + \overline{b})(cQ + d) - (aQ + b)(\overline{c}\overline{Q}(\frac{h_0}{h_1}) + \overline{d}) \pmod{I_X}.$$

Hence

$$(\overline{a}\overline{Q}(\frac{h_0}{h_1}) + \overline{b})(cQ + d) - (aQ + b)(\overline{c}\overline{Q}(\frac{h_0}{h_1}) + \overline{d}) \tag{16}$$
$$\equiv (cQ + d) \prod_{\alpha \in \mathbb{F}_q} [(a - \alpha c)Q + (b - \alpha d)] \pmod{I_X}.$$

Multiplying (16) by h_1^D yields

$$(\overline{a}\widetilde{Q} + \overline{b}h_1^D)(cQ + d) - (aQ + b)(\overline{c}\widetilde{Q} + \overline{d}h_1^D) \tag{17}$$
$$\equiv h_1^D \cdot (cQ + d) \cdot \prod_{\alpha \in \mathbb{F}_q} [(a - \alpha c)Q + (b - \alpha d)] \pmod{I_X},$$

where $\widetilde{Q}(X) = h_1^D \cdot \overline{Q}(h_0/h_1)$. Note that the polynomial on the left side of (17) has degree $\leq 3D$. If this polynomial is m-smooth, then (17) yields a linear relation of the logarithms of some degree-m polynomials and logarithms of translates of Q. After collecting slightly more than q^2 such relations, one searches for a linear combination of these relations that eliminates all translates of Q except for Q itself. To achieve this, consider row vectors in $(\mathbb{Z}_N)^{q^2}$ with coordinates indexed by elements $\lambda \in \mathbb{F}_{q^2}$. For each relation, we define a vector v whose entry v_λ is 1 if $Q - \lambda$ appears in the right side of (17), and 0 otherwise. If the resulting matrix $\mathcal{H}(Q)$ of row vectors has full column rank, then one obtains an expression for $\log_g Q$ in terms of the logarithms of polynomials of degree $\leq m$. The number of distinct polynomials of degree $\leq m$ in this expression is expected to be $A_{q^2}(m, 3D) \cdot q^2$; in the analysis we shall assume that each of these polynomials has degree exactly m.

Since the probability that a degree-$3D$ polynomial is m-smooth is $N_{q^2}(m, 3D)/(q^2)^{3D}$, one must have

$$\frac{N_{q^2}(m, 3D)}{q^{6D}} \cdot (q^3 + q) \gg q^2 \tag{18}$$

in order to ensure that $\mathcal{H}(Q)$ has $\gg q^2$ rows, whereby $\mathcal{H}(Q)$ can be expected to have full rank.

The expected cost of the relation generation portion of QPA descent is

$$\frac{q^{6D}}{N_{q^2}(m, 3D)} q^2 \cdot S_{q^2}(m, 3D),$$

while the cost of the linear algebra is $q^5 \cdot A_N$.

3.7   Gröbner Bases Descent

Let $Q \in \mathbb{F}_{q^2}[X]$ with $\deg Q = D$, and let $m = \lceil (D+1)/2 \rceil$. In Joux's new descent method [34, §5.3], one finds degree-m polynomials[3] $k_1, k_2 \in \mathbb{F}_{q^2}[X]$ such that $Q \mid G$, where

$$G = h_1^m (k_1^q k_2 - k_1 k_2^q) \bmod I_X.$$

We then have

$$h_1^m \cdot k_2 \cdot \prod_{\alpha \in \mathbb{F}_q} (k_1 - \alpha k_2) \equiv G(X) \pmod{I_X}$$

as can be seen by making the substitution $Y \mapsto k_1/k_2$ into the systematic equation (9) and clearing denominators. Define $\widetilde{k}(X) = h_1^m \cdot \overline{k}(h_0/h_1)$ and note that $\deg \widetilde{k} = 2m$. We thus have $G \equiv \widetilde{k}_1 k_2 - k_1 \widetilde{k}_2 \pmod{I_X}$, and consequently $G = \widetilde{k}_1 k_2 - k_1 \widetilde{k}_2$ provided that $3m < n$. It follows that $G(X) = Q(X)R(X)$ for some $R \in \mathbb{F}_{q^2}[X]$ with $\deg R = 3m - D$. If R is m-smooth, we obtain a linear relationship between $\log_g Q$ and logs of degree-m polynomials by taking logarithms of both sides of the following:

$$h_1^m \cdot k_2 \cdot \prod_{\alpha \in \mathbb{F}_q} (k_1 - \alpha k_2) \equiv Q(X)R(X) \pmod{I_X}. \tag{19}$$

To determine (k_1, k_2, R) that satisfy

$$\widetilde{k}_1 k_2 - k_1 \widetilde{k}_2 = Q(X)R(X), \tag{20}$$

one can transform (20) into a system of multivariate bilinear equations over $\mathbb{F}_q$. Specifically, each coefficient of k_1, k_2 and R is written using two variables over $\mathbb{F}_q$, the two variables representing the real and imaginary parts of that coefficient (which is in $\mathbb{F}_{q^2}$). The coefficients of $\widetilde{k}_1$ and $\widetilde{k}_2$ can then be written in terms of the coefficients of k_1 and k_2. Hence, equating coefficients of X^i of both sides of (20) yields $3m + 1$ quadratic equations. The real and imaginary parts of each of these equations are equated, yielding $6m + 2$ bilinear equations in $10m - 2D + 6$ variables over $\mathbb{F}_q$. This system of equations can be solved by finding a Gröbner basis for the ideal it generates. Finally, solutions (k_1, k_2, R) are tested until one is found for which R is m-smooth. This yields an expression for $\log_g Q$ in terms of the logarithms of approximately $q + 1 + A_{q^2}(m, 3m - D)$ polynomials of degree (at most) m; in the analysis we shall assume that each of the polynomials has degree exactly m.

Now, the number of candidate pairs (k_1, k_2) is $((q^2)^{m+1})^2 = q^{4(m+1)}$. Since $(q^2)^{3m-D+1}$ of the $(q^2)^{3m+1}$ degree-$(3m)$ polynomials in $\mathbb{F}_{q^2}[X]$ are divisible by $Q(X)$, the number of solutions (k_1, k_2, R) is expected to be approximately

$$\frac{q^{2(3m-D+1)}}{q^{2(3m+1)}} \cdot q^{4(m+1)} = q^{4(m+1)-2D}.$$

---

[3] More generally, the degrees of k_1 and k_2 can be different.

However, the number of distinct R obtained will be much less than $q^{4(m+1)-2D}$. For example, any two pairs (k_1', k_2') and (k_1'', k_2'') with $k_1'/k_2' = k_1''/k_2''$ will generate the same R, so the expected number of distinct R is at most $q^{4(m+1)-2D}/(q^2-1)$. Let us denote by $R(m, D)$ the expected number of distinct R obtainable. Then the condition

$$R(m, D) \gg \frac{q^{2(3m-D)}}{N_{q^2}(m, 3m - D)}, \tag{21}$$

can ensure that there exists a solution (k_1, k_2, R) for which R is m-smooth.

The number $R(m, D)$ has not been determined in general. For the case $m = 1$ and $D = 2$, one must select $k_1 = aX + b$ and $k_2 = cX + d$ with $(a, b, c, d) \in \mathcal{P}_q$ to avoid collisions; hence $R(1, 2) \leq \frac{q^4}{q^8}(q^3 + q) \approx \frac{1}{q}$ and descending from 2 to 1 can be expected to succeed only for 1 out of every q quadratics; this is indeed what we observed in our experiments. In general, the success of the Gröbner bases descent step is best determined experimentally (cf. §4.7).

It is difficult to determine the exact cost $G_{q^2}(m, D)$ of the Gröbner basis finding step. After the Gröbner basis is found, the cost to find an m-smooth R is $(q^2)^{3m-D}/N_{q^2}(m, 3m - D) \cdot S_{q^2}(m, 3m - D)$.

4   Computing Discrete Logarithms in $\mathbb{F}_{3^{6 \cdot 509}}$

We present a concrete analysis of the DLP algorithm described in §3 for computing discrete logarithms in $\mathbb{F}_{3^{6 \cdot 509}}$. In fact, this field is embedded in the quadratic extension field $\mathbb{F}_{3^{12 \cdot 509}}$, and it is the latter field where the DLP algorithm of §3 is executed. Thus, we have $q = 3^6 = 729$, $n = 509$, and $N = 3^{12 \cdot 509} - 1$. Note that $3^{12 \cdot 509} \approx 2^{9681}$. We wish to find $\log_g h$, where g is a generator of $\mathbb{F}_{3^{12 \cdot 509}}^*$ and $h \in \mathbb{F}_{3^{12 \cdot 509}}^*$.

As mentioned in §1, our main motivation for finding discrete logarithms in $\mathbb{F}_{3^{6 \cdot 509}}$ is to attack the elliptic curve discrete logarithm problem in $E(\mathbb{F}_{3^{509}})$, where E is the supersingular elliptic curve $Y^2 = X^3 - X + 1$ with $\#E(\mathbb{F}_{3^{509}}) = 7r$, and where $r = (3^{509} - 3^{255} + 1)/7$ is an 804-bit prime. Note that $r^2 \nmid N$. The elliptic curve discrete logarithm problem in the order-r subgroup of $E(\mathbb{F}_{3^{509}})$ can be efficiently reduced to the discrete logarithm problem in the order-r subgroup of $\mathbb{F}_{3^{12 \cdot 509}}^*$. In the latter problem, we are given two elements α, β of order r in $\mathbb{F}_{3^{12 \cdot 509}}^*$ and we wish to find $\log_\alpha \beta$. It can readily be seen that $\log_\alpha \beta = (\log_g \beta)/(\log_g \alpha) \bmod r$. Thus, we will henceforth assume that h has order r and that we only need to find $\log_g h \bmod r$. An immediate consequence of this restriction is that all the linear algebra in the new algorithm has to be performed modulo the 804-bit r instead of modulo the 9681-bit N.

The parameters for each step of the algorithm were carefully chosen in order to balance the running time of the steps. We also took into account the degree to which each step could be parallelized on conventional computers. A summary of the parameter choices for the descent is given in Figure 1. The costs of each step are given in Table 2.

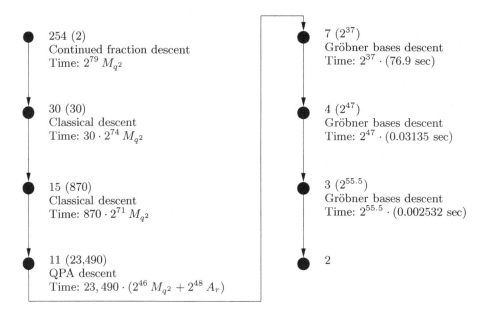

Fig. 1. A typical path of the descent tree for computing an individual logarithm in $\mathbb{F}_{3^{12 \cdot 509}}$ ($q = 3^6$). The numbers in parentheses next to each node are the expected number of nodes at that level. 'Time' is the expected time to generate all nodes at a level.

Table 2. Estimated costs of the main steps of the new DLP algorithm for computing discrete logarithms in $\mathbb{F}_{3^{12 \cdot 509}}$ ($q = 3^6$). A_r and M_{q^2} denote the costs of an addition modulo the 804-bit prime $r = (3^{509} - 3^{255} + 1)/7$ and a multiplication in $\mathbb{F}_{3^{12}}$. We use the cost ratio $A_r/M_{q^2} = 4$, and also assume that 2^{30} multiplications in $\mathbb{F}_{3^{12}}$ can be performed in 1 second (cf. §4.8).

Finding logarithms of linear polynomials		
Relation generation	$2^{30} M_{q^2}$	$2^{30} M_{q^2}$
Linear algebra	$2^{48} A_r$	$2^{50} M_{q^2}$
Finding logarithms of irreducible quadratic polynomials		
Relation generation	$3^{12} \cdot 2^{39} M_{q^2}$	$2^{58} M_{q^2}$
Linear algebra	$3^{12} \cdot 2^{48} A_r$	$2^{69} M_{q^2}$
Descent		
Continued-fraction (254 to 30)	$2^{79} M_{q^2}$	$2^{79} M_{q^2}$
Classical (30 to 15)	$30 \cdot 2^{74} M_{q^2}$	$2^{79} M_{q^2}$
Classical (15 to 11)	$870 \cdot 2^{71} M_{q^2}$	$2^{81} M_{q^2}$
QPA (11 to 7)	$23,490 \cdot (2^{46} M_{q^2} + 2^{48} A_r)$	$2^{65} M_{q^2}$
Gröbner bases (7 to 4)	$2^{37} \cdot (76.9 \text{ seconds})$	$2^{73} M_{q^2}$
Gröbner bases (4 to 3)	$2^{47} \cdot (0.03135 \text{ seconds})$	$2^{72} M_{q^2}$
Gröbner bases (3 to 2)	$2^{55.5} \cdot (0.002532 \text{ seconds})$	$2^{77} M_{q^2}$

4.1   Setup

We chose the representations

$$\mathbb{F}_{3^6} = \mathbb{F}_3[U]/(U^6 + 2U^4 + U^2 + 2U + 2)$$

and

$$\mathbb{F}_{3^{12}} = \mathbb{F}_{3^6}[V]/(V^2 + U^{365}).$$

We selected

$$h_0 = (U^{553}V + U^{343})X^2 + (U^{535}V + U^{417})X + (U^{172}V + U^{89}) \in \mathbb{F}_{3^{12}}[X]$$

and $h_1 = 1$, and $I_X \in \mathbb{F}_{3^{12}}[X]$ to be the degree-509 monic irreducible factor of $X^{3^6} - h_0$. The other irreducible factors have degrees 43, 55 and 122.

4.2   Finding Logarithms of Linear Polynomials

The factor base $\mathcal{B}_1$ has size $3^{12} \approx 2^{19}$. The cost of relation generation is approximately $2^{30}M_{q^2}$, whereas the cost of the linear algebra is approximately $2^{48}A_r$.

4.3   Finding Logarithms of Irreducible Quadratic Polynomials

For each $u \in \mathbb{F}_{3^{12}}$, the expected cost of computing logarithms of all quadratics in $\mathcal{B}_{2,u}$ is $2^{39}M_{q^2}$ for the computation of $\mathcal{H}(Q)$, and $2^{48}A_r$ for the linear algebra. Note that the number of columns in $\mathcal{H}(Q)$ can be halved since the logarithms of all reducible quadratics are known. Since the expected number of relations obtainable is

$$\frac{N_{q^2}(1,6)}{q^{12}} \cdot (q^3 + q) \approx \frac{1}{719.98} \cdot (q^3 + q) \approx q^2 + 6659,$$

one can expect that the matrix $\mathcal{H}(Q)$ will have full rank.

4.4   Continued-Fraction Descent

For the continued-fraction descent, we selected $m = 30$. The expected cost of this descent is $2^{79}M_{q^2}$. The expected number of distinct irreducible factors of degree (at most) 30 obtained is $2A_{3^{12}}(30, 254) \approx 30$.

4.5   Classical Descent

Two classical descent stages are employed. In the first stage, we have $D = 30$ and select $m = 15$, $s = 3$, $d_1 = 5$, $d_2 = 5$, and $\delta = 4$. The set of $D + \delta$ pairs (i, j) selected was

$$([0, 3] \times [0, 5]) \cup \{(4, 0), (4, 1), (4, 2), (4, 3), (4, 4), (5, 0), (5, 1), (5, 2), (5, 3), (5, 4)\},$$

yielding $t_1 = 138$ and $t_2 = 143$. Note that inequality (13) is satisfied. The expected cost of the descent for each of the 30 degree-30 polynomials is approximately $2^{52} \cdot S_{q^2}(15, 108)$. The expected total number of distinct irreducible polynomials of degree (at most) 15 obtained is approximately 870.

In the second classical descent stage, we have $D = 15$ and select $m = 11$, $s = 3$, $d_1 = 3$, $d_2 = 4$, and $\delta = 4$. The set of $D + \delta$ pairs (i, j) selected was

$$([0, 2] \times [0, 4]) \cup \{(3, 0), (3, 1), (3, 2), (3, 3)\},$$

yielding $t_1 = 110$ and $t_2 = 87$. Note that inequality (13) is satisfied. The expected cost of the descent for each of the 870 degree-15 polynomials is approximately $2^{50} \cdot S_{q^2}(11, 87)$. The expected total number of distinct irreducible polynomials of degree (at most) 11 obtained is approximately 23,490.

4.6 QPA Descent

The QPA descent method is then applied to each of the 23,490 degree-11 polynomials Q obtained from the classical descent stage. We have $D = 11$ and $m = 7$. For each Q, the expected number of rows in $\mathcal{H}(Q)$ is 570,172, so we can expect this matrix to have full column rank (namely, $q^2 = 531, 441$). For each Q, the expected cost of relation generation is $2^{29} \cdot S_{q^2}(7, 33)$ and the cost of the linear algebra is $2^{48} A_r$. Also for each Q, the expected number of distinct polynomials of degree at most 7 obtained is expected to be $A_{q^2}(7, 33) \cdot q^2 \approx 2^{22}$. Thus, the total number of distinct polynomials of degree at most 7 obtained after the QPA descent stage is approximately 2^{37}.

4.7 Gröbner Bases Descent

The Gröbner bases descent method is applied to each of the 2^{37} polynomials of degree (at most) 7 obtained after QPA descent. Our experiments were run using Magma v2.19-7 [41] on a 2.9 GHz Intel core i7-3520M.

First, one descends from 7 to 4, i.e., $D = 7$ and $m = 4$. For each degree-7 polynomial Q, we have to solve a system of 26 quadratic polynomial equations in 32 variables over $\mathbb{F}_q$ (cf. (20)). Since the ideal generated by these polynomials typically has dimension greater than 0, we randomly fix some of the variables in the hope of obtaining a 0-dimensional ideal. (More precisely, we added some linear constraints involving pairs of variables, one variable from k_1 and the other from k_2.) Each degree-5 R obtained from the variety of the resulting ideal is tested for 4-smoothness. If no 4-smooth R is obtained, we randomly fix some other subset of variables and repeat. We ran 17,510 Gröbner bases descent experiments with randomly-selected degree-7 polynomials Q. On average, we had to find 1.831 Gröbner bases for each Q. The average number of R's tested for 4-smoothness for each Q was 1.252, which agrees with the expected number $q^{10}/N_{q^2}(4, 5) \approx 1.25$. The average time to find each Gröbner basis was 42.0 seconds, and the memory consumption was 64 Mbytes. In total, the expected number of polynomials of degree at most 4 obtained is $2^{37}(q + 1 + A_{q^2}(4, 5)) \approx 2^{47}$.

Next, one descends from 4 to 3, i.e., $D = 4$ and $m = 3$. For each degree-4 polynomial Q, we have to solve a system of 20 quadratic polynomial equations in 28 variables over $\mathbb{F}_q$. We proceed as above, by fixing some of the 28 variables. We ran 1,230,000 Gröbner bases descent experiments with randomly-selected degree-4 polynomials Q. On average, we had to find 2.361 Gröbner bases for each Q. The average number of R's tested for 3-smoothness for each Q was 1.815, which agrees with the expected number $q^{10}/N_{q^2}(3,5) \approx 1.818$. The average time to find each Gröbner basis was 0.01328 seconds, and the memory consumption was 32 Mbytes. In total, the expected number of polynomials of degree at most 3 obtained is $2^{47}(q + 1 + A_{q^2}(3,5)) \approx 2^{57}$.

Finally, one descends from 3 to 2, i.e., $D = 3$ and $m = 2$. Since the total number of monic irreducible cubics over $\mathbb{F}_{q^2}$ is approximately $2^{55.5}$, which is less than 2^{57}, we perform the 3 to 2 descent for all monic irreducible cubics. For each such polynomial Q, we have to solve a system of 14 quadratic polynomial equations in 20 variables over $\mathbb{F}_q$. We proceed as above, by fixing some of the 20 variables. We ran 8,100,000 Gröbner bases descent experiments with randomly-selected degree-3 polynomials Q. On average, we had to find 2.026 Gröbner bases for each Q. The average number of R's tested for 2-smoothness for each Q was 1.499, which agrees with the expected number $q^6/N_{q^2}(2,3) \approx 1.5$. The average time to find each Gröbner basis was 0.00125 seconds, and the memory consumption was 32 Mbytes.

4.8 Overall Running Time

The second column of Table 2 gives the running time estimates for the main steps of the new DLP algorithm in three units of time: A_r, M_{q^2}, and seconds. In order to assess the overall time, we make some assumptions about the ratios of these units of time.

First, we shall assume that $A_r/M_{q^2} = 4$. To justify this, we observe that an 804-bit integer can be stored in thirteen 64-bit words. The X86-64 instruction set has an **ADD** operation that adds two 64-bit unsigned integers in one clock cycle. Hence, integer addition can be completed in 13 clock cycles. Modular reductions comprises one conditional statement plus one subtraction (required in roughly half of all modular additions). One can use a lazy reduction technique that amortizes the cost of a modular reduction among many integer additions. All in all, the cost of A_r can be estimated to be 13 clock cycles. Unlike for 64-bit integer multiplication, there is no native support for $\mathbb{F}_{3^{12}}$ multiplication on an Intel Core i7 machine. However, we expect that a specially designed multiplier could be built to achieve a multiplication cost of 4 clock cycles. While building such a native multiplier would certainly be costly, this expense can be expected to be within the budget of a well-funded adversary who is contemplating implementing the new DLP algorithm. This gives us an A_r/M_{q^2} ratio of approximately 4.

Next, since a multiplication in $\mathbb{F}_{3^{12}}$ can be done in 4 clock cycles, we will transform one second on a 2.9 GHz machine (on which the Gröbner bases descent experiments were performed) into $2^{30}M_{q^2}$.

Using these estimates, we see from the third column of Table 2 that the overall running time of the new algorithm is approximately $2^{81.7} M_{q^2}$. We note that the relation generation, continued-fraction descent, classical descent, and Gröbner bases descent steps, and also the relation generation portion of QPA descent, are effectively parallelizable in the sense that one can essentially achieve a factor-C speedup if C processors are available. Using the experimental results in [32,5] as a guide, we can safely estimate that each linear system of equations can be solved in less than one day of using a small number of GPUs and CPUs. Thus, we conclude that the linear system of equations for finding logarithms of linear polynomials, the $3^{12} \approx 2^{19}$ linear systems of equations for finding logarithms of irreducible quadratic polynomials, and the $23,490$ linear systems of equations in QPA can be effectively parallelized on conventional computers.

Remark 2. (*caveat emptor*) Although our analysis is concrete rather than asymptotic, it must be emphasized that the analysis makes several heuristic assumptions and approximations. For example, there are the usual heuristic assumptions that certain polynomials encountered are uniformly distributed over the set of all polynomials of the same degree. Furthermore, we have assumed that the matrix $\mathcal{H}(Q)$ in QPA descent indeed has full column rank. Also, our run time analysis ignores operations such as additions in $\mathbb{F}_{3^{12}}$ and memory accesses. Thus, further analysis and experimentation is needed before one can conclude with certainty that the $2^{81.7} M_{q^2}$ running time estimate is an accurate measure of the efficiency of the new DLP algorithm for computing logarithms in the order-r subgroup of $\mathbb{F}_{3^{6 \cdot 509}}^*$.

Remark 3. (*looseness of our upper bound on the running time*) Remark 2 notwithstanding, our analysis is quite conservative and there are several possible ways in which the upper bound on the running time could be improved. (i) In our estimates for the number of branches in a descent step, we assume that each distinct irreducible polynomial obtained has degree exactly m, whereas in practice many of these polynomials will have degree significantly less than m. Thus, it would appear that our upper bound on the number of nodes in the descent tree is quite loose. (ii) The Gröbner bases descent running times reported in §4.7 can be expected to be significantly improved by a native implementation of the F4 [21] or F5 [22] Gröbner basis finding algorithms optimized for characteristic-three finite fields. (Magma implements the F4 algorithm, but is not optimized for characteristic-three finite fields.) (iii) An optimized Gröbner basis implementation might be successful in performing the descent from $D = 11$ to $D = 6$, thereby replacing the QPA descent from $D = 11$ to $D = 7$ and significantly reducing the number of nodes in the descent tree. (iv) Bernstein's smoothness testing method [11] might be faster in practice than the basic method described in §2.2. (v) Sieving can be expected to significantly speedup the continued-fraction descent stage [6].

4.9   Comparisons with Joux-Lercier

Shinohara et al. [44] estimated that the running time of the Joux-Lercier algorithm [37] for computing discrete logarithms in $\mathbb{F}_{3^{6 \cdot 509}}$ is $2^{111.35}$ for the relation generation stage, and $2^{102.69}$ for the linear algebra stage; the units of time were not specified. The relation generation time can be significantly decreased using Joux's pinpointing technique [33] without having a noticeable impact on the linear algebra time. We note also that the linear algebra cost of $2^{102.69}$ is an underestimation since it does not account for the number of nonzero coefficients in each equation. In any case, since the relation generation is effectively parallelizable on conventional computers whereas the linear algebra is not, the linear algebra stage is the dominant step of the Joux-Lercier algorithm. Due to its large size, the linear algebra stage will remain infeasible for the foreseeable future.

In contrast, the new algorithm is effectively parallelizable and has an overall running time of $2^{81.7} M_{q^2}$. If one had access to a massive number of processors (e.g., 2^{30} processors), then the new algorithm could be executed within one year.

We believe that these comparisons justify the claim made in the abstract about the weakness of the field $\mathbb{F}_{3^{6 \cdot 509}}$, and thereby also the supersingular elliptic curve over $\mathbb{F}_{3^{509}}$ with embedding degree 6.

5   Concluding Remarks

Our concrete analysis of the new algorithm of Joux and Barbulescu et al. has shown that the supersingular elliptic curve over $\mathbb{F}_{3^{509}}$ with embedding degree 6 is significantly less resistant to attacks on the elliptic curve discrete logarithm problem than previously believed. Consequently, this elliptic curve is not suitable for implementing pairing-based cryptosystems. Our analysis applies equally well to the supersingular elliptic curve over $\mathbb{F}_{3^{5 \cdot 97}}$ with embedding degree 6 that has been proposed for compact hardware implementation of pairing-based cryptosystems by Estibals [20], and to the genus-2 curves over $\mathbb{F}_{2^{12 \cdot 367}}$ and $\mathbb{F}_{2^{12 \cdot 439}}$ with embedding degree 12 (see Appendix A).

An important open question is whether the new algorithm or its implementation can be improved to the extent that the discrete logarithm problem in $\mathbb{F}_{3^{6 \cdot 509}}$ can be feasibly solved using existing computer technology.

Another important question is whether the new attack is effective for finding discrete logarithms in other small-characteristic finite fields of interest in pairing-based cryptography. Our preliminary analysis suggests that the new algorithm is ineffective for computing discrete logarithms in $\mathbb{F}_{2^{4 \cdot 1223}}$.

Acknowledgements. We would like to thank Pierre-Jean Spaenlehauer for answering our questions about Gröbner basis finding algorithms.

References

1. Adikari, J., Anwar Hasan, M., Negre, C.: Towards faster and greener cryptoprocessor for eta pairing on supersingular elliptic curve over $\mathbb{F}_{2^{1223}}$. In: Knudsen, L.R., Wu, H. (eds.) SAC 2012. LNCS, vol. 7707, pp. 166–183. Springer, Heidelberg (2013)
2. Adleman, L., Huang, M.-D.: Function field sieve method for discrete logarithms over finite fields. Information and Computation 151, 5–16 (1999)

3. Ahmadi, O., Hankerson, D., Menezes, A.: Software implementation of arithmetic in $\mathbb{F}_{3^m}$. In: Carlet, C., Sunar, B. (eds.) WAIFI 2007. LNCS, vol. 4547, pp. 85–102. Springer, Heidelberg (2007)
4. Aranha, D., Beuchat, J., Detrey, J., Estibals, N.: Optimal eta pairing on supersingular genus-2 binary hyperelliptic curves. In: Dunkelman, O. (ed.) CT-RSA 2012. LNCS, vol. 7178, pp. 98–115. Springer, Heidelberg (2012)
5. Barbulescu, R., Bouvier, C., Detrey, J., Gaudry, P., Jeljeli, H., Thomé, E., Videau, M., Zimmermann, P.: Discrete logarithm in GF(2^{809}) with FFS, http://eprint.iacr.org/2013/197
6. Barbulescu, R., Gaudry, P.: Personal communication (August 12, 2013)
7. Barbulescu, R., Gaudry, P., Joux, A., Thomé, E.: A quasi-polynomial algorithm for discrete logarithm in finite fields of small characteristic: Improvements over FFS in small to medium characteristic, http://eprint.iacr.org/2013/400
8. Barreto, P., Galbraith, S., ÓhÉigeartaigh, C., Scott, M.: Efficient pairing computation on supersingular abelian varieties. Designs, Codes and Cryptography 42, 239–271 (2007)
9. Barreto, P., Kim, H., Lynn, B., Scott, M.: Efficient algorithms for pairing-based cryptosystems. In: Yung, M. (ed.) CRYPTO 2002. LNCS, vol. 2442, pp. 354–368. Springer, Heidelberg (2002)
10. Barrett, P.: Implementing the Rivest Shamir and Adleman public key encryption algorithm on a standard digital signal processor. In: Odlyzko, A.M. (ed.) CRYPTO 1986. LNCS, vol. 263, pp. 311–323. Springer, Heidelberg (1987)
11. Bernstein, D.: How to find small factors of integers (2002) (manuscript), http://cr.yp.to/papers/sf.pdf
12. Beuchat, J., Detrey, J., Estibals, N., Okamoto, E., Rodríguez-Henríquez, F.: Fast architectures for the η_T pairing over small-characteristic supersingular elliptic curves. IEEE Transactions on Computers 60, 266–281 (2011)
13. Beuchat, J., López-Trejo, E., Martínez-Ramos, L., Mitsunari, S., Rodríguez-Henríquez, F.: Multi-core implementation of the Tate pairing over supersingular elliptic curves. In: Garay, J.A., Miyaji, A., Otsuka, A. (eds.) CANS 2009. LNCS, vol. 5888, pp. 413–432. Springer, Heidelberg (2009)
14. Blake, I., Fuji-Hara, R., Mullin, R., Vanstone, S.: Computing logarithms in finite fields of characteristic two. SIAM Journal on Algebraic and Discrete Methods 5, 276–285 (1984)
15. Boneh, D., Lynn, B., Shacham, H.: Short signatures from the Weil pairing. Journal of Cryptology 17, 297–319 (2004)
16. Chatterjee, S., Hankerson, D., Menezes, A.: On the efficiency and security of pairing-based protocols in the type 1 and type 4 settings. In: Hasan, M.A., Helleseth, T. (eds.) WAIFI 2010. LNCS, vol. 6087, pp. 114–134. Springer, Heidelberg (2010)
17. Cheng, Q., Wan, D., Zhuang, J.: Traps to the BGJT-algorithm for discrete logarithms, http://eprint.iacr.org/2013/673
18. Coppersmith, D.: Fast evaluation of logarithms in fields of characteristic two. IEEE Transactions on Information Theory 30, 587–594 (1984)
19. Coppersmith, D.: Solving homogeneous linear equations over $GF(2)$ via block Wiedemann algorithm. Mathematics of Computation 62, 333–350 (1994)
20. Estibals, N.: Compact hardware for computing the Tate pairing over 128-bit-security supersingular curves. In: Joye, M., Miyaji, A., Otsuka, A. (eds.) Pairing 2010. LNCS, vol. 6487, pp. 397–416. Springer, Heidelberg (2010)
21. Faugère, J.: A new efficient algorithm for computing Gröbner bases (F_4). Journal of Pure and Applied Algebra 139, 61–88 (1999)

22. Faugère, J.: A new efficient algorithm for computing Gröbner bases without reduction to zero (F_5). In: Proceedings of the 2002 International Symposium on Symbolic and Algebraic Computation (ISSAC 2002), pp. 75–83 (2002)
23. Galbraith, S.: Supersingular curves in cryptography. In: Boyd, C. (ed.) ASIACRYPT 2001. LNCS, vol. 2248, pp. 495–513. Springer, Heidelberg (2001)
24. Galbraith, S., Harrison, K., Soldera, D.: Implementing the Tate pairing. In: Fieker, C., Kohel, D.R. (eds.) ANTS 2002. LNCS, vol. 2369, pp. 324–337. Springer, Heidelberg (2002)
25. Galbraith, S., Paterson, K., Smart, N.: Pairings for cryptographers. Discrete Applied Mathematics 156, 3113–3121 (2008)
26. Geiselmann, W., Shamir, A., Steinwandt, R., Tromer, E.: Scalable hardware for sparse systems of linear equations, with applications to integer factorization. In: Rao, J.R., Sunar, B. (eds.) CHES 2005. LNCS, vol. 3659, pp. 131–146. Springer, Heidelberg (2005)
27. Göloğlu, F., Granger, R., McGuire, G., Zumbrägel, J.: On the function field sieve and the impact of higher splitting probabilities. In: Canetti, R., Garay, J.A. (eds.) CRYPTO 2013, Part II. LNCS, vol. 8043, pp. 109–128. Springer, Heidelberg (2013)
28. Göloğlu, F., Granger, R., McGuire, G., Zumbrägel, J.: Solving a 6120-bit DLP on a desktop computer, http://eprint.iacr.org/2013/306
29. Granger, R., Page, D., Stam, M.: Hardware and software normal basis arithmetic for pairing based cryptography in characteristic three. IEEE Transactions on Computers 54, 852–860 (2005)
30. Hankerson, D., Menezes, A., Scott, M.: Software implementation of pairings. In: Joye, M., Neven, G. (eds.) Identity-Based Cryptography. IOS Press (2008)
31. Hayashi, T., Shimoyama, T., Shinohara, N., Takagi, T.: Breaking pairing-based cryptosystems using η_T pairing over $GF(3^{97})$. In: Wang, X., Sako, K. (eds.) ASIACRYPT 2012. LNCS, vol. 7658, pp. 43–60. Springer, Heidelberg (2012)
32. Jeljeli, H.: Accelerating iterative SpMV for discrete logarithm problem using GPUs, http://arxiv.org/abs/1209.5520
33. Joux, A.: Faster index calculus for the medium prime case: Application to 1175-bit and 1425-bit finite fields. In: Johansson, T., Nguyen, P.Q. (eds.) EUROCRYPT 2013. LNCS, vol. 7881, pp. 177–193. Springer, Heidelberg (2013)
34. Joux, A.: A new index calculus algorithm with complexity $L(1/4 + o(1))$ in very small characteristic, http://eprint.iacr.org/2013/095
35. Joux, A.: Discrete logarithm in GF(2^{6128}). Number Theory List (May 21, 2013)
36. Joux, A., Lercier, R.: The function field sieve is quite special. In: Fieker, C., Kohel, D.R. (eds.) ANTS 2002. LNCS, vol. 2369, pp. 431–445. Springer, Heidelberg (2002)
37. Joux, A., Lercier, R.: The function field sieve in the medium prime case. In: Vaudenay, S. (ed.) EUROCRYPT 2006. LNCS, vol. 4004, pp. 254–270. Springer, Heidelberg (2006)
38. LaMacchia, B., Odlyzko, A.: Solving large sparse linear systems over finite fields. In: Menezes, A., Vanstone, S.A. (eds.) CRYPTO 1990. LNCS, vol. 537, pp. 109–133. Springer, Heidelberg (1991)
39. Lenstra, A.K.: Unbelievable security: Matching AES security using public key systems. In: Boyd, C. (ed.) ASIACRYPT 2001. LNCS, vol. 2248, pp. 67–86. Springer, Heidelberg (2001)
40. Lenstra, A.K., Shamir, A., Tomlinson, J., Tromer, E.: Analysis of bernstein's factorization circuit. In: Zheng, Y. (ed.) ASIACRYPT 2002. LNCS, vol. 2501, pp. 1–26. Springer, Heidelberg (2002)
41. Magma v2.19-7, http://magma.maths.usyd.edu.au/magma/

42. Maple 17, http://www.maplesoft.com/products/maple/
43. Page, D., Smart, N., Vercauteren, F.: A comparison of MNT curves and supersingular curves. Applicable Algebra in Engineering, Communication and Computing 17, 379–392 (2006)
44. Shinohara, N., Shimoyama, T., Hayashi, T., Takagi, T.: Key length estimation of pairing-based cryptosystems using η_T pairing. In: Ryan, M.D., Smyth, B., Wang, G. (eds.) ISPEC 2012. LNCS, vol. 7232, pp. 228–244. Springer, Heidelberg (2012)
45. Wiedemann, D.: Solving sparse linear equations over finite fields. IEEE Transactions on Information Theory 32, 54–62 (1986)

A   Computing Discrete Logarithms in $\mathbb{F}_{2^{12 \cdot 367}}$

We present a concrete analysis of the DLP algorithm described in §3 for computing discrete logarithms in $\mathbb{F}_{2^{12 \cdot 367}}$. In fact, this field is embedded in the quadratic extension field $\mathbb{F}_{2^{24 \cdot 367}}$, and it is the latter field where the DLP algorithm of §3 is executed. Thus, we have $q = 2^{12}$, $n = 367$, and $N = 2^{24 \cdot 367} - 1$. Note that $2^{24 \cdot 367} \approx 2^{8808}$. We wish to find $\log_g h$, where g is a generator of $\mathbb{F}_{2^{24 \cdot 367}}^*$ and $h \in \mathbb{F}_{2^{24 \cdot 367}}^*$.

As mentioned in §1, our main motivation for finding discrete logarithms in $\mathbb{F}_{2^{12 \cdot 367}}$ is to attack the discrete logarithm problem in $\mathrm{Jac}_C(\mathbb{F}_{2^{367}})$, where C is the supersingular genus-2 curve $Y^2 + Y = X^5 + X^3$ with $\#\mathrm{Jac}_C(\mathbb{F}_{2^{367}}) = 13 \cdot 7170258097 \cdot r$, and where $r = (2^{734} + 2^{551} + 2^{367} + 2^{184} + 1)/(13 \cdot 7170258097)$ is a 698-bit prime. Note that $r^2 \nmid N$. The discrete logarithm problem in the order-r subgroup of $\mathrm{Jac}_C(\mathbb{F}_{2^{367}})$ can be efficiently reduced to the discrete logarithm

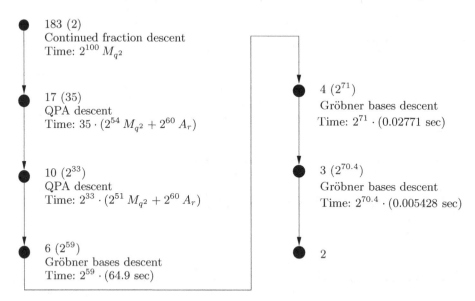

Fig. 2. A typical path of the descent tree for computing an individual logarithm in $\mathbb{F}_{2^{24 \cdot 367}}$ ($q = 2^{12}$). The numbers in parentheses next to each node are the expected number of nodes at that level. 'Time' is the expected time to generate all nodes at a level.

Table 3. Estimated costs of the main steps of the new DLP algorithm for computing discrete logarithms in $\mathbb{F}_{2^{24\cdot367}}$ $(q = 2^{12})$. A_r and M_{q^2} denote the costs of an addition modulo the 698-bit prime $r = (2^{734} + 2^{551} + 2^{367} + 2^{184} + 1)/(13 \cdot 7170258097)$ and a multiplication in $\mathbb{F}_{2^{24}}$. We use the cost ratio $A_r/M_{q^2} = 1$, and also assume that 2^{28} multiplications in $\mathbb{F}_{2^{24}}$ can be performed in 1 second (cf. §A).

Finding logarithms of linear polynomials		
Relation generation	$2^{35} M_{q^2}$	$2^{35} M_{q^2}$
Linear algebra	$2^{60} A_r$	$2^{60} M_{q^2}$
Finding logarithms of irreducible quadratic polynomials		
Relation generation	$2^{24} \cdot 2^{44} M_{q^2}$	$2^{68} M_{q^2}$
Linear algebra	$2^{24} \cdot 2^{60} A_r$	$2^{84} M_{q^2}$
Descent		
Continued-fraction (183 to 17)	$2^{100} M_{q^2}$	$2^{100} M_{q^2}$
QPA (17 to 10)	$35 \cdot (2^{54} M_{q^2} + 2^{60} A_r)$	$2^{65} M_{q^2}$
QPA (10 to 6)	$2^{33} \cdot (2^{51} M_{q^2} + 2^{60} A_r)$	$2^{93} M_{q^2}$
Gröbner bases (6 to 4)	$2^{59} \cdot (64.9 \text{ seconds})$	$2^{93} M_{q^2}$
Gröbner bases (4 to 3)	$2^{71} \cdot (0.02771 \text{ seconds})$	$2^{94} M_{q^2}$
Gröbner bases (3 to 2)	$2^{70.4} \cdot (0.005428 \text{ seconds})$	$2^{91} M_{q^2}$

problem in the order-r subgroup of $\mathbb{F}^*_{2^{12\cdot367}}$. Thus, we will henceforth assume that h has order r and that we only need to find $\log_g h \bmod r$. An immediate consequence of this restriction is that all the linear algebra in the new algorithm has to be performed modulo the 698-bit r instead of modulo the 8808-bit N.

The parameters for each step of the algorithm were chosen in order to balance the running time of the steps. We also took into account the degree to which each step could be parallelized on conventional computers. A summary of the parameter choices for the descent is given in Figure 2. The costs of each step are given in Table 3.

If $f \in \mathbb{F}_q[X]$ has degree d, then $X^q \bmod f$ can be determined by first precomputing $X^4, X^8, \dots, X^{4(d-1)} \bmod f$ by repeated multiplication by X. Thereafter, computing the fourth power of a polynomial modulo f can be accomplished by computing fourth powers of the coefficients of the polynomial, and then multiplying the precomputed polynomials by these fourth powers (and adding the results). In this way, we get a loose upper bound of $4d^2 + 11d^2 = 15d^2$ $\mathbb{F}_{2^{24}}$-multiplications of the cost to compute $X^{2^{24}} \bmod f$, and the total cost for testing m-smoothness of f (cf. §2.2) becomes

$$S_{2^{24}}(m, d) = 2d^2(d + m + 7.5) \quad \mathbb{F}_{2^{24}}\text{-multiplications.} \qquad (22)$$

A.1 Setup. We chose the representations

$$\mathbb{F}_{2^{12}} = \mathbb{F}_2[U]/(U^{12} + U^7 + U^6 + U^5 + U^3 + U + 1)$$

and

$$\mathbb{F}_{2^{24}} = \mathbb{F}_{2^{12}}[V]/(V^2 + U^{152}V + U^{3307}).$$

We selected

$$h_0 = (U^{2111}V + U^{2844})X^2 + (U^{428}V + U^{2059})X + (U^{1973}V + U^{827}) \in \mathbb{F}_{2^{24}}[X]$$

and

$$h_1 = X + U^{2904}V + U^{401} \in \mathbb{F}_{2^{24}}[X],$$

and $I_X \in \mathbb{F}_{2^{24}}[X]$ to be the degree-367 monic irreducible factor of $h_1 X^{2^{12}} - h_0$. The other irreducible factors of $h_1 X^{2^{12}} - h_0$ have degrees 23, 103, 162, 298 and 3144.

A.2 Finding Logarithms of Linear Polynomials. The factor base $\mathcal{B}_1$ has size 2^{24}. The cost of relation generation is approximately $2^{35} M_{q^2}$, whereas the cost of the linear algebra is approximately $2^{60} A_r$.

A.3 Finding Logarithms of Irreducible Quadratic Polynomials. For each $u \in \mathbb{F}_{2^{24}}$, the expected cost of computing logarithms of all quadratics in $\mathcal{B}_{2,u}$ is $2^{44} M_{q^2}$ for the computation of $\mathcal{H}(Q)$, and $2^{60} A_r$ for the linear algebra.

A.4 Continued-Fraction Descent. We selected $m = 17$. The expected cost of this descent is $2^{100} M_{q^2}$. The expected number of distinct irreducible factors of degree (at most) 17 obtained is $2 A_{2^{24}}(17, 183) \approx 35$.

A.5 Classical Descent. When applicable, classical descent is preferable to QPA descent since the former produces a far smaller number of branches when descending from a polynomial Q. However, in the field under consideration we have $q = 2^{12}$, so at least one of X^{2^s} and $X^{2^{12-s}}$ has degree at least 64. This means that at least one of the polynomials $R_1 = R(X, X^{2^s})$ and $R_2 = R'(X^{2^{12-s}}, h_0)$ (cf. §3.5) has very large degree, rendering classical descent ineffective.

A.6 QPA Descent. The QPA descent method is applied to each of the 35 degree-17 polynomials Q obtained from the continued-fraction descent stage. We have $D = 17$ and $m = 10$. For each Q, the expected cost of relation generation is $2^{54} M_{q^2}$ and the cost of the linear algebra is $2^{60} A_r$. Also for each Q, the expected number of distinct polynomials of degree at most 6 obtained is expected to be $A_{q^2}(10, 51) \cdot q^2 \approx 2^{28}$. Thus, the total number of distinct polynomials of degree at most 10 obtained after the first QPA descent stage is approximately 2^{33}.

The QPA descent method is then applied to each of these 2^{33} degree-10 polynomials Q. We have $D = 10$ and $m = 6$. For each Q, the expected cost of relation generation is $2^{51} M_{q^2}$ and the cost of the linear algebra is $2^{60} A_r$. Also for each Q, the expected number of distinct polynomials of degree at most 6 obtained is expected to be $A_{q^2}(6, 30) \cdot q^2 \approx 2^{26}$. Thus, the total number of distinct polynomials of degree at most 6 obtained after the second QPA descent stage is approximately 2^{59}.

A.7 Gröbner Bases Descent. The Gröbner bases descent method is applied to each of the 2^{59} polynomials of degree (at most) 6 obtained after QPA descent. Our experiments were run using Magma v2.19-7 [41] on a 2.9 GHz Intel core i7-3520M.

First, one descends from 6 to 4, i.e., $D = 6$ and $m = 4$. For each degree-6 polynomial Q, we have to solve a system of 26 quadratic polynomial equations in 34 variables over $\mathbb{F}_q$ (cf. (20)). After fixing some variables, each degree-6 R obtained from the variety of the resulting ideal is tested for 4-smoothness. If no 4-smooth R is obtained, we randomly fix some other subset of variables and repeat. We ran 11,810 Gröbner bases descent experiments with randomly-selected degree-6 polynomials Q. On average, we had to find 2.112 Gröbner bases for each Q. The average number of R's tested for 4-smoothness for each Q was 1.585, which agrees with the expected number $q^{12}/N_{q^2}(4,6) \approx 1.579$. The average time to find each Gröbner basis was 30.74 seconds. In total, the expected number of polynomials of degree at most 4 obtained is $2^{59}(q+1+A_{q^2}(4,6)) \approx 2^{71}$.

Next, one descends from 4 to 3, i.e., $D = 4$ and $m = 3$. For each degree-4 polynomial Q, we have to solve a system of 20 quadratic polynomial equations in 28 variables over $\mathbb{F}_q$. We proceed as above, by fixing some of the 28 variables. We ran 3,608,000 Gröbner bases descent experiments with randomly-selected degree-4 polynomials Q. On average, we had to find 2.362 Gröbner bases for each Q. The average number of R's tested for 3-smoothness for each Q was 1.817, which agrees with the expected number $q^{10}/N_{q^2}(3,5) \approx 1.818$. The average time to find each Gröbner basis was 0.01173 seconds. In total, the expected number of polynomials of degree at most 3 obtained is $2^{71}(q+1+A_{q^2}(3,5)) \approx 2^{83}$.

Finally, one descends from 3 to 2, i.e., $D = 3$ and $m = 2$. Since the total number of monic irreducible cubics over $\mathbb{F}_{q^2}$ is approximately $2^{70.4}$, which is less than 2^{83}, we perform the 3 to 2 descent for all monic irreducible cubics. For each such polynomial Q, we have to solve a system of 14 quadratic polynomial equations in 20 variables over $\mathbb{F}_q$. We proceed as above, by fixing some of the 20 variables. We ran 1,080,000 Gröbner bases descent experiments with randomly-selected degree-3 polynomials Q. On average, we had to find 2.024 Gröbner bases for each Q. The average number of R's tested for 2-smoothness for each Q was 1.5, which agrees with the expected number $q^6/N_{q^2}(2,3) \approx 1.5$. The average time to find each Gröbner basis was 0.002682 seconds.

A.8 Overall Running Time. In order to assess the overall time, we make some assumptions about the ratios of units of time used in Table 3, namely A_r, M_{q^2}, and seconds.

First, we shall assume that $A_r/M_{q^2} = 1$. To justify this, we use estimates similar to the ones in §4.8. An integer modulo r can be accommodated in eleven 64-bit words, so we estimate A_r to be 11 clock cycles. Using the carry-less multiplication instruction PCLMULQDQ, a multiplication in $\mathbb{F}_{2^{24}}$ can be performed at a price of approximately 10 clock cycles. This gives us an A_r/M_{q^2} ratio of approximately 1.

Next, since a multiplication in $\mathbb{F}_{2^{24}}$ can be done in approximately 10 clock cycles, we will transform one second on a 2.9 GHz machine (on which the Gröbner bases descent experiments were performed) into $2^{28}M_{q^2}$.

Using these estimates, we see from the third column of Table 2 that the overall running time of the new algorithm is approximately $2^{100}M_{q^2}$. As with the case of $\mathbb{F}_{3^{12\cdot509}}$, the relation generation, continued-fraction descent, classical descent, and Gröbner bases descent steps, and also the relation generation portion of QPA descent, are effectively parallelizable on conventional computers. Moreover, the linear system of equations for finding logarithms of linear polynomials, the 2^{24} linear systems of equations for finding logarithms of irreducible quadratic polynomials, and the 2^{33} linear systems of equations are also effectively parallelizable on conventional computers since each linear system of equations can be expected to be solvable in less than 12 days using a small number of GPUs and CPUs (cf. [32,5]).

A.9 Comparisons with Joux-Lercier. The Joux-Lercier algorithm [37] with pinpointing [33] is an alternative method for computing discrete logarithms in the order-r subgroup of $\mathbb{F}_{2^{12\cdot367}}^*$. The algorithm works with two polynomial representations of $\mathbb{F}_{2^{12\cdot367}}$.

The factor base can be taken to be the set of all monic irreducible polynomials of degree at most 4 over $\mathbb{F}_{2^{12}}$ in each of the two representations. The action of the 2^{12}-power Frobenius is used to reduce the factor base size by a factor of 12, yielding a factor base of size $2^{43.4}$. Taking $d_1 = 37$ and $d_2 = 10$ (see Section 2 of [33] for the definitions of d_1 and d_2), the running time of relation generation is approximately $2^{94.0}M_q$, where M_q denotes the cost of a multiplication in $\mathbb{F}_{2^{12}}$ (cf. Section 4 of [33]). The (sparse) matrix in the linear algebra stage has $2^{43.4}$ rows and columns, and approximately 28 nonzero entries per row. Using standard techniques for solving sparse systems of linear equations [38], the expected cost of the linear algebra is approximately $2^{91.6}$ operations modulo r. Since relation generation is effectively parallelizable, whereas the linear algebra is not amenable to parallelization due to its large size, the dominant step in the Joux-Lercier algorithms is the linear algebra.

In contrast, even though the new algorithm has a greater overall running time of $2^{100}M_{q^2}$, it is effectively parallelizable. Thus a reasonable conclusion is that the new algorithm is more effective than Joux-Lercier for computing logarithms in $\mathbb{F}_{2^{12\cdot367}}$.

To lend further weight to this conclusion, we observe that special-purpose hardware for solving the relatively-small linear systems of equations in the new algorithm can reasonably be expected to be built at a cost that is well within the budget of a well-funded organization. In 2005, Geiselmann et al. [26] estimated that the cost of special-purpose hardware for solving a linear system where the matrix has 2^{33} rows and columns, and approximately 2^7 nonzero entries (integers modulo 2) per row would be approximately U.S. \$2 million; the linear system would be solvable in 2.4 months. For $\mathbb{F}_{2^{12\cdot367}}$, each matrix in the new algorithm has 2^{24} rows and columns, and approximately 2^{12} nonzero entries (integers modulo r) per row. On the other hand, the cost of special-purpose hardware for solving the linear system encountered in the Joux-Lercier algorithm would be prohibitive.

Our conclusion about the relative weakness of $\mathbb{F}_{2^{12\cdot367}}$ for discrete logarithm cryptography also applies to the field $\mathbb{F}_{2^{12\cdot439}}$. Both these conclusions are subject to the caveats in Remark 2 in §4.8.

The Special Number Field Sieve in $\mathbb{F}_{p^n}$
Application to Pairing-Friendly Constructions

Antoine Joux[1,2,4,5,6] and Cécile Pierrot[3,4,5,6]

[1] CryptoExperts
[2] Chaire de Cryptologie de la Fondation de l'UPMC,
4 place Jussieu, 75005 Paris, France
[3] Université de Versailles Saint-Quentin, Laboratoire PRISM,
45 avenue des États-Unis, 78000 Versailles, France
[4] UPMC, Univ Paris 06, LIP6
[5] INRIA, Paris-Rocquencourt Center, PolSys Project
[6] CNRS, UMR 7606, LIP6
Antoine.Joux@m4x.org, Cecile.Pierrot@lip6.fr

Abstract. In this paper, we study the discrete logarithm problem in finite fields related to pairing-based curves. We start with a precise analysis of the state-of-the-art algorithms for computing discrete logarithms that are suitable for finite fields related to pairing-friendly constructions. To improve upon these algorithms, we extend the Special Number Field Sieve to compute discrete logarithms in $\mathbb{F}_{p^n}$, where p has an adequate sparse representation. Our improved algorithm works for the whole range of applicability of the Number Field Sieve.

1 Introduction

Since its introduction, pairing-based cryptography has permitted the development of many cryptographic schemes, including identity-based cryptographic primitives [BF03, SK03, CC03, Pat02], short signature schemes [BLS04], or one-round three-way key exchange [Jou04]. Some of these schemes have already been deployed in the marketplace.

One very important challenge necessary for practical pairing-based cryptography is to construct pairing-friendly curves suitable for efficient asymmetric schemes offering a high security level and to estimate precisely their concrete security. This is not a simple task, since it requires to construct a pairing-based curve, while balancing the complexities of the various discrete logarithm algorithms that can be used. This challenge has been studied in many articles such as [BLS03, KM05]. To evaluate the security of a given construction, the traditional approach is to balance the complexity of square-root algorithms for computing discrete logarithms in the relevant subgroup of the elliptic curve and an estimate of the complexity of the Number Field Sieve (NFS) algorithm in the finite field where the pairing takes its values. The complexity of solving the discrete logarithm problem in the finite field in this context is usually estimated by using keysize tables such as [Nat03, LV01]. This approach makes an *implicit assumption*, namely it considers that the complexity of NFS in the finite field is close to the complexity of factoring an integer

Z. Cao and F. Zhang (Eds.): Pairing 2013, LNCS 8365, pp. 45–61, 2014.

of the same size. As far as we know, this implicit assumption has not been checked in the relevant literature.

Our goal in this paper is twofold. First, we show that for current parameters of high-security pairing-based cryptography, the implicit assumption is incorrect and that the state-of-the-art algorithm for discrete logarithms in this case is the High-Degree variant of the Number Field Sieve introduced in [JLSV06], whose complexity is higher than the complexity of factoring. Second, we revisit discrete logarithm algorithms and show that, thanks to the specific form of the characteristic of the field of definition of pairing-friendly curves that appears with classical constructions, such as Barreto-Naehrig [BN05], it is possible to devise improved algorithms by generalizing the Special Number Field Sieve (SNFS) [Gor93, Sch08]. In truth, we go beyond this goal and present SNFS variations for the whole range of finite fields covered by the NFS, assuming that the characteristic of the field admits an adequate sparse representation.

As a side bonus, we also improve the complexity analysis given in [JLSV06] for the boundary case between FFS and NFS and show that in this boundary case, the complexity of NFS is, in fact, not higher than in the general case.

This paper is organized as follows: in Sections 2 and 3 we make a short refresher on tools and on the Number Field Sieve used in the medium prime case. This includes our improvement of the boundary case in Section 3.1. We explain in Section 4 the state-of-the-art algorithm for discrete logarithms for pairing-based cryptography. In Section 5 we develop our variation on the special index calculus algorithm for $\mathbb{F}_{p^n}$ involved in pairing-friendly constructions. The Section 6 gives finally a precise heuristic analysis of the algorithm.

2   Tools and Notations

When dealing with index calculus algorithms, the complexities are usually expressed using the following notation:

$$L_q(\alpha, c) = \exp\left((c + o(1))(\log q)^\alpha (\log \log q)^{1-\alpha}\right)$$

where α and c are constants such that $0 < \alpha < 1$ and $c > 0$ and log denotes natural logarithm. The notation $L_q(\alpha)$ is also used when the constant c is not explicitly specified. These functions arise from the probability for values to be smooth. More precisely, it comes from the well-known theorem of Canfield, Erdös and Pomerance. Let us introduce the quantity $\psi(x, y)$ to denote the number of positive numbers up to x which are y-smooth. Then $\log(\psi(x, y)/x)$ is close to:

$$-\frac{\log x}{\log y}\left(\log\left(\frac{\log x}{\log y}\right)\right).$$

In particular, when both x and y are given as L_q expressions, we have the following theorem.

Theorem 21 (Canfield, Erdös, Pomerance). *Let $C \subset \mathbb{R}^4$ be a compact set such that for all $(r, s, \gamma, \delta) \in C$ one has $\gamma > 0$, $\delta > 0$ and $0 < s < r < 1$. Let $\mathcal{P}$ denote the probability that a random positive integer below $L_q(r, \gamma)$ splits into primes lower than $L_q(s, \delta)$. Then we have:*

$$\mathcal{P} = L_q(r - s, -\gamma(r - s)/\delta + o(1))$$

for $q \to \infty$, uniformly for (r, s, γ, δ) in C.

As often the case in articles studying index calculus algorithms, we also use the *heuristic generalization* of Theorem 21 to the probability of smoothness of integers which are not selected uniformly and to pairs of integers which are not independent.

3   A Short Refresher on Discrete Logarithms in the Medium Prime Case

Thoughout the rest of the paper, Q denotes the size of the finite field being considered, *i.e.* $Q = p^n$.

3.1   The $p = L_Q(l_p, c_p)$ Case, with $1/3 \leqslant l_p < 2/3$

We first recall the Number Field Sieve variant proposed in [JLSV06] in the case where $p = L_Q(l_p, c_p)$, with $1/3 < l_p < 2/3$. We extend afterwards the algorithm to the configuration $p = L_Q(1/3, c_p)$.

3.1.1   The $l_p \neq 1/3$ Case

Setup

General setting. In order to compute discrete logarithms in $\mathbb{F}_{p^n}$, a degree n extension of the base field $\mathbb{F}_p$, we start by choosing two polynomials f_1 and f_2 in $\mathbb{Z}[X]$ with a common root in $\mathbb{F}_{p^n}$. In other words, we choose f_1 and f_2 such that the greatest common divisor of these two polynomials has an irreducible factor of degree n in $\mathbb{F}_p$. As a consequence, we can draw the commutative diagram in Figure 1.

Let $\mathbb{Q}[\theta_1]$ denote $\mathbb{Q}[X]/(f_1(X))$ and $\mathbb{Q}[\theta_2]$ denote $\mathbb{Q}[X]/(f_2(X))$, the two number fields defined by f_1 and f_2, *i.e.* θ_1 and θ_2 are roots of these polynomials in $\mathbb{C}$.

Choice of polynomials. In [JLSV06], f_1 is chosen as a degree n polynomial, with small coefficients and irreducible over $\mathbb{F}_p$, while f_2 is defined as the polynomial $f_1 + p$. To balance the size of the norms computed during the algorithm, another approach is also mentioned. This variant uses continued fractions and involves changing the polynomial selection such that the coefficients of both polynomials are of the same size. The authors of [JLSV06] propose for instance to choose f_1 such that at least one of its coefficients, let us say c, is of the order of $\sqrt{p}$. More

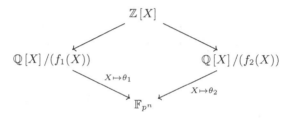

Fig. 1. Commutative diagram for the algorithm of [JLSV06]

precisely, such that $f_1 = g + c \cdot h$ where g and h are polynomials with small coefficients. Since we can write $c \equiv a/b \pmod{p}$ with a and b also of the order of $\sqrt{p}$, we define $f_2 \equiv bf_1 \pmod{p}$. The coefficients of f_2 are $O(\sqrt{p})$ instead of $O(p)$.

The key contribution of our variation of the SNFS in Section 5 is to introduce a different way to reduce the size of the coefficients that appear in f_1 and f_2.

Sieving
We then denote by $t - 1$ the degree[1] of the polynomials which we are going to sieve on and the two following bounds: A a sieve limit and B a smoothness bound. We consider all t-uples of the form $(a_0, \cdots, a_{t-1})$ such that the norms of the $a_0 + \cdots + a_{t-1}\theta_1^{t-1}$ and $a_0 + \cdots + a_{t-1}\theta_2^{t-1}$ are both B-smooth. After some post-processing described in [JLSV06], each such t-uple yields a linear equation between "logarithms of ideals" coming from both number fields and belonging to the smoothness basis.

Linear Algebra
Once the sieving phase is complete, we solve the resulting sparse system of equations modulo $p^n - 1$, the cardinality of $\mathbb{F}_{p^n}^*$, and recover logarithms of ideals in the smoothness basis. To be more precise, the linear algebra is done modulo a large factor of this cardinality, while small prime factors are considered separately, using a combination of Pollard's rho and Pohlig-Hellman algorithm.

Individual Discrete Logarithms
Once the sieving and the linear algebra phases have been performed, we know the logarithms of all the ideals in the smoothness basis. The important phase that remains is the individual discrete logarithms phase which allows to compute the discrete logarithm of an arbitrary element in the finite field. The approach proposed in [JLSV06] is based on a "special-q" descent. In a nutshell, in order to compute the discrete logarithm of an arbitrary element y of $\mathbb{F}_{p^n}$, represented as $\mathbb{F}_p[X]/(f_1(X))$, we search for a multiplicative relation of the form $z = y^i X^j$ for some $i, j \in \mathbb{N}$. We expect z to satisfy the two properties: if $B' = L_Q(2/3, 1/3^{1/3})$ and $\bar{z}$ denotes the lift of z to the number field $\mathbb{Q}[\theta_1]$, the norm of $\bar{z}$ should be

---

[1] While this notation might seems awkward, it is in fact quite convenient, because a polynomial of degree $t - 1$ gives dimension t to the sieving space.

B'-smooth and squarefree. The second condition implies that only degree one prime ideals will appear in the factorization of $(\bar{z})$. This is required since only logarithms of such ideals are computed during the sieving and linear algebra phases. After finding such a z, we factor the principal ideal generated by $\bar{z}$ into degree one prime ideals of small norm. Some of them are not in the factor base (those whose norm is smaller than B' but bigger than B). To compute the logarithm of such an ideal $\mathbf{q}$ we start a "special-$\mathbf{q}$" descent, progressively lowering the bound B' until it reaches B. We finally backtrack to recover the logarithm of $\bar{z}$ and consequently the logarithm of y.

3.1.2   The $p = L_Q(1/3, c_p)$ Case

Again, we sieve on polynomials of degree $t - 1$ and follow the phases described above. However, the analysis of [JLSV06] no longer applies directly and we need to refine the bound on norms to extend the analysis to this case.

A Short Analysis of the Extended NFS

Let us recall that the parameters of the algorithm taking part in the analysis are the extension degree n, the smoothness bound [2], the degree $t - 1$ of the elements we are sieving over and the bound A on the coefficients of these elements. We assume that we can write:

$$n = \frac{1}{c_p} \left(\frac{\log Q}{\log \log Q} \right)^{2/3}, \quad t = \frac{c_t}{c_p} \left(\frac{\log Q}{\log \log Q} \right)^{1/3}, \quad A^t = L_Q(1/3, c_a c_t),$$

where c_a and c_t will be determined later on.

The difference between the case $p = L_Q(1/3, c_p)$ and the case $p = L_Q(l_p, c_p)$ with $1/3 < l_p < 2/3$ appears when computing the bound on the norms of polynomials. More precisely, for each polynomial involved in the sieving, the two norms are easily bounded by $n^t t^n A^n$ and $n^t t^n A^n p^t$ respectively on the $\mathbb{Q}[\theta_1]$ and on the $\mathbb{Q}[\theta_2]$ side. When $l_p > 1/3$, the $n^t t^n$ term is negligible compared to A^n and p^t and vanishes from the complexity analysis. However, due to the size of t and n in the $l_p = 1/3$ case, the t^n term is no longer negligible. This leads to an extra term in the product of the norms and yields a $L_Q(1/3)$ complexity with a constant higher than $(128/9)^{1/3}$.

We now improve the bound on these two norms in order to restore a complexity of $L_Q(1/3, (128/9)^{1/3})$ in this extended case of NFS.

First, each norm can be expressed as the determinant of the Sylvester matrix $M(f_i, h)$ of f_i and h, with $i = 1$ or $i = 2$. Let $m_{j,k}$ represents the coefficient at the j-th row and k-th column of $M(f_i, h)$. Using the formula:

$$\det M(f_i, h) = \sum_{\sigma_j \in S_{n+t}} \operatorname{sign}(\sigma_j) \prod_{k=1}^{n+t} m_{k, \sigma_j(k)}, \tag{1}$$

we remark that the two norms are bounded by ΘA^n and $\Theta A^n p^t$ respectively on the $\mathbb{Q}[\theta_1]$ and on the $\mathbb{Q}[\theta_2]$ side, where Θ is the number of permutations

---

[2] Which is not required in this section, where we simply improve the bound on norms.

of S_{n+t} leading to a non zero product in (1). Kalkbrener gives a majoration of Θ in the second theorem of [Kal97]. With our notations this bound becomes: $\Theta \leqslant \binom{n+t}{n} \cdot \binom{n+t-1}{t}$. Because of the following inequalities:

$$
\begin{aligned}
\binom{n+t}{n} \cdot \binom{n+t-1}{t} &= \frac{n}{n+t} \left(\frac{(n+t)!}{n!t!} \right)^2 \\
&\leq \frac{n}{n+t} \left(\frac{(n+1)\cdots(n+t)}{t!} \right)^2 \\
&\leq \frac{n}{n+t} \left(\prod_{i=1}^{t} \frac{(n+i)}{i} \right)^2 \\
&\leq \frac{n}{n+t} \prod_{i=1}^{t} \left(\frac{n}{i} + 1 \right)^2
\end{aligned}
$$

we obtain that $\Theta \leqslant (n+1)^{2t}$. Hence the two norms are bounded by $(n+1)^{2t} A^n$ and $(n+1)^{2t} A^n p^t$ respectively. Due to the size of n and t in this case, we have $(n+1)^{2t} \approx L_Q(1/3, 4c_t/3c_p)$ and thus the coefficient $(n+1)^{2t}$ is negligible (when Q tends to infinity) compared to the $L_Q(2/3)$ contribution of A^n and p^t. As a

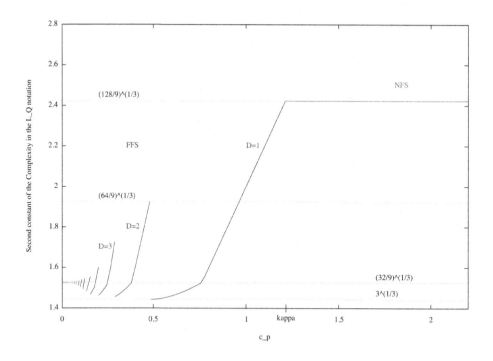

Fig. 2. Asymptotic complexities at the $p = L_Q(1/3, c_p)$ boundary case. The graph represents the second constant c of the complexity $L_Q(1/3, c)$ as a function of c_p.

consequence, we recover the two usual bounds so this allows us to continue with the same analysis of NFS as before. We conclude that the asymptotic complexity of the extended NFS when $l_p = 1/3$ is also:

$$L_Q(1/3, (128/9)^{1/3}).$$

Yet the $p = L_Q(1/3, c_p)$ case remains particular because we have to consider both the extended version of the NFS algorithm and the Function Field Sieve algorithm (FFS) from [JL06]. It is not our main point here to develop the analysis of this boundary case in the FFS part but we need to know which algorithm gives the best asymptotic complexity depending on the constant c_p. The Figure 2 addresses this need by showing how complexities vary with c_p in this case. The intersection between the FFS and the NFS approach is at $c_p = \kappa$ with $\kappa = (16/9)^{1/3}$. It is also indicated which algorithm has to be chosen in each case: the FFS algorithm when c_p is smaller than κ, and the NFS algorithm when c_p is higher. This figure is the juxtaposition of two analyses: the NFS analysis performed above and the FFS analysis from [JL06].

3.2   The $p = L_Q(l_p, c_p)$ Case with $2/3 \leqslant l_p \leqslant 1$

In this case, we modify both settings and sieving phase. First, the choice of the polynomials has to be changed, since the size of the coefficients of f_2 is too high when f_2 is defined as $f_1 + p$. In [JLSV06] the authors propose to select the polynomial f_2 using lattice reduction. We do not give details on this method since it does not affect our new algorithm developed further.

The second modification concerns the sieving space. Indeed, for these values of l_p it is possible to collect enough relations with a smaller sieving space than the one involved above. More precisely, it suffices to set $t = 2$, *i.e.* to sieve on linear polynomials only. The linear algebra and the individual discrete logarithms phases are left unchanged.

4   Applicable Discrete Logarithms for Pairing-Based Cryptography

Constructing pairing-based elliptic curves with a high security level implies taking into account the complexities of the various discrete logarithm algorithms that can be used. The traditional approach is to balance the complexity of a generic algorithm for computing discrete logarithms in the relevant subgroup of the elliptic curve and an estimate of the complexity of the NFS algorithm in the finite field where the pairing takes its values. This requires that $\sqrt{p} = L_Q(1/3, c)$, for some constant c. Equivalently, we have:

$$p = L_Q(1/3, 2c). \tag{2}$$

It is relevant to notice that this constraint imposed on curves gives an indication on the form of the characteristic p, and that this explicit form permits conversely to estimate the actual complexity of computing discrete logarithms in the finite field considered. As a consequence of (2), we consider the case discussed in section 3.1. To determine which algorithm is applicable for computing discrete logarithms in $\mathbb{F}_Q$ with $p = L_Q(1/3, 2c)$, we have to evaluate the constant $2c$. As said in the introduction, we notice that current constructions select keys implicitly as if the complexity in the finite field was $L_Q(1/3, c)$ with a constant $c = (64/9)^{1/3}$. This leads to $2c \approx 3.845998854$, which is clearly higher than the boundary point κ. This points out that the extended NFS is the algorithm applicable here.

As a consequence, the actual choice of parameters and, in particular, the usual implicit assumption that $c = (64/9)^{1/3}$ are too pessimistic compared with the state-of-the-art. In fact, the analysis of section 3.1 shows that, using the best currently known variant of the Number Field Sieve algorithm, we have to choose $c = (128/9)^{1/3}$. We still have $2c > \kappa$.

5   SNFS Polynomials for Pairing-Based Finite Fields

5.1   Pairing-Based Finite Fields

Instead of proceeding as in Section 3 in the case of finite fields of general form we consider now the specificity of finite fields obtained with some particular curves. In practice, pairings require elliptic curves to be computationally very simple to use, and, often, not too difficult to generate. With this aim, families of such curves are frequently characterized by three simple polynomials, including P which defines after evaluation the characteristic of $\mathbb{F}_{p^n}$ where $\varphi : E \times E \to \mathbb{F}_{p^n}$ is the pairing considered, E a particular curve in the family and n its embedding degree. Several families have been proposed [FST10] and most of them have in common to set P as a polynomial of small degree and with constant coefficients. Until now, we consider the case of a particular family of curves where p the characteristic of $\mathbb{F}_{p^n}$ is given by the evaluation of such a polynomial. In other words, we consider a family where p can be written as:

$$p = P(u),$$

with P a polynomial of small degree λ and small coefficients and u small compared to p. We want to underline that λ is fixed beforehand and only depends on the family considered. Thus λ does not depend on p. In the following subsection 5.2, we explain how to use this sparse representation of p to lower the asymptotic heuristic complexity for the whole range of finite fields covered by the NFS – see the complete analysis in Section 6.

5.2   Choice of Polynomials for the SNFS Algorithm

We explain now how to use the specific structure of the polynomials characterizing pairing-friendly curves. Only a slight change has to be made in the algorithm described above: it concerns the choice of the two polynomials f_1 and f_2. We choose f_1 as an irreducible polynomial over $\mathbb{F}_p$, with degree equals to n, such as:

$$f_1(X) = X^n + R(X) - u$$

with $R(X)$ a polynomial of small degree and with coefficients 0, 1 or -1. Since we have $P(u) = p$, the size of the coefficients of f_1 is bounded by $p^{1/\lambda}$. Let us be more precise about the degree d_R of R. f_1 is a polynomial of degree n and has consequently approximatively one chance over n to be irreducible over the finite field: thus we need to keep enough degree of freedom concerning the choice of the coefficients of f_1. Hence we assume that the degree d_R is such as $d_R = O(\log n / \log 3)$. Since $3^{\log n / \log 3} = n$, this permits us to have enough choices for R, thus for f_1, and finally to obtain an irreducible polynomial [3].

Moreover, the second polynomial is chosen as follows:

$$f_2(X) = P(X^n + R(X)).$$

Indeed, f_2 has degree λn and the size of its coefficients is bounded by $O(\log(n)^\lambda)$. This mostly comes from the $R(X)^\lambda$ term that appears in the decomposition of f_2, which provides the highest coefficients of f_2. Its coefficients are in fact bounded by $(d_R + 2)^\lambda = O(\log(n)^\lambda)$, with some multinomials in λ hidden in the O notation. Furthermore, we have:

$$f_2(X) = P(f_1(X) + u) \equiv P(u) = p,$$

where $\equiv$ denotes equivalence $\bmod f_1(X)$.

Thus there exists a polynomial h such that $f_2(X) - p = h(X)f_1(X)$, and this implies that $f_2(X)$ is a multiple of $f_1(X)$ modulo p. Due to the fact that the $\gcd(f_1(X), f_2(X))$ is irreducible with degree n, they correctly define the commutative diagram previously drawn. The main interest of this choice is to keep small degrees while forcing a very small product of the two size of coefficients: the polynomials have respectively $(n, p^{1/\lambda})$ and $(\lambda n, O(\log(n)^\lambda))$ as degree and size of coefficients.

A Short Example

We give here both an example of a finite field based on a usual pairing construction and a possible choice for the two polynomials f_1 and f_2. We consider the Barreto-Naehrig family which is optimal for the polynomial:

$$P(x) = 36x^4 + 36x^3 + 24x^2 + 6x + 1.$$

---

[3] Other possibilities are available for the polynomial R, all without any influence over the final asymptotic complexities. In the opposite way of our choice (small degree and constant coefficients), we could take R of constant degree d_R and with coefficients bounded by $O(n^{1/(d_R+1)})$. An interesting configuration is to consider the intermediate case and to balance the degree of R with the size of its coefficients. If we force the coefficients to be bounded by d_r, the irreducibility of f_1 leads to the condition $d_r^{d_r} \approx n$ and finally to take $d_r = O(\log n / \log \log n)$. This impacts on the coefficients of f_2 which become bounded by $O((\log n / \log \log n)^\lambda)$ instead of $O(\log(n)^\lambda)$.

For $u = 6521908912666445631$ we get the characteristic

$$p = P(u) = 6513305019599253805152425835527202156406008609274450191912835466146347850 4083$$

and the elliptic curve defined over $\mathbb{F}_p$ by the equation:

$$Y^2 = X^3 + 3.$$

We recall that the embedding degree of an elliptic curve in this family is 12, thus the target field of the pairing is $\mathbb{F}_{p^{12}}$. We choose the following irreducible polynomial over $\mathbb{F}_p$:

$$f_1(X) = X^{12} + X - 6521908912666445631$$

and we define f_2 as:

$$\begin{aligned}
f_2(X) = {} & 36X^{48} + 144X^{37} + 36X^{36} + 216X^{26} + 108X^{25} + 24X^{24} \\
& + 144X^{15} + 108X^{14} + 48X^{13} + 6X^{12} + 36X^4 + 36X^3 + 24X^2 + 6X + 1.
\end{aligned}$$

The reader can check that the resultant of f_1 and f_2 is equal to p^{12} and that f_1 divides f_2 modulo p.

6   Asymptotic Heuristic Complexity

In order to analyze the asymptotic heuristic complexity of the algorithm described above, we first write the relations between n, p and $Q = p^n$ in the following form:

$$p = \exp\left(c_p (\log Q)^{l_p} (\log \log Q)^{1 - l_p}\right), \qquad n = \frac{1}{c_p}\left(\frac{\log Q}{\log \log Q}\right)^{1 - l_p}.$$

The parameters of the algorithm that appear in the analysis are the smoothness bound B, the degree of the elements in the sieving space $t - 1$ and the bound A on the coefficients of these elements. We recall that we note λ the degree of the polynomial P mentioned in Section 5.

6.1   The $p = L_Q(l_p, c_p)$ Case with $1/3 \leqslant l_p < 2/3$

We assume that we can express t, A and B as

$$t = \frac{c_t}{c_p}\left(\frac{\log Q}{\log \log Q}\right)^{2/3 - l_p}, \qquad A^t = L_Q(1/3, c_a c_t), \qquad B = L_Q(1/3, c_b)$$

where c_a, c_b and c_t will be determined later on.

In order to minimize the total runtime of the algorithm, we want to balance the complexities of the sieving phase and of the linear algebra phase. Since the total sieving space contains A^t elements, and the linear algebra phase costs approximately B^2 operations, we require that t, A and B satisfy $A^t = B^2$. This leads to the first condition:

$$c_b = \frac{c_a c_t}{2}. \tag{3}$$

Since we need to have enough good relations after sieving, we also require that $A^t \mathcal{P} \approx B$, where $\mathcal{P}$ denotes the probability that an element of the sieving space yields a good relation, *i.e.* the probability that its norms (in each of the two number fields) split into primes number smaller than B. Put together with the previous remark, this means:

$$B \approx 1/\mathcal{P}. \tag{4}$$

Let us note N_i the norm coming from the polynomial $h = a_{t-1}X^{t-1} + \cdots + a_0$ in $\mathbb{Q}[X]/(f_i(X))$ (for $i = 1$ and $i = 2$ to account for both sides). We can bound the two norms as follows. Keeping the notations of Section 3.1, N_1 is smaller than $\Theta A^n p^{t/\lambda}$, because f_1 is of degree n and its coefficients are bounded by $p^{1/\lambda}$ and h is of degree $t-1$ and its coefficients are bounded by A. Similarly we have N_2 smaller than $\Theta A^{\lambda n} \log(n)^{\lambda t}$. Thus, $\mathcal{P}$ is the probability that $\Theta^2 \log(n)^{\lambda t} A^{(\lambda+1)n} p^{t/\lambda}$ splits into primes lower than B. Besides, the calculus of $A^{(\lambda+1)n} p^{t/\lambda}$ gives $L_Q(2/3, (\lambda+1)c_a + c_t/\lambda)$. We remark that both Θ^2 and $\log(n)^{\lambda t}$ are negligible in this case: in fact, both terms are smaller than $(n+1)^{4\lambda t}$ and $(n+1)^{4\lambda t} \approx L_Q(2/3 - l_p)$. We now make the usual heuristic hypothesis, and assume that $\mathcal{P}$ follows the theorem of Canfield, Erdös and Pomerance: a random number below $L_q(r, \gamma)$ splits into primes lower than $L_q(s, \delta)$ with probability $L_q(r - s, -\gamma(r - s)/\delta)$. As a result, after plugging in our values, we find that:

$$\mathcal{P} = L_Q\left(\frac{1}{3}, \frac{-1}{3c_b}((\lambda+1)c_a + c_t/\lambda)\right). \tag{5}$$

Putting together (4) and (5), we finally obtain the second condition involving the various constants:

$$3c_b^2 = (\lambda+1)c_a + c_t/\lambda. \tag{6}$$

We now want to minimize c_b under the two conditions (3) and (6). Hence, the complexity will be $L_Q(1/3, 2\,c_b^{min})$, where c_b^{min} is naturally the minimum we are looking for. Let us introduce two new variables μ and x and rewrite (3):

$$c_t = x, \qquad c_a = \mu x, \qquad c_b = \frac{\mu x^2}{2}.$$

Then (6) becomes:

$$3\left(\frac{\mu x^2}{2}\right)^2 = (\lambda+1)\mu x + \frac{x}{\lambda} \qquad \Leftrightarrow \qquad x^3 = \frac{4}{3} \cdot \left(\frac{(\lambda+1)\mu + 1/\lambda}{\mu^2}\right)$$

Minimizing $2\,c_b = \mu x^2$ is clearly equivalent to minimizing $(\mu x^2)^3$, so we calculate:

$$(\mu x^2)^3 = \left(\frac{4}{3}\right)^2 \cdot \left(\frac{(\lambda+1)^2\mu^2 + 1/\lambda^2 + 2\mu(\lambda+1)/\lambda}{\mu}\right).$$

Finally, forcing the derivative of the right member with respect to μ to vanish implies $(\lambda + 1)^2 \mu^2 - 1/\lambda^2 = 0$ and at the end $\mu = 1/(\lambda(\lambda + 1))$. As a result, $(2\,c_b^{min})^3 = (\mu x^2)^3 = (64/9) \cdot (\lambda + 1)/\lambda$. Thus, the complexity of the algorithm in this case is:

$$L_Q\left(\frac{1}{3}, \left(\frac{64}{9} \cdot \frac{\lambda + 1}{\lambda}\right)^{1/3}\right).$$

As soon as $\lambda \geqslant 2$, the complexity is clearly better than the one in the general case, which is $L_Q(1/3, (128/9)^{1/3})$.

6.2   The $p = L_Q(2/3, c_p)$ Case

In this case, we consider a family of algorithms indexed by the degree $t - 1$ of the polynomials we are sieving on and we compute the asymptotic complexity of each algorithms. Figure 3 shows which algorithm has to be chosen, depending on the constant c_p, in order to get the best asymptotic complexity. The analysis made here follows exactly the previous one, except that the round-off error in t is no longer negligible. This explains why the final complexity varies with c_p. We continue the analysis in the general case while the two extreme cases $t \to \infty$ and $t = 2$ are discussed further. When t tends to infinity, we recover the asymptotic complexity of the $p = L_Q(l_p, c_p)$ case with $1/3 \leqslant l_p < 2/3$. Furthermore, the asymptotic complexity is minimal for the choice of p that are compatible with $t = 2$, i.e. that allows sieving on linear polynomials. Thus we explicitly compute the complexity in this case.

Sieving on Polynomials of Degree $t - 1$

We assume that we can express A and B as:

$$A = L_Q(1/3, c_a) \qquad \text{and} \qquad B = L_Q(1/3, c_b).$$

The sieving space contains in this case A^t elements since the polynomials involved are of degree $t - 1$. Thus, balancing the size of the sieving space and the runtime of the linear algebra we deduce $c_a = 2c_b/t$. Keeping the same notations as above and neglecting again the Θ and $\log(n)^\lambda$ terms, we can write the two norms $N_1 = A^n p^{(t-1)/\lambda}$ and $N_2 = A^{\lambda n}$. So the product of the two norms is $A^{(\lambda+1)n} p^{(t-1)/\lambda}$, which can also be written as:

$$N_1 \cdot N_2 = L_Q\left(\frac{2}{3}, \frac{2(\lambda + 1)c_b}{c_p t} + \frac{(t - 1)c_p}{\lambda}\right).$$

In order to get enough relations we force B to be equal to the inverse of the probability of smoothness $\mathcal{P}$, i.e. $B = L_Q\left(\frac{1}{3}, \frac{1}{3c_b}\left(\frac{2(\lambda+1)c_b}{c_p t} + \frac{(t-1)c_p}{\lambda}\right)\right)$. This leads to the following equation:

$$3\,c_b^2 = \frac{2(\lambda + 1)c_b}{c_p t} + \frac{(t - 1)c_p}{\lambda}.$$

Consequently, the sieving on polynomials of degree $t - 1$ has complexity $L_Q(1/3, C_\lambda(c_p))$ with:

$$C_\lambda(c_p) = 2\,c_b = \frac{2}{3}\left(\frac{\lambda+1}{c_p t} + \sqrt{\left(\frac{\lambda+1}{c_p t}\right)^2 + \frac{3(t-1)c_p}{\lambda}}\right). \qquad (7)$$

This has to be compared with the asymptotic complexity in the General Number Field Sieve (GNFS) for the same case which is $L_Q(1/3, C(c_p))$ with:

$$C(c_p) = \frac{2}{3}\left(\frac{2}{c_p t} + \sqrt{\left(\frac{2}{c_p t}\right)^2 + 3(t-1)c_p}\right).$$

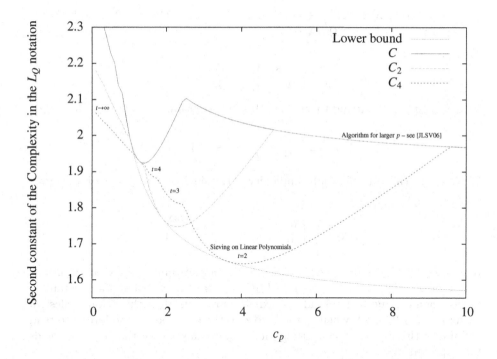

Fig. 3. Asymptotic complexities $L_Q(1/3, C(c_p))$, $L_Q(1/3, C_2(c_p))$ and $L_Q(1/3, C_4(c_p))$ as a function of c_p with $p = L_Q(2/3, c_p)$. The red curve shows the variation of the second constant of the complexity for the GNFS while the green and blue ones present the amelioration obtained by our SNFS in two cases $\lambda = 2$ and $\lambda = 4$. The degree $t - 1$ of the elements in the sieving space is also indicated for the blue curve. The pink curve corresponds to the minimal complexity that can be obtained. The value of the optimal degree of P depends on the value of c_p – see Section 6.3, *The Boundary Case $l_p = 2/3$.*

In Figure 3 we have plotted the constant $C(c_p)$ which determines the complexity $L_Q(1/3, C(c_p))$ as a function of the constant c_p. The red curve represents the constant $C(c_p)$ obtained with the GNFS [JLSV06] while the other ones are obtained with our SNFS for $\lambda = 2$ (green curve) and $\lambda = 4$ (blue curve). Those values of λ correspond respectively to the family of MNT curves and to the family of Barreto-Naehrig elliptic curves.

Splicing the $p = L_Q(2/3, c_p)$ Case to the $p = L_Q(l_p, c_p)$ Case with $l_p < 2/3$
We consider c_p as a variable and compute the value of c_p which minimize the complexity $L_Q(1/3, C_\lambda(c_p))$ given in the previous subsection 6.2. We note it again c_p^{min}. $C_\lambda(c_p)$ comes to a minimum when:

$$\frac{\lambda + 1}{c_p^2 t} = \frac{-2(\lambda+1)^2 t^{-2} c_p^{-3} + 3(t-1)\lambda^{-1}}{2\sqrt{\left(\frac{\lambda+1}{c_p t}\right)^2 + \frac{3(t-1)c_p}{\lambda}}}$$

$$\Leftrightarrow 4(\lambda+1)^4 \lambda^2 + 12t^2(t-1)\lambda(\lambda+1)^2 c_p^3 = (3(t-1)t^2 c_p^3 - 2\lambda(\lambda+1))^2$$
$$\Leftrightarrow t^2(t-1)c_p^3 = (8/3)\lambda(\lambda+1)^2.$$

Thus we take:

$$c_p^{min} = \left(\frac{8}{3} \cdot \frac{\lambda(\lambda+1)^2}{(t-1)t^2}\right)^{1/3}.$$

As a consequence, putting together with (7) we obtain:

$$c_b = 2\left(\frac{1}{3^2} \cdot \frac{t-1}{t} \cdot \frac{\lambda+1}{\lambda}\right)^{1/3}.$$

We conclude that the minimal complexity of the sieving on polynomials of degree $t-1$ in this case is:

$$L_Q\left(\frac{1}{3}, \left(\frac{64}{9} \cdot \frac{t-1}{t} \cdot \frac{\lambda+1}{\lambda}\right)^{1/3}\right). \tag{8}$$

If $p = L_Q(2/3, c_p)$ can only be written with a constant c_p close to zero, it is better in practice to write it as $p = L_Q(l_p, c_p')$ with $l_p < 2/3$ and a constant c_p' higher than c_p, and to apply afterwards the previous algorithm. Nonetheless, if we fix $p = L_Q(2/3, c_p)$, when c_p tends to zero the best choice is to force t to tend to infinity (Figure 3). Theoretically, it is interesting to see that $t \to \infty$ yields the expected limit:

$$L_Q\left(\frac{1}{3}, \left(\frac{64}{9} \cdot \frac{\lambda+1}{\lambda}\right)^{1/3}\right)$$

which is the asymptotic complexity of the $p = L_Q(l_p, c_p)$ case with $1/3 \leqslant l_p < 2/3$.

Looking at the Optimal Case: Sieving on Linear Polynomials
Let us go back to the minimal complexity that appears in (8). Considering that the asymptotic complexity in GNFS [JLSV06] for the same case is

$L_Q(1/3, (128/9).(t - 1/t)^{1/3})$, we remark that for each algorithm our variant multiplied by a factor $\frac{\lambda+1}{2\lambda}$ the cube of the second constant of the complexity in the L_q notation. In particular, this gives an interesting result when we are sieving on linear polynomials, i.e. when $t - 1 = 1$. Replacing t by 2 in (8), we find that sieving on linear polynomials leads to the following complexity:

$$L_Q\left(\frac{1}{3}, \left(\frac{32}{9} \cdot \frac{\lambda+1}{\lambda}\right)^{1/3}\right).$$

This has to be compared with the asymptotic complexity in GNFS [JLSV06] for the same case which is $L_Q(1/3, (64/9)^{1/3})$. Again, as soon as $\lambda \geqslant 2$, the complexity of our SNFS is clearly better than the one in the general case.

6.3   Algorithm for Larger p

The $p = L_Q(l_p, c_p)$ Case with $2/3 < l_p < 1$
We recall that sieving on linear polynomials in this case is sufficient. Let A be the bound on the coefficients of the polynomials we are sieving over, and B the smoothness bound. Again, balancing the size of the sieving space A^2 and the runtime of the linear algebra B^2 leads to $A = B$. We assume that we can express B as $B = L_Q(1/3, c_b)$. The product of the two norms is as usual bounded by $\Theta^2 \log(n)^\lambda B^{(\lambda+1)n} p^{1/\lambda}$. Due to the size of n in this case, Θ^2 and $\log(n)^\lambda$ are negligible compared to $B^{(\lambda+1)n} p^{1/\lambda}$. Let us develop the logarithm of this new bound: $\log(B^{(\lambda+1)n} p^{1/\lambda}) = n \log B + \lambda n \log B + (1/\lambda) \log p$. First, we remark that we have $n \log B = \log L_Q(4/3 - l_p) = \log L_Q(l)$ with $l < 2/3$. Setting besides:

$$\lambda n = c_l \left(\frac{\log Q}{\log \log Q}\right)^{1/3} \tag{9}$$

with c_l to be determined later on, we obtain $\lambda n \log B + (1/\lambda) \log p = \log(L_Q(2/3, c_b c_l + 1/c_l))$. Thus B^n is negligible compared to $B^{\lambda n} p^{1/\lambda}$. Moreover, $B^{\lambda n} p^{1/\lambda}$ comes to a minimum when:

$$c_l = 1/\sqrt{c_b}. \tag{10}$$

The product of the two norms is so bounded by $L_Q(2/3, 2\sqrt{c_b})$. Hence the probability that it is B-smooth is $L_Q(1/3, -2/(3\sqrt{c_b}))$. As usual, we equalize B with the inverse of the probability. This yields $c_b = 2/(3\sqrt{c_b})$ and then $c_b = (4/9)^{1/3}$. Putting this value in (10), we get $c_l = (3/2)^{1/3}$. The constraint (9) over λ becomes:

$$\lambda = \frac{1}{n}\left(\frac{3 \log Q}{2 \log \log Q}\right)^{1/3}.$$

Finally, the asymptotic complexity of the algorithm for this degree λ is:

$$L_Q(1/3, (32/9)^{1/3}).$$

This has to be compared with the complexity of GNFS in the same case, which is $L_Q(1/3, (64/9)^{1/3})$.

The Boundary Case : $l_p = 2/3$
When $l_p = 2/3$ matters are more complicated since B^n is no more negligible. The product of the norms is now rewritten as $L_Q(2/3, c_b(c_l + 1/c_p) + 1/c_l)$. Again, this is minimized at $c_l = 1/\sqrt{c_b}$. However, it now becomes $L_Q(2/3, 2\sqrt{c_b} + c_b/c_p)$ and the probability of smoothness is $L_Q(1/3, -(1/3).(2/\sqrt{c_b}) + 1/c_p))$. Equating the opposite of the second constant to c_b yields $(3c_b + 1/c_p)^2 = 4/c_b$ and finally:

$$9c_b^3 - \frac{6}{c_p}c_b^2 + \frac{1}{c_p^2}c_b - 4 = 0.$$

This equation leads to the pink curve represented in Figure 3. When c_p tends to infinity, we recover the $(32/9)^{1/3}$ constant in the complexity.

The $p = L_Q(1, c_p)$ Case
The analysis follows exactly the previous one, except that we have a simpler expression of the extension degree $n = 1/c_p$. Setting again $\lambda = c_p(3\log Q)^{1/3}(2\log\log Q)^{-1/3}$, we obtain the final asymptotic complexity $L_Q(1/3, (32/9)^{1/3})$. In particular, this applies on finite fields of prime order, since $n = 1$ implies that p can be written as $p = L_p(1, 1)$. We recall that the original SNFS applies on such fields of prime order and has the same complexity $L_Q(1/3, (32/9)^{1/3})$ – see [Sch10, Sch08, HT11].

7   Conclusion

In this paper, we adapted the Special Number Field Sieve to compute discrete logarithms in $\mathbb{F}_{p^n}$ when p is obtained by evaluation of a polynomial with small coefficients. More precisely, for $p = L_Q(l_p, c_p)$ with $1/3 \leqslant l_p < 2/3$ our variation yields a complexity of $L_Q(1/3, [(64/9) \cdot (\lambda + 1)/\lambda]^{1/3})$ where λ is the small degree of the polynomial P which gives the characteristic p after evaluation. This should be compared with the previous $L_Q(1/3, (128/9)^{1/3})$ in the General High Degree Number Field Sieve. Likewise, for $p = L_Q(2/3, c_p)$ we make the asymptotic heuristic complexity drop from $L_Q(1/3, (64/9)^{1/3})$ to $L_Q(1/3, [(32/9) \cdot (\lambda + 1)/\lambda]^{1/3})$. For larger p ($p = L_Q(l_p, c_p)$ with $2/3 < l_p < 1$), it goes down from $L_Q(1/3, (64/9)^{1/3})$ to $L_Q(1/3, (32/9)^{1/3})$ for some λ with a suitable size compared with p.

Thankfully, our improved NFS in the pairing-based case essentially counterbalances a technical mistake in the analysis of the security of many pairing-based curves. As a consequence, it is not necessary to change the practical parameters of current pairing-based cryptosystems in large characteristic.

References

[BF03]   Boneh, D., Franklin, M.K.: Identity-based encryption from the Weil pairing. SIAM J. Comput. 32(3), 586–615 (2003)

[BLS03]   Barreto, P.S.L.M., Lynn, B., Scott, M.: On the selection of pairing-friendly groups. In: Matsui, M., Zuccherato, R.J. (eds.) SAC 2003. LNCS, vol. 3006, pp. 17–25. Springer, Heidelberg (2004)

[BLS04]   Boneh, D., Lynn, B., Shacham, H.: Short signatures from the Weil pairing. J. Cryptology 17(4), 297–319 (2004)

[BN05]   Barreto, P.S.L.M., Naehrig, M.: Pairing-friendly elliptic curves of prime order. In: Preneel, B., Tavares, S. (eds.) SAC 2005. LNCS, vol. 3897, pp. 319–331. Springer, Heidelberg (2006)

[CC03]   Cha, J.C., Cheon, J.H.: An identity-based signature from gap diffie-hellman groups. In: Desmedt, Y.G. (ed.) PKC 2003. LNCS, vol. 2567, pp. 18–30. Springer, Heidelberg (2002)

[FST10]   Freeman, D., Scott, M., Teske, E.: A taxonomy of pairing-friendly elliptic curves. J. Cryptology 23(2), 224–280 (2010)

[Gor93]   Gordon, D.M.: Discrete logarithms in GF(p) using the number field sieve. SIAM J. Discrete Math. 6(1), 124–138 (1993)

[HT11]   Hayasaka, K., Takagi, T.: An experiment of number field sieve over gF(p) of low hamming weight characteristic. In: Chee, Y.M., Guo, Z., Ling, S., Shao, F., Tang, Y., Wang, H., Xing, C. (eds.) IWCC 2011. LNCS, vol. 6639, pp. 191–200. Springer, Heidelberg (2011)

[JL06]   Joux, A., Lercier, R.: The function field sieve in the medium prime case. In: Vaudenay, S. (ed.) EUROCRYPT 2006. LNCS, vol. 4004, pp. 254–270. Springer, Heidelberg (2006)

[JLSV06]   Joux, A., Lercier, R., Smart, N.P., Vercauteren, F.: The number field sieve in the medium prime case. In: Dwork, C. (ed.) CRYPTO 2006. LNCS, vol. 4117, pp. 326–344. Springer, Heidelberg (2006)

[Jou04]   Joux, A.: A one round protocol for tripartite Diffie-Hellman. J. Cryptology 17(4), 263–276 (2004)

[Kal97]   Kalkbrener, M.: An upper bound on the number of monomials in determinants of sparse matrices with symbolic entries. Mathematica Pannonica 8, 73–82 (1997)

[KM05]   Koblitz, N., Menezes, A.: Pairing-based cryptography at high security levels. In: IMA Int. Conf., pp. 13–36 (2005)

[LV01]   Lenstra, A.K., Verheul, E.R.: Selecting cryptographic key sizes. J. Cryptology 14(4), 255–293 (2001)

[Nat03]   National Institute of Standards and Technology. Special publication 800-56: Recommendation on key establishment schemes, Draft 2.0 (2003)

[Pat02]   Paterson, K.G.: Id-based signatures from pairings on elliptic curves. IACR Cryptology ePrint Archive, 2002:4 (2002)

[Sch08]   Schirokauer, O.: The impact of the number field sieve on the discrete logarithm problem in finite fields. Algorithmic Number Theory 44 (2008)

[Sch10]   Schirokauer, O.: The number field sieve for integers of low weight. Math. Comput. 79(269), 583–602 (2010)

[SK03]   Sakai, R., Kasahara, M.: Id based cryptosystems with pairing on elliptic curve. IACR Cryptology ePrint Archive, 2003:54 (2003)

Efficient Semi-static Secure Broadcast Encryption Scheme

Jongkil Kim, Willy Susilo, Man Ho Au, and Jennifer Seberry

Centre for Computer and Information Security Research
School of Computer Science and Software Engineering
University of Wollongong, Australia
jk057@uowmail.edu.au, {wsusilo,aau,jennie}@uow.edu.au

Abstract. In this paper, we propose a semi-static secure broadcast encryption scheme with constant-sized private keys and ciphertexts. Our result improves the semi-static secure broadcast encryption scheme introduced by Gentry and Waters. Specifically, we reduce the private key and ciphertext size by half. By applying the generic transformation proposed by Gentry and Waters, our scheme also achieves adaptive security. Finally, we present an improved implementation idea which can reduce the ciphertext size in the aforementioned generic transformation.

Keywords: semi-static, broadcast encryption, constant size.

1 Introduction

A broadcast encryption [7] is a cryptographic primitive that allows a sender to encrypt a message to a set of users so that only the users within that set can decrypt it and obtain the message. In addition, the set of receivers is not fixed and an arbitrary set of users can be chosen by the sender at the time of encryption. Broadcast encryption is suggested as being efficient in a system having a large number of group members, and it also has many practical applications such as its use in secure database system, DRM (digital right management) and group communications. In a broadcast encryption system, any subset of users can be included in a broadcast, but decryption of the chiphertexts is only possible for users included in the broadcast using their own private keys.

There are many desirable properties of broadcast encryption. It can be *fully collusion resistant*, which means that a ciphertext cannot be decrypted even if all users who are not included in the broadcast encryption collude. This is an essential property of a secure broadcast encryption. Having *stateless receivers* [15] is another desirable property. In a broadcast encryption with stateless receivers, any set of receivers can be included in a broadcast encryption without requiring any update of private keys.

Multi-receiver key encapsulation [22] (mKEM) is a key encapsulation scheme, which allows multiple parties to share a secret key efficiently, and the notion of mKEM has been extended to multi-receiver identity-based key encapsulation [1] [2] (mID-KEM) by combining it with an identity-based encryption [20].

Z. Cao and F. Zhang (Eds.): Pairing 2013, LNCS 8365, pp. 62–76, 2014.

Identity-based broadcast encryption [5,19] is a combination of broadcast encryption and identity-based encryption. Although it shares many similar concepts with mID-KEM, an identity-based broadcast encryption focuses more on a broadcast encryption as a generalization of an identity-based encryption. This means that an identity-based encryption is a special case of an identity-based broadcast encryption with a single receiver in the broadcast. In an identity-based broadcast encryption, encryptions and decryptions are based on receivers' identities, in which the recipients in a normal broadcast encryption are usually indexed sequentially from 1 to n. The most important difference between broadcast encryption and identity-based broadcast encryption is the number of users in the system. Identity-based broadcast encryptions are usually designed to support exponentially many users since user identities are merely bit-strings of arbitrary-size and hence, they are unknown during the system setup.

Adaptive security, also known as *full security*, of a broadcast encryption was introduced by Gentry and Waters [9]. In this security model, an adversary can adaptively select a target set by using public parameters and previously compromised private keys. *Static security*, as defined by [3], is a weaker version of adaptive security of a broadcast encryption. In the static security model, an adversary must declare the target set he/she wants to attack before observing public parameters. A *Semi-static security* model [9] is half-way between a static and an adaptive security model. Similar to the case in a static security model, an adversary is still required to declare a potential target set prior to setting public keys in a semi-static security model. However, the adversary can select any target set to be challenged, provided that the target set is a subset of the previously declared potential target set.

In this paper, we improve the semi-static secure broadcast encryption of Gentry and Waters. As in Gentry and Waters' scheme, our scheme offers semi-static security and is fully collusion-resistant. In addition, receivers are stateless receivers, and the sizes of the public key and the private key do not depend on the total number of users. Our scheme also features very short private keys and ciphertexts and is computationally more efficient than Gentry and Waters' scheme. Based on the transformation technique from [9], our scheme can achieve adaptive security while maintaining efficiency.

The rest of this paper is organized as follows. In the next section, we will review some related work. We will highlight our contributions and compare them to existing schemes in the literature. In Section 3, we will review some definitions and complexity assumptions that will be used throughout the paper. In Section 4, we will first describe semi-static secure broadcast encryption and subsequently revisit the construction by Gentry and Waters. In Section 5, we will present our construction that will improve Gentry and Waters' scheme, together with its security analysis. In Section 6, we will present the transformation of our scheme to achieve adaptive security, following the transformation technique from [9]. We will also present a technique in the implementation of the scheme to remove the linear-sized tag required in the generic transformation. Finally, Section 7 concludes the paper.

2   Related Works

Since the introduction of broadcast encryption as a revocation system [15], a number of several fully collusion resistant broadcast encryption schemes have been proposed. [6,10,11] A fully collusion resistant broadcast encryption scheme which has short ciphertext was proposed by Boneh, Gentry and Waters (BGW) [3]. They introduced a broadcast encryption scheme with a constant size private key and ciphertext in the static security model, then generalized it to achieve $O(\sqrt{n})$ size ciphertext. As a compensation for generalization, they reduced the size of the public key from $O(n)$ to $O(\sqrt{n})$. A similar achievement in identity-based broadcast encryption scheme was introduced Delerablée [5]. Delerablée's work offers constant size private keys and ciphertexts, and it supports exponentially many identities in the random oracle model.

Gentry and Waters [9] considered adaptive security from a different approach. They first introduced semi-static security, in which efficient schemes can be constructed. Then, they presented a generic transformation to achieve adaptive security with only a small impact on the ciphertext size. Specifically, the resulting ciphertext size is doubled and a component, called a 'tag' is added, which has a space complexity of $O(|S|)$ where S is the set of receivers of a broadcast. For a normal broadcast encryption, this tag is of $|S|$-bit and can be removed in the random oracle model. In addition, they introduced two broadcast encryption schemes that satisfy semi-static security. Both of the schemes have constant sized ciphertext. In contrast, the first scheme has $O(n)$ private key size, while the second scheme has a constant size private key.

A *revocation system* [15,16] where only non-revoked users can decrypt ciphertexts is a type of broadcast encryption system and is comparable to semi-static broadcast encryption. Indeed, the selective secure revocation system and semi-static broadcast encryption offer similar functions when the encrypter in the semi-static broadcast encryption only chooses the set of non-revoked users to be included in the broadcast. However, it seems that Gentry and Waters' technique is not applicable to transform selectively secure revocation to offer adaptive security, as noted in [13].

Although our scheme and [9] can achieve adaptive security in broadcast encryption, it is only adaptive chosen plaintext attack (CPA) secure. Recently, a few adaptively chosen ciphertext attack (CCA) secure schemes were introduced, including the schemes by Malek and Miri [14] and Ren and Gu [18], which feature constant size ciphertexts and private keys of size $O(n)$. In addition, Phan et al. [17] suggested a broadcast encryption scheme with constant size private key and ciphertext under a non standard assumption.

2.1   Our Contributions

Compared with Gentry and Waters' semi-static broadcast encryption scheme with constant size private key and ciphertext (denoted as GW_{SS} throughout this paper), our construction offers a reduced-size private key and ciphertext. Also, in terms of computation, the number of pairing and exponentiation computations are reduced. While several adaptively secure broadcast encryption schemes have been introduced recently, our semi-static secure scheme is still important because a semi-static secure broadcast encryption scheme can be transformed into an adaptively secure broadcast encryption scheme. We compare the efficiency of our scheme with other broadcast encryption schemes in Table 1. Our scheme is quite competitive when we consider both efficiency and security. The only scheme offering better efficiency is the broadcast encryption scheme that was suggested by Phan et al. [17]. Unfortunately, this scheme is based on a non-standard assumption.

Table 1. Comparison of efficiency and security of Broadcast Encryption schemes

	Pub. Key	Priv. Key	Ciphertext	Pairing	Exponentiation	Security
MM [14]	$O(n)$	$O(n)$	$O(1)$	0/2	$O(\lvert S\rvert)/O(\lvert S\rvert)$	ACCA
RG [18]	$O(n)$	$O(n)$	$O(1)$	3/3	$O(\lvert S\rvert)/O(1)$	ACCA
PPSS [17]	$O(n)$	$O(1)$	$O(1)$	1/2	$O(1)/O(1)$	ACCA
CD^b [5]	$O(\ell)$	$O(1)$	$O(1)$	0/2	$O(\lvert S\rvert)/O(\lvert S\rvert)$	SCCA
BGW [3]	$O(n)$	$O(1)$	$O(1)$	1/2	$O(1)/O(1)$	SCCA
GW$_{SS}$ [9]	$O(\ell)$	$O(1)$	$O(1)$	2/2	$O(\ell)/O(\ell)$	SSCPA
GW$_{SS}^a$ [9]	$O(\ell)$	$O(1)$	$O(\lvert S\rvert)$	4/2	$O(\ell)/O(\ell)$	ACPA
GW$_{IBBE}$ [9]	$O(\sqrt{\lvert S\rvert})$	$O(1)$	$O(\sqrt{\lvert S\rvert})$	$O(\sqrt{\lvert S\rvert})/2$	$O(\lvert S\rvert)/O(\sqrt{\lvert S\rvert})$	ACPA
Our scheme	$O(\ell)$	$O(1)$	$O(1)$	1/2	$O(\ell)/O(\ell)$	SSCPA
Our scheme^a	$O(\ell)$	$O(1)$	$O(1)\ or\ O(\ell)$	2/2	$O(\ell)/O(\ell)$	ACPA

^{a} An adaptively secure scheme transformed from semi-static secure schemes
^{b} In the random oracle model

3   Definitions and Complexity Assumptions

3.1   Broadcast Encryption System

For simplicity, the definition of a broadcast encryption system is often replaced by a key encapsulation system. Through a key encapsulation system, multiple receivers participating in a broadcast share a symmetric key for further secure communications. We introduce the definition of a semi-static broadcast encryption system, which is useful to understand our scheme, based on the definition of an adaptively secure broadcast encryption system [9]. It consists of four algorithms, setup (**Setup**), private key generation (**KeyGen**), encapsulation (**Enc**), and decapsulation (**Dec**) as defined below.

Setup(λ, n, ℓ) takes as input the number of receivers (n) and the maximal size of a broadcast recipient group ℓ ($\leq n$). It outputs a public/master secret key pair $\langle PK, MSK \rangle$.

KeyGen(i, MSK) takes as input an index $i \in \{1, ..., n\}$ and the secret key MSK. It outputs a private key d_i.

Enc(S, PK) takes as input a subset $S \subseteq \{1, ..., n\}$, a public key PK and a message M to encrypt. If $|S| \leq \ell$, it outputs a pair $\langle Hdr, K \rangle$ where Hdr is called the header and $K \in \mathcal{K}$ is a message encryption key.

Dec(S, i, d_i, Hdr, PK) takes as input a subset $S \subseteq \{1, ..., n\}$ an index $i \in \{1, ..., n\}$, a private key d_i for i, a header Hdr, and the public key PK. If $|S| \leq \ell$ and $i \in S$, then the algorithm outputs the message encryption key $K \in \mathcal{K}$.

Correctness Property. For the correctness, the following property must be satisfied.

For $S = \{1, ..., n\}$ where $|S| \leq \ell \leq n$, let $(PK, SK_1, ..., SK_n) \leftarrow Setup(\lambda, n, \ell)$, and $\langle Hdr, K \rangle \leftarrow Enc(S, PK)$. Then, if $i \in S$, $Dec(S, i, d_i, Hdr, PK) = K$.

It should be noted that the definition of a semi-static secure broadcast encryption system above can be easily extended to encrypt messages using the standard key encapsulation mechanism/data encapsulation mechanism (KEM/DEM) transformation [21] [4].

3.2 Bilinear Maps

Let p be a large prime number. Let $\mathbb{G}_1$, $\mathbb{G}_2$ be two groups of order p, and g be a generator of $\mathbb{G}_1$. $e : \mathbb{G}_1 \times \mathbb{G}_1 \rightarrow \mathbb{G}_2$ is a bilinear map satisfying the following properties:

1. Bilinearity: For all, $u, v \in \mathbb{G}_1$ and $a, b \in \mathbb{Z}, e(u^a, u^b) = e(u, v)^{ab}$.
2. Non-degeneracy: $e(g, g) \notin 1$.
3. Computability: There exists an efficient algorithm to compute $e(u, v), \forall u, v \in \mathbb{G}_1$.

3.3 Complexity Assumptions

Definition 1. *(The Decision Bilinear Diffie-Hellman Exponent (DB-DHE) Sum Problem for (S, m))[8] Fix $S \subset \mathbb{Z}$ and $m \in Z \setminus (S + S)$. Let $\mathbb{G}$ and $\mathbb{G}_T$ be groups of order p with bilinear map $e : \mathbb{G} \times \mathbb{G} \rightarrow \mathbb{G}_T$, and let g be a generator for $\mathbb{G}$. Set $\alpha \leftarrow \mathbb{Z}_p^*$ and $b \leftarrow \{0,1\}$. If $b = 0$, set $Z \leftarrow e(g, g)^{\alpha^m}$;otherwise, set $Z \leftarrow \mathbb{G}_T$. Output*

$$\{g^{\alpha^i} : i \in S\} \text{ and } Z$$

The problem is to guess b. The specific BDHE Sum instance we use in our security analysis is for $m = 4d + 4\ell - 1$ and

$$S = [0, \ell - 2] \cup [d + \ell, 2d + \ell - 1] \cup [2d + 2\ell, 2d + 3\ell - 1]$$

$$\cup [3d + 3\ell, 4d + 3\ell] \cup [4d + 4\ell, 5d + 4\ell + 1]$$

where $d = n + 2\ell$.

Also, we define $AdvBDHES_{\mathcal{A},n,\ell}(\lambda)$ as the advantage of an algorithm $\mathcal{A}$ to solve the decision BDHE Sum problem as defined above.

$$AdvBDHES_{\mathcal{A},n,\ell}(\lambda) = |Pr[b = b'] - 1/2|.$$

4   Semi-static Secure Broadcast Encryption

4.1   Security Definition

Static secure broadcast encryption is a weaker notion of adaptively secure broadcast encryption. In a static secure broadcast encryption, the adversary must declare the target set he/she wants to attack before **Setup**, and ask a challenge against exactly the same target set in **Challenge**. Semi-static secure broadcast encryption is in between static security and adaptive security. In a semi-static secure broadcast encryption, the adversary must also let the challenger know the target set before **Setup** in the same way that static secure requires, but the adversary makes a challenge for any subsets of the target set which the adversary has declared. We review the definition given in Gentry and Waters [9], which is a game between the challenger and the adversary.

Both the adversary and the challenger are given as input ℓ, i.e., the maximal size of a set of receivers S.

Init: The adversary $\mathcal{A}$ first outputs a set $S^* \subseteq \{1, ..., n\}$ of identities that he/she wants to attack (with $|S| \leq \ell$), and let k $= |S|$.

Setup: The challenger runs **Setup**(λ, ℓ) to obtain a public key PK. He/she gives $\mathcal{A}$ the public key PK.

Extract: The adversary $\mathcal{A}$ adaptively issues queries $q_1, ..., q_{n-k}$, where q_i is that the challenger runs **KeyGen** on ith element of $S^{*c} = \{1, ..., n\} - S^*$ and forwards the resulting private key to the adversary.

Challenge: If **Extract** is over, the challenger runs **Encrypt** algorithm to obtain $(Hdr^*, K) = $ **Encrypt**$(\tilde{S}, PK)$ where $K \in \mathcal{K}$, and any $\tilde{S} \subseteq S^*$. The challenger set $K_0 = K$, and K_1 to a random value in $\mathcal{K}$, then randomly selects $b \leftarrow \{0, 1\}$. The challenger returns (Hdr^*, K_b) to $\mathcal{A}$.

Guess: Finally, the adversary $\mathcal{A}$ outputs a guess $b' \in \{0, 1\}$ and wins the game if $b = b'$.

In the definition above, the indices of users were noted as ID. However, this is only for the generalization of the definition. For a normal broadcast encryption, the values of ID are taken from the set $\{1, ..., n\}$ where n is an integer representing the total number of users and is polynomial in the security parameter. Also, we define $AdvBr_{\mathcal{A},n,\ell}^{SS}(\lambda)$ be the advantage of algorithm $\mathcal{A}$ in winning the semi-static security game through at most ℓ users that can be included a broadcast if the system has total n users. It should be noted that the maximum number of extraction queries in this case is $n - k$ in the definition above because $\mathcal{A}$ cannot make private key queries for users in S^*.

4.2   Semi-static Secure Broadcast Encryption by Gentry and Waters [9]

Our main contribution is to improve the efficiency of the semi-static secure broadcast encryption from [9]. However, their construction of semi-static secure broadcast encryption was not separately written down because it can be obtained by simplifying adaptively secure identity-based broadcast encryption. For comparison with our algorithm, it is helpful to rewrite their semi-static secure broadcast encryption scheme clearly based on their description and proof. Let $GroupGen(\lambda, n, \ell)$ be an algorithm that outputs suitable bilinear group parameters $\langle \mathbb{G}, \mathbb{G}_T, e \rangle$, where $\mathbb{G}$ is of order $p \geq n + \ell$.

Setup(n, ℓ): Run $\langle \mathbb{G}, \mathbb{G}_T, e \rangle \leftarrow GroupGen(\lambda, n, \ell)$. Set $g_1, g_2 \xleftarrow{R} \mathbb{G}$. Set $\alpha, \beta, \gamma \xleftarrow{R} \mathbb{Z}_p$. Set $\hat{g}_1 \leftarrow g_1^\beta$ and $\hat{g}_2 \leftarrow g_2^\beta$. PK contains a description of $\langle \mathbb{G}, \mathbb{G}_T, e \rangle$, the parameters n and ℓ, along with g_1^γ, $g_1^{\gamma \cdot \alpha}$ and the set

$$\{g_1^{\alpha^j}, \hat{g}_1^{\alpha^j}, \hat{g}_2^{\alpha^k} : j \in [0, \ell], k \in [0, \ell - 2]\}.$$

Generate a random key κ for a PRF $\Psi : [1, n] \rightarrow \mathbb{Z}_p$. The private key is $SK \leftarrow (\alpha, \gamma, g_2, \kappa)$.

KeyGen(i, SK): set $r_i \leftarrow \Psi_\kappa(i)$ and output the private key

$$d_i \leftarrow \langle r_i, h_i \rangle, \text{ where } h_i \leftarrow g_2^{\frac{\gamma - r_i}{\alpha - i}}.$$

Enc(S, PK): Let $k = |S|$. Parse S as $\{i_1, ..., i_k\}$. Set $i_j \leftarrow n + j$ for $j \in [k+1, \ell]$. Set $P(x) = \prod_{j=1}^\ell (x - i_j)$. Set $t \xleftarrow{R} \mathbb{Z}_p$ and set $K \leftarrow e(g_1, \hat{g}_2)^{\gamma \cdot \alpha^{\ell-1} \cdot t}$. Next, set

$$Hdr \leftarrow \langle C_1, C_2, C_3, C_4 \rangle \leftarrow \langle \hat{g}_1^{P(\alpha) \cdot t}, g_1^{\gamma \cdot t}, g_1^t, e(g_1, \hat{g}_2)^{\alpha^{\ell-1} \cdot t} \rangle.$$

Output $\langle Hdr, K \rangle$.

Dec(S, i, d_i, Hdr, PK): Suppose $i \in S = \{i_1, ..., i_k\}$. Define $P(x)$ as above. Let $P_i(x) = x^{\ell-1} - \frac{P(x)}{x-i}$. Set

$$K = e(C_1, h_i) \cdot e(C_2 \cdot C_3^{-r_i}, \hat{g}_2^{P_i(\alpha)}) \cdot C_4^{r_i}.$$

Correctness. Note that $K = K_1 \cdot K_2$, where we gather the terms containing a γ in K_1, and the other terms in K_2.

$$K_1 = e(C_1, g_2^\gamma)^{1/(\alpha-i)} \cdot e(C_2, \hat{g}_2^{P_i(\alpha)}).$$

$$K_2 = e(C_1, g_2^{-r_i/(\alpha-i)}) \cdot e(C_3, \hat{g}_2^{P_i(\alpha)})^{-r_i} \cdot C_4^{r_i}.$$

We have that

$$K_1^{1/t} = e(g_1, \hat{g}_2)^{\gamma(P(\alpha)/(\alpha-i) + P_i(\alpha))} = e(g_1, \hat{g}_2)^{\gamma \cdot \alpha^{\ell-1}}.$$

We also have that

$$K_2^{1/t} = e(g_1, \hat{g}_2)^{-r_i \cdot P(\alpha)/(\alpha-i) - r_i \cdot P_i(\alpha) + r_i \cdot \alpha^{\ell-1}}$$
$$= e(g_1, \hat{g}_2)^{r_i \cdot (\alpha^{\ell-1} - P_i(\alpha) - P(\alpha)/(\alpha-i))}$$
$$= e(g_1, \hat{g}_2)^0 = 1$$

as required.

5 Our Scheme

Our scheme reduces the size of private keys by removing the randomness r_i in GW scheme. Below we give an intuition for the reason that we are able to reduce the private key size (which in turn allows reduction in ciphertext size). Roughly speaking, the key structure, $(r_i, g_2^{\frac{\gamma - r_i}{\alpha - i}})$ for master key (γ, α) and generator g_2, of the GW scheme is commonly used to handle adaptive private key queries. However, we observe that this capability is not required since the goal is to achieve semi-static security. Based on this observation, we are able to remove the randomness r_i in the private key. Additionally, upon successful removal of r_i, we are also able to reduce the ciphertext size by half though removing the component (C_3, C_4) which was used to cancel the effect of r_i in the private key.

To be more specific, recall that in the security proof of GW scheme, the problem instance given to the simulator contains various power of α in the exponents. That is, g^{α^j} for a set of j and a generator g. The simulator chooses a polynomial $f(x)$ of some suitable degree and sets $\gamma = f(\alpha)$. While the simulator cannot compute the value γ, the public key is computable because it is at the form of $g^\gamma = g^{f(\alpha)}$. In order to generate a private key for value i, the simulator is required to compute a value related to $g^{\frac{\gamma - r_i}{\alpha - i}}$. This is where r_i is needed in GW's proof: for any value i, the simulator can set $r_i = f(i)$. Since γ is $f(\alpha)$, this ensures $(\alpha - i)$ is a factor of $\gamma - r_i$ because the latter is equivalent to $f(\alpha) - f(i)$. Note that indeed the simulator is capable of generating private key for any i.

As discussed, our goal is to achieve semi-static security and thus the capability of handling adaptive private key queries is not necessary. Our simple key structure can be proven as follows. Since any query i must come from the set $\dot{S} = \{1, \ldots, n\} \setminus S^*$, the simulator in our scheme sets the polynomial $f(x)$ to be divisible by $(x - i)$ for all $i \in \dot{S}$. That is, $f(x) = \prod_{i \in \dot{S}} (x + i) f'(x)^1$ for some random polynomial $f'(x)$ that is also chosen by the simulator. The master key γ is then set to be $f(\alpha)$. Since the adversary in the semi-static setting is restricted to query private keys from the set $\dot{S}$, the simulator can always compute the corresponding private key since $\gamma = f(\alpha)$ is always divisible by $(x + i)$ for all $i \in \dot{S}$. As such, we eliminate the need of randomness r_i which in turns remove the ciphertext component (C_3, C_4).

Our scheme has identical **Setup** with GW_{SS}, which means the public key remains the same as GW_{SS}. However, in **KeyGen**, the random element r_i of a private key in GW_{SS} was removed. As a result of the removal, **Enc** and **Dec** become simpler. Also, the size of private keys and ciphertexts are reduced by 50% and less computation are required. The detail of the scheme is as follows.

Let $GroupGen(\lambda, n, \ell)$ be an algorithm that outputs suitable bilinear group parameters $\langle \mathbb{G}, \mathbb{G}_T, e \rangle$, where $\mathbb{G}$ is of order $p \geq n + \ell$.

Setup(n, ℓ): Run $\langle \mathbb{G}, \mathbb{G}_T, e \rangle \leftarrow GroupGen(\lambda, n, \ell)$. Set $g_1, g_2 \xleftarrow{R} \mathbb{G}$. Set $\alpha, \beta, \gamma \xleftarrow{R} \mathbb{Z}_p$. Set $\hat{g}_1 \leftarrow g_1^\beta$ and $\hat{g}_2 \leftarrow g_2^\beta$. PK contains a description of

---

[1] We use the $(x + i)$ instead of $(x - i)$ as the factor since it appears to be easier to work with in our case.

$\langle \mathbb{G}, \mathbb{G}_T, e \rangle$, the parameters n and ℓ, along with g_1^γ, $g_1^{\gamma \cdot \alpha}$ and the set

$$\{g_1^{\alpha^j}, \hat{g}_1^{\alpha^j}, \hat{g}_2^{\alpha^k} : j \in [0, \ell], k \in [0, \ell - 2]\}.$$

The private key is $SK \leftarrow (\alpha, \gamma, g_2)$.

KeyGen(i, SK): Output the private key

$$d_i \leftarrow g_2^{\frac{\gamma}{\alpha+i}}.$$

Enc (S, PK): Let $k = |S|$. Parse S as $\{i_1, ..., i_k\}$. Set $i_j \leftarrow n+j$ for $j \in [k+1, \ell]$. Set $P(x) = \prod_{j=1}^\ell (x + i_j)$. Set $t \xleftarrow{R} \mathbb{Z}_p$ and set $K \leftarrow e(g_1, \hat{g}_2)^{\gamma \cdot \alpha^{\ell-1} \cdot t}$. Next, set

$$Hdr \leftarrow \langle C_1, C_2 \rangle \leftarrow \langle \hat{g}_1^{P(\alpha) \cdot t}, g_1^{\gamma \cdot t} \rangle.$$

Output $\langle Hdr, K \rangle$.

Dec (S, i, d_i, Hdr, PK): Suppose $i \in S = \{i_1, ..., i_k\}$. Define $P(x)$ as above. Let $P_i(x) = x^{\ell-1} - \frac{P(x)}{x+i}$. Set

$$K = e(C_1, d_i) \cdot e(C_2, \hat{g}_2^{P_i(\alpha)}).$$

Correctness. The correctness of our scheme is shown as follows.

$$\begin{aligned} K^{1/t} &= e(\hat{g}_1^{P(\alpha)}, g_2^\gamma)^{1/(\alpha+i)} \cdot e(g_1^\gamma, \hat{g}_2^{P_i(\alpha)}) \\ &= e(g_1, \hat{g}_2)^{\gamma(P(\alpha)/(\alpha+i)+P_i(\alpha))} \\ &= e(g_1, \hat{g}_2)^{\gamma \cdot \alpha^{\ell-1}}. \end{aligned}$$

$\square$

It was modified to a semi-static construction to achieve constant size private key and ciphertext. Thus, as a broadcast encryption in the semi-static security model, this construction can be optimized as per our scheme.

5.1   Security Analysis

In this section, we shall prove that our scheme remains semi-static secure.

Theorem 1. Let $\mathcal{A}$ be a semi-static adversary against the above broadcast encryption system that makes at most $n - |S^*|$ queries. Then, there exists algorithm $\mathcal{B}$ such that

$$AdvBr_{\mathcal{A},n,\ell}^{SS}(\lambda) \leq AdvBDHES_{\mathcal{B},q,\ell}(\lambda) + 2/p$$

where $\mathcal{B}$ runs in time $t(A) + O((n + \ell)^2 \cdot \lambda^3)$ at most, assuming exponentiations take time $O(\lambda^3)$.

Proof. Let us assume that BDHE Sum instance $\{g^{\alpha^i} : i \in S\}$ is given for $m = 4d + 4\ell - 1$ and

$$S = [0, \ell - 2] \cup [d + \ell, 2d + \ell - 1] \cup [2d + 2\ell, 2d + 3\ell - 1]$$

$$\cup[3d + 3\ell, 4d + 3\ell] \cup [4d + 4\ell, 5d + 4\ell + 1]$$

where $d = n + 2\ell$.

Init $\mathcal{A}$ selects $S^* \subseteq [1, n]$ and sends S^* to $\mathcal{B}$.

Setup $\mathcal{B}$ randomly generates $a_0, a_1, a_2 \xleftarrow{R} \mathbb{Z}_p^*$, and implicitly sets $k = |S^*|$. Then, $\mathcal{B}$ parses S^* as $\{i_1, ..., i_k\}$ and sets $i_j \leftarrow n + j$ for $j \in [k + 1, \ell]$ and $P(x) = \prod_{j=1}^{\ell}(x + i_j)$. Also, let $f(x) = \prod_{i \in [1,n] \setminus S^*}(x + i) \cdot f'(x)$, and randomly construct $f'(x)$ that is a $d - n + k$ degree polynomial not to have common roots with $P(x)$. $f(x)$ is constructed in this way because $f(x)$ has to be divided by $(x + i)$ to generate valid private keys if identity i does not belong to the target set S^*.

Now, $\mathcal{B}$ sets

$$\beta \leftarrow a_0 \cdot \alpha^{-d-\ell}, \ \gamma \leftarrow f(\alpha),$$

and

$$g_1 \leftarrow g^{a_1 \cdot \alpha^{4d + 4\ell}}, \ g_2 \leftarrow g^{a_2 \cdot \alpha^{d + \ell}}, \ \hat{g}_1 \leftarrow g_1^{\beta}, \ \hat{g}_2 \leftarrow g_2^{\beta}.$$

Then, all public keys which are g_1^{γ}, $g_1^{\gamma \cdot \alpha}$ and

$$\{g_1^{\alpha^j}, \hat{g}_1^{\alpha^j}, \hat{g}_2^{\alpha^k} : j \in [0, \ell], k \in [0, \ell - 2]\}$$

can be computed from the instance. Then, $\mathcal{B}$ send PK to $\mathcal{A}$.

Extract. If $\mathcal{A}$ makes a private key query against i, $\mathcal{B}$ computes

$$d_i \leftarrow g_2^{\frac{\gamma}{\alpha + i}}$$

and sends d_i to $\mathcal{A}$. Notice that $f_i(x) \leftarrow f(x)/(x + i)$ is a polynomial of degree $d - 1$ for all $i \in [1, n] \setminus S^*$. Hence, $\mathcal{B}$ can calculate

$$g_2^{\frac{f(\alpha)}{\alpha + i}} = g^{a_2 \alpha^{d + \ell} \cdot f_i(\alpha)}$$

because $\{g^{\alpha^i} : i \in [d + \ell, 2d + \ell - 1]\}$ is given in the instance.

Challenge. For simplifying the notations, let $g_3 = g_1^{\alpha^{-d-\ell}} = g^{a_1 \cdot \alpha^{3d + 3\ell}}$, and $\hat{g}_3 = g_3^{\beta}$. Then, g_3 and $\hat{g}_3$ are only possible to be computed from the BDHE Sum instance

$$\{g_3^{\alpha^j}, \hat{g}_3^{\alpha^k} : j \in [0, d] \cup [d + \ell, 2d + \ell + 1], k \in [0, \ell - 1] \cup [d + \ell, 2d + \ell]\}.$$

If $\mathcal{A}$ sends a set $\tilde{S} \subseteq S^*$, $\mathcal{B}$ computes a polynomial $t(x)$ of degree $d + \ell - 1$ satisfying

$$t(x)f(x)|_i = 0, \text{ if } i \in [d + 1, d + \ell - 1] \quad t(x)f(x)|_d = 1.$$

$$t(x)P(x)|_i = 0, \text{ if } i \in [\ell, d + \ell - 1].$$

where $f(x)|_i$ is the coefficient of x^i in function f.
$t(x)$ exists due to Lemma 1 of [9]. $\mathcal{B}$ now sets the ciphertext values:

$$Hdr^* \leftarrow \langle C_1, C_2 \rangle \leftarrow \langle \hat{g}_3^{P(\alpha) \cdot t(\alpha)}, g_3^{f(\alpha) \cdot t(\alpha)} \rangle.$$

$$K \leftarrow Z^{a_0 a_1 a_2} \cdot e(g, g)^{a_0 a_1 a_2 (f(\alpha) \cdot t(\alpha) \cdot \alpha^{3d+4\ell-1} - \alpha^{4d+4\ell-1})}.$$

It should be noted that if $Z = e(g,g)^{\alpha^{4d+4\ell-1}}$, K is valid because $t(x)f(x)|_d = 1$.

Guess. Finally, $\mathcal{A}$ outputs a bit b'. $\mathcal{B}$ sends b' to the challenger.

Almost Perfect Simulation. We show that $\mathcal{B}$'s simulation is almost perfect from the point of $\mathcal{A}$. Most of our analysis is identical with GW's analysis [9]. In a semi-static security model, the maximum number of extraction queries is limited as $n - k$ because $\mathcal{A}$ only queries private keys for receivers not in $\tilde{S}$.

- PK is uniformly distributed since a_0, a_1, a_2, and α are random.
- Private key is uniformly distributed if $f(x)$ is uniformly distributed. In order to verify the uniformity of $f(x)$, the information leaking to $\mathcal{A}$ is formalized as follows.
  - In **Init**, $\mathcal{A}$ gets

    $$f(-i) \neq 0 \text{ for } i \in \{S^* \cup [n+1, n+\ell]\}.$$

  - In **Setup**, From the PK, $\mathcal{A}$ gets

    $$f(\alpha) = DL_{g_1}(g_1^\gamma).$$

  - In **Extract**, to $\mathcal{A}$, each private key query reveals

    $$f(-i) = 0 \text{ for } i \notin S^*.$$

  Since at most $n-k$ extraction queries can be made, therefore the information about $f(x)$ to $\mathcal{A}$ can be formulated by total $n+\ell-k+1$ equations described above even if we consider all non-zero equations. Because degree of $f(x)$ is $n + 2\ell$, $f(x)$ can be random and independent. This implies that the private key is also appropriately distributed.
- Suppose Z is random, then the statistical difference from uniform distribution is less than $2/p$. Let $Z = e(g,g)^{\delta + \alpha^{4d+4\ell-1}}$, then $K = e(g,g)^{\delta a_0 a_1 a_2} \cdot K'$ where K' is the correct key for Hdr^*. When $\delta = 0$, there is only one possible value of K. However, when $\delta \neq 0$, there are $p - 1$ equally probable values of K depending on $a_0 a_1 a_2$ which is non-zero.

Abort. There is no additional abortion which gives advantages to $\mathcal{A}$ except the cases we mentioned in *Almost Perfect Simulation* part.

Running Time of Simulation. The running time of this game is dominated by two computations, computing $g_2^{f_i(\alpha)}$ and $t(x)$. $O(n + \ell)$ exponentiation is necessary to calculate $g_2^{f_i(\alpha)}$ for each private key query, and $n - k$ private key queries can be made at most. Also, for computing $t(x)$, the algorithm must calculate at least one column of a $(d + \ell - 1)$ dimension Sylvester matrix. This requires $O(\ell(n + \ell))$ algorithm with the current knowledge [9]. Therefore, the running time of this simulation is at most about $O((n + \ell)^2)$. $\qquad\square$

6   Transforming Semi-static Security to Adaptive Security

The adaptive security model [9] is the strongest and most realistic notion in broadcast encryption. An adversary is not required to declare any target set before observing public keys. As such, there is no **Init** phase. Moreover, the set for a challenge cipertext can be any subsets of the set of identities that has never been queried in the **Extract** phase.

6.1   Transforming Semi-static Security to Adaptive Security

In addition to the semi-static security model, Gentry and Waters also showed how to transform a semi-static secure broadcast encryption scheme to an adaptively secure broadcast algorithm based on the two key technique [12]. In their technique, two keys are assigned for each user, but only one private key is allocated randomly to an individual user to respond extraction queries adaptively. Since the sender does not know which key each receiver has, the ciphertext must be constructed for both keys. Furthermore, users can also figure out which ciphertext can be decrypted by their private keys through a bit included in their private key.

We basically follow GW's approaches to make our semi-static secure broadcast encryption scheme be adaptively secure. In addition to their technique, we suggest an implementation technique to remove a linearly increasing element in GW's transformation. Let S be the set of receivers. The original transformation requires that for all $i \in S$, a bit $b_i \in \{0, 1\}$ is also included in the ciphertext. In other words, the ciphertext contains an additional component of $|S|$-bit.

Let $S = \{ID_1, \ldots, ID_{|S|}\}$ be the set of receivers. The original transformation requires an additional one bit information for each identity ID_i, denoted as b_{ID_i}, to be transmitted along the ciphertext. In order to transmit this information, the transformation includes an additional bit-string t of length $|S|$ such that $t[i] = b_{ID_i}$, where $t[i]$ represents the i-th bit of t.

In the transformation, the i-th receiver $ID_i \in S$ is associated with a bit $t[i]$. And therefore, the $|S|$-bit t is required.

Since decryption requires the knowledge of S, it is possible that in some scenarios, S has to be transmitted along the ciphertext. In this case, we describe an implementation trick that reduces the component t from $|S|$ bits to one bit. As the set S is normally not counted as part of the ciphertext, truly constant size ciphertext can be achieved.

Our Implementation Technique

Based on the observation that transmitting a set S and a sequence $\tilde{S}$, such that for any $i \in \tilde{S}$, $i \in S$, requires the same space complexity, we are able to replace $\{b_i\}$ with one single bit as follows. Denote i_s as the smallest value in S. Let $S_{b0} = \{i \in S \setminus \{i_s\} | b_i = 0\}$ and $S_{b1} = \{i \in S \setminus \{i_s\} | b_i = 1\}$. In other words, S_{b0} and S_{b1} are *the partition* of $S \setminus \{i_s\}$ based on the bit b_i.

We can construct a sequence $(S_{separated})$ as $\mathsf{seq}(S_{b0}), i_s, \mathsf{seq}(S_{b1})$ where $\mathsf{seq}(S)$ represents the random arrangement of elements of a set S to form a sequence (for simplicity, it can be in the normal ascending order). The sequence $S_{separated}$, together with a bit b_{i_s} would be sufficient to recover b_i for all i. For instance, the receiver first recovers the smallest identity i_s from the sequence $S_{separated}$. For any i in the sequence $S_{separated}$, $b_i = 0$ if i is before i_s and $b_i = 1$ otherwise. The only bit that needs to be transmitted along with the ciphertext is therefore b_{i_s}. Note that the cost of transmitting the sequence $S_{separated}$ is identical to that of S. We do not claim significant reduction in transmission cost in practice despite the saving in asymptotic complexity is from $O(|S|)$ to $O(1)$. In practice, if the set of receivers is to be transmitted together with the ciphertext, which is possibly true in some cases when S is highly dynamic, the actual saving of our tricks is $\lceil \log(|S|) \rceil - 1$ bits only. However, if the set S is known to the set of receivers, the trick is not applicable as in those cases, S does not need to be transmitted repeatedly.

Our construction using $S_{separated}$ is as follows. Note that the size of $S_{separated}$ is identical that of S.

Setup(n, ℓ): Run $\langle PK', SK' \rangle \leftarrow Setup_{SS}(2n, \ell)$. Set $s \leftarrow \{0,1\}^n$, Set $PK \leftarrow PK'$ and $SK \leftarrow (SK', s)$. Output $\langle PK, SK \rangle$.

KeyGen(i, SK): Run $d'_i \leftarrow KeyGen_{SS}(i + n \cdot s_i, SK')$. Set $d_i \leftarrow \langle d'_i, s_i \rangle$. Output d_i.

Enc(S, PK): Generate a random set of $|S|$ bits: $t \leftarrow \{t_i \leftarrow \{0,1\} : i \in S\}$. Generate $K \leftarrow \mathcal{K}$. Set

$$S_{t_0} \leftarrow \{i \text{ if } t_i = 0 : i \in S\}, \quad S_{t_1} \leftarrow \{i \text{ if } t_i = 1 : i \in S\}$$
$$S_0 \leftarrow S_{t_0} \cup \{i + n : i \in S_{t_1}\}, \quad \langle Hdr_0, k_0 \rangle \leftarrow Enc_{SS}(S_0, PK')$$
$$S_1 \leftarrow \{i + n : i \in S_{t_0}\} \cup S_{t_1}, \quad \langle Hdr_1, k_1 \rangle \leftarrow Enc_{SS}(S_1, PK').$$

Set $C_0 \leftarrow SymEnc(k_0, K)$, $C_1 \leftarrow SymEnc(k_1, K)$, $Hdr \leftarrow \langle Hdr_0, C_0, Hdr_1, C_1, b_{i_s} \rangle$ where b_{i_s} is the bit for the smallest identity in $i_s \in S$. Output $\langle Hdr, K \rangle$. Also, replace S with the sequence $S_{separated} \leftarrow \{\mathsf{seq}(S_{b0}), i_s, \mathsf{seq}(S_{b1})\}$ where

$$S_{b0} \leftarrow S_{t_0} \setminus \{i_s\}, \quad S_{b1} \leftarrow S_{t_1} \setminus \{i_s\}.$$

Dec$(S_{separated}, i, d_i, Hdr, PK)$: Parse d_i as $\langle d'_i, s_i \rangle$ and Hdr as $\langle Hdr_0, C_0, Hdr_1, C_1, b_{i_s} \rangle$. Set S_0 and S_1. Run

$$k_{s_i \oplus t_i} \leftarrow Dec_{SS}(S_{s_i \oplus t_i}, i, d'_i, Hdr_{s_i \oplus t_i}, PK').$$

Run $K \leftarrow SymDec(k_{s_i \oplus t_i}, C_{s_i \oplus t_i})$. Output K.

Since we just compress t to S through $S_{seperated}$, the security analysis remains the same as in the original Gentry and Waters' proof. Our adaptive broadcast encryption, following this generic transformation, compares favourably to the transformation of GW_{SS} since the impact of the transformation on efficiency is linear.

7 Conclusion

Gentry and Waters [9] introduced the security model and constructions for semi-static broadcast encryption, which can be transformed to an adaptively secure broadcast encryption. Based on their contributions, we introduced a more efficient semi-static broadcast encryption scheme. Our scheme enjoys smaller ciphertexts, shorter private keys and is more efficient in terms of computation cost.

We also showed that an adaptively secure broadcast encryption scheme transformed from our semi-static broadcast encryption scheme is still competitive against other adaptively secure broadcast encryption schemes that have been introduced recently. In addition, we elaborated an implementation technique to add to Gentry and Waters' transformation technique, which removes the linearly increasing part in the ciphertext. By adopting this idea, the resulting adaptively secure broadcast encryption scheme has a constant ciphertext if the underlying semi-static secure broadcast encryption scheme has a constant size ciphertext.

Furthermore, our scheme can be used as an identity-based broadcast encryption, but limited for polynomially many users. Extending our scheme for exponentially many users might be possible following the approach introduced by Delerablée [5], but it will rely on a random oracle.

Acknowledgements. We would like to thank the anonymous referees of Pairing 2013 for their constructive feedback to improve our paper. Additionally, we would like to thank Madeleine Cincotta for her thorough check to improve the linguistic quality of our paper. Finally, we would like to thank Dario Fiore who helped us to improve the quality of our paper. The second author is supported by ARC Future Fellowship FT0991397 and partly supported by the Natural Science Foundation of China through project 61370190.

References

1. Baek, J., Safavi-Naini, R., Susilo, W.: Efficient multi-receiver identity-based encryption and its application to broadcast encryption. In: Vaudenay, S. (ed.) PKC 2005. LNCS, vol. 3386, pp. 380–397. Springer, Heidelberg (2005)
2. Barbosa, M., Farshim, P.: Efficient identity-based key encapsulation to multiple parties. In: Smart, N.P. (ed.) Cryptography and Coding 2005. LNCS, vol. 3796, pp. 428–441. Springer, Heidelberg (2005)
3. Boneh, D., Gentry, C., Waters, B.: Collusion resistant broadcast encryption with short ciphertexts and private keys. In: Shoup, V. (ed.) CRYPTO 2005. LNCS, vol. 3621, pp. 258–275. Springer, Heidelberg (2005)

4. Cramer, R., Shoup, V.: Design and analysis of practical public-key encryption schemes secure against adaptive chosen ciphertext attack. SIAM Journal on Computing 33(1), 167–226 (2003)
5. Delerablée, C.: Identity-based broadcast encryption with constant size ciphertexts and private keys. In: Kurosawa, K. (ed.) ASIACRYPT 2007. LNCS, vol. 4833, pp. 200–215. Springer, Heidelberg (2007)
6. Dodis, Y., Fazio, N.: Public key broadcast encryption for stateless receivers. In: Feigenbaum, J. (ed.) DRM 2002. LNCS, vol. 2696, pp. 61–80. Springer, Heidelberg (2003)
7. Fiat, A., Naor, M.: Broadcast encryption. In: Stinson, D.R. (ed.) CRYPTO 1993. LNCS, vol. 773, pp. 480–491. Springer, Heidelberg (1994)
8. Gentry, C., Halevi, S.: Hierarchical identity based encryption with polynomially many levels. In: Reingold, O. (ed.) TCC 2009. LNCS, vol. 5444, pp. 437–456. Springer, Heidelberg (2009)
9. Gentry, C., Waters, B.: Adaptive security in broadcast encryption systems (with short ciphertexts). In: Joux, A. (ed.) EUROCRYPT 2009. LNCS, vol. 5479, pp. 171–188. Springer, Heidelberg (2009)
10. Goodrich, M.T., Sun, J.Z., Tamassia, R.: Efficient tree-based revocation in groups of low-state devices. In: Franklin, M. (ed.) CRYPTO 2004. LNCS, vol. 3152, pp. 511–527. Springer, Heidelberg (2004)
11. Halevy, D., Shamir, A.: The LSD broadcast encryption scheme. In: Yung, M. (ed.) CRYPTO 2002. LNCS, vol. 2442, pp. 47–60. Springer, Heidelberg (2002)
12. Katz, J., Wang, N.: Efficiency improvements for signature schemes with tight security reductions. In: Jajodia, S., Atluri, V., Jaeger, T. (eds.) ACM Conference on Computer and Communications Security, pp. 155–164. ACM (2003)
13. Lewko, A.B., Sahai, A., Waters, B.: Revocation systems with very small private keys. In: IEEE Symposium on Security and Privacy, pp. 273–285. IEEE Computer Society (2010)
14. Malek, B., Miri, A.: Adaptively secure broadcast encryption with short ciphertexts. I. J. Network Security 14(2), 71–79 (2012)
15. Naor, D., Naor, M., Lotspiech, J.: Revocation and tracing schemes for stateless receivers. In: Kilian, J. (ed.) CRYPTO 2001. LNCS, vol. 2139, pp. 41–62. Springer, Heidelberg (2001)
16. Naor, M., Pinkas, B.: Efficient trace and revoke schemes. In: Frankel, Y. (ed.) FC 2000. LNCS, vol. 1962, pp. 1–20. Springer, Heidelberg (2001)
17. Phan, D.-H., Pointcheval, D., Shahandashti, S.F., Strefler, M.: Adaptive CCA broadcast encryption with constant-size secret keys and ciphertexts. In: Susilo, W., Mu, Y., Seberry, J. (eds.) ACISP 2012. LNCS, vol. 7372, pp. 308–321. Springer, Heidelberg (2012)
18. Ren, Y., Gu, D.: Fully CCA2 secure identity based broadcast encryption without random oracles. Inf. Process. Lett. 109(11), 527–533 (2009)
19. Sakai, R., Furukawa, J.: Identity-based broadcast encryption. IACR Cryptology ePrint Archive, 2007:217 (2007)
20. Shamir, A.: Identity-based cryptosystems and signature schemes. In: Blakely, G.R., Chaum, D. (eds.) CRYPTO 1984. LNCS, vol. 196, pp. 47–53. Springer, Heidelberg (1985)
21. Shoup, V.: A proposal for an iso standard for public key encryption. IACR Cryptology ePrint Archive, 2001:112 (2001)
22. Smart, N.P.: Efficient key encapsulation to multiple parties. In: Blundo, C., Cimato, S. (eds.) SCN 2004. LNCS, vol. 3352, pp. 208–219. Springer, Heidelberg (2005)

Pairing Inversion via Non-degenerate
Auxiliary Pairings

Seunghwan Chang[1], Hoon Hong[2], Eunjeong Lee[3], and Hyang-Sook Lee[4]

[1] Institute of Mathematical Sciences, Ewha Womans University, Seoul, S. Korea
schang@ewha.ac.kr
[2] Department of Mathematics, North Carolina State University, Raleigh, USA
hong@ncsu.edu
[3] Institute of Mathematical Sciences, Ewha Womans University, Seoul, S. Korea
ejlee127@ewha.ac.kr
[4] Department of Mathematics, Ewha Womans University, Seoul, S. Korea
hsl@ewha.ac.kr

Abstract. The security of pairing-based cryptosystems is closely related to the difficulty of the pairing inversion problem(PI). In this paper, we discuss the difficulty of pairing inversion on the generalized ate pairings of Vercauteren. First, we provide a simpler approach for PI by generalizing and simplifying Kanayama-Okamoto's approach; our approach involves modifications of exponentiation inversion(EI) and Miller inversion(MI), via an auxiliary pairing. Then we provide a complexity of the modified MI, showing that the complexity depends on the sum-norm of the integer vector defining the auxiliary pairing. Next, we observe that *degenerate* auxiliary pairings expect to make modified EI harder. We provide a sufficient condition on the integer vector, in terms of its max norm, so that the corresponding auxiliary paring is *non*-degenerate. Finally, we define an infinite set of curve parameters, which includes those of typical pairing friendly curves, and we show that, within those parameters, PI of arbitrarily given generalized ate pairing can be reduced to modified EI in polynomial time.

1 Introduction

Pairings [1, 9, 12, 13, 18, 25, 29] play an important role in cryptography [2–4, 14, 27]. The security of pairing-based cryptosystems is closely related to the difficulty of the pairing inversion problem (PI): for a given pairing $\langle \cdot, \cdot \rangle$, an argument Q(or P) and a pairing value z, compute the other argument P(or Q) such that $z = \langle P, Q \rangle$.

PI on elliptic curves was first recognized by Verheul [26] as a potentially hard cryptographic computational problem. Satoh [23, 24] considered the polynomial interpolations to find the x-coordinate of P for given Q and z, providing evidences that support the difficulty of PI. Galbraith-Hess-Vercauteren [11] defined PI formally and discussed two approaches for PI. (1) Try to solve PI in a single step. (2) Solve PI by inverting exponentiation first and then inverting Miller step

Z. Cao and F. Zhang (Eds.): Pairing 2013, LNCS 8365, pp. 77–96, 2014.

- Since pairings on elliptic curves are computed in two steps, namely the Miller step and the exponentiation step, they suggested inverting them in reverse order to solve PI, i.e. exponentiation inversion(EI) and then Miller inversion (MI). They discussed the possibilities on the reduction of MI to PI (precisely FAPI-1) vice versa for Tate-Lichtenbaum pairing after the observation that the EI for Tate-Lichtenbaum pairing can be defined as returning a random value satisfying its exponentiation relation, which is very easy. They remarked that the situation, of EI, is quite different for the ate pairing. Recently, [17] showed that, when a preimage of Tate-Lichtenbaum pairing was restricted, its PI was equivalent to the PI of the ate pairing. Kanayama-Okamoto [15] studied the PI on the ate_i pairings and suggested a clever idea for a reduction of PI to EI.

In this paper, inspired by significant previous works [26, 22–24, 11, 20, 28, 15, 7], we provide further contributions toward understanding the difficulty of pairing inversion. In order to provide the context and the motivation for the main contributions of this paper, we first review informally some of the previous works particular [11, 15] on PI by recasting them for the generalized ate pairing of Vercauteren [25], which currently is one of the most general constructions of cryptographic pairings.

For a given integer vector ε, the generalized ate pairing $a_\varepsilon : G_2 \times G_1 \to G_3$ takes two points $P \in G_1, Q \in G_2$ and produces a value z. It is carried out in two steps: Miller step (M) [19] and Exponentiation step (E).

1. $[\mathsf{M}_\varepsilon]$ $\quad \gamma_\varepsilon = Z_\varepsilon(Q, P)$
2. $[\mathsf{E}_\varepsilon]$ $\quad z = \gamma_\varepsilon^L$

where Z_ε is a certain rational function depending on the integer vector ε and L is a certain natural number. Depending on the choice of ε, one gets a different pairing (see [25] and Section 2.2 for details).

Pairing inversion problems are defined in two types [11]. In this paper, we consider one of them (FAPI-1): for given $Q \in G_2$, $z \in G_3$, find P such that $z = a_\varepsilon(Q, P)$. Following [11, 15], we consider the two-step approach i.e., first inverting the exponentiation step (EI) and then inverting the Miller step (MI).

For the generalized ate pairings, there is a *subtlety* in the formulation of EI, as observed for example in [17], due to the fact that, for a fixed Q, the map $a_\varepsilon(Q, \cdot) : G_1 \to G_3$ is one-to-one, unlike for Tate-Lichtenbaum pairing. One could think of three possible formulations of EI. For a given L and z, find

F1: any γ such that $z = \gamma^L$. (γ might not be γ_ε)
F2: all γ's such that $z = \gamma^L$. (one of them will be γ_ε)
F3: the "right" γ such that $z = \gamma^L$. ($\gamma = \gamma_\varepsilon$)

In [15], it is *not* stated explicitly which formulation of EI is intended. From the context, we conclude that it cannot be F1. If it were F1, then we get into a strange conclusion that PI could be solvable in polynomial time since F1 is obviously solvable in polynomial time (due to fact that L is relatively prime to the order of z) and [15] showed that PI can be reduced to EI. We also conclude that it cannot be F2 either. If it were F2, then one would have to carry out

MI for each of the exponentially many γ's, contradicting the claim of [15] that PI can be reduced to EI in polynomial time. Hence, the only formulation of EI which is consistent with the claim of [15] is F3. Therefore, we will use F3 as the formulation of EI. Summarizing, we have the following formulation of PI :

1. [EI_ε] Find the "right" γ_ε from the set $\{\gamma : z = \gamma^L\}$
2. [MI_ε] Find P from $\gamma_\varepsilon = Z_\varepsilon(Q, P)$

In [15], Kanayama-Okamoto proposed an interesting modification of the natural approach for PI, which amounts to the following:

1. [Choice] Choose an integer vector e (which might be different from ε), giving rise to another generalized ate pairing, which we will call *an auxiliary pairing*, which may or may not be non-degenerate.
2. [$EI_{\varepsilon,e}$] Find the "right" γ_e by carrying out several "related" exponentiation inversions (See Section 2.3).
3. [MI_e]   Find P from $\gamma_e = Z_e(Q, P)$

From now on, we will call $EI_{\varepsilon,e}$ and MI_e as the *modified* exponentiation inversion and the *modified* Miller inversion, respectively. If $e = \varepsilon$, then $EI_{\varepsilon,e}$ and MI_e are exactly same as EI_ε and MI_ε. The key idea is to choose an integer vector e which may be different from ε, but which may be better for PI. Specifically, Kanayama-Okamoto suggested that the integer vector e is chosen from either coefficients of cyclotomic polynomials or $(1, \ldots, 1)$, because such e yields Z_e of low degree, making MI_e easy.

This concludes the informal review of the previous works on PI (recast for the generalized ate pairing). Finally we are ready to describe informally the main contributions of this paper.

1. In Section 3, we provide another approach for pairing inversion (Approach 1), by simplifying the step $EI_{\varepsilon,e}$ of Kanayama-Okamoto's approach. The simplicity of the proposed approach significantly facilitates the subsequent investigation. We prove its correctness (Theorem 1), and then compare the two approaches with respect to the search spaces(Theorem 2).
2. In Section 4, we provide a complexity analysis of MI_e (Theorem 3). It essentially says that the complexity is bounded by $||e||_1^2$ where $||e||_1$ stands for the sum norm of the chosen integer vector e. Hence, in order to reduce the complexity of MI_e, one needs to choose e with small sum norm.
3. In Section 5, we provide an incremental result toward the understanding of the complexity of $EI_{\varepsilon,e}$. We begin by observing that the degeneracy of the auxiliary pairing has a potential impact on the difficulty of $EI_{\varepsilon,e}$ (Proposition 1 and Remark 2). More precisely, if the auxiliary paring defined by the choice of e is degenerate, then the exponential relation in $EI_{\varepsilon,e}$ step becomes independent of the input z, that is, the exponential relation does not capture any information about the input. As a result, $EI_{\varepsilon,e}$ is expected to be harder than EI_ε, when such e is chosen. If the auxiliary pairing corresponding to e is non-degenerate, then $EI_{\varepsilon,e}$ is likely as hard as EI_ε. Hence, in order to

reduce the complexity of $\mathsf{EI}_{\varepsilon,e}$, one better choose e such that the auxiliary paring defined by e is non-degenerate. We provide a sufficient condition on e, in terms of the max norm of e, so that the pairing corresponding to e is non-degenerate (Theorem 4).

4. In Section 6, we discuss when pairing inversion can be reduced to modified exponentiation inversion $\mathsf{EI}_{\varepsilon,e}$. This was inspired by Kanayama-Okamoto [15] where pairing inversion was reduced to several (unmodified) exponentiation inversions. Specifically we are looking for a condition on e so that MI_e is easy. As explained above, we need to find *small e*. Thus, one might be naturally tempted to choose the integer vector e from either coefficients of cyclotomic polynomials or $(1, \ldots, 1)$. However such e makes the corresponding auxiliary pairing degenerate. Hence the modified exponentiation inversion $\mathsf{EI}_{\varepsilon,e}$ is expected to be hard. Therefore, in order to meaningfully reduce pairing inversion to modified exponentiation inversion, one needs find e such that it is *small* and the corresponding auxiliary pairing is *non-degenerate*. In this section, we investigate the existence of such e in various cases. In particular, we define an infinite set of curve parameters (Definition 1), which includes those of typical pairing friendly curves as in Table 1 of [10] and show that, within those parameters, pairing inversion of an arbitrarily given pairing can be reduced to modified exponentiation inversion in polynomial time (Theorem 5). We furthermore provide tighter upper bounds on the number of bit operations needed by such reductions for several concrete cases (Table 1).

2   Preliminaries

In this section, we briefly review elliptic curves, the generalized ate pairings due to Vercauteren [25] and an approach to pairing inversion due to Kanayama-Okamoto [15]. We encourage all the readers to skim through them, as the notations and the assumptions therein will be extensively used throughout the subsequent sections.

2.1   Elliptic Curves

We fix the basic notations for elliptic curves. Let q be a power of a prime and let r be a prime such that $\gcd(q, r) = 1$. Let k be the embedding degree defined as the multiplicative order of q in $\mathbb{F}_r^*$, denoted by $k = \mathrm{ord}_r(q)$, and $L = (q^k - 1)/r$. Let E be an elliptic curve defined over $\mathbb{F}_q$ such that $r \mid \#E(\mathbb{F}_q)$. Let $G_1 = E[r] \cap \ker(\pi_q - [1])$ and $G_2 = E[r] \cap \ker(\pi_q - [q])$ where $\pi_q : E \to E$ denotes the q-power Frobenius endomorphism.

2.2   Vercauteren's Generalized Ate Pairings

We review the generalized ate pairings [25]. Let $\mu_r = \left\{ u \in \mathbb{F}_{q^k}^\times : u^r = 1 \right\}$. Let $f_{n,Q}, l_{P,Q}$ and v_P be the normalized functions with divisors $n(Q) - ([n]Q) -$

$(n-1)(O)$, $(P)+(Q)+(-(P+Q))-3(O)$ and $(P)+(-P)-2(O)$ respectively, where O denotes the identity element of the group E. Let

$$g(X) = X^k - 1, \quad \lambda_\varepsilon(X) = \sum_{j=0}^{k-1} \varepsilon_j X^j, \quad W_\varepsilon(X) = \det\begin{pmatrix} g(X) & \lambda_\varepsilon(X) \\ g'(X) & \lambda'_\varepsilon(X) \end{pmatrix}$$

for $\varepsilon = (\varepsilon_0, \ldots, \varepsilon_{k-1}) \in \mathbb{Z}^k$. Vercauteren [25] defined a map $a_\varepsilon : G_2 \times G_1 \to \mu_r$ such that, for all $P \in G_1, Q \in G_2$,

$$a_\varepsilon(Q, P) = Z_\varepsilon(Q, P)^L, \quad \text{where}$$

$$Z_\varepsilon(Q, P) = \prod_{j=0}^{k-1} f_{\varepsilon_j, q^j Q}(P) \prod_{j=0}^{k-2} \frac{l_{\varepsilon_j q^j Q, (\varepsilon_{j+1}q^{j+1}+\cdots+\varepsilon_{k-1}q^{k-1})Q}}{v_{(\varepsilon_j q^j+\cdots+\varepsilon_{k-1}q^{k-1})Q}}(P)$$

and showed that it is a well-defined bilinear map if $r \mid \lambda_\varepsilon(q)$, $r^2 \nmid \lambda_\varepsilon(q)$ and $r^2 \nmid g(q)$. He also showed that a_ε is non-degenerate if and only if $r^2 \nmid W_\varepsilon(q)$.

From now on, we will assume $r \mid \lambda_\varepsilon(q)$, $r^2 \nmid \lambda_\varepsilon(q)$, $r^2 \nmid g(q)$ and $r^2 \nmid W_\varepsilon(q)$, so that a_ε is a non-degenerate pairing. We will also assume, without losing generality, that $\gcd(\varepsilon_0, \ldots, \varepsilon_{k-1}) = 1$ because the vector ε is selected as small as possible for faster pairing computation. In summary, Vercauteren proposed the following approach for pairings.

In: $P \in G_1, Q \in G_2$
Out: $z = a_\varepsilon(Q, P)$

1. $[M_\varepsilon]$ $\gamma_\varepsilon \leftarrow Z_\epsilon(P, Q)$
2. $[E_\varepsilon]$ $z \leftarrow \gamma_\epsilon^L$

2.3 Kanayama-Okamoto's Approach to Pairing Inversion

We review an approach for pairing inversion due to Kanayama-Okamoto [15]. They proposed the following approach and proved its correctness.

In: $Q \in G_2, z \in \mu_r$
Out: $P \in G_1$ such that $z = a_e(Q, P)$.

1. [Choice] Choose $e \in \mathbb{Z}^k$ such that $r \mid \lambda_e(q)$ and $\gcd(e_0, \ldots, e_{k-1}) = 1$.
2. $[EI_{\varepsilon,e}]$ Find γ_e by carrying out the following.
   (a) $T_j \leftarrow \text{rem}(q^j, r)$, the remainder of q^j modulo r
   (b) $a_j \leftarrow \text{ord}_r(T_j)$
   (c) $n_j \leftarrow \frac{T_j^{a_j} - 1}{r}$
   (d) $N_j \leftarrow \gcd(T_j^{a_j} - 1, q^k - 1)$
   (e) $d_j \leftarrow \sum_{h=0}^{a_j-1} T_j^{a_j-1-h} q^{jh}$
   (f) $c_j \leftarrow \text{rem}(d_j, N_j)$
   (g) $c'_j \leftarrow c_j^{-1} \mod r$.
   (h) $U_e \leftarrow \frac{1}{r} \sum_{j=0}^{k-1} e_j T_j$

(i) $U_\varepsilon \leftarrow \frac{1}{r} \sum_{j=0}^{k-1} \varepsilon_j T_j$

(j) $\psi_\varepsilon \leftarrow U_\varepsilon - \sum_{j=0}^{k-1} \varepsilon_j c'_j n_j$

(k) $\psi'_\varepsilon \leftarrow \psi_\varepsilon^{-1} \bmod r$.

(l) Find the "right" τ such that $\tau^L = z^{\psi'_\varepsilon}$

(m) Find the "right" α_j such that $\alpha_j^L = \tau^{L c'_j n_j}$

(n) $\gamma_e \leftarrow \dfrac{\tau^{U_e}}{\prod_{j=0}^{k-1} \alpha_j^{e_j}}$.

3. [MI$_e$] Find P from $\gamma_e = Z_e(Q, P)$.

By the "right" τ and the "right" α_j, we mean the ones satisfying the condition $\tau = f_{r,Q}(P)$ and $\alpha_j = f_{T_j,Q}(P)$ for some $P \in G_1$.

Remark 1. The above description is a bit different from the original one by Kanayama-Okamoto [15] in three ways.

- They used the quantity $\dfrac{\prod_{j=0}^{k-1} \alpha_j^{e_j}}{\tau^{U_e}}$ for γ_e, which is the reciprocal of the quantity shown above. We changed it in the current form, because it is more consistent with the notation used in Vercauteren's generalized pairings [25].
- They elaborated their idea for ate_i pairing (corresponding to a particular class of ε) and indicated that it could be extended to the generalized ate pairing of Vercauteren [25] (corresponding to a general class of ε). Indeed, such an extension is straightforward. The above description allows arbitrary ε.
- They elaborated their idea for particular choices of e such as coefficients of cyclotomic polynomials or $(1, \ldots, 1)$. The extension to arbitrary e is also straightforward. The above description allows arbitrary e.

3   A Simpler Approach for Paring Inversion

In this section, we describe an approach for inverting the generalized ate pairing of Vercauteren (Approach 1). We will use the notations introduced in Section 2.2. Comparing to Kanayama-Okamoto's approach (See Section 2.3), one sees that the modified exponentiation inversion step EI$_{\varepsilon,e}$ is simplified. The simplicity of the proposed approach facilitates the subsequent investigation. We prove its correctness (Theorem 1). Then we compare the simpler approach with Kanayama-Okamoto's approach (Theorem 2). We let $a \equiv_n b$ abbreviate $a \equiv b \pmod{n}$ for simplicity.

Approach 1 Pairing Inversion

In: $Q \in G_2$, $z \in \mu_r$
Out: $P \in G_1$ such that $z = a_\varepsilon(Q, P)$.

1. [Choice]   Choose $e \in \mathbb{Z}^k$ such that $r \mid \lambda_e(q)$ and $\gcd(e_0, \ldots, e_{k-1}) = 1$.

2. [EI$_{\varepsilon,e}$]   Find the "right" γ_e from $\Gamma_{\varepsilon,e,z} = \left\{ \gamma \in \mathbb{F}_{q^k}^\times : \gamma^L = z^{\delta_{\varepsilon,e}} \right\}$, where $\delta_{\varepsilon,e} \equiv_r w_e/w_\varepsilon$ and $w_\eta = \frac{1}{r} W_\eta(q)$.

3. [MI$_e$]   Find P from $\gamma_e = Z_e(Q, P)$.

By the "right" γ_e, we mean the ones satisfying the condition $\gamma_e = Z_e\,(Q, P)$ for some $P \in G_1$.

Theorem 1 (Correctness). *If* $\gamma_e = Z_e\,(Q, P)$, *then* $\gamma_e^L = z^{\delta_{\varepsilon,e}}$.

Proof. Recall that $\gamma_e^L = a_e(Q, P)$ and $z = a_\varepsilon(Q, P)$. Hence we need to show that

$$a_e(Q, P) = a_\varepsilon(Q, P)^{\delta_{\varepsilon,e}}.$$

Recall, from the proof of Theorem 4 in [25], that

$$f_{q,Q}(P)^{L\frac{\lambda_e(q)}{r}g'(q)\left(\frac{g(q)}{r}\right)^{-1}} = f_{q,Q}(P)^{L\lambda_e'(q)} \cdot a_e(Q, P).$$

and thus

$$a_e(Q, P) = f_{q,Q}(P)^{L\left(\frac{\lambda_e(q)}{r}g'(q)\left(\frac{g(q)}{r}\right)^{-1} - \lambda_e'(q)\right)} = f_{q,Q}(P)^{L\left(-\left(\frac{g(q)}{r}\right)^{-1}w_e\right)}.$$

Similarly, one gets

$$a_\varepsilon(Q, P) = f_{q,Q}(P)^{L\left(-\left(\frac{g(q)}{r}\right)^{-1}w_\varepsilon\right)}.$$

Thus,

$$a_e(Q, P) = f_{q,Q}(P)^{L\left(-\left(\frac{g(q)}{r}\right)^{-1}w_e\right)} = a_\varepsilon(Q, P)^{w_e w_\varepsilon^{-1}} = a_\varepsilon(Q, P)^{\delta_{\varepsilon,e}}. \qquad \square$$

One may wonder how the above approach compares to the approach of Kanayama-Okamoto. Since the MI_e steps are the same, we only need to compare $\mathsf{EI}_{\varepsilon,e}$ steps. Since $\mathsf{EI}_{\varepsilon,e}$ is essentially a search problem (finding the "right" elements), we need to compare the search spaces. Recall that the search space of Approach 1 is $\Gamma_{\varepsilon,e,z}$ when "brute-force" search is used. Likewise, the search space for the approach of Kanayama-Okamoto (see Section 2.3) amounts to

$$\Theta_{\varepsilon,e,z} = \left\{ \frac{\tau^{U_e}}{\prod_{j=0}^{k-1}\alpha_j^{e_j}} \;:\; \exists \tau, \alpha_j \in \mathbb{F}_{q^k}^\times \quad \alpha_j^L = \tau^{Lc_j'n_j} \wedge \tau^L = z^{\psi_\varepsilon'} \right\}$$

The following theorem states that the two "brute-force" search spaces are the same.

Theorem 2. *We have*

$$\Gamma_{\varepsilon,e,z} = \Theta_{\varepsilon,e,z}.$$

Proof. We will prove the inclusion in both directions.

Claim 1: $\Theta_{\varepsilon,e,z} \subset \Gamma_{\varepsilon,e,z}$

Let $\tau \in \mathbb{F}_{q^k}^\times$ and $\alpha_j \in \mathbb{F}_{q^k}^\times$ be such that $\alpha_j^L = \tau^{Lc_j'n_j}$ and $\tau^L = z^{\psi_\varepsilon'}$. Let $\theta = \frac{\tau^{U_e}}{\prod_{j=0}^{k-1}\alpha_j^{e_j}}$. We need to show that $\theta^L = z^{\delta_{\varepsilon,e}}$. Note

$$\theta^L = \left(\frac{\tau^{U_e}}{\prod_{j=0}^{k-1}\alpha_j^{e_j}}\right)^L = \frac{\tau^{LU_e}}{\prod_{j=0}^{k-1}\alpha_j^{Le_j}} = \frac{\tau^{LU_e}}{\prod_{j=0}^{k-1}\tau^{Le_jc_j'n_j}} = \tau^{L\left(U_e - \sum_{j=0}^{k-1}e_jc_j'n_j\right)} = \tau^{L\psi_e}$$

As $z = \tau^{L\psi_\varepsilon}$, we have $\theta^L = z^{\psi_e \psi_\varepsilon'}$. Since $Z_e(Q, P) \in \Theta_{e,z}$ as [15] showed, we also have $Z_e(Q, P)^L = z^{\psi_e \psi_\varepsilon'}$. Recall $Z_e(Q, P)^L = a_\varepsilon(Q, P)^{w_e w_\varepsilon'} = z^{w_e w_\varepsilon'}$. Thus,

$$\theta^L = z^{\psi_e \psi_\varepsilon'} = Z_e(Q, P)^L = a_\varepsilon(Q, P)^{w_e w_\varepsilon'} = z^{w_e w_\varepsilon'} = z^{\delta_{\varepsilon,e}}.$$

Claim 2: $\Gamma_{\varepsilon,e,z} \subset \Theta_{\varepsilon,e,z}$

Let $\gamma \in \mathbb{F}_{q^k}^\times$ be such that $\gamma^L = z^{\delta_{\varepsilon,e}}$. We need to find τ and α_j such that $\alpha_j^L = \tau^{Lc_j' n_j}$ and $\tau^L = z^{\psi_\varepsilon'}$ and $\gamma = \frac{\tau^{U_e}}{\prod_{j=0}^{k-1} \alpha_j^{e_j}}$. Let $P \in G_1$ and $Q \in G_2$ be such that $z = a_\varepsilon(Q, P)$. Such P, Q exist because the map $G_1 \to \mu_r, P \mapsto a_\varepsilon(Q, P)$ is bijective if $Q \in G_2 - \{O\}$. Let $\tilde{\tau} = f_{r,Q}(P)$ and $\tilde{\alpha}_j = f_{T_j,Q}(P)$ and $\tilde{\gamma} = \frac{\tilde{\tau}^{U_e}}{\prod_{j=1}^{k-1} \tilde{\alpha}_j^{e_j}}$. Let $h \in \mathbb{Z}^k$ be such that $\sum_{j=0}^{k-1} h_j e_j = 1$. Such h exists because $\gcd(e_0, \ldots, e_{k-1}) = 1$. Let

$$\tau = \tilde{\tau}, \qquad \alpha_j = \tilde{\alpha}_j \left(\frac{\tilde{\gamma}}{\gamma} \right)^{h_j}$$

Then we have

$$\tau^L = \tilde{\tau}^L = z^{\psi_\varepsilon'}$$

$$\alpha_j^L = \left(\tilde{\alpha}_j \left(\frac{\tilde{\gamma}}{\gamma} \right)^{h_j} \right)^L = \tilde{\alpha}_j^L \left(\frac{\tilde{\gamma}}{\gamma} \right)^{Lh_j} = \tilde{\alpha}_j^L \left(\frac{z^{\delta_{\varepsilon,e}}}{z^{\delta_{\varepsilon,e}}} \right)^{h_j} = \tilde{\tau}^{Lc_j' n_j} = \tau^{Lc_j' n_j}$$

$$\gamma = \tilde{\gamma} \frac{\gamma}{\tilde{\gamma}} = \frac{\tilde{\tau}^{U_e}}{\prod_{j=0}^{k-1} \tilde{\alpha}_j^{e_j}} \prod_{j=0}^{k-1} \left(\frac{\gamma}{\tilde{\gamma}} \right)^{h_j e_j} = \frac{\tilde{\tau}^{U_e}}{\prod_{j=0}^{k-1} \left(\tilde{\alpha}_j \left(\frac{\tilde{\gamma}}{\gamma} \right)^{h_j} \right)^{e_j}} = \frac{\tau^{U_e}}{\prod_{j=1}^{k-1} \alpha_j^{e_j}}$$

$\square$

4   Complexity of Modified Miller Inversion

In this section, we provide a bit-complexity of the modified Miller inversion step MI_e. It essentially says that, when q and k are fixed, the complexity is bounded by $||e||_1^2$ where $||e||_1$ stands for the sum norm of the integer vector e. Hence in order to reduce the complexity of MI_e, one needs to choose e with small sum norm. This result can be viewed as an adaptation of the results/ideas [11] to the generalized ate pairing.

Theorem 3 (Complexity of MI_e). *There exists an algorithm for MI_e requiring at most*

$$2^8 ||e||_1^2 k^2 (\log_2 q)^3$$

bit operations.

In the remainder of this section, we will prove Theorem 3. We will divide the proof into several lemmas that are interesting on their own. We begin with a slight reformulation of the expression for the generalized ate pairing [25], because it greatly simplifies the derivation of the above upper bound.

Lemma 1. *Let* $e^{(+)}, e^{(-)} \in \mathbb{Z}^k$ *be*

$$e_i^{(+)} = \begin{cases} e_i \ if \ e_i > 0 \\ 0 \ else \end{cases} \qquad and \qquad e_j^{(-)} = \begin{cases} e_j \ if \ e_j < 0 \\ 0 \ else \end{cases}$$

Then, for all $Q \in G_2$ *and all* $P \in G_1$, *we have*

$$Z_e(Q, P) = \frac{Z_{e^{(+)}}(Q, P)}{Z_{-e^{(-)}}(Q, P)}$$

Proof. See the Appendix.   □

Lemma 2. *For every* $Q \in G_2$, $\theta \in \mathbb{F}_{q^k}^*$ *and* $e \in \mathbb{Z}^\ell$, *there exists a bivariate polynomial* h *over* $\mathbb{F}_{q^k}$ *such that*

(a) $\forall (x, y) \in G_1 \quad \theta = Z_e(Q, (x, y)) \implies h(x, y) = 0$
(b) $\deg_X (h) \le ||e||_1$
(c) $\deg_Y (h) \le 2 \max\{s, t\}$, *where* $s := \#\{j : e_j > 0\}$ *and* $t := \#\{j : e_j < 0\}$.

Proof. See the Appendix..   □

Proof (Proof of Theorem 3). To solve MI_e for given $Q \in G_2$ and $e \in \mathbb{Z}^\ell$, we have to find $P = (x, y) \in G_1$ such that

$$\theta = Z_e(Q, (x, y)), \qquad\qquad y^2 = x^3 + ax + b \qquad (1)$$

Let h be a bivariate polynomial over $\mathbb{F}_{q^k}$ satisfying the three conditions in Lemma 2 and let, for the h,

$$F(X, Y) = Y^2 - X^3 - aX - b$$
$$u(X) = \mathrm{res}_Y (h(X, Y), F(X, Y)).$$

Note, for all $(x, y) \in G_1$, if $\theta = Z_e(Q, (x, y))$, then $u(x) = 0$ and

$$\deg u \ \le \ \deg_Y F \deg_X h + \deg_Y h \deg_X F \ \le \ 2 \cdot ||e||_1 + 2||e||_1 \cdot 3 \ = \ 8 \, ||e||_1.$$

From [11], there exists an algorithm for solving a polynomial of degree d in $\mathbb{F}_q$ whose complexity is $O(d^2 k^2 (\log q)^3)$. In fact, a more detailed analysis shows that the algorithm requires at most $4 \, d^2 \, k^2 \, (\log_2 q)^3$ bit operations. Since solving $u(X) = 0$ is enough to solve the system of equations (1), we see that MI_e can be solved within

$$4 \, (8 \, ||e||_1)^2 \, k^2 \, (\log_2 q)^3 = 2^8 \, ||e||_1^2 \, k^2 \, (\log_2 q)^3 \, .$$

bit operations.   □

5 Toward Complexity of Modified Exponentiation Inversion

It would be nice to have a complexity estimate for the modified exponentiation inversion $\mathsf{EI}_{\varepsilon,e}$, just as for the modified Miller inversion MI_e (Theorem 3). Unfortunately, we do *not* have a result on it. We are not aware of any results in the literature either. We expect it to be a very non-trivial task, most likely requiring patient and long arduous efforts of many researchers, each making an incremental contribution. In this section, we report on an incremental finding toward complexity of $\mathsf{EI}_{\varepsilon,e}$.

Recall that $\mathsf{EI}_{\varepsilon,e}$ asks to find the "right" γ_e from the search space $\Gamma_{\varepsilon,e,z}$. Hence it is reasonable to begin with the study of the relationship between the search space $\Gamma_{\varepsilon,e,z}$ and the chosen vector e.

Proposition 1. *We have*

1. *If the auxiliary pairing a_e is degenerate, then $\Gamma_{\varepsilon,e,z} = \Gamma_{\varepsilon,\varepsilon,1} = \mu_L$.*
2. *If the auxiliary pairing a_e is non-degenerate, then $\Gamma_{\varepsilon,e,z} = \Gamma_{\varepsilon,\varepsilon,z^{\delta_{\varepsilon,e}}}$.*

Proof. Note that $\delta_{\varepsilon,\varepsilon} = 1$. Recall that $\delta_{\varepsilon,e} \equiv_r w_e/w_\varepsilon$ and $w_e = \frac{1}{r}W_e(q) \in \mathbb{Z}$. Therefore we have

$$a_e \text{ is degenerate} \iff r^2 | W_e(q) \iff w_e \equiv_r 0 \iff \delta_{\varepsilon,e} \equiv_r 0$$

If a_e is degenerate, then we have

$$\Gamma_{\varepsilon,e,z} = \left\{\gamma \in \mathbb{F}_{q^k}^\times : \gamma^L = z^0\right\} = \left\{\gamma \in \mathbb{F}_{q^k}^\times : \gamma^L = 1^{\delta_{\varepsilon,e}}\right\} = \Gamma_{\varepsilon,\varepsilon,1} = \mu_L$$

If a_e is non-degenerate, then we have

$$\Gamma_{\varepsilon,e,z} = \left\{\gamma \in \mathbb{F}_{q^k}^\times : \gamma^L = z^{\delta_{\varepsilon,e}}\right\} = \left\{\gamma \in \mathbb{F}_{q^k}^\times : \gamma^L = \left(z^{\delta_{\varepsilon,e}}\right)^{\delta_{\varepsilon,\varepsilon}}\right\} = \Gamma_{\varepsilon,\varepsilon,z^{\delta_{\varepsilon,e}}}$$

$\square$

Remark 2. From the above proposition, we observe the followings:

- If a_e is degenerate then the search space of $\mathsf{EI}_{\varepsilon,e}$ is *independent* of the input z, that is, the exponential relation in $\mathsf{EI}_{\varepsilon,e}$ does not capture any information about the input. Thus the modified exponentiation inversion $\mathsf{EI}_{\varepsilon,e}$ will be most likely *harder* when a_e is degenerate than when a_e is non-degenerate.
- If a_e is non-degenerate then the search space of $\mathsf{EI}_{\varepsilon,e}$ for an input z is the same as that of EI_ε for *another* input $z^{\delta_{\varepsilon,e}}$. Thus the modified exponentiation inversion $\mathsf{EI}_{\varepsilon,e}$ is likely as hard as the original exponentiation inversion EI_ε.

Therefore, as a first step toward finding an efficient method for $\mathsf{EI}_{\varepsilon,e}$, we better ensure that a_e is non-degenerate. The following theorem (Theorem 4) gives a sufficient condition on e, in terms of the max norm of e, for the non-degeneracy of a_e. We will use the following lemma in the proof of the theorem, hence we state it first.

Lemma 3. *Let s be a primitive k-th root of unity modulo r^2 and $s \equiv q \mod r$. Then $r^2 \nmid \lambda_e(s)$ iff a_e is non-degenerate.*

Proof. The claim follows easily from the proof of [12, Theorem 3]. See the Appendix for a detailed proof in terms of our terminologies.

Theorem 4. *Let $e \in \mathbb{Z}^k$ be such that $r \mid \lambda_e(q)$ and $\Phi_k(X) \nmid \lambda_e(X)$. Let $m_e = [\mathbb{Q}(\zeta_k) : \mathbb{Q}(\lambda_e(\zeta_k))]$. If*

$$||e||_\infty < \frac{r^{2m_e/\varphi(k)}}{\varphi(k)}$$

then a_e is non-degenerate.

Proof. We will prove the contra-positive. Assume that a_e is degenerate. We claim

$$||e||_\infty \geq \frac{r^{2m_e/\varphi(k)}}{\varphi(k)}.$$

Let $s \in \mathbb{Z}$ be such that $s \equiv q \pmod{r}$ and $\operatorname{ord}_{r^2}(s) = k$. To prove the claim, we will use the fact that a_e is degenerate if and only if $r^2 \mid \lambda_e(s)$ (Lemma 3). Note $r^2 \mid (s^k - 1) = \prod_{d|k} \Phi_d(s)$. Since $r \mid \Phi_d(s) = \Phi_d(q + \iota r)$ implies $r \mid \Phi_d(q)$, r divides only $\Phi_k(s)$ and $r \nmid \Phi_d(s)$ for all $d < k$. Therefore, $r^2 \mid \Phi_k(s)$.

Let $\mu_e(X) = \operatorname{rem}(\lambda_e(X), \Phi_k(X))$ and $\zeta_k \in \mathbb{C}$ be a primitive k-th root of unity. Note that $\mu_e \neq 0$ from the assumption. Let $v(X) \in \mathbb{Q}[X]$ be the minimal polynomial of $\mu_e(\zeta_k)$ over $\mathbb{Q}$. Note that $v(x) \in \mathbb{Z}[x]$ as $\mu_e(\zeta_k) \in \mathbb{Z}[\zeta_k]$, the ring of integers of $\mathbb{Q}(\zeta_k)$. Since $v(\mu_e(X))$ is zero at ζ_k and $\Phi_k(x)$ is monic, we have

$$v(\mu_e(X)) = \Phi_k(X)h(X) \quad \text{for some} \quad h(X) \in \mathbb{Z}[X].$$

From $r^2 \mid \lambda_e(s)$ and $r^2 \mid \Phi_k(s)$, we have $r^2 \mid \mu_e(s)$ and

$$v(0) \equiv_{r^2} v(\mu_e(s)) \equiv_{r^2} \Phi_k(s)h(s) \equiv_{r^2} 0$$

Therefore, we have either $v(0) = 0$ or $|v(0)| \geq r^2$. Noting that, by [6, Proposition 4.3.2] and the fact that v is monic,

$$|v(0)| = |\operatorname{Norm}(\mu_e(\zeta_k))| = \left|\operatorname{Norm}_{\mathbb{Q}(\zeta_k)/\mathbb{Q}}(\mu_e(\zeta_k))\right|^{\frac{1}{m_e}} = \left|\prod_{\gcd(j,k)=1} \mu_e(\zeta_k^j)\right|^{\frac{1}{m_e}},$$

we conclude that $v(0) \neq 0$. Indeed if $v(0) = 0$, then $\Phi_k \mid \lambda_e$, a contradiction to $\mu_e \neq 0$. Thus, we have

$$r^2 \leq |v(0)| = \left|\prod_{\gcd(j,k)=1} \mu_e(\zeta_k^j)\right|^{\frac{1}{m_e}} \leq \left(\prod_{\gcd(j,k)=1} \varphi(k)||e||_\infty\right)^{\frac{1}{m_e}} = (\varphi(k)||e||_\infty)^{\frac{\varphi(k)}{m_e}}$$

Therefore, we finally have the claim. $\qquad\square$

6   Reducing Paring Inversion to Modified Exponentiation Inversion

In this section, we discuss when pairing inversion can be reduced to modified exponentiation inversion $\mathsf{EI}_{\varepsilon,e}$.

Specifically we are looking for a condition on e so that MI_e is easy. According to Theorem 3, we need to find *small e*. One might be naturally tempted to choose the integer vector e from either coefficients of cyclotomic polynomials or $(1,\ldots,1)$. However according to Corollary 6 of Vercauteren [25], such e makes the corresponding auxiliary pairing degenerate. Hence, from Proposition 1, the modified exponentiation inversion $\mathsf{EI}_{\varepsilon,e}$ is expected to be hard because the search space does *not* depend on z. Therefore, in order to meaningfully reduce pairing inversion to modified exponentiation inversion, one needs find e such that it is *small* and the corresponding auxiliary pairing is *non-degenerate*. In this section, we investigate the existence of such e in various cases (Theorem 5 and the subsequent examples in Table 1). We begin by introducing a definition that was inspired by the discussions in[11].

Definition 1. *Let C_α be the set of all $(r,k) \in \mathbb{Z}_{>0}^2$ satisfying*

C1: $r^{1/\varphi(k)} > \varphi(k)$
C2: $r^{1/\varphi(k)} \le (\log_2 r)^\alpha$

Remark 3. In the following figure, the bottom curve is from the condition C1 in Definition 1 and the top curve is from the condition C2 when $\alpha = 10$. Thus, the regions between the two curves is the set C_{10}, The black dots represent typical pairing friendly curves from Table 1 in [10]. Note that the parameters for the typical pairing friendly curves belong to C_{10}.

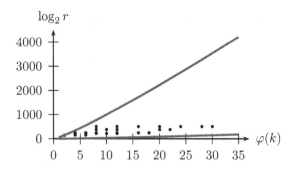

Lemma 4. *If $\alpha > 1$, then C_α is an infinite set.*

Proof. See the Appendix.   □

Theorem 5. *Let $\alpha > 1$, $(r,k) \in C_\alpha$ and $r \ge \sqrt{q}$. Then the inversion of every generalized ate pairing can be reduced to modified exponentiation inversion* *in polynomial time in* $\log_2 r$. *Specifically, there exists e such that the auxiliary pairing a_e is non-degenerate and MI_e can be carried out in at most*

$$2^{13} \ (\log_2 r)^{8\alpha+3}$$

bit operations.

Proof. Let $(q, r) \in C_\alpha$ and $r \geq \sqrt{q}$. We need to find a "witness" e such that a_e is non-degenerate and MI_e can be carried out in the claimed number of bit operations. From Minkowski's theorem (see III.C of [25]), there exists $e \in \mathbb{Z}^k$ with $r \mid \lambda_e(q)$ such that the last $k - \varphi(k)$ elements of e are zero and

$$||e||_\infty \leq r^{1/\varphi(k)}$$

We will take it as the witness.

First we show that a_e is non-degenerate. Since the last $k - \varphi(k)$ elements of e are zero, we have $\lambda_e(X) \nmid \Phi_k(X)$. From the condition that $r^{1/\varphi(k)} > \varphi(k)$, we have

$$\frac{r^{(2m_e-1)/\varphi(k)}}{\varphi(k)} \geq \frac{r^{1/\varphi(k)}}{\varphi(k)} > 1$$

and thus

$$||e||_\infty \leq r^{1/\varphi(k)} < r^{1/\varphi(k)} \frac{r^{(2m_e-1)/\varphi(k)}}{\varphi(k)} = \frac{r^{2m_e/\varphi(k)}}{\varphi(k)}$$

Therefore, by Theorem 4, a_e is non-degenerate.

Next we show that MI_e can be carried out in the claimed number of bit operations. Let N be the number of bit operations for MI_e. Note that $||e||_1 \leq \varphi(k) ||e||_\infty$. Hence $||e||_1 \leq \varphi(k) r^{1/\varphi(k)}$. Therefore, from Theorem 3, we have

$$N \leq 2^8 \left(\varphi(k) r^{1/\varphi(k)} \right)^2 k^2 \ (\log_2 q)^3$$

From the condition $r \geq \sqrt{q}$, we have

$$N \leq 2^8 \left(\varphi(k) r^{1/\varphi(k)} \right)^2 k^2 \ (2\log_2 r)^3 = 2^{11} \ \varphi(k)^2 \ r^{2/\varphi(k)} \ k^2 \ (\log_2 r)^3$$

Since $\sqrt{k} \leq \sqrt{2}\varphi(k)$ and $\varphi(k) < r^{1/\varphi(k)}$, we have

$$N \leq 2^{11} \ \varphi(k)^2 \ r^{2/\varphi(k)} \ 4 \ \varphi(k)^4 \ (\log_2 r)^3 = 2^{13} \ r^{8/\varphi(k)} \ (\log_2 r)^3$$

Since $r^{1/\varphi(k)} \leq (\log_2 r)^\alpha$, we have

$$N < 2^{13} \ (\log_2 r)^{8\alpha} \ (\log_2 r)^3 = 2^{13} \ (\log_2 r)^{8\alpha+3} \qquad \square$$

The upper bound in Theorem 5 is not tight. In Table 1, we provide tighter upper bounds for several examples. For each example, the first row of the table shows $k, \varphi(k), \log_2 r, \alpha$ with which we can estimate an upper bound of the bit complexity for reducing PI to $\mathsf{El}_{\varepsilon,e}$, using Theorem 5. The next rows show actual

Table 1. Estimates on time needed for reducing pairing inversion to exponentiation inversion

BN	$k,\ \varphi(k),\ \log_2 r,\ \alpha$	12, 4, 158, 6
	q	2063276713607373024910158007441390334505910272219
	r	2063276713607373024910153465110806135060608358413
	e	$[-550292684801, 0, -550292684802, 1]$
	$\|e_1\|$	$\approx 2^{41}$
	bit ops	$< 2^{118} \approx 5.7 \times 10^8$ years
KSS1	$k,\ \varphi(k),\ \log_2 r,\ \alpha$	40, 16, 270, 3
	q	17832670971324521726062757296872438734385533246858199397670289787762755378 369096459615195260462717384342962017722458889
	r	10333609989585926391763339467648162217044412785537436596479947661501694341 18209921
	e	$[-89353, -1, 0, 0, 0, 0, 0, 0, 0, 0, -178706, 0, 0, 0, 0, 0, 0, 0, 0, 0, 0, 0, 0, 0, 0, 0, 0, 0, 0, 0,$ $0, 0, 0, 0, 0, 0, 0, 0, 0, 0]$
	$\|e_1\|$	$\approx 2^{19}$
	bit ops	$< 2^{81} \approx 1.5$ days
KSS2	$k,\ \varphi(k),\ \log_2 r,\ \alpha$	36, 12, 169, 2
	q	2751543160631368260054651194751592326705827593927804159297383466 9
	r	7057085270285284208731356322531945870927284566673193
	e	$[644, 966, 2899, -2255, 8697, 10307, 12562, -2577, 5798, 0, 6120, 2577, 0, 0, 0, 0, 0, 0,$ $0, 0, 0, 0, 0, 0, 0, 0, 0, 0, 0, 0, 0, 0, 0, 0, 0, 0]$
	$\|e_1\|$	$\approx 2^{16}$
	bit ops	$< 2^{74} \approx 17.1$ minutes
CP1	$k,\ \varphi(k),\ \log_2 r,\ \alpha$	23, 22, 257, 2
	q	14581195760274460834017340459207397113118390962271666876151276230048512680 03597885800006313754045399948707280439848940248906689382680399441035897388 657793
	r	17116282357765890892357712305726339622924416691441071745853644550112128595 6693
	e	$[-196, -527, -851, -89, -648, 115, 1086, -14, 547, -1053, 409, -611, 680, -1368, -$ $891, -1808, -3226, -1664, 577, 22, 213, 15, 0]$
	$\|e_1\|$	$\approx 2^{15}$
	bit ops	$< 2^{73} \approx 8.5$ minutes
C6.6	$k,\ \varphi(k),\ \log_2 r,\ \alpha$	33, 20, 265, 2
	q	17156052909325454315949246639981773625245302303247192926147820123623493657 4795328339355710502059
	r	57482237782367522519498203534411140773179333661921340353191781776555783843 120129
	e	$[0, 0, 0, 0, 0, 0, 0, 0, 0, 1, 0, 0, 0, 0, 0, 0, 0, 0, 0, -9727, 0, 0, 0, 0, 0, 0, 0, 0, 0, 0, 0, 0, 0]$
	$\|e_1\|$	$\approx 2^{14}$
	bit ops	$< 2^{70} \approx 1.1$ minutes

parameters q, r and a vector $e \in \mathbb{Z}^{\varphi(k)}$. The vector e is the one with smallest sum norm among the LLL reduced vectors for the lattice with respect to q, r, k [25]. The vector e is verified to yield non-degenerate a_e. For the vector e, the last row has been calculated using Theorem 3, which estimates the bit complexity of MI_e on the curve more precisely. The estimated upper bounds on the computing times are based on the assumption that one uses the currently fastest super-computer [8], which can perform about $17 \cdot 10^{15}$ flops $\times\, 1000\dfrac{\text{bops}}{\text{flops}} = 2^{64}\text{bops}$ (bit operations per second).

The first example BN is the smallest value taken from Table 1 in [21]. Since $\varphi(k)$ for the BN curves [5] are small ($\varphi(k) = 4$), they easily satisfy the condition C1 in Definition 1 but large α values are needed to satisfy C2. Therefore, from Theorem 5, we expect that it will be difficult to reduce PI to $\mathsf{EI}_{\varepsilon,e}$ for BN curves. The tighter upper bound on the bit operation on the last row, based on Theorem 3, supports the observation. Next two examples are the KSS curves described in Example 4.6 and Example 4.7 in [16]. The parameters are obtained by evaluating the polynomials in the Examples in [16] at $x_0 = -188$ for KSS1 and $x_0 = 107$ for KSS2. The example CP1 is constructed by Cocks-Pinch method to have small α and "typical" parameters $(k, \log_2 r)$ in Table 1 in [10]. The example C6.6 is obtained from evaluating the polynomials in Construction 6.6 with $k = 33$ in [10] at $x_0 = -9727$, which is also a pairing-friendly curve (Definition 2.3 in [10]). The $\varphi(k)$ for these curves are small enough to satisfy C1, and big enough for small α values to satisfy C2. Therefore, from Theorem 5, we expect that it will be relatively easy to reduce PI to $\mathsf{EI}_{\varepsilon,e}$ for these curves. The tighter upper bound on the bit operations on the last row, based on Theorem 3, supports the observation.

Acknowledgements. The authors[1,3,4] were supported by Basic Science Research Program through the National Research Foundation of Korea(NRF) funded by the Ministry of Science, ICT and Future Planning(Grant Number: 2012R1A2A1A03006706). The author[3] was also supported by Basic Science Research Program (Grant No. 2011-0022600). The authors would like to thank Steven Galbraith and anonymous referees for their insightful and helpful suggestions.

References

1. Barreto, P., Galbraith, S., ÓhÉigeartaigh, C., Scott, M.: Efficient Pairing Computation on Supersingular Abelian Varieties. Designs, Codes and Cryptography 42(3), 239–271 (2007)
2. Boneh, D., Franklin, M.: Identity-based encryption from the Weil pairing. SIAM J. of Computing 32(3), 586–615 (2003)
3. Boneh, D., Goh, E., Nissim, K.: Evaluating 2-DNF formulas on ciphertexts. In: Kilian, J. (ed.) TCC 2005. LNCS, vol. 3378, pp. 325–341. Springer, Heidelberg (2005)
4. Boneh, D., Lynn, B., Shacham, H.: Short signatures from the Weil pairing. J. of Cryptology 17(4), 297–319 (2004)

5. Barreto, P., Naehrig, M.: Pairing-friendly elliptic curves of prime order. In: Preneel, B., Tavares, S. (eds.) SAC 2005. LNCS, vol. 3897, pp. 319–331. Springer, Heidelberg (2006)

6. Cohen, H.: A Course in Computational Algebraic Number Theory. Springer, Heidelberg (2000)

7. Duc, A., Jetchev, D.: Hardness of Computing Individual Bits for One-way Functions on Elliptic Curves. In: Safavi-Naini, R., Canetti, R. (eds.) CRYPTO 2012. LNCS, vol. 7417, pp. 832–849. Springer, Heidelberg (2012)

8. Cray Titan, olcf.ornl.gov/titan/, en.wikipedia.org/wiki/Titan_(supercomputer)

9. Duursma, I., Lee, H.-S.: Tate pairing implementation for hyperelliptic curves $y^2 = x^p - x + d$. In: Laih, C.-S. (ed.) ASIACRYPT 2003. LNCS, vol. 2894, pp. 111–123. Springer, Heidelberg (2003)

10. Freeman, D., Scott, M., Teske, E.: A taxonomy of pairing-friendly elliptic curves. J. of Cryptology 23, 224–280 (2010)

11. Galbraith, S., Hess, F., Vercauteren, F.: Aspects of Pairing Inversion. IEEE Trans. Information Theory 54, 5719–5728 (2008)

12. Hess, F.: Pairing Lattices. In: Galbraith, S.D., Paterson, K.G. (eds.) Pairing 2008. LNCS, vol. 5209, pp. 18–38. Springer, Heidelberg (2008)

13. Hess, F., Smart, N., Vercauteren, F.: The Eta Pairing Revisited. IEEE Trans. Information Theory 52, 4595–4602 (2006)

14. Joux, A.: A one round protocol for tripartite Diffie-Hellman. J. of Cryptology 17(4), 263–276 (2004)

15. Kanayama, N., Okamoto, E.: Approach to Pairing Inversions Without Solving Miller Inversion. IEEE Trans. Information Theory 58, 1248–1253 (2012)

16. Kachisa, E.J., Schaefer, E.F., Scott, M.: Constructing Brezing-Weng Pairing-Friendly Elliptic Curves Using Elements in the Cyclotomic Field. In: Galbraith, S.D., Paterson, K.G. (eds.) Pairing 2008. LNCS, vol. 5209, pp. 126–135. Springer, Heidelberg (2008)

17. Kim, S., Cheon, J.: Fixed Argument Pairing Inversion on Elliptic Curves (2012) (preprint), http://eprint.iacr.org/2012/657

18. Lee, E., Lee, H.-S., Park, C.: Efficient and Generalized Pairing Computation on Abelian Varieties. IEEE Trans. Information Theory 55(4), 1793–1803 (2009)

19. Miller, V.: The Weil pairing and its efficient calculation. J. of Cryptology 17, 235–261 (2004)

20. El Mrabet, N.: What about Vulnerability to a Fault Attack of the Miller's Algorithm During an Identity Based Protocol? In: Park, J.H., Chen, H.-H., Atiquzzaman, M., Lee, C., Kim, T.-h., Yeo, S.-S. (eds.) ISA 2009. LNCS, vol. 5576, pp. 122–134. Springer, Heidelberg (2009)

21. Pereira, G., Simplício, M., Naehrig, M., Barreto, P.: A Family of Implementation-Friendly BN Elliptic Curves. J. of Systems and Software 84(8), 1319–1326 (2011)

22. Page, D., Vercauteren, F.: A Fault Attack on Pairing Based Cryptography. IEEE Trans. Computers 55(9), 1075–1080 (2006)

23. Satoh, T.: On polynomial interpolations related to Verheul homomorphisms. J. Comput. Math. 9, 135–158 (2006)

24. Satoh, T.: On pairing inversion problems. In: Takagi, T., Okamoto, T., Okamoto, E., Okamoto, T. (eds.) Pairing 2007. LNCS, vol. 4575, pp. 317–328. Springer, Heidelberg (2007)

25. Vercauteren, F.: Optimal Pairings. IEEE Trans. Information Theory 56(1), 455–461 (2010)

26. Verheul, E.: Evidence that XTR is more secure than supersingular elliptic curve cryptosystems. J. Cryptology 17(4), 277–296 (2004)
27. Waters, B.: Efficient Identity-Based Encryption Without Random Oracles. In: Cramer, R. (ed.) EUROCRYPT 2005. LNCS, vol. 3494, pp. 114–127. Springer, Heidelberg (2005)
28. Weng, J., Dou, Y., Ma, C.: Fault Attacks against the Miller Algorithm in Hessian Coordinates. In: Wu, C.-K., Yung, M., Lin, D. (eds.) Inscrypt 2011. LNCS, vol. 7537, pp. 102–112. Springer, Heidelberg (2012)
29. Zhao, C., Zhang, F., Huang, J.: A Note on the Ate Pairing. International J. of Information Security 7(6), 379–382 (2008)

Appendix

In this appendix, we provide proofs of several technical lemmas.

Proof (Proof of Lemma 1). Let $e_{m_1}, \ldots, e_{m_s} > 0$ and $e_{n_1}, \ldots, e_{n_t} < 0$ and all other components of e are zero. Then we have

$$e_{m_i}^{(+)} = e_{m_i} \qquad\qquad e_{n_j}^{(-)} = e_{n_j}$$

and all other components of $e^{(+)}$ and $e^{(-)}$ are zero. Note

$$U_e r - e_{n_1} q^{n_1} - \cdots - e_{n_t} q^{n_t} = e_{m_1} q^{m_1} + \cdots + e_{m_s} q^{m_s}$$

Thus

$$f_{e_{m_1} q^{m_1} + \cdots + e_{m_s} q^{m_s}, Q}$$

$$= \prod_{i=1}^{s} f_{q^{m_i}, Q}^{e_{m_i}} \prod_{i=1}^{s} f_{e_{m_i}, q^{m_i} Q} \prod_{i=1}^{s-1} \frac{l_{e_{m_i} q^{m_i} Q, (e_{m_{i+1}} q^{m_{i+1}} + \cdots + e_{m_s} q^{m_s}) Q}}{v_{(e_{m_i} q^{m_i} + \cdots + e_{m_s} q^{m_s}) Q}}$$

$$= \prod_{i=1}^{s} f_{q^{m_i}, Q}^{e_{m_i}}(P) \cdot Z_{e^{(+)}}(Q, P)$$

$$f_{U_e r - e_{n_1} q^{n_1} - \cdots - e_{n_t} q^{n_t}, Q}$$

$$= f_{U_e r, Q} f_{-e_{n_1} q^{n_1} - \cdots - e_{n_t} q^{n_t}, Q}$$

$$= f_{r, Q}^{U_e}(P) \prod_{j=1}^{t} f_{q^{n_j}, Q}^{-e_{n_j}}(P) \cdot Z_{-e^{(-)}}(Q, P)$$

Hence

$$f_{r, Q}^{U_e}(P) \prod_{j=1}^{t} f_{q^{n_j}, Q}^{-e_{n_j}}(P) \cdot Z_{-e^{(-)}}(Q, P) = \prod_{i=1}^{s} f_{q^{m_i}, Q}^{e_{m_i}} \cdot Z_{e^{(+)}}(Q, P)$$

and, from [25], we have

$$Z_e(Q, P) = \frac{f_{r, Q}^{U_e}(P)}{\prod_{i=0}^{k-1} f_{q^i, Q}^{e_i}(P)} = \frac{Z_{e^{(+)}}(Q, P)}{Z_{-e^{(-)}}(Q, P)}$$

$\square$

Proof (Proof of Lemma 2). Let $Q \in G_2$, $\theta \in \mathbb{F}_{q^k}^*$ and $e \in \mathbb{Z}^\ell$. We will construct a witness for the existentially quantified h. From Lemma 14 of [11], we have

$$f_{\mu, \nu Q}(X, Y) = \begin{cases} 1 & \mu = 1 \\ \dfrac{f_{\mu,\nu,1}(X) + Y f_{\mu,\nu,2}(X)}{v_{\mu\nu Q}} & \mu > 1 \end{cases}$$

where $f_{\mu,\nu,1}, f_{\mu,\nu,2} \in \mathbb{F}_{q^k}[X]$ such that

$$\deg(f_{\mu,\nu,1}) \leq \left\lfloor \frac{\mu+1}{2} \right\rfloor, \qquad \deg(f_{\mu,\nu,2}) \leq \left\lfloor \frac{\mu}{2} - 1 \right\rfloor$$

From Lemma 1, we have

$$Z_e(Q, (x,y)) = \frac{Z_{e^{(+)}}(x,y)}{Z_{-e^{(-)}}(x,y)} =: \frac{A(x,y)}{B(x,y)} \quad \text{for all } (x,y) \in G_1$$

where

$$A = \prod_{\substack{1 \leq i \leq s \\ e_{m_i} \geq 2}} \left(f_{e_{m_i}, q^{m_i}, 1} + Y f_{e_{m_i}, q^{m_i}, 2} \right) \prod_{\substack{1 \leq j \leq t \\ e_{n_j} \leq -2}} v_{-e_{n_j} q^{n_j} Q}$$

$$\prod_{i=1}^{s-1} l_{e_{m_i} q^{m_i} Q, \left(e_{m_{i+1}} q^{m_{i+1}} + \cdots + e_{m_s} q^{m_s} \right) Q} \prod_{j=1}^{t-1} v_{\left(-e_{n_{j+1}} q^{n_{j+1}} - \cdots - e_{n_t} q^{n_t} \right) Q}$$

$$B = \prod_{\substack{1 \leq j \leq t \\ e_{n_j} \leq -2}} \left(f_{-e_{n_j}, q^{n_j}, 1} + Y f_{-e_{n_j}, q^{n_j}, 2} \right) \prod_{\substack{1 \leq i \leq s \\ e_{m_i} \geq 2}} v_{e_{m_i} q^{m_i} Q}$$

$$\prod_{j=1}^{t-1} l_{-e_{n_j} q^{n_j} Q, \left(-e_{n_{j+1}} q^{n_{j+1}} - \cdots - e_{n_t} q^{n_t} \right) Q} \prod_{i=1}^{s-1} v_{\left(e_{m_i} q^{m_i} + \cdots + e_{m_s} q^{m_s} \right) Q}$$

Finally, we propose the following h as a witness for the existential quantification:

$$h = A - \theta B.$$

We will show that h is indeed a witness satisfying the three conditions.

(a) $\forall (x,y) \in G_1$, $Z_e(Q, (x,y)) = \theta \implies h(x,y) = 0.$: Let $(x,y) \in G_1$. Assume that $\theta = Z_e(Q, (x,y))$. Then Obviously $\theta = \frac{A(x,y)}{B(x,y)}$. Thus $h(x,y) = A(x,y) - \theta B(x,y) = 0$.

(b) $\deg_X (h) \leq \|e\|_1$: Note

$$\deg_X(A) \leq \sum_{e_i \geq 2} \left\lfloor \frac{e_i+1}{2} \right\rfloor \; + \; \sum_{e_i \leq -2} 1 \; + \sum_{e_i \geq 1} 1 + \sum_{e_i \leq -1} 1$$

$$= \sum_{e_i \geq 2} \left\lfloor \frac{e_i+3}{2} \right\rfloor \; + \; \sum_{e_i \leq -2} 2 \; + \sum_{e_i = 1} 1 + \sum_{e_i = -1} 1$$

$$\leq \sum_{e_i \geq 2} |e_i| + \sum_{e_i \leq -2} |e_i| \; + \sum_{e_i = 1} |e_i| + \sum_{e_i = -1} |e_i|$$

$$= \|e\|_1$$

$$\deg_X (B) \leq \sum_{e_i \leq -2} \left\lfloor \frac{-e_i+1}{2} \right\rfloor \; + \; \sum_{e_i \geq 2} 1 \; + \sum_{e_i \leq -1} 1 + \sum_{e_i \geq 1} 1$$

$$= \sum_{e_i \leq -2} \left\lfloor \frac{-e_i+3}{2} \right\rfloor \; + \; \sum_{e_i \geq 2} 2 + \sum_{e_i = -1} 1 + \sum_{e_i = 1} 1$$

$$\leq \sum_{e_i \leq -2} |e_i| + \sum_{e_i \geq 2} |e_i| \; + \sum_{e_i = -1} |e_i| + \sum_{e_i = 1} |e_i|$$

$$= \|e\|_1$$

Hence $\deg_X(h) \leq \|e\|_1$.

(c) $\deg_Y (h) \leq 2 \max\{s,t\}$: Note

$$\deg_Y (A) \leq s + s \leq 2s, \qquad\qquad \deg_Y(B) \leq t + t \leq 2t$$

Hence $\deg_Y (h) \leq 2 \max\{s,t\}$.

$\square$

Proof (Proof of Lemma 3). Note

$$f_{r,Q}^{\frac{s^k-1}{r}} = f_{s^k-1,Q} = f_{s^k,Q} = f_{s,Q}^{s^{k-1}} f_{s,sQ}^{s^{k-2}} \cdots f_{s,s^{k-1}Q}$$

Since $s \equiv q \pmod{r}$ and $f_{s,sQ} = f_{s,qQ} = f_{s,Q}^q$, we have

$$f_{r,Q}^{\frac{s^k-1}{r}} = f_{s,Q}^{s^{k-1}} f_{s,Q}^{qs^{k-2}} \cdots f_{s,s^{k-2}Q}^q = f_{s,Q}^{s^{k-1}+qs^{k-2}+\cdots+q^{k-1}} \tag{2}$$

Let $u = s^{k-1} + qs^{k-2} + \cdots + q^{k-1}$. Then $u \equiv kq^{k-1} \bmod r$. Raising Eq. (2) to the power $(q^k - 1)/r$, we have

$$t(Q,P)^{\frac{s^k-1}{r}} = f_{s,Q}(P)^{\frac{(q^k-1)}{r} \cdot u}.$$

Since $r \mid \frac{s^k-1}{r}$, we have

$$t(Q,P)^{\frac{s^k-1}{r}} = 1$$

$$f_{s,Q}(P)^{\frac{(q^k-1)}{r}} = 1.$$

Therefore, $f_{s^i,Q}(P)^{\frac{q^k-1}{r}} = f_{s,Q}^{(s^{i-1}+s^{i-2}q+\dots+q^{i-1})\frac{q^k-1}{r}} = 1$ for $0 \leq i \leq k-1$. Note

$$t(Q,P)^{\frac{\lambda_e(s)}{r}} = f_{r,Q}(P)^{\frac{\lambda_e(s)}{r}\frac{q^k-1}{r}}$$

$$= f_{\lambda_e(s),Q}(P)^{\frac{q^k-1}{r}}$$

$$= f_{e_0+\dots+e_{k-1}s^{k-1},Q}(P)^{\frac{q^k-1}{r}}$$

$$= \prod_{j=0}^{k-1} f_{e_j s^j,Q}(P)^{\frac{q^k-1}{r}} \left(\prod_{j=0}^{k-2} \frac{\ell_{e_j s^j Q,(e_{j+1}s^{j+1}+\dots+e_{k-1}s^{k-1})Q}(P)}{v_{(e_j s^j+\dots+e_{k-1}s^{k-1})Q}(P)} \right)^{\frac{q^k-1}{r}}$$

$$= \prod_{j=0}^{k-1} f_{s^j,Q}(P)^{e_j \frac{q^k-1}{r}} \prod_{j=0}^{k-1} f_{e_j,q^j Q}(P)^{\frac{q^k-1}{r}} \left(\prod_{j=0}^{k-2} \frac{\ell_{e_j q^j Q,(e_{j+1}q^{j+1}+\dots+e_{k-1}q^{k-1})Q}(P)}{v_{(e_j q^j+\dots+e_{k-1}q^{k-1})Q}(P)} \right)^{\frac{q^k-1}{r}}$$

$$= \prod_{j=0}^{k-1} 1^{e_j} \left(\prod_{j=0}^{k-1} f_{e_j,Q}^{q^j}(P) \prod_{j=0}^{k-2} \frac{\ell_{e_j q^j Q,(e_{j+1}q^{j+1}+\dots+e_{k-1}q^{k-1})Q}(P)}{v_{(e_j q^j+\dots+e_{k-1}q^{k-1})Q}(P)} \right)^{\frac{q^k-1}{r}}$$

$$= Z_e(Q,P)^{\frac{q^k-1}{r}} = a_e(Q,P)$$

The claim follows immediately from the relation $t(Q,P)^{\frac{\lambda_e(s)}{r}} = a_e(Q,P)$. $\square$

Proof (Proof of Lemma 4). We first observe that $r = 9$ and $\varphi(k) = 2$ satisfy the above two conditions. We will show that the two curves defined by

$$r^{1/\varphi(k)} = \varphi(k), \qquad\qquad r^{1/\varphi(k)} = (\log_2 r)^\alpha$$

do not meet when $\varphi(k) > 2$. The above system is equivalent to

$$r^{1/\varphi(k)} = \varphi(k)$$
$$(\log_2 r)^\alpha = \varphi(k)$$

The first equation is equivalent to

$$\log_2 r = \varphi(k) \log_2 \varphi(k)$$

By substituting it into the second equation, we have

$$\varphi(k)^\alpha (\log_2 \varphi(k))^\alpha = \varphi(k),$$

which does not have a solution when $\varphi(k) > 2$. Thus the above two curves do not meet when $\varphi(k) > 2$. Therefore, we conclude that C_α is an infinite set. $\square$

Constructing Symmetric Pairings over Supersingular Elliptic Curves with Embedding Degree Three

Tadanori Teruya[1], Kazutaka Saito[2,*], Naoki Kanayama[3],
Yuto Kawahara[4], Tetsutaro Kobayashi[4], and Eiji Okamoto[3]

[1] Research Institute for Secure Systems,
National Institute of Advanced Industrial Science and Technology,
1-1-1 Umezono, Tsukuba-shi, Ibaraki-ken 305-8568, Japan
[2] Internet Initiative Japan Inc.,
Jinbocho Mitsui Bldg., 1-105 Kanda Jinbo-cho, Chiyoda-ku, Tokyo 101-0051, Japan
[3] Faculty of Systems and Information Engineering,
University of Tsukuba,
1-1-1, Ten-nohdai, Tsukuba-shi, Ibaraki-ken, 305-8573 Japan
[4] NTT Secure Platform Laboratories,
3-9-11, Midori-cho, Musashino-shi, Tokyo 180-8585, Japan

Abstract. In the present paper, we propose constructing symmetric pairings by applying the Ate pairing to supersingular elliptic curves over finite fields that have large characteristics with embedding degree three. We also propose an efficient algorithm of the Ate pairing on these curves. To construct the algorithm, we apply the denominator elimination technique and the signed-binary approach to the Miller's algorithm, and improve the final exponentiation. We then show the efficiency of the proposed method through an experimental implementation.

Keywords: supersingular elliptic curves, symmetric pairings.

1 Introduction

Since Sakai et al. [26] and Boneh et al. [6,7] independently proposed pairing-based cryptosystems, many other novel cryptographic schemes that use pairings have been proposed.

An admissible pairing e is a mapping from two source groups $\mathbb{G}_1$ and $\mathbb{G}_2$, both of order r, to target group $\mathbb{G}_T$, also of order r. The mapping must be bilinear, nondegenerate, and able to be computed efficiently. Typically, $\mathbb{G}_1$ and $\mathbb{G}_2$ are denoted as additive groups, and $\mathbb{G}_T$ is denoted as a multiplicative group. The bilinearity is described as follows:

$$e(P_1 + P_2, Q) = e(P_1, Q)e(P_2, Q),$$
$$e(P, Q_1 + Q_2) = e(P, Q_1)e(P, Q_2),$$

---

* Part of this work was done while the second author was a student at the University of Tsukuba.

Z. Cao and F. Zhang (Eds.): Pairing 2013, LNCS 8365, pp. 97–112, 2014.
© Springer International Publishing Switzerland 2014

where $P, P_1, P_2 \in \mathbb{G}_1$ and $Q, Q_1, Q_2 \in \mathbb{G}_2$. In the present paper, the case $\mathbb{G}_1 = \mathbb{G}_2$ of pairings from $\mathbb{G}_1 \times \mathbb{G}_1$ to $\mathbb{G}_T$ is referred to as a *symmetric pairing* (the "type 1" pairing in [11]), and the other case, i.e., $\mathbb{G}_1 \neq \mathbb{G}_2$, is referred to as an *asymmetric pairing*. Symmetric pairings and asymmetric pairings are similar in some ways, but they differ in their mathematical structures and the security assumptions used to construct cryptographic schemes. It has been reported for several implementations that asymmetric pairings are the best choice for higher levels of security. However, symmetric pairings are often used to construct cryptographic schemes because their mathematical structures are simpler than asymmetric pairings. Currently, the most popular way to construct symmetric pairings is to use supersingular (hyper)elliptic curves. These curves have many properties that are friendly to the computations for symmetric parings, for example, the existence of distortion maps. In particular, supersingular elliptic curves over finite fields of small characteristic have been widely used for computing symmetric pairings.

However, there have also been several proposals of security analysis for solving the discrete logarithm problem (DLP) on $\mathbb{G}_T$ in the case of small characteristic [15,1]. Hayashi et al. [15] showed that the DLP over $\mathbb{F}_{3^{97 \cdot 6}}$ can be solved. Subsequently, Adj et al. [1] reported that the actual security level of the curves with characteristic 3 is lower than was previously estimated. In the case of characteristic 2, Joux [17] reported that the DLP in $\mathbb{F}_{2^{254 \cdot 24}}$ can be solved in practical time. $\mathbb{G}_T$ is included in the extension field of degree 4 or 12, thus $\mathbb{G}_T$ is also included in $\mathbb{F}^*_{2^{254 \cdot 24}}$. These results will lead to the reevaluation of their security level, and the key length, and performance of them are expected to be worse.

As mentioned above, asymmetric pairings currently perform the best. The constructions of cryptographic schemes on asymmetric pairings that are similar to those that have been proposed on symmetric pairings have been considered. Chatterjee et al. [9] investigated the construction of several cryptographic schemes built on asymmetric pairings and compared their performance. The most interesting result of Chatterjee et al. is the construction of a Waters signature scheme [31] on an asymmetric pairing. The original Waters scheme is constructed on a symmetric pairing, and the public key, private key, and signature are all very small. On the other hand, in order to construct, the modified Waters signature schemes proposed by Chatterjee et al., they require either larger public and private keys or a public parameter generated by a trusted third party. Hence, there are several trade-offs between using symmetric or asymmetric pairings.

Contribution

In the present paper, we consider efficient algorithms for supersingular elliptic curves that are defined over extension fields that have large characteristics. Supersingular curves defined over finite fields that have large characteristics are classified into two types. These curves are summarized in Table 1. The type 1 curve is defined over prime fields, and the type 2 curve is defined over extension fields.

The use of the type 1 curve in the construction of pairing-based cryptosystems was demonstrated by Boneh et al. [6,7]. The type 2 curve was introduced by Verheul [29,30] in a different context. However, using these curves for pairing-based cryptosystems is not as popular as using supersingular curves over fields with small characteristics. One of the reasons is that the type 1 elliptic curves have not been commonly used in recent cryptographic pairings (such as the η_T pairing [3] and the Ate pairing [16]). For supersingular elliptic curves over small-characteristic finite fields, we can use the η_T pairing $f_{T,P}(Q)$ instead of the Tate pairing $f_{r,P}(Q)$, since, in this case, the bit length of T is half that of r. Thus, for these curves, the η_T pairing can be computed much faster than the Tate pairing. There is, however, almost no advantage to using the Eta or the Ate pairing for type 1 supersingular elliptic curves because their trace is 0.

On the other hand, computing pairings over type 2 supersingular elliptic curves has not been extensively investigated. One of the reasons for this is that the embedding degree k of such curves is 3. This is smaller than that of the super-singular elliptic curves over small characteristic fields (in these cases, $k = 4, 6$), and it thus would seem that there would not be much advantage to using type 2 elliptic curves. Furthermore, the η_T pairing is not applicable for type 2 curves because their k is odd, and we cannot directly use the denominator elimination technique [4] that is used when k is even. However, Lin et al. [21] proposed a denominator elimination technique for elliptic curves with an odd embedding degree. Also note that the embedding degree $k = 3$ of a type 2 elliptic curve is slightly larger than the degree $k = 2$ of elliptic curves over prime fields.

Another advantage of using a type 2 elliptic curve is that we can use the efficient method for scalar multiplication that was proposed by Gallant et al. [12] because the group order r is of the form $r = p^2 \pm p + 1$. This can save much computation time.

In the present paper, we propose a method for efficiently computing symmetric pairings over type 2 elliptic curves.

The remainder of this paper is organized as follows. Section 2 presents a brief mathematical description of pairings. Section 3 presents the reduced Ate pairings on type 2 elliptic curves; this is the main result of the present study. Section 4 presents an experimental implementation of the proposed method. Finally, conclusions are presented in Section 5.

2   Mathematical Preliminaries

2.1   Pairings

Let E be an elliptic curve over a finite field $\mathbb{F}_q$ with q elements. The set of $\mathbb{F}_q$-rational points of E is denoted as $E(\mathbb{F}_q)$. Let $E(\mathbb{F}_q)[r]$ denote the subgroup of r-torsion points in $E(\mathbb{F}_q)$. We write O for the point at infinity on E. Consider a large prime r such that $r \mid \#E(\mathbb{F}_q)$, and denote the embedding degree by k, which is the smallest positive integer such that r divides $q^k - 1$. Let π_q be the q-power Frobenius endomorphism $\pi_q : E \to E, (x, y) \mapsto (x^q, y^q)$. We denote the

Table 1. Summary of supersingular elliptic curves defined over large characteristic finite fields

Type	1		2
Base Field	$\mathbb{F}_p$, where $p > 3$ and $p \equiv 3 \pmod 4$	$\mathbb{F}_p$, where $p > 3$ and $p \equiv 2 \pmod 3$	$\mathbb{F}_{p^2}$, where $p > 3$ and $p \equiv 5 \pmod 6$
Curve	$E/\mathbb{F}_p : Y^2 = X^3 + X$	$E/\mathbb{F}_p : Y^2 = X^3 + 1$	$E/\mathbb{F}_{p^2} : Y^2 = X^3 + b$, where b is a square but not a cube in $\mathbb{F}_{p^2}$
Order	$\#E(\mathbb{F}_p) = p + 1$	$\#E(\mathbb{F}_p) = p + 1$	$\#E(\mathbb{F}_{p^2}) = p^2 + 1 - t,$ $t = \pm p$
Embedding Degree	2	2	$\begin{cases} 3 & \text{if } t = p, \\ 3/2 & \text{otherwise} \end{cases}$
Distortion Map	$\iota : (x,y) \mapsto (-x, \zeta_4 y),$ where ζ_4 is a proper element in $\mathbb{F}_{p^2}$ and $\zeta_4^4 = 1$	$\iota : (x,y) \mapsto (\zeta_3 x, y),$ where ζ_3 is a proper element in $\mathbb{F}_{p^2}$ and $\zeta_3^3 = 1$	$\iota : (x,y) \mapsto (u^2 x^p, u^3 y^p),$ where u is a proper element in $\mathbb{F}_{p^6}$ and $u^6 = b/b^p$

trace of Frobenius by t, i.e., $\#E(\mathbb{F}_q) = q + 1 - t$. Finally, let $\mu_r(\subset \mathbb{F}_{q^k}^\times)$ be the group of r-th roots of unity.

Tate Pairing. Let $P \in E(\mathbb{F}_{q^k})[r]$ and $Q \in E(\mathbb{F}_{q^k})$. Choose a point $R \in E(\mathbb{F}_{q^k})$ such that the supports of $\operatorname{div}(f_{r,P}) = r(P) - r(O)$ and $D_Q := (Q + R) - (R)$ are disjoint. Then, the Tate pairing (Tate–Lichtenbaum pairing) is defined by:

$$\langle \cdot, \cdot \rangle_r : E(\mathbb{F}_{q^k})[r] \times E(\mathbb{F}_{q^k})/rE(\mathbb{F}_{q^k}) \to \mathbb{F}_{q^k}^\times/(\mathbb{F}_{q^k}^\times)^r,$$
$$(P, Q) \mapsto \langle P, Q \rangle_r := f_{r,P}(D_Q) \bmod (\mathbb{F}_{q^k}^\times)^r .$$

It has been shown that $\langle P, Q \rangle_r$ is bilinear and nondegenerate.

For cryptography applications, it is convenient to define pairings for which the outputs are unique values rather than equivalence classes. Thus, we consider the reduced Tate pairing defined by:

$$\tau_r : E(\mathbb{F}_{q^k})[r] \times E(\mathbb{F}_{q^k})/rE(\mathbb{F}_{q^k}) \to \mu_r,$$
$$\tau_r(P, Q) = \langle P, Q \rangle_r^{(q^k-1)/r}.$$

We call the operation $z \mapsto z^{(q^k-1)/r}$ final exponentiation.

Ate Pairing. The Ate pairing, proposed by Hess et al. [16], is a generalization of the η_T pairing [3]. The Ate pairing can be applied to not only supersingular but also to ordinary elliptic curves.

Let $T = t - 1$. We choose integers N and L such that $N = \gcd(T^k - 1, q^k - 1)$ and $T^k - 1 = LN$. We assume that r^2 does not divide $q^k - 1$.

Definition 1. *The reduced Ate pairing (on $\mathbb{G}_2 \times \mathbb{G}_1$) is defined by*

$$a_T : \ \mathbb{G}_2 \times \mathbb{G}_1 \to \mu_r;$$
$$(Q, \ P) \mapsto f_{T,Q}(P)^{(q^k - 1)/r},$$

where the rational function $f_{T,Q}$ on E is the normalized function that satisfies

$$(f_{T,Q}) = T(Q) - ([T]Q) - (T - 1)(O).$$

The definition for the normalization of rational functions is given in [22].

Many variants of the Ate pairing have been proposed, including the Ate$_i$ pairing [32], the R-Ate pairing [20], and the optimal pairing [28]. These pairings are defined on $\mathbb{G}_2 \times \mathbb{G}_1$ using normalization functions. The Ate pairing and its variants are also defined in $\mathbb{G}_1 \times \mathbb{G}_2$[1], there is no need to consider normalization [25].

2.2   Supersingular Elliptic Curves Defined over an Extension Field

We propose a method for the efficient computation of a symmetric pairing over a supersingular elliptic curve $E/\mathbb{F}_q$, as characterized in [30]:

$$E/\mathbb{F}_q : Y^2 = X^3 + b, \tag{1}$$

where $q = p^2$ and the quantities in (1) satisfy the following conditions:

- p is a prime larger than 3;
- $p \equiv 5 \pmod 6$;
- $b \in \mathbb{F}_q$ is a square in $\mathbb{F}_q$ but is not a cube in $\mathbb{F}_q$.

The trace t of the q-power Frobenius endmorphism π_q on $E/\mathbb{F}_q$ and the cardinality $\#E(\mathbb{F}_q)$ are determined, respectively, by:

$$t = p,$$
$$\#E(\mathbb{F}_q) = p^2 - p + 1. \tag{2}$$

Therefore, the embedding degree of $E/\mathbb{F}_q$ is $k = 3$.

Let r be the largest prime divisor of $\#E(\mathbb{F}_q)$, and let $h = \#E(\mathbb{F}_q)/r$. We assume that $r^2 \nmid \#E/\mathbb{F}_q$. Hereafter, we write $\mathbb{G}_1 := E(\mathbb{F}_q)[r]$ and call $\mathbb{G}_1$ the source group of pairings.

---

[1] When E is supersingular, the Ate pairing is defined using the same formula. When E is ordinary, the Ate pairing is defined using a slightly different formula. In this case, the Ate pairing is called the twisted Ate pairing; for more information see [16].

2.3   Distortion Map

The distortion map on $E/\mathbb{F}_q$ is defined as follows.

Lemma 1 (distortion map, [30]). *Let* $E/\mathbb{F}_q : Y^2 = X^3 + b$ *be an elliptic curve, and let* u *be a proper element in* $\mathbb{F}_{q^3}$ *such that* $u^6 = b/b^p$.
Then

$$\iota : E(\mathbb{F}_q) \to E(\mathbb{F}_{q^3}) \setminus E(\mathbb{F}_q), (x, y) \mapsto (u^2 x^p, u^3 y^p) \tag{3}$$

is a distortion map on E.

We can construct a symmetric pairing $e(\cdot, \cdot)$ by "compositing" the distortion map ι to the Tate pairing $\langle \cdot, \cdot \rangle$ on E, that is,

$$e(\cdot, \cdot) := \langle \cdot, \iota(\cdot) \rangle .$$

3   The Main Result

As mentioned in Section 1, there is almost no advantage to using the Ate pairing for type 1 supersingular elliptic curves defined over prime fields, because $t = 0$ for them. However, the Ate pairing for a type 2 curve, as discussed in Section 2.2, can be computed efficiently. In the present section, we propose an algorithm for computing Ate pairings over type 2 curves.

First, we compare type 2 curves with type 1 curves from the viewpoint of pairing-based cryptography.

3.1   Comparison between Type 1 and Type 2 Curves

When we use elliptic curves over $\mathbb{F}_{p^2}$, we need to consider the hardness of the elliptic curve discrete logarithm problem (ECDLP) on $E/\mathbb{F}_{p^2}$ against a Gaudry–Hess–Smart (GHS) attack or an attack by one of its variants. Let $E/\mathbb{F}_{p^2} : Y^2 = F(X)$ be an elliptic curve. According to Momose et al. [23], if $F(X)$ is irreducible over $\mathbb{F}_{p^2}$ or can be factored as a product of linear factors, then E is equivalent to the elliptic curves of the Scholten form [27], and we can use degree 2 Weil restrictions to make a genus 2 hyperelliptic curve $C/\mathbb{F}_p$. Hence, the ECDLP on $E/\mathbb{F}_{p^2}$ is reduced to the hyperelliptic curve discrete logarithm problem (HECDLP) on the Jacobian group of $C/\mathbb{F}_p$. In the case of our target curve $\mathbb{F}_{p^2}$, $F(X) = X^3 + b$ is generally irreducible since b is not a cube in $\mathbb{F}_{p^2}$. Hence, degree 2 Weil restrictions are applicable to $E/\mathbb{F}_{p^2}$, and we must choose parameters $(q(= p^2), r, t)$ to protect against this attack. When we solve the HECDLP on the Jacobian of $C/\mathbb{F}_p$, which is obtained by applying degree 2 Weil restrictions to $E/\mathbb{F}_{p^2}$ and using the double-large prime variation-of-index calculus of Gaudry et al. [13] and Nagao [24]. The running cost is $\tilde{O}(q)$ when the genus of C is 2.

When we choose (q, r, t) such that q^3 is at least 960 bits, then $q = p^2$ is at least 320 bits. Hence, the running cost $\tilde{O}(q)$ is larger than $O(2^{320})$ when the characteristic p is 160 bits. We now need to choose a larger q; for example, if p

is 200 bits, we can choose a q^3 that is 1200 bits. We can thus obtain parameters that are secure against the Weil restrictions.

Next, we consider the hardness of finite-field discrete logarithm problem (FFDLP) on $\mathbb{G}_T$. To guarantee security, the FFDLP must be hard. The elliptic curve introduced in Section 2.2 is defined over a large characteristic extension field. Freeman et al. [10] suggested that the size of q^k needs 2200-3600 bits in order to guarantee the 112-bit level of security. We can also consider another setting, which based on the function-field sieve attack [2], and its complexity is:

$$\exp\left(\left(\frac{32}{9} + o(1)\right)^{\frac{1}{3}} \cdot (\log q^k)^{\frac{1}{3}} \cdot (\log \log q^k)^{\frac{2}{3}}\right). \tag{4}$$

Recently, Joux and Pierrot [18] proposed the extended special number field sieve to compute FFDLP in $\mathbb{F}_{p^n}$, where p has an adequate sparse representation. The concern with the security analysis of FFDLP has been growing by their investigations. It is interesting to follow up their results further, but it is not our present concern.

Next, we compare the parameters of the type 1 and type 2 elliptic curves for the 112-bit level of security based on Equation (4). We suppose $o(1)$ in Equation (4) is 0, namely, we need that the size of the resulting $\mathbb{F}_{p^k}$, which includes $\mathbb{G}_T$, is around 3132 bits. The summary of the comparison of parameters is shown in Table 2. The base field of the type 2 curve is smaller than that of the type 1 curve. Moreover, the base field of the type 2 curve is an extension field. Thus, the characteristic of the type 2 curve is small, its arithmetic is implementation friendly, and the representation of the elements in $\mathbb{G}_1$ is smaller than it is for the type 1 curve. However, the order of the type 2 curve is larger than that of the type 1 curve. If the method proposed by Gallant et al. [12] (GLV) is used for scalar multiplication on $\mathbb{G}_1$ for the type 2 elliptic curves, then the length of this operation is cut in half; nevertheless, the reduced length is still larger than that for type 1 curves. Scalar multiplication on type 2 curves is considerably slower than it is for type 1 curves. But the final exponentiation is faster for type 2 curves because the costly part of this operation on type 2 curves is smaller than it is for type 1 curves. Hence, the Weil pairing is considerable for type 1 curves. This means that Miller's algorithm is evaluated in twice the time it takes to calculate a pairing on type 1 curves. The actual Miller loop parameters for the type 1 and type 2 curves are $2 \cdot 224$ bits and 522 bits, respectively, so that of the type 2 curves is still larger. However, the arithmetic of the type 2 curves can be implemented efficiently by using the pseudo-Mersenne prime [14], and we show several instances of them in Section 4.1.

3.2 Miller's Algorithm

We now present an algorithm for computing the Ate pairing over type 2 curves.

In this algorithm, we use a denominator elimination technique based on the following lemma.

Table 2. Summary of parameter comparison for the 112-bit security level which is discussed in Section 3.1, where "GLV Method" is the method proposed by Gallant et al. [12], "Miller Loop Parameter" is the integer that determines the number of iterations of Miller's algorithm, and "Final Exp." is the exponents of operations in the final exponentiation

Type	1	2
Base Field	$\mathbb{F}_p$: p is a 1566-bit prime number	$\mathbb{F}_{p^2}$: 1044-bit size and p is a 522-bit prime number
Order	r: 224-bit prime number such that $p + 1 = hr$	r: prime number such that hr is a 1044-bit integer and h is small
GLV Method	Not applicable	Applicable by using $\phi : (x, y) \mapsto (\zeta_3 x, y)$, where $\zeta_3 \in \mu_3 \subset \mathbb{F}_{p^2}^*$
Miller Loop Parameter	r: 224-bit prime number with low Hamming weight	$p - 1$: 522-bit integer with small number of non-zero components in NAF encoding
Final Exp.	$(p^2 - 1)/r = (p - 1)h$, where h is a 1342-bit integer	$(p^6 - 1)/r = (p^3 - 1)(p + 1)h$, where h is a small integer

Lemma 2 ([21])

$$\frac{1}{x_P - x_Q} = \frac{x_P^2 + x_P x_Q + x_Q^2}{(y_P + y_Q)(y_P - y_Q)} \tag{5}$$

Lemma 1 and Lemma 2 derive the following theorem.

Theorem 1 (denominator elimination). *Let* $P = (x_P, y_P)$ *and* $Q = (x_Q, y_Q) \in \mathbb{G}_1$, *let* ι *be a distortion map defined as in Equation* (3), *and let* $Q' = \iota(Q)$.

Then, without changing the output of the reduced Tate pairing, division by $x_P - x_{Q'}$ *can be replaced with multiplication by* $x_P^2 + x_P x_{Q'} + x_{Q'}^2$.

Proof. In Equation (5), $x_P - x_{Q'} \neq 0$ and $x_P^2 + x_P x_{Q'} + x_{Q'}^2 \neq 0$ for all possible $x_P, x_{Q'}$ in the Miller loop. Then, the denominator in Miller's algorithm is replaced as in Lemma 2, and we note that the denominator in Equation (5) is as follows:

$$(y_P + y_{Q'})(y_P - y_{Q'}) = (y_P + u^3 y_Q)(y_P - u^3 y_Q)$$
$$= y_P^2 - u^6 y_Q^2 \in \mathbb{F}_q. \tag{6}$$

In the final exponentiation, the exponent can be decomposed as $(q^3 - 1)/r = (q - 1)(p^2 + p + 1)h$, and resulting value of the final exponentiation with input the value of Equation (6) becomes one.   □

Miller's Algorithm with Signed-Binary Representation. Miller's algorithm to compute $f_{p-1,P}(\iota(Q))$ is defined on the standard binary representation, and it is also known as the double-and-add approach. It can be extended to the signed-binary representation, and it is then known as the double-and-add/subtract approach. If the number of non-zero components of the non-adjacent form (NAF) of $p - 1$ is smaller than the Hamming weight of its binary representation, then the computation time can be improved.

Beuchat et al. [5] proposed using Miller's algorithm on the signed-binary representation of the Miller's algorithm on the Barreto–Naehrig curves; however, their algorithm does not work on the curves introduced in Section 2.2. As the definition of the Miller function implies,

$$(f_{-a,P}) = \left(\frac{1}{f_{a,P} \cdot v_{[a]P}} \right). \tag{7}$$

The algorithm presented by Beuchat et al. does not handle $v_{[a]P}$.

To extend the original Miller's algorithm for the signed-binary representation, we consider the subtraction of Miller's formula as follows:

$$
\begin{aligned}
(f_{a-1,P}) &= \left(f_{a,P} \cdot f_{-1,P} \cdot \frac{l_{[a]P,-P}}{v_{[a-1]P}} \right) \\
&= \left(f_{a,P} \cdot \frac{l_{[a]P,-P}}{v_{-P} \cdot v_{[a-1]P}} \right).
\end{aligned}
\tag{8}
$$

Theorem 1 derives the following subtraction procedure:

$$f_{a-1,P}(Q) = \left(f_{a,P} \cdot l_{[a]P,-P} \cdot S_{[a-1]P} \cdot S_{-P} \right)(Q), \tag{9}$$

where S_V is a polynomial function on the elliptic curve defined as $S_V(Q) = x_V^2 + x_V x_Q + x_Q^2$. Equation (9) allows us to extend Miller's algorithm for the signed-binary representation with the elimination of the denominator to the curves introduced in Section 2.2.

3.3   Final Exponentiation

The output of Miller's algorithm is defined as an element of $\mathbb{F}_{q^k}^* / (\mathbb{F}_{q^k}^*)^r$. An exponentiation by $(q^3 - 1)/r$ is necessary in order to obtain a unique value of $\mu_r \in \mathbb{F}_{q^3}^*$, where μ_r is the r-th roots of unity. Typically, this exponentiation is called *final exponentiation*. This operation is computed in $\mathbb{F}_{q^3}$, and so it is one of the more expensive parts of a pairing computation.

From the definition of type 2 elliptic curves in Section 2.2, we can transform the exponent for the final exponentiation as follows:

$$
\begin{aligned}
(p^6 - 1)/r &= h(p^6 - 1)/\#E(\mathbb{F}_q) \\
&= h(p^6 - 1)/(p^2 - p + 1) \\
&= h(p^3 - 1)(p + 1),
\end{aligned}
\tag{10}
$$

where $h = \#E(\mathbb{F}_q)/r$. Hence, the final exponentiation is efficiently calculated by one inversion over $\mathbb{F}_{q^k}$, two multiplications over $\mathbb{F}_{q^k}$, two Frobenius maps, and an exponentiation by h. The most expensive part is the exponentiation by h. However, since we can choose an elliptic curve such that h is a very small integer in almost all cases, this operation can be done quickly. We call this faster version *fast final exponentiation*.

Algorithm 1. Reduced Ate pairing on $E/\mathbb{F}_{p^2}$

Input: T, P, Q: $T = t - 1 = 2^\ell + \sum_{i=0}^{\ell-1} s_i 2^i$, where $s_i \in \{0, \pm 1\}$, and $P, Q \in \mathbb{G}_1$.

Output: Reduced Ate pairing $f_{T,P}\left(\iota(Q)\right)^{(q^k-1)/r} \in \mathbb{G}_T$.

1: $Q' \leftarrow \iota(Q);$ // $6M_2$
2: $t_0 \leftarrow x_{Q'}^2;$ // S_6
3: $t_1 \leftarrow S'_{-P}(Q', t_0);$ // $3M_2$
4: $V \leftarrow P;$
5: $f \leftarrow 1;$
6: **for** $i \leftarrow \ell - 1$ **down to** 0 **do**
7:     $(f, V) \leftarrow \left(f^2 \cdot l_{V,V}(Q') \cdot S'_{[2]V}(Q', t_0), [2]V\right);$
8:     **if** $s_i = 1$ **then**
9:       $(f, V) \leftarrow \left(f \cdot l_{V,P}(Q') \cdot S'_{V+P}(Q', t_0), V + P\right);$
10:    **else if** $s_i = -1$ **then**
11:      $(f, V) \leftarrow \left(f \cdot l_{V,-P}(Q') \cdot S'_{V-P}(Q', t_0) \cdot t_1, V - P\right);$
12:    **end if**;
13: **end for**;
14: $f \leftarrow f^{p^3} \cdot f^{-1};$ // $\pi_{p^3} + I_6 + M_6$
15: $f \leftarrow f \cdot f^p;$ // $\pi_p + M_6$
16: $f \leftarrow f^h;$ // Exp_h
17: **return** f;

3.4 Estimation of Computational Cost

In this section, we estimate computational cost of our algorithm performing the reduced Ate pairing. We will show the algorithm for the reduced Ate pairing on the elliptic curve $E/\mathbb{F}_{p^2}$ introduced in Section 2.2; see Algorithm 1. We note that $S'_V(Q, t) := x_V(x_V + x_Q) + t$ and $S'_P(Q, x_Q^2) = x_P^2 + x_P x_Q + x_Q^2 = S_P(Q)$ in Algorithm 1. In Algorithm 1, lines 1-13 and lines 14-16 correspond to the Miller's algorithm and the final exponentiation, respectively.

In this paper, we use the affine coordinate to implement the group operation of $\mathbb{G}_1$. The details of lines 7 and 9 in Algorithm 1 are described in Algorithm 2 and 3, respectively. The detail of line 11 in Algorithm 1 is easily derived by Algorithm 3, the difference is a multiplication by $t_1 \in \mathbb{F}_{p^6}$ and P is replaced by $-P$. We then show the computational cost of Algorithm 1 at Table 3. We note that the number of additions and subtractions are ignored and assume two Frobenius maps π_p and π_{p^3} over $\mathbb{F}_{p^6}$ have same computational cost in Table 3.

4 Experimental Implementation

In this section, we show the results from an experimental implementation of our proposed method. First, we show the environment in Table 4.

Algorithm 2. Doubling step of the reduced Ate pairing on $E/\mathbb{F}_{p^2}$ (at the line 7 in Algorithm 1)

Input: f, V, Q', t_0: $f \in \mathbb{F}_{p^6}$, $V \in E(\mathbb{F}_{p^2})$, $Q' = \iota(Q) \in E(\mathbb{F}_{p^6})$, and $t_0 = x_{Q'}^2 \in \mathbb{F}_{p^6}$.
    Note that Q' and t_0 are computed at lines 1 and 2, respectively, in Algorithm 1.
Output: $\left(f^2 \cdot l_{V,V}(Q') \cdot S'_{[2]V}(Q', t_0), [2]V \right) \in \mathbb{F}_{p^6} \times E(\mathbb{F}_{p^2})$.

1: $m \leftarrow 3x_V^2$;   // S_2
2: $n \leftarrow 2y_V$;
3: $\lambda \leftarrow m/n$;   // $I_2 + M_2$
4: $g \leftarrow y_{Q'} - y_V - \lambda(x_{Q'} - x_V)$;   // $3M_2$
5: $f \leftarrow f^2$;   // S_6
6: $f \leftarrow fg$;   // M_6
7: $\lambda' \leftarrow \lambda^2$;   // S_2
8: $x_{V'} \leftarrow \lambda' - 2x_V$;
9: $y_{V'} \leftarrow \lambda(x_V - x_{V'}) - y_V$;   // M_2
10: $V' \leftarrow (x_{V'}, y_{V'})$;
11: $v \leftarrow x_{V'}(x_{V'} + x_{Q'}) + t_0$;   // $3M_2$
12: $f \leftarrow fv$;   // M_6
13: **return** (f, V');

4.1 Parameters

In our experiment, we generated two parameters, Curve 1 and Curve 2. In the class of our target elliptic curves described in Section 3, the characteristic p of a base field can be chosen as the pseudo-Mersenne prime ($p = 2^n - c$ and $\log_2 |c| \le n/2$) [14]. Moreover, a tower field $\mathbb{F}_{q^3} = \mathbb{F}_{p^6}$ containing $\mathbb{G}_T$ can be defined by an irreducible binomial of $W^3 - \beta \in \mathbb{F}_q[W]$.

For our experiments, we generated two elliptic curves, Curves 1 and 2, as defined above. The length of their characteristics are $n = 367$ and 522, respectively. The parameter setting of Curve 1 is based on the least size of suggestions described in [10], and Curve 2 is based on Equation (4) with the assumption described in Section 3.1. Note that these two curves were generated randomly. We note that w_{NAF}^+ and w_{NAF}^- denote the numbers of 1 components and -1 components, respectively, in NAF encoding of $p - 1$.

Curve 1 (the sizes of p, r, and q^3 are 367 bits, 718 bits, and 2202 bits, respectively):

$E/\mathbb{F}_{p^2} : Y^2 = X^3 + \beta$,
$p = 2^{367} - c$, where $c = 6441$,
$w_{\mathrm{NAF}}^+ = 2$ and $w_{\mathrm{NAF}}^- = 5$,
$q = p^2$, and $t = p$,
$r = \#E(\mathbb{F}_{p^2})/h = (p^2 - p + 1)/h$, where $h = 110937$,
$\mathbb{F}_q = \mathbb{F}_{p^2} := \mathbb{F}_p[V]/(V^2 - \alpha)$, where α is

    26742451583095328073256740694549729056517160227393088628
    7889216699870470962170359843916380575606965024714761 9722,

Algorithm 3. Addition step of the reduced Ate pairing on $E/\mathbb{F}_{p^2}$ (at the line 9 in Algorithm 1)

Input: f, V, P, Q', t_0: $f \in \mathbb{F}_{p^6}$, $V, P \in E(\mathbb{F}_{p^2})$, $Q' = \iota(Q) \in E(\mathbb{F}_{p^6})$, and $t_0 = x_{Q'}^2 \in \mathbb{F}_{p^6}$. Note that Q' and t_0 are computed at lines 1 and 2, respectively, in Algorithm 1, and P is a one of inputs of Algorithm 1.

Output: $\left(f \cdot l_{V,P}(Q') \cdot S'_{V+P}(Q', t_0), V + P\right) \in \mathbb{F}_{p^6} \times E(\mathbb{F}_{p^2})$.

```
1:  m ← (y_P − y_V);
2:  n ← (x_P − x_V);
3:  λ ← m/n;                           // I₂ + M₂
4:  g ← y_Q' − y_V − λ(x_Q' − x_V);    // 3M₂
5:  f ← fg;                            // M₆
6:  λ' ← λ²;                           // S₂
7:  x_V' ← λ' − x_V − x_P;
8:  y_V' ← λ(x_P − x_V') − y_P;        // M₂
9:  V' ← (x_V', y_V');
10: v ← x_V'(x_V' + x_Q') + t₀;        // 3M₂
11: f ← fv;                            // M₆
12: return f;
```

$\mathbb{F}_{q^3} := \mathbb{F}_q[W]/(W^3 - \beta)$, where β is

> 252896440908710958673537029450843684969101759712604153865507223365991977183853605246047387340418369769543384088$2V+$
> 205884167423125302598766820160225408190302010691030952352459948502700795868754014808684134161442322034832833606,

and distortion map is $\iota : (x, y) \mapsto (u^2 x^p, u^3 y^p)$ where u is

> 991433029351457151646257206920379907879751919331832750358817801101527156847957824504707603087720411781675899$00W$.

Curve 2 (the sizes of p, r, and q^3 are 522 bits, 1038 bits, and 3132 bits, respectively):

$E/\mathbb{F}_{p^2} : Y^2 = X^3 + \beta$,

$p = 2^{522} - c$, where $c = 29087$,

$w_{\text{NAF}}^+ = 3$ and $w_{\text{NAF}}^- = 3$,

$q = p^2$, and $t = p$,

$r = \#E(\mathbb{F}_{p^2})/h = (p^2 - p + 1)/h$, where $h = 93$,

$\mathbb{F}_q = \mathbb{F}_{p^2} := \mathbb{F}_p[V]/(V^2 - \alpha)$, where α is

> 258383455985381145943216612442768350216739157485898965452144420032289993162361593970361156761409673509807439865701651847527304215126376997355248221059380187 9,

$\mathbb{F}_{q^3} := \mathbb{F}_q[W]/(W^3 - \beta)$, where β is

> 554049680523485864905407793012859943661570904888476938766039686205977417020547370576767363281773235534834319379101136395933609254025785131451054428029717140$1V+$
> 572961158262123787867811990708439070426770284787172621 4

Table 3. Computational cost of our algorithm, where M_k, S_k, and I_k denote the multiplication, squaring, and inversion over $\mathbb{F}_{p^k}$, π denotes Frobenius map over $\mathbb{F}_{p^6}$, $p = 2^{\ell} - c$ and it is a prime number, w_{NAF}^{+} denotes the number of 1 components and w_{NAF}^{-} denotes the number of -1 components in NAF encoding of $p - 1$, and Exp_h denotes exponentiation by h over $\mathbb{F}_{p^6}$

Part of Algorithm 1	Computational Cost
$l_{V,V}(Q')$ and $[2]V$ in line 7	$5M_2 + 2S_2 + I_2$
$S'_{[2]V}(Q', t_0)$ in line 7	$3M_2$
$l_{V,\pm P}(Q')$ and $V \pm P$ in lines 9 and 11	$5M_2 + S_2 + I_2$
$S'_{V \pm P}(Q', t_0)$ in lines 9 and 11	$3M_2$
Line 7	$8M_2 + 2S_2 + I_2 + 2M_6 + S_6$
Line 9	$8M_2 + S_2 + I_2 + 2M_6$
Line 11	$8M_2 + S_2 + I_2 + 3M_6$
Miller's algorithm (lines 1-13)	$9M_2 + S_6 + (8M_2 + 2S_2 + I_2 + 2M_6 + S_6)\ell$ $+(w_{\mathrm{NAF}}^{+} + w_{\mathrm{NAF}}^{-})(8M_2 + S_2 + I_2 + 2M_6)$ $+w_{\mathrm{NAF}}^{-}M_6$
Final exponentiation (lines 14-16)	$2M_6 + 2\pi + I_6 + \mathrm{Exp}_h$

Table 4. Experimental environment

	Environment
OS	Linux 3.5.0-37 (Ubuntu 12.04.2 LTS)
CPU	Core i7-4770 (3.4 GHz)
Memory	32 GB
Language	Magma version 2.19-8 [8]

3429775029040573419091832483405499148515483815456512633
3272840656234717693494535091798944547219519692 9, and
distortion map is $\iota : (x, y) \mapsto (u^2 x^p, u^3 y^p)$ where u is
1810455431901709610502451144154632135017017586718473396
1873794180953915455128081305700723007474055399866147491
2257979473021331073785338117339271976581905545 5W

4.2   Performance of the Proposed Method

We computed the pairings and compared the running time of the Tate pairing and the Ate pairing with the signed-binary approach on $E/\mathbb{F}_q$. The parameters used in Miller's algorithm were r and $p - 1$, and these were represented in NAF encoding. We ran the pairings 1000 times and computed the averages of Miller's algorithm for the Tate pairing, the Ate pairing, and the fast final exponentiation. Table 5 shows these averages. It is clear that the Ate pairing computation on $E/\mathbb{F}_q$ is efficiently computable. We note that our experimental implementation is written in Magma [8], we did not implement efficient arithmetic based on the pseudo-Mersenne prime, and generated curves are randomly generated. Thus, there is room for further optimization.

Table 5. Running time of pairing computations (unit: milliseconds)

	Curve 1	Curve 2
$f_{r,P}\big(\iota(Q)\big)$ with NAF	88.28	157.87
$f_{T,P}\big(\iota(Q)\big)$ with NAF	34.38	62.06
Fast Final Exp.	0.25	0.21
Reduced Tate	88.53	158.08
Reduced Ate	34.63	62.27

5   Conclusion

In the present paper, we proposed a method to construct symmetric pairings by applying the Ate pairing to supersingular elliptic curves over finite fields with large characteristics and embedding degree three. We also proposed an efficient algorithm of the Ate pairing on these curves. We then generated several curves in order to show the existence of curves that our method is applicable to, and implemented experimental programs of our method and demonstrated that it is efficiently computable.

Acknowledgements. The authors would like to thank Goichiro Hanaoka and Takahiro Matsuda for the valuable comments. We gratefully thank the members of Shin-Akarui-Angou-Benkyou-Kai for the valuable discussion and comments. We also thank the anonymous reviewers of Pairing 2013 for the valuable comments.

References

1. Adj, G., Menezes, A., Oliveira, T., Rodríguez-Henríquez, F.: Weakness of $\mathbb{F}_{3^{6\cdot509}}$ for discrete logarithm cryptography. In: Cao, Z., Zhang, F. (eds.) Pairing 2013. LNCS, vol. 8365, pp. 19–43. Springer, Heidelberg (2014)
2. Adleman, L.M.: The function field sieve. In: Huang, M.-D.A., Adleman, L.M. (eds.) ANTS 1994. LNCS, vol. 877, pp. 108–121. Springer, Heidelberg (1994)
3. Barreto, P.S.L.M., Galbraith, S.D., ÓhÉigeartaigh, C., Scott, M.: Efficient pairing computation on supersingular abelian varieties. Des. Codes Cryptography 42(3), 239–271 (2007)
4. Barreto, P.S.L.M., Kim, H.Y., Lynn, B., Scott, M.: Efficient algorithms for pairing-based cryptosystems. In: Yung, M. (ed.) CRYPTO 2002. LNCS, vol. 2442, pp. 354–368. Springer, Heidelberg (2002)
5. Beuchat, J.-L., González-Díaz, J.E., Mitsunari, S., Okamoto, E., Rodríguez-Henríquez, F., Teruya, T.: High-speed software implementation of the optimal ate pairing over barreto–naehrig curves. In: Joye, M., Miyaji, A., Otsuka, A. (eds.) Pairing 2010. LNCS, vol. 6487, pp. 21–39. Springer, Heidelberg (2010)
6. Boneh, D., Franklin, M.K.: Identity-based encryption from the Weil pairing. In: [19], pp. 213–229
7. Boneh, D., Franklin, M.K.: Identity-based encryption from the Weil pairing. SIAM J. Comput. 32(3), 586–615 (2003)

8. Bosma, W., Cannon, J., Playoust, C.: The Magma algebra system. I. The user language. J. Symbolic Comput. 24(3-4), 235–265 (1997); Computational algebra and number theory, London (1993)

9. Chatterjee, S., Hankerson, D., Knapp, E., Menezes, A.: Comparing two pairing-based aggregate signature schemes. Des. Codes Cryptography 55(2-3), 141–167 (2010)

10. Freeman, D., Scott, M., Teske, E.: A taxonomy of pairing-friendly elliptic curves. J. Cryptology 23(2), 224–280 (2010)

11. Galbraith, S.D., Paterson, K.G., Smart, N.P.: Pairings for cryptographers. Discrete Applied Mathematics 156(16), 3113–3121 (2008)

12. Gallant, R., Lambert, R., Vanstone, S.: Faster point multiplication on elliptic curves with efficient endomorphisms. In: [19], pp. 190–200 (2001)

13. Gaudry, P., Thomé, E., Thériault, N., Diem, C.: A double large prime variation for small genus hyperelliptic index calculus. Mathematics of Computation 76, 475–492 (2004)

14. Hankerson, D., Menezes, A.J., Vanstone, S.: Guide to Elliptic Curve Cryptography. Springer-Verlag New York, Inc., Secaucus (2004)

15. Hayashi, T., Shimoyama, T., Shinohara, N., Takagi, T.: Breaking pairing-based cryptosystems using η_T pairing over $GF(3^{97})$. In: Wang, X., Sako, K. (eds.) ASIACRYPT 2012. LNCS, vol. 7658, pp. 43–60. Springer, Heidelberg (2012)

16. Hess, F., Smart, N.P., Vercauteren, F.: The eta pairing revisited. IEEE Transactions on Information Theory 52(10), 4595–4602 (2006)

17. Joux, A.: Discrete logarithms in GF(2^{6168}) [= GF(($2^{257})^{24}$)]. NMBRTHRY list (May 21, 2013), https://listserv.nodak.edu/cgi-bin/wa.exe?A2=NMBRTHRY;49bb494e.1305

18. Joux, A., Pierrot, C.: The special number field sieve in $\mathbb{F}_{p^n}$, application to pairing-friendly constructions. In: Cao, Z., Zhang, F. (eds.) Pairing 2013. LNCS, vol. 8365, pp. 45–61. Springer, Heidelberg (2014)

19. Kilian, J. (ed.): CRYPTO 2001. LNCS, vol. 2139. Springer, Heidelberg (2001)

20. Lee, E., Lee, H.S., Park, C.M.: Efficient and generalized pairing computation on abelian varieties. IEEE Transactions on Information Theory 55(4), 1793–1803 (2009)

21. Lin, X., Zhao, C., Zhang, F., Wang, Y.: Computing the ate pairing on elliptic curves with embedding degree $k = 9$. IEICE Transactions 91-A(9), 2387–2393 (2008)

22. Miller, V.S.: The Weil pairing, and its efficient calculation. J. Cryptology 17(4), 235–261 (2004)

23. Momose, F., Chao, J.: Scholten forms and elliptic/hyperelliptic curves with weak Weil restrictions. Cryptology ePrint Archive, Report 2005/277 (2005), http://eprint.iacr.org/2005/277

24. Nagao, K.: Improvement of Thériault algorithm of index calculus for Jacobian of hyperelliptic curves of small genus. Cryptology ePrint Archive, Report 2004/161 (2004), http://eprint.iacr.org/2004/161

25. Ogura, N., Uchiyama, S., Kanayama, N., Okamoato, E.: A note on the pairing computation using normalized Miller functions. IEICE Transactions on Fundamentals of Electronics, Communications and Computer Sciences E95-A(1), 196–203 (2012)

26. Sakai, R., Ohgishi, K., Kasahara, M.: Cryptosystems based on pairing. In: 2000 Symposium on Cryptography and Information Security (SCIS 2000), pp. 26–28 (January 2000) C20

27. Scholten, J.: Weil restriction of an elliptic curve over a quadratic extension (2003) (preprint), http://www.esat.kuleuven.ac.be/~jscholte/weilres.ps

28. Vercauteren, F.: Optimal pairings. IEEE Transactions on Information Theory 56(1), 455–461 (2010)

29. Verheul, E.R.: Evidence that XTR is more secure than supersingular elliptic curve cryptosystems. In: Pfitzmann, B. (ed.) EUROCRYPT 2001. LNCS, vol. 2045, pp. 195–210. Springer, Heidelberg (2001)

30. Verheul, E.R.: Evidence that XTR is more secure than supersingular elliptic curve cryptosystems. J. Cryptology 17(4), 277–296 (2004)

31. Waters, B.: Efficient identity-based encryption without random oracles. In: Cramer, R. (ed.) EUROCRYPT 2005. LNCS, vol. 3494, pp. 114–127. Springer, Heidelberg (2005)

32. Zhao, C., Zhang, F., Huang, J.: A note on the ate pairing. Int. J. Inf. Sec. 7(6), 379–382 (2008)

Predicate- and Attribute-Hiding Inner Product Encryption in a Public Key Setting

Yutaka Kawai and Katsuyuki Takashima

Mitsubishi Electric, 5-1-1 Ofuna, Kamakura, Kanagawa 247-8501, Japan
Kawai.Yutaka@da.MitsubishiElectric.co.jp,
Takashima.Katsuyuki@aj.MitsubishiElectric.co.jp

Abstract. In this paper, we propose a *reasonable* definition of *predicate-hiding* inner product encryption (IPE) *in a public key setting*, which we call inner product encryption with ciphertext conversion (IPE-CC), where original ciphertexts are converted to predicate-searchable ones by an helper in possession of a conversion key. We then define a notion of *full* security for IPE-CC, which comprises three security properties of being adaptively *predicate-* and attribute-hiding in the public key setting, adaptively *(fully-)attribute-hiding against the helper*, and usefully secure even *against the private-key generator (PKG)*. We then present *the first fully secure IPE-CC* scheme, and convert it into the *first fully secure symmetric-key IPE (SIPE)* scheme, where the security is defined in the sense of Shen, Shi, Waters. All the security properties are proven under the decisional linear assumption in the standard model. The IPE-CC scheme is comparably as efficient as existing attribute-hiding (not predicate-hiding) IPE schemes. We also present a variant of the proposed IPE-CC scheme with the same security that achieves shorter public and secret keys. We employ two key techniques, *trapdoor basis setup*, in which a new trapdoor is embedded in a public key, and *multi-system proof technique*, which further generalizes an extended dual system approach given by Okamoto and Takashima recently.

1 Introduction

1.1 Background

The notion of *predicate encryption* (PE) was explicitly presented by Katz, Sahai and Waters [12] for achieving fine-grained control over revealed information on encrypted data for various predicate-searchable token key owners. In the encryption system, the owner of a (master) secret key can create and issue tokens to system users. Informally, tokens in a predicate encryption scheme correspond to predicates in some class $\mathcal{F}$, and a sender associates a ciphertext with an attribute in a set Σ; a ciphertext ct_x associated with the attribute (or plaintext) $x \in \Sigma$ can be evaluated by token tk_f corresponding to the predicate $f \in \mathcal{F}$ to learn whether $f(x) = 1$. In this paper, we only consider this *predicate-only* PE [12, 21], in which attribute x can be treated as a plaintext in a general functional encryption framework [8]. (However, we treat x as an attribute hereafter.)

Z. Cao and F. Zhang (Eds.): Pairing 2013, LNCS 8365, pp. 113–130, 2014.

In addition, a security notion for PE, *attribute-hiding*, was defined in [12], where, roughly speaking, a ciphertext conceals the associated attribute. More specifically, it requires that an adversary in possession of tokens $\mathsf{tk}_{f_1}, \ldots, \mathsf{tk}_{f_h}$ for predicates $f_1, \ldots, f_h$ cannot derive any information on attribute x from ciphertext ct_x other than the values of $f_1(x), \ldots, f_h(x)$.

Katz, Sahai and Waters [12] also presented a concrete construction of PE for a class of predicates called *inner product* predicates, which represents a wide class of predicates that includes an equality test (for IBE [2–4, 10] and HVE [9]), range queries [22], disjunctions or conjunctions of equality tests, and, more generally, arbitrary CNF or DNF formulas. Informally, an attribute of inner product predicates is expressed as vector $\vec{x}$ and predicate $f_{\vec{v}}$ is associated with vector $\vec{v}$, where $f_{\vec{v}}(\vec{x}) = 1$ iff $\vec{v} \cdot \vec{x} = 0$. (Here, $\vec{v} \cdot \vec{x}$ denotes the standard inner product.)

The attribute-hiding security achieved in [13–15] is more limited or weaker than that achieved in [12, 17]. The former is called weakly-attribute-hiding, and the latter *fully-attribute-hiding*. Although the IPE scheme [12] achieved fully-attribute-hiding, it is *selectively* secure under non-standard assumptions. Subsequently, several attribute-hiding IPE schemes have been proposed [13–16, 20], for aiming at an IPE scheme with better security, e.g., adaptive security, fully-attribute-hiding and weaker (standard) assumptions. This research direction culminated in *adaptively secure* and *fully-attribute-hiding* IPE scheme under the *decisional linear (DLIN)* assumption [17]. The basic scheme in [17] has a variant with shorter public and tokens based on the technique in [16]. A hierarchical IPE (HIPE) scheme can be realized with the same security. (For a practical variant of the schemes, refer to [19].)

However, all previous public key IPE schemes have a problem to be applied in a practical system, that is, *predicate token queries may leak some sensitive information*, e.g., medical personal history, patent strategy, or corporate sensitive data. This is unavoidable in a *plain public key IPE* system, since anyone can generate a ciphertext associated with any attribute, and then, by using it, check the predicate associated in (target) token. In order to avoid this problem, Shen-Shi-Waters [21] proposed a *symmetric*-key IPE (SIPE) scheme, where predicate in a token is hidden from any malicious users [21, 23]. The property is called *predicate-hiding*. They [21] defined a strong security notion "full security", which implies predicate- and attribute-hiding, however, only constructed a weakly secure (selectively secure, single challenge) SIPE scheme since it is based on a weakly secure public key IPE given in [12]. Therefore, to construct a fully secure SIPE remains an interesting open problem.

Moreover, we require such an IPE functionality in a *public key setting*. To see the importance of *predicate- and attribute-hiding* IPE in a *public key setting*, let us consider an example on electronic medical record (EMR) storing and managing system that allows multiple hospitals to export EMRs to a remote server. By sharing EMRs among the hospitals, patient care and cost savings are greatly improved. Moreover, the database system provides a large source of medical research for physicians, biologists, and pharmacists, etc. For example, pharmaceutical companies use it for developing a new medicine.

Here, it is desirable that such a sensitive data be treated as encrypted data even for data processing and retrievals, which protects privacy of data provider. In addition, in the above example, multiple competitors, e.g., pharmaceutical companies, like to hide their access histories from each other. Hence, to apply PE technology to the remote EMR server setting, we require

1. For providing and sharing EMRs among multiple medical institutes, PE should be realized in a public key setting.
2. Attribute-hiding (for data-provider's privacy) and predicate-hiding (for data-retriever's privacy) must be assured.

In other applications with remote storage servers, a PE-encrypted file system with the above properties also highly improves user availability and removes privacy concerns. Recently, Boneh et al.[6, 7] proposed function-private PE (including IPE) schemes, which assure predicate-hiding only when used predicates are sampled from any *sufficiently unpredictable* distribution. The schemes does not guarantee predicate-hiding in the above setting, in general. Hence, to give a *reasonable and useful definition* of predicate-hiding IPE in a public key setting which is applicable in the above, is also an interesting open problem from a practical and theoretical point of view.[1]

1.2   Our Results

1. This paper introduces a reasonable and useful definition of IPE for achieving predicate-hiding in a public-key setting, i.e., *IPE with ciphertext conversion (IPE-CC)*.

    Here, two types of ciphertexts, original and converted, are introduced, and a new type of key, conversion key, is used as well as public and secret keys: Each user encrypts an attribute $\vec{x}$ by using public key, and the generated ciphertext $\mathsf{ct}_{\vec{x}}$ is called original. The ciphertext is converted to a predicate-searchable one $\mathsf{CT}_{\vec{x}}$ by a helper in possession of the conversion key ck.

    IPE-CC has two types of secret (or trapdoor) keys, sk and ck. Depending on which key an adversary has, we have three security requirements:
    (a) predicate-hiding of token key $\mathsf{tk}_{\vec{v}}$ and attribute-hiding of ciphertexts ($\mathsf{ct}_{\vec{x}}$, $\mathsf{CT}_{\vec{x}}$) against any malicious user with no secret key sk nor conversion key ck,
    (b) (fully-)attribute-hiding of ciphertexts ($\mathsf{ct}_{\vec{x}}$, $\mathsf{CT}_{\vec{x}}$) against any malicious helper with no secret key sk,
    (c) predicate-hiding of token key $\mathsf{tk}_{\vec{v}}$ and attribute-hiding of ciphertext $\mathsf{ct}_{\vec{x}}$ against any malicious PKG with no conversion key ck.
    An IPE-CC scheme is called *fully secure* iff it satisfies all the above three security requirements.

---

[1] Boneh et al. [5] approached the problem based on PIR, which is a communication protocol, while our solution is provided just by an encryption scheme (with much more efficient communication).

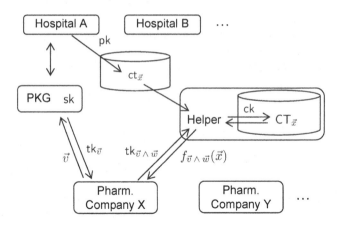

Fig. 1. Application to EMR storing and managing system, in which original encrypted data $\mathsf{ct}_{\vec{x}}$ are publicly accessible but converted ciphertexts $\mathsf{CT}_{\vec{x}}$ are not made public. Pharmaceutical Company X retrieves medical data with some medical predicate $\vec{w}$ as well as a predetermined condition $\vec{v}$.

2. This paper proposes *the first fully-secure* IPE-CC scheme, where all the security properties are proven under the DLIN assumption in the standard model (Section 4).

   Remark: Our IPE-CC scheme addresses privacy concerns given in the above remote server system, which is illustrated in Figure 1. Every data-provider, e.g., Hospital A, B,.., can put his encrypted data $\mathsf{ct}_{\vec{x}}$ for data $\vec{x}$ on the shared server, and each data-retriever, e.g., Pharmaceutical Company X, Y,..., obtains his own token $\mathsf{tk}_{\vec{v}}$ associated with a predicate category $\vec{v}$ from PKG. Here, a predicate category indicates an available range for specific predicate searches, e.g., Company X is assigned for accessing patient-data in the south of the U.S., and Y is assigned for accessing patient-data in the north. (The predicate category may be empty condition.) The data-retriever delegates the (high-level) token $\mathsf{tk}_{\vec{v}}$ to a specific predicate token $\mathsf{tk}_{\vec{v} \wedge \vec{w}}$, where $\vec{w}$ indicates some medical predicate, e.g., records for cardiac patients aged 60 and above. (Refer to Appendix A for the 2-level hierarchical IPE-CC scheme.) Helper converts original encrypted data $\mathsf{ct}_{\vec{x}}$ to searchable ones, $\mathsf{CT}_{\vec{x}}$, using conversion key ck (in some extra time). Note that the converted ciphertexts are not made public (while original encrypted data on the database are publicly accessible). In the figure, Company X sends a search query with delegated token $\mathsf{tk}_{\vec{v} \wedge \vec{w}}$, and he obtains search result, $f_{\vec{v} \wedge \vec{w}}(\vec{x}) \in \{0, 1\}$. The basic security (a) protects privacy for both data-providers and data-retrievers from dishonest users, e.g., competing companies. The security condition (b) assures no information leakage to the server administrator (i.e., helper) from ciphertexts on the server. Moreover, since converted ciphertexts are not public, security (c) assures both predicate-hiding in tokens and attribute-hiding in ciphertexts *against PKG*. Since to mitigate the power of PKG is important in PE systems, this security against PKG is useful and interesting. Thus, to

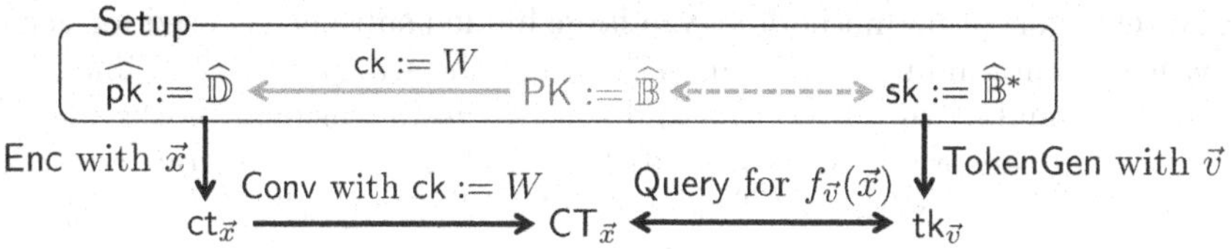

$$\boxed{\begin{array}{c} \text{Setup} \\ \widehat{\mathsf{pk}} := \widehat{\mathbb{D}} \xleftarrow{\quad \mathsf{ck} := W \quad} \mathsf{PK} := \widehat{\mathbb{B}} \xleftrightarrow{\quad\quad} \mathsf{sk} := \widehat{\mathbb{B}}^* \end{array}}$$

Enc with $\vec{x}$ $\downarrow$ Conv with ck $:= W$ Query for $f_{\vec{v}}(\vec{x})$ $\downarrow$ TokenGen with $\vec{v}$

$\mathsf{ct}_{\vec{x}} \xrightarrow{\quad\quad\quad} \mathsf{CT}_{\vec{x}} \xleftrightarrow{\quad\quad\quad} \mathsf{tk}_{\vec{v}}$

Fig. 2. Trapdoor basis setup with conversion key ck for public key $\widehat{\mathsf{pk}}$ and (master) secret key sk, in which $\mathsf{PK} := \widehat{\mathbb{B}}$ is not directly used (with Enc, TokenGen, Conv, Query)

summarize, the proposed scheme provides attribute-hiding for ciphertexts as in [17] and predicate-hiding for tokens from any malicious users but the helper. The technique can be applied to unbounded IPE in [18].

3. We propose *the first fully secure* symmetric-key IPE (SIPE) scheme in the sense of the definition by Shen, Shi and Waters [21] (Section 5). The scheme is (generically) converted from our public key setting IPE-CC by including public key and conversion key into (master) secret key. The security is also proven under the DLIN assumption in the standard model.

4. We also present a variant of the proposed IPE-CC scheme with the same security that achieves shorter public key and shorter (master) secret key (Section 6). Table 1 in Section 7 compares the proposed IPE-CC scheme (resp. SIPE scheme) with existing attribute-hiding IPE schemes in the public key setting (resp. the existing SIPE scheme).

1.3 Key Techniques

Trapdoor Basis Setup: A full security notion of IPE-CC (in the public key setting) consists of three types of hiding properties against various type adversaries, i.e., malicious users, helper, or PKG. For achieving such a rich security property, we employ a new trapdoor embedded in a public key. See Figure 2. The setup algorithm produces a pair of random dual bases $(\mathbb{B}, \mathbb{B}^*)$ on a dual pairing vector space (DPVS), and by using random matrix $\mathsf{ck} := W$, linearly transforms a part of the basis, $\widehat{\mathbb{B}}$ $(\subset \mathbb{B})$, to a new basis $\widehat{\mathbb{D}} := \widehat{\mathbb{B}} \cdot W$, which is uniformly and independently distributed from $\mathbb{B}$. It outputs $\widehat{\mathsf{pk}} := \widehat{\mathbb{D}}$ as a part of a public key and the corresponding $\mathsf{sk} := \widehat{\mathbb{B}}^*$ as a secret key, where the bases are independent from each other if W is not considered. Original ciphrtexts and tokens inherit this independence property from the master key pair. The trapdoor (i.e., conversion key) W transforms the original ciphertexts to searchable ones, which are related to tokens through the dual orthonormal property of $(\mathbb{B}, \mathbb{B}^*)$. We establish security properties against various level adversaries based on this *trapdoor basis setup* construction.

Multi-system Proof Technique: As we observed, our IPE-CC scheme implies the *first* fully secure SIPE scheme. Since no previous SIPE schemes are fully secure, we develop a new technique to obtain the scheme, we call *multi-system proof technique*, which extends the approach given in [17]. Based on Waters' dual system encryption methodology, a large hidden subspace is used for achieving *fully*-attribute-hiding of IPE in [17], where the subspace is $2n$-dimensional for n-dimensional attribute vectors and the two n-dimensional blocks play different roles in the proof. Moreover, to hide a challenge bit b from adversary, *unbiased* ciphertexts with $\omega_0 \vec{x}^{(0)} + \omega_1 \vec{x}^{(1)}$ for challenge $\vec{x}^{(0)}, \vec{x}^{(1)} \in \mathbb{F}_q^n$ (and $\omega_0, \omega_1 \xleftarrow{\mathsf{U}} \mathbb{F}_q$) plays a key role in the security proof. For both *fully* predicate- and attribute-hiding security of our schemes, a simulator must deal with two types of challenges $(\vec{x}^{(0)}, \vec{x}^{(1)})$ and $(\vec{v}^{(0)}, \vec{v}^{(1)})$ simultaneously. Since the above unbiased ciphertext (or token) construction is not enough for this purpose, we use larger, $3n$-dimensional, multi-system hidden subspace, and refined game hopping.[2] See the full version of this paper for the details.

1.4   Notations

When A is a random variable or distribution, $y \xleftarrow{\mathsf{R}} A$ denotes that y is randomly selected from A according to its distribution. When A is a set, $y \xleftarrow{\mathsf{U}} A$ denotes that y is uniformly selected from A. We denote the finite field of order q by $\mathbb{F}_q$, and $\mathbb{F}_q \setminus \{0\}$ by $\mathbb{F}_q^\times$. A vector symbol denotes a vector representation over $\mathbb{F}_q$, e.g., $\vec{x}$ denotes $(x_1, \ldots, x_n) \in \mathbb{F}_q^n$. For two vectors $\vec{x} = (x_1, \ldots, x_n)$ and $\vec{v} = (v_1, \ldots, v_n)$, $\vec{x} \cdot \vec{v}$ denotes the inner product $\sum_{i=1}^n x_i v_i$. The vector $\vec{0}$ is abused as the zero vector in $\mathbb{F}_q^n$ for any n. X^T denotes the transpose of matrix X. I_ℓ and 0_ℓ denote the $\ell \times \ell$ identity matrix and the $\ell \times \ell$ zero matrix, respectively. A bold face letter denotes an element of vector space $\mathbb{V}$, e.g., $\boldsymbol{x} \in \mathbb{V}$. When $\boldsymbol{b}_i \in \mathbb{V}$ ($i = 1, \ldots, n$), $\mathsf{span}\langle \boldsymbol{b}_1, \ldots, \boldsymbol{b}_n \rangle \subseteq \mathbb{V}$ (resp. $\mathsf{span}\langle \vec{x}_1, \ldots, \vec{x}_n \rangle$) denotes the subspace generated by $\boldsymbol{b}_1, \ldots, \boldsymbol{b}_n$ (resp. $\vec{x}_1, \ldots, \vec{x}_n$). For bases $\mathbb{B} := (\boldsymbol{b}_1, \ldots, \boldsymbol{b}_N)$ and $\mathbb{B}^* := (\boldsymbol{b}_1^*, \ldots, \boldsymbol{b}_N^*)$, $(x_1, \ldots, x_N)_\mathbb{B} := \sum_{i=1}^N x_i \boldsymbol{b}_i$ and $(y_1, \ldots, y_N)_{\mathbb{B}^*} := \sum_{i=1}^N y_i \boldsymbol{b}_i^*$. For a dimension n, $\vec{e}_j$ denotes the canonical basis vector $(\overbrace{0 \cdots 0}^{j-1}, 1, \overbrace{0 \cdots 0}^{n-j}) \in \mathbb{F}_q^n$ for $j = 1, \ldots, n$. $GL(n, \mathbb{F}_q)$ denotes the general linear group of degree n over $\mathbb{F}_q$.

2   Dual Pairing Vector Spaces (DPVS)

In this paper, for simplicity of description, we will present the proposed schemes on the symmetric version of dual pairing vector spaces (DPVS) [14, 13, 15] constructed using symmetric bilinear pairing groups given in Definition 1. Owing to the abstraction of DPVS, the presentation and the security proof of the proposed schemes are essentially the same as those on the asymmetric version of DPVS, $(q, \mathbb{V}, \mathbb{V}^*, \mathbb{G}_T, \mathbb{A}, \mathbb{A}^*, e)$, for which see Appendix A.2 in the full version of [15]. The symmetric version is a specific (self-dual) case of the asymmetric version, where $\mathbb{V} = \mathbb{V}^*$ and $\mathbb{A} = \mathbb{A}^*$.

---

[2] In [21], a generic conversion from an adaptively secure single-challenge SIPE to a fully secure (multi-challenge) SIPE is given. By using the conversion, we may take an approach to fully secure SIPE via single challenge secure SIPE based on IPE in [17]. However, since the conversion loses efficiency, our SIPE in Section 5 is better.

Definition 1. *"Symmetric bilinear pairing groups" $(q, \mathbb{G}, \mathbb{G}_T, G, e)$ are a tuple of a prime q, cyclic additive group $\mathbb{G}$ and multiplicative group $\mathbb{G}_T$ of order q, $G \neq 0 \in \mathbb{G}$, and a polynomial-time computable nondegenerate bilinear pairing $e : \mathbb{G} \times \mathbb{G} \to \mathbb{G}_T$ i.e., $e(sG, tG) = e(G, G)^{st}$ and $e(G, G) \neq 1$. Let $\mathcal{G}_{\mathsf{bpg}}$ be an algorithm that takes input 1^λ and outputs a description of bilinear pairing groups $(q, \mathbb{G}, \mathbb{G}_T, G, e)$ with security parameter λ.*

Definition 2. *"Dual pairing vector spaces (DPVS)" $(q, \mathbb{V}, \mathbb{G}_T, \mathbb{A}, e)$ by a direct product of symmetric pairing groups $(q, \mathbb{G}, \mathbb{G}_T, G, e)$ are a tuple of prime q, N-dimensional vector space $\mathbb{V} := \overbrace{\mathbb{G} \times \cdots \times \mathbb{G}}^{N}$ over $\mathbb{F}_q$, cyclic group $\mathbb{G}_T$ of order q, canonical basis $\mathbb{A} := (\boldsymbol{a}_1, \ldots, \boldsymbol{a}_N)$ of $\mathbb{V}$, where $\boldsymbol{a}_i := (\overbrace{0, .., 0}^{i-1}, G, \overbrace{0, .., 0}^{N-i})$, and pairing $e : \mathbb{V} \times \mathbb{V} \to \mathbb{G}_T$. The pairing is defined by $e(\boldsymbol{x}, \boldsymbol{y}) := \prod_{i=1}^{N} e(G_i, H_i) \in \mathbb{G}_T$ where $\boldsymbol{x} := (G_1, .., G_N) \in \mathbb{V}$ and $\boldsymbol{y} := (H_1, .., H_N) \in \mathbb{V}$. This is nondegenerate bilinear i.e., $e(s\boldsymbol{x}, t\boldsymbol{y}) = e(\boldsymbol{x}, \boldsymbol{y})^{st}$ and if $e(\boldsymbol{x}, \boldsymbol{y}) = 1$ for all $\boldsymbol{y} \in \mathbb{V}$, then $\boldsymbol{x} = \boldsymbol{0}$. For all i and j, $e(\boldsymbol{a}_i, \boldsymbol{a}_j) = e(G, G)^{\delta_{i,j}}$ where $\delta_{i,j} = 1$ if $i = j$, and 0 otherwise, and $e(G, G) \neq 1 \in \mathbb{G}_T$. DPVS generation algorithm $\mathcal{G}_{\mathsf{dpvs}}$ takes input 1^λ $(\lambda \in \mathbb{N})$ and $N \in \mathbb{N}$, and outputs a description of $\mathsf{param}'_{\mathbb{V}} := (q, \mathbb{V}, \mathbb{G}_T, \mathbb{A}, e)$ with security parameter λ and N-dimensional $\mathbb{V}$. It can be constructed by using $\mathcal{G}_{\mathsf{bpg}}$.*

3   Definition of Inner Product Encryption with Ciphertext Conversion (IPE-CC)

This section defines inner product encryption with ciphertext conversion (IPE-CC) and its security. An attribute (or plaintext) of inner product predicates is expressed as a vector $\vec{x} \in \mathbb{F}_q^n \setminus \{\vec{0}\}$ and a predicate $f_{\vec{v}}$ is associated with a vector $\vec{v}$, where $f_{\vec{v}}(\vec{x}) = 1$ iff $\vec{v} \cdot \vec{x} = 0$. Let $\Sigma := \mathbb{F}_q^n \setminus \{\vec{0}\}$, i.e., the set of the attributes, and $\mathcal{F} := \{f_{\vec{v}} | \vec{v} \in \mathbb{F}_q^n \setminus \{\vec{0}\}\}$ i.e., the set of the predicates.

Definition 3. *An inner product encryption with ciphertext conversion (IPE-CC) scheme (for predicates $\mathcal{F}$ and attributes Σ) consists of probabilistic polynomial-time algorithms* Setup, TokenGen, Enc, Conv *and* Query. *They are given as follows:*

- Setup *takes as input security parameter 1^λ, and it outputs a public key* pk, *a conversion key* ck, *and a (master) secret key* sk.
- TokenGen *takes as input a public key* pk, *a (master) secret key* sk, *and a predicate vector $\vec{v}$. It outputs a corresponding token* $\mathsf{tk}_{\vec{v}}$.
- Enc *takes as input a public key* pk *and an attribute (or plaintext) vector $\vec{x}$. It returns an original ciphertext* $\mathsf{ct}_{\vec{x}}$.
- Conv *takes as input a public key* pk, *a conversion key* ck, *and an original ciphertext* $\mathsf{ct}_{\vec{x}}$. *It returns a converted ciphertext* $\mathsf{CT}_{\vec{x}}$.
- Query *takes as input a public key* pk, *a token* $\mathsf{tk}_{\vec{v}}$ *and a converted ciphertext* $\mathsf{CT}_{\vec{x}}$. *It outputs either 0 or 1, indicating the value of the predicate $f_{\vec{v}}$ evaluated on the underlying attribute $\vec{x}$.*

Remark 1. In the introduction, we give an application example using a delegation from $\mathsf{tk}_{\vec{v}}$ to $\mathsf{tk}_{\vec{v} \wedge \vec{w}} (:= \mathsf{tk}_{(\vec{v},\vec{w})})$. While we can add this functionality, the explicit description of the delegation is not included here for simple presentation. Refer to Appendix A for the 2-level hierarchical IPE-CC scheme.

An IPE-CC scheme should have the following correctness property: for all $(\mathsf{pk}, \mathsf{ck}, \mathsf{sk}) \xleftarrow{\mathsf{R}} \mathsf{Setup}(1^\lambda, n)$, all $f_{\vec{v}} \in \mathcal{F}$ and $\vec{x} \in \Sigma$, all $\mathsf{tk}_{\vec{v}} \xleftarrow{\mathsf{R}} \mathsf{TokenGen}(\mathsf{pk}, \mathsf{sk}, \vec{v})$, all original ciphertexts $\mathsf{ct}_{\vec{x}} \xleftarrow{\mathsf{R}} \mathsf{Enc}(\mathsf{pk}, \vec{x})$ and converted ciphertexts $\mathsf{CT}_{\vec{x}} \xleftarrow{\mathsf{R}} \mathsf{Conv}(\mathsf{pk}, \mathsf{ck}, \mathsf{ct}_{\vec{x}})$, it holds that $1 = \mathsf{Query}(\mathsf{tk}_{\vec{v}}, \mathsf{CT}_{\vec{x}})$ if $f_{\vec{v}}(\vec{x}) = 1$. Otherwise, it holds only with negligible probability.

We then define the *full* security notion of IPE-CC, which consists of three security notions, i.e., security against *malicious users*, *malicious helper*, and *malicious PKG*.

Definition 4 (Full Security of IPE-CC). *An IPE-CC scheme is fully secure if for all probabilistic polynomial-time adversaries $\mathcal{A}$, all $\mathsf{Adv}_{\mathcal{A}}^{\mathsf{DisU}}(\lambda)$, $\mathsf{Adv}_{\mathcal{A}}^{\mathsf{DisH}}(\lambda)$ and $\mathsf{Adv}_{\mathcal{A}}^{\mathsf{DisPKG}}(\lambda)$ are negligible.*

[Dishonest-User Game]   *The model for defining the adaptively predicate-hiding and adaptively attribute-hiding security of IPE-CC against malicious user $\mathcal{A}$ is given as follows:*

1. *The challenger runs* Setup *to generate keys* pk, ck *and* sk, *and* pk *is given to $\mathcal{A}$. The challenger picks a random bit b.*
2. *$\mathcal{A}$ may adaptively make a polynomial number of queries, where each query is one of two types:*
   - *On the ℓ-th ciphertext query, $\mathcal{A}$ outputs two attribute vectors $(\vec{x}_\ell^{(0)}, \vec{x}_\ell^{(1)})$. The challenger responds with $(\mathsf{ct}_\ell, \mathsf{CT}_\ell)$, where $\mathsf{ct}_\ell \xleftarrow{\mathsf{R}} \mathsf{Enc}(\mathsf{pk}, \vec{x}_\ell^{(b)})$ and $\mathsf{CT}_\ell \xleftarrow{\mathsf{R}} \mathsf{Conv}(\mathsf{pk}, \mathsf{ck}, \mathsf{ct}_\ell)$.*
   - *On the h-th token query, $\mathcal{A}$ outputs two predicate vectors, $(\vec{v}_h^{(0)}, \vec{v}_h^{(1)})$. The challenger responds with $\mathsf{tk}_h \xleftarrow{\mathsf{R}} \mathsf{TokenGen}(\mathsf{pk}, \mathsf{sk}, \vec{v}_h^{(b)})$.*
   $\mathcal{A}$'s queries are subject to the restriction that, for all ciphertext queries $(\vec{x}_\ell^{(0)}, \vec{x}_\ell^{(1)})$ and all token queries $(\vec{v}_h^{(0)}, \vec{v}_h^{(1)})$, $f_{\vec{v}_h^{(0)}}(\vec{x}_\ell^{(0)}) = f_{\vec{v}_h^{(1)}}(\vec{x}_\ell^{(1)})$.
3. *$\mathcal{A}$ outputs a guess b' of b.*

The success experiment in the above game, i.e., $b' = b$, is denoted by $\mathsf{Succ}_{\mathcal{A}}^{\mathsf{DisU}}(\lambda)$, and the advantage of $\mathcal{A}$ is defined as $\mathsf{Adv}_{\mathcal{A}}^{\mathsf{DisU}}(\lambda) := \Pr[\mathsf{Succ}_{\mathcal{A}}^{\mathsf{DisU}}(\lambda)] - 1/2$ for any security parameter λ.

[Dishonest-Helper Game]   *The model for defining the adaptively (fully-)attribute-hiding security of IPE-CC against malicious helper $\mathcal{A}$ is given as follows:*

1. *The challenger runs* Setup *to generate keys* pk, ck *and* sk, *and* pk *and* ck *are given to $\mathcal{A}$. The challenger picks a random bit b.*
2. *$\mathcal{A}$ may adaptively make a polynomial number of queries, where each query is one of two types:*

- On the ℓ-th ciphertext query, $\mathcal{A}$ outputs two attribute vectors $(\vec{x}_\ell^{(0)}, \vec{x}_\ell^{(1)})$. The challenger responds with $\mathsf{ct}_\ell \xleftarrow{\mathsf{R}} \mathsf{Enc}(\mathsf{pk}, \vec{x}_\ell^{(b)})$.
- On the h-th token query, $\mathcal{A}$ outputs a predicate vector, $\vec{v}_h$. The challenger responds with $\mathsf{tk}_h \xleftarrow{\mathsf{R}} \mathsf{TokenGen}(\mathsf{pk}, \mathsf{sk}, \vec{v}_h)$.

$\mathcal{A}$'s queries are subject to the restriction that, for all ciphertext queries $(\vec{x}_\ell^{(0)}, \vec{x}_\ell^{(1)})$ and all token queries $\vec{v}_h$, $f_{\vec{v}_h}(\vec{x}_\ell^{(0)}) = f_{\vec{v}_h}(\vec{x}_\ell^{(1)})$.
3. $\mathcal{A}$ outputs a guess b' of b.

The success experiment in the above game, i.e., $b' = b$, is denoted by $\mathsf{Succ}_{\mathcal{A}}^{\mathsf{DisH}}(\lambda)$, and the advantage of $\mathcal{A}$ is defined as $\mathsf{Adv}_{\mathcal{A}}^{\mathsf{DisH}}(\lambda) := \Pr[\mathsf{Succ}_{\mathcal{A}}^{\mathsf{DisH}}(\lambda)] - 1/2$ for any security parameter λ.

[Dishonest-PKG Game]   The model for defining the adaptively attribute-hiding and predicate-hiding security of IPE-CC against malicious-PKG $\mathcal{A}$ is given as follows:

1. The challenger runs Setup to generate keys pk, ck and sk, and pk and sk are given to $\mathcal{A}$. The challenger picks a random bit b.
2. $\mathcal{A}$ may adaptively make a polynomial number of queries, where each query is one of two types:
   - On the ℓ-th ciphertext query, $\mathcal{A}$ outputs two attribute vectors $(\vec{x}_\ell^{(0)}, \vec{x}_\ell^{(1)})$. The challenger responds with $\mathsf{ct}_\ell \xleftarrow{\mathsf{R}} \mathsf{Enc}(\mathsf{pk}, \vec{x}_\ell^{(b)})$.
   - On the h-th token query, $\mathcal{A}$ outputs two predicate vectors, $(\vec{v}_h^{(0)}, \vec{v}_h^{(1)})$. The challenger responds with $\mathsf{tk}_h \xleftarrow{\mathsf{R}} \mathsf{TokenGen}(\mathsf{pk}, \mathsf{sk}, \vec{v}_h^{(b)})$.

   $\mathcal{A}$'s queries are subject to no restrictions.
3. $\mathcal{A}$ outputs a guess b' of b.

The success experiment in the above, i.e., $b' = b$, is denoted by $\mathsf{Succ}_{\mathcal{A}}^{\mathsf{DisPKG}}(\lambda)$, and the advantage of $\mathcal{A}$ is defined as $\mathsf{Adv}_{\mathcal{A}}^{\mathsf{DisPKG}}(\lambda) := \Pr[\mathsf{Succ}_{\mathcal{A}}^{\mathsf{DisPKG}}(\lambda)] - 1/2$ for any security parameter λ.

Since a converted ciphertext is not publicly available, it is not given to the adversary in the above Dishonest-PKG game.

4 Proposed (Basic) IPE-CC Scheme

4.1 Construction

We describe random dual orthonormal basis generator $\mathcal{G}_{\mathsf{ob}}^{\mathsf{IPE}}$ below, which is used as a subroutine in the proposed IPE-CC and SIPE schemes.

$\mathcal{G}_{\mathsf{ob}}^{\mathsf{IPE}}(1^\lambda, N):$ $\mathsf{param}_{\mathbb{V}}' := (q, \mathbb{V}, \mathbb{G}_T, \mathbb{A}, e) \xleftarrow{\mathsf{R}} \mathcal{G}_{\mathsf{dpvs}}(1^\lambda, N), \psi \xleftarrow{\mathsf{U}} \mathbb{F}_q^\times, g_T := e(G, G)^\psi,$

$X := (\chi_{i,j}) \xleftarrow{\mathsf{U}} GL(N, \mathbb{F}_q), (\vartheta_{i,j}) := \psi \cdot (X^{\mathsf{T}})^{-1}, \mathsf{param}_{\mathbb{V}} := (\mathsf{param}_{\mathbb{V}}', g_T),$

$\boldsymbol{b}_i := \sum_{j=1}^N \chi_{i,j} \boldsymbol{a}_j, \mathbb{B} := (\boldsymbol{b}_1, \ldots, \boldsymbol{b}_N), \boldsymbol{b}_i^* := \sum_{j=1}^N \vartheta_{i,j} \boldsymbol{a}_j, \mathbb{B}^* := (\boldsymbol{b}_1^*, \ldots, \boldsymbol{b}_N^*),$

return $(\mathsf{param}_{\mathbb{V}}, \mathbb{B}, \mathbb{B}^*).$

We refer to Section 1.4 for notations on DPVS. For matrix $W :=$ $(w_{i,j})_{i,j=1,\ldots,N} \in \mathbb{F}_q^{N \times N}$ and element $\boldsymbol{g} := (G_1, \ldots, G_N)$ in N-dimensional $\mathbb{V}$, $\boldsymbol{g}W$ denotes $(\sum_{i=1}^N G_i w_{i,1}, \ldots, \sum_{i=1}^N G_i w_{i,N}) = (\sum_{i=1}^N w_{i,1} G_i, \ldots, \sum_{i=1}^N w_{i,N} G_i)$ by a natural multiplication of a N-dim. row vector and a $N \times N$ matrix. Thus it holds an associative law like $(\boldsymbol{g}W)W^{-1} = \boldsymbol{g}(WW^{-1}) = \boldsymbol{g}$. The proposed scheme is given as:

$\mathsf{Setup}(1^\lambda, n) : (\mathsf{param}_\mathbb{V}, \mathbb{B} := (\boldsymbol{b}_1, .., \boldsymbol{b}_{6n}), \mathbb{B}^* := (\boldsymbol{b}_1^*, .., \boldsymbol{b}_{6n}^*)) \xleftarrow{\mathsf{R}} \mathcal{G}_{\mathsf{ob}}^{\mathsf{IPE}}(1^\lambda, N := 6n)$,

$\quad W \xleftarrow{\mathsf{U}} GL(N, \mathbb{F}_q), \quad \boldsymbol{d}_i := \boldsymbol{b}_i W \text{ for } i = 1, \ldots, 6n, \quad \mathbb{D} := (\boldsymbol{d}_1, \ldots, \boldsymbol{d}_{6n})$,

$\quad \widehat{\mathbb{D}} := (\boldsymbol{d}_1, \ldots, \boldsymbol{d}_n, \boldsymbol{d}_{5n+1}, \ldots, \boldsymbol{d}_{6n}), \quad \widehat{\mathbb{B}}^* := (\boldsymbol{b}_1^*, \ldots, \boldsymbol{b}_n^*, \boldsymbol{b}_{4n+1}^*, \ldots, \boldsymbol{b}_{5n}^*)$,

$\quad$ return $\mathsf{pk} := (1^\lambda, \mathsf{param}_\mathbb{V}, \widehat{\mathbb{D}}), \quad \mathsf{ck} := W, \quad \mathsf{sk} := \widehat{\mathbb{B}}^*$.

$\mathsf{TokenGen}(\mathsf{pk}, \mathsf{sk}, \vec{v} \in \mathbb{F}_q^n \setminus \{\vec{0}\}) : \quad \sigma \xleftarrow{\mathsf{U}} \mathbb{F}_q, \quad \vec{\eta} \xleftarrow{\mathsf{U}} \mathbb{F}_q^n$,

$$\boldsymbol{k}^* := (\quad \overbrace{\sigma \vec{v}}^{n}, \quad \overbrace{0^{3n}}^{3n}, \quad \overbrace{\vec{\eta}}^{n}, \quad \overbrace{0^n}^{n} \quad)_{\mathbb{B}^*}, \quad \text{return } \mathsf{tk}_{\vec{v}} := \boldsymbol{k}^*.$$

$\mathsf{Enc}(\mathsf{pk}, \vec{x} \in \mathbb{F}_q^n \setminus \{\vec{0}\}) : \quad \tau \xleftarrow{\mathsf{U}} \mathbb{F}_q, \quad \vec{\xi} \xleftarrow{\mathsf{U}} \mathbb{F}_q^n$,

$$\boldsymbol{f} := (\quad \overbrace{\tau \vec{x}}^{n}, \quad \overbrace{0^{3n}}^{3n}, \quad \overbrace{0^n}^{n}, \quad \overbrace{\vec{\xi}}^{n} \quad)_{\mathbb{D}}, \quad \text{return } \mathsf{ct}_{\vec{x}} := \boldsymbol{f}.$$

$\mathsf{Conv}(\mathsf{pk}, \mathsf{ck} := W, \mathsf{ct}_{\vec{x}} := \boldsymbol{f}) : \quad \rho \xleftarrow{\mathsf{U}} \mathbb{F}_q, \quad \boldsymbol{y} \xleftarrow{\mathsf{U}} \mathsf{span}\langle \boldsymbol{d}_{5n+1}, \ldots, \boldsymbol{d}_{6n} \rangle$,

$\quad \boldsymbol{c} := (\rho \boldsymbol{f} + \boldsymbol{y}) W^{-1}, \quad \text{return } \mathsf{CT}_{\vec{x}} := \boldsymbol{c}$.

$\mathsf{Query}(\mathsf{pk}, \mathsf{tk}_{\vec{v}} := \boldsymbol{k}^*, \mathsf{CT}_{\vec{x}} := \boldsymbol{c}) :$

$\quad$ if $e(\boldsymbol{c}, \boldsymbol{k}^*) = 1$, output 1, otherwise, output 0.

Remark 2. To realize a delegation from $\mathsf{tk}_{\vec{v}}$ to $\mathsf{tk}_{\vec{v} \wedge \vec{w}} (:= \mathsf{tk}_{(\vec{v}, \vec{w})})$ given in the introduction, we can construct a natural delegation algorithm in a similar manner to [14–17]. We give the 2-level hierarchical IPE-CC (HIPE-CC) scheme in Appendix A.

[Correctness] Since $\mathbb{D} \cdot W^{-1} := (\boldsymbol{d}_1 W^{-1}, \ldots, \boldsymbol{d}_{6n} W^{-1})$ is equal to $\mathbb{B} := (\boldsymbol{b}_1, \ldots, \boldsymbol{b}_{6n})$, $\boldsymbol{c} := (\rho \boldsymbol{f} + \boldsymbol{u}) W^{-1} = (\omega \vec{x}, 0^{3n}, 0^n, \vec{\varphi})_{\mathbb{D}} \cdot W^{-1} = (\omega \vec{x}, 0^{3n}, 0^n, \vec{\varphi})_{\mathbb{D} \cdot W^{-1}} = (\omega \vec{x}, 0^{3n}, 0^n, \vec{\varphi})_{\mathbb{B}}$, where $\omega \in \mathbb{F}_q$ and $\vec{\varphi} \in \mathbb{F}_q^n$ are uniformly and independently distributed. Therefore, if $\vec{v} \cdot \vec{x} = 0$, then $e(\boldsymbol{c}, \boldsymbol{k}^*) = g_T^{\omega \sigma \vec{v} \cdot \vec{x}} = 1$.

4.2 Security

The DLIN assumption is standard [15–17] (and given in the full paper).

Theorem 1. *The proposed IPE-CC scheme is fully secure under the DLIN assumption, i.e., for any adversary $\mathcal{A}$, all $\mathsf{Adv}_{\mathcal{A}}^{\mathsf{DisU}}(\lambda)$, $\mathsf{Adv}_{\mathcal{A}}^{\mathsf{DisH}}(\lambda)$ and $\mathsf{Adv}_{\mathcal{A}}^{\mathsf{DisPKG}}(\lambda)$ are negligible under the DLIN assumption.*

Proof. The proof of Theorem 1 is reduced to those of Lemmas 1–3. □

Lemma 1. *For any adversary $\mathcal{A}$, $\mathsf{Adv}_{\mathcal{A}}^{\mathsf{DisU}}(\lambda)$ is negligible under the DLIN assumption.*

Lemma 2. *For any adversary $\mathcal{A}$, $\mathsf{Adv}_{\mathcal{A}}^{\mathsf{DisH}}(\lambda)$ is negligible under the DLIN assumption.*

Lemma 3. *For any adversary $\mathcal{A}$, $\mathsf{Adv}_{\mathcal{A}}^{\mathsf{DisPKG}}(\lambda)$ is negligible under the DLIN assumption.*

The proofs of Lemmas 1–3 are given in the full version of this paper.

5 Fully Secure SIPE

The definitions of symmetric-key IPE (SIPE) and full security of SIPE are given in Appendix B.

From the above IPE-CC scheme, we obtain the first fully secure SIPE scheme. Namely, using the IPE-CC scheme, $\Pi_{\mathsf{IPE\text{-}CC}} := (\mathsf{Setup}, \mathsf{TokenGen}, \mathsf{Enc}, \mathsf{Conv}, \mathsf{Query})$, a modified setup algorithm $\mathsf{Setup}'(1^\lambda, n)$ outputs a (master) secret key $\mathsf{sk}' := (\mathsf{pk}, \mathsf{ck}, \mathsf{sk})$, where $(\mathsf{pk}, \mathsf{ck}, \mathsf{sk}) \xleftarrow{\mathsf{R}} \mathsf{Setup}(1^\lambda, n)$, and a modified encryption algorithm $\mathsf{Enc}'(\mathsf{sk}', \vec{x})$ outputs a ciphertext $\mathsf{CT}'_{\vec{x}} \xleftarrow{\mathsf{R}} \mathsf{Conv}(\mathsf{pk}, \mathsf{ck}, \mathsf{ct}_{\vec{x}})$, where $\mathsf{ct}_{\vec{x}} \xleftarrow{\mathsf{R}} \mathsf{Enc}(\mathsf{pk}, \vec{x})$, and the rest of algorithms, $\mathsf{TokenGen}$ and Query are the same as those of the IPE-CC scheme since an input sk' of $\mathsf{TokenGen}$ includes $(\mathsf{pk}, \mathsf{sk})$. Hence, we obtain a (converted) SIPE, $\Pi_{\mathsf{SIPE}} := (\mathsf{Setup}', \mathsf{TokenGen}, \mathsf{Enc}', \mathsf{Query})$.

Theorem 2. *The proposed SIPE scheme is fully secure under the DLIN assumption.*

Proof. By the construction, the full security for SIPE Π_{SIPE} is reduced from the Dishonest-User Game security for IPE-CC $\Pi_{\mathsf{IPE\text{-}CC}}$, i.e., for any adversary $\mathcal{A}$, we can construct $\mathcal{A}'$ from $\mathcal{A}$ s.t. $\mathsf{Adv}_{\mathcal{A}}^{\mathsf{SIPE}}(\lambda)$ for Π_{SIPE} in Def. 6 is less than or equal to $\mathsf{Adv}_{\mathcal{A}'}^{\mathsf{DisU}}(\lambda)$ for $\Pi_{\mathsf{IPE\text{-}CC}}$ in Def. 4. Hence, Lemma 1 implies Theorem 2.   □

6 A Variant for Achieving Shorter Public and Secret Keys

A variant of the proposed (basic) IPE-CC scheme with the same security, that achieves a shorter ($O(n)$-size) public key and secret key, can be constructed by combining with the techniques in [16], where n is the dimension of vectors of the IPE-CC scheme. Here, we show this variant.

6.1 Construction and Security

Let $N := 6n$ and

$$
\mathcal{H}(n, \mathbb{F}_q) := \left\{ \left.
\begin{pmatrix}
\mu_1'' & \mu_2'' & \cdots & \mu_{n-1}'' & \mu''' \\
\mu & & & & \mu_2' \\
& & \ddots & & \vdots \\
& & & \mu & \mu_{n-1}' \\
& & & & \mu_n'
\end{pmatrix}
\right|
\begin{array}{l}
\mu, \mu_2', \dots, \mu_n', \\
\mu_1'', \dots, \mu_{n-1}'', \mu''' \in \mathbb{F}_q, \\
\text{a blank element in the matrix} \\
\text{denotes } 0 \in \mathbb{F}_q
\end{array}
\right\},
$$

$$\mathcal{L}(6, n, \mathbb{F}_q) := \left\{ X := \begin{pmatrix} X_{1,1} & \cdots & X_{1,6} \\ \vdots & & \vdots \\ X_{6,1} & \cdots & X_{6,6} \end{pmatrix} \middle| \begin{array}{l} X_{i,j} \in \mathcal{H}(n, \mathbb{F}_q) \\ \text{for } i, j = 1, \ldots, 6 \end{array} \right\} \bigcap GL(N, \mathbb{F}_q).$$

We note that $\mathcal{L}(6, n, \mathbb{F}_q)$ is a subgroup of $GL(N, \mathbb{F}_q)$ (Lemma 4). For $X \in \mathcal{L}(6, n, \mathbb{F}_q)$, we denote ($\psi$-times) its adjoint matrix $(X^{-1})^{\mathrm{T}}$ as a sparse form

$$(X^{-1})^{\mathrm{T}} := \begin{pmatrix} Y_{1,1} & \cdots & Y_{1,6} \\ \vdots & & \vdots \\ Y_{6,1} & \cdots & Y_{6,6} \end{pmatrix}, \quad \text{where } Y_{i,j} := \begin{pmatrix} \vartheta''_{i,j,1} & & & \\ \vartheta''_{i,j,2} & \vartheta_{i,j} & & \\ \vdots & & \ddots & \\ \vartheta''_{i,j,n-1} & & & \vartheta_{i,j} \\ \vartheta'''_{i,j} & \vartheta'_{i,j,2} & \cdots & \vartheta'_{i,j,n} \end{pmatrix}$$

for $i, j = 1, \ldots, 6$. Here, a blank element in the above matrix denotes $0 \in \mathbb{F}_q$. That is, $X \in \mathcal{L}(6, n, \mathbb{F}_q)$ is represented by $72n$ non-zero entries $\{\mu_{i,j}, \mu'_{i,j,2}, \ldots, \mu'_{i,j,n},$ $\mu''_{i,j,1}, \ldots, \mu''_{i,j,n-1}, \mu'''_{i,j}\}_{i,j=1,\ldots 6}$, and $\psi(X^{-1})^{\mathrm{T}}$ is represented by $72n$ non-zero entries $\{\vartheta_{i,j}, \vartheta'_{i,j,2}, \ldots, \vartheta'_{i,j,n}, \vartheta''_{i,j,1}, \ldots, \vartheta''_{i,j,n-1}, \vartheta'''_{i,j}\}_{i,j=1,\ldots 6}$.

Random dual orthonormal basis generator $\mathcal{G}^{\mathsf{IPE}}_{\mathsf{ob,sp}}$ with *sparse* matrices below is used as a subroutine in the proposed variants of IPE-CC and SIPE schemes.

$\mathcal{G}^{\mathsf{IPE}}_{\mathsf{ob,sp}}(1^\lambda, 6, n):$ $\mathsf{param}_{\mathbb{G}} := (q, \mathbb{G}, \mathbb{G}_T, G, e) \xleftarrow{\mathsf{R}} \mathcal{G}_{\mathsf{bpg}}(1^\lambda),$ $N := 6n,$

$\psi \xleftarrow{\mathsf{U}} \mathbb{F}_q^\times,$ $g_T := e(G, G)^\psi,$ $\mathsf{param}_{\mathbb{V}} := (q, \mathbb{V}, \mathbb{G}_T, \mathbb{A}, e) := \mathcal{G}_{\mathsf{dpvs}}(1^\lambda, N, \mathsf{param}_{\mathbb{G}}),$

$\mathsf{param}_{\mathbb{V}} := (\mathsf{param}'_{\mathbb{V}}, g_T),$ $X \xleftarrow{\mathsf{U}} \mathcal{L}(6, n, \mathbb{F}_q),$

hereafter, $\{\mu_{i,j}, \mu'_{i,j,2}, .., \mu'_{i,j,n}, \mu''_{i,j,1}, .., \mu''_{i,j,n-1}, \mu'''_{i,j}\}_{i,j=1,\ldots 6}$ denotes

non-zero entries of X, and $\{\vartheta_{i,j}, \vartheta'_{i,j,2}, .., \vartheta'_{i,j,n}, \vartheta''_{i,j,1}, .., \vartheta''_{i,j,n-1}, \vartheta'''_{i,j}\}_{i,j=1,\ldots 6}$

denotes non-zero entries of $\psi(X^{-1})^{\mathrm{T}}$,

$\{B_{i,j} := \mu_{i,j}G, B'_{i,j,2} := \mu'_{i,j,2}G, \ldots, B'_{i,j,n} := \mu'_{i,j,n}G,$

$\quad B''_{i,j,1} := \mu''_{i,j,1}G, \ldots, B''_{i,j,n-1} := \mu''_{i,j,n-1}G, B'''_{i,j} := \mu'''_{i,j}G\}_{i,j=1,\ldots 6},$

$\{B^*_{i,j} := \vartheta_{i,j}G, B'^*_{i,j,2} := \vartheta'_{i,j,2}G, \ldots, B'^*_{i,j,n} := \vartheta'_{i,j,n}G,$

$\quad B''^*_{i,j,1} := \vartheta''_{i,j,1}G, \ldots, B''^*_{i,j,n-1} := \vartheta''_{i,j,n-1}G, B'''^*_{i,j} := \vartheta'''_{i,j}G\}_{i,j=1,\ldots 6},$

return $(\mathsf{param}_{\mathbb{V}}, \{B_{i,j}, B'_{i,j,2}, \ldots, B'_{i,j,n}, B''_{i,j,1}, \ldots, B''_{i,j,n-1}, B'''_{i,j}\}_{i,j=1,\ldots 6},$

$\quad \{B^*_{i,j}, B'^*_{i,j,2}, \ldots, B'^*_{i,j,n}, B''^*_{i,j,1}, \ldots, B''^*_{i,j,n-1}, B'''^*_{i,j}\}_{i,j=1,\ldots 6}).$

Remark 3. Let

$$\begin{pmatrix} \boldsymbol{b}_{(i-1)n+1} \\ \vdots \\ \boldsymbol{b}_{in} \end{pmatrix} := \begin{pmatrix} B''_{i,1,1} & B''_{i,1,2} & \cdots & B'''_{i,1} & B''_{i,6,1} & B'''_{i,6,2} & \cdots & B'''_{i,6} \\ & B_{i,1} & & B'_{i,1,2} & & B_{i,6} & & B'_{i,6,2} \\ & & \ddots & \vdots & \cdots & & \ddots & \vdots \\ & & & B'_{i,1,n} & & & & B'_{i,6,n} \end{pmatrix} \tag{1}$$

$$\begin{pmatrix} \boldsymbol{b}^*_{(i-1)n+1} \\ \vdots \\ \boldsymbol{b}^*_{in} \end{pmatrix} := \begin{pmatrix} B''^*_{i,1,1} & & & & B''^*_{i,6,1} \\ B''^*_{i,1,2} & B^*_{i,1} & & & B''^*_{i,6,2} & B^*_{i,6} \\ \vdots & & \ddots & \cdots & \vdots & & \ddots \\ B'''^*_{i,1} & B'^*_{i,1,2} & \cdots & B'^*_{i,1,n} & B'''^*_{i,6} & B'^*_{i,6,2} & \cdots & B'^*_{i,6,n} \end{pmatrix}$$

for $i = 1, \ldots, 6$, and $\mathbb{B} := (\boldsymbol{b}_1, \ldots, \boldsymbol{b}_{6n})$, $\mathbb{B}^* := (\boldsymbol{b}^*_1, \ldots, \boldsymbol{b}^*_{6n})$, where a blank element in the matrices denotes $0 \in \mathbb{G}$. $(\mathbb{B}, \mathbb{B}^*)$ are the dual orthonormal bases, i.e., $e(\boldsymbol{b}_i, \boldsymbol{b}^*_i) = g_T$ and $e(\boldsymbol{b}_i, \boldsymbol{b}^*_j) = 1$ for $1 \le i \ne j \le 6n$.

Here, we assume that input vectors, $\vec{x} := (x_1, \ldots, x_n)$ and $\vec{v} := (v_1, \ldots, v_n)$, satisfies $x_1 \ne 0$ and $v_n \ne 0$. The proposed scheme is given as:

Setup$(1^\lambda, n)$:

$(\mathsf{param}_\mathbb{V}, \{B_{i,j}, B'_{i,j,2}, \ldots, B'_{i,j,n}, B''_{i,j,1}, \ldots, B''_{i,j,n-1}, B'''_{i,j}\}_{i,j=1,\ldots6},$

$\{B^*_{i,j}, B'^*_{i,j,2}, \ldots, B'^*_{i,j,n}, B''^*_{i,j,1}, \ldots, B''^*_{i,j,n-1}, B'''^*_{i,j}\}_{i,j=1,\ldots6}) \xleftarrow{\mathsf{R}} \mathcal{G}^{\mathsf{IPE}}_{\mathsf{ob,sp}}(1^\lambda, 6, n),$

$W \xleftarrow{\mathsf{U}} \mathcal{L}(6, n, \mathbb{F}_q), \quad \begin{pmatrix} \boldsymbol{d}_1 \\ \vdots \\ \boldsymbol{d}_{6n} \end{pmatrix} := \begin{pmatrix} \boldsymbol{b}_1 \\ \vdots \\ \boldsymbol{b}_{6n} \end{pmatrix} \cdot W,$ where $(\boldsymbol{b}_i)_{i=1,\ldots,6n}$ is given in Eq. (1), and $(\boldsymbol{d}_i)_{i=1,\ldots,6n}$ is represented as in Eq. (1) using

$\{D_{i,j}, D'_{i,j,2}, \ldots, D'_{i,j,n}, D''_{i,j,1}, \ldots, D''_{i,j,n-1}, D'''_{i,j}\}_{i,j=1,\ldots6},$

return pk$:= (1^\lambda, \mathsf{param}_\mathbb{V}, \{D_{i,j}, D'_{i,j,2}, .., D'_{i,j,n}, D''_{i,j,1}, .., D''_{i,j,n-1}, D'''_{i,j}\}_{i=1,6; j=1,\ldots,6}),$

ck $:= W, \quad$ sk $:= \{B^*_{i,j}, B'^*_{i,j,2}, .., B'^*_{i,j,n}, B''^*_{i,j,1}, .., B''^*_{i,j,n-1}, B'''^*_{i,j}\}_{i=1,5; j=1,\ldots,6}.$

TokenGen(pk, sk, $\vec{v}$) : $\quad \sigma, \eta_1, \ldots, \eta_n \xleftarrow{\mathsf{U}} \mathbb{F}_q,$

for $j = 1, .., 6, \quad K^*_{j,1} := \sum_{l=1}^{n-1}(\sigma v_l B''^*_{1,j,l} + \eta_l B''^*_{5,j,l}) + \sigma v_n B'''^*_{1,j} + \eta_n B'''^*_{5,j},$

$K^*_{j,l} := \sigma(v_l B'^*_{1,j} + v_n B'^*_{1,j,l}) + \eta_l B^*_{5,j} + \eta_n B'^*_{5,j,l}$ for $l = 2, \ldots, n-1,$

$K^*_{j,n} := \sigma v_n B'^*_{1,j,n} + \eta_n B'^*_{5,j,n},$

$\boldsymbol{k}^* := (K^*_{1,1}, \ldots, K^*_{1,n}, \ldots, K^*_{6,1}, \ldots, K^*_{6,n}) \in \mathbb{G}^{6n}, \quad$ return tk$_{\vec{v}} := \boldsymbol{k}^*.$

Enc(pk, $\vec{x}$) : $\quad \omega, \varphi_1, \ldots, \varphi_n \xleftarrow{\mathsf{U}} \mathbb{F}_q,$

for $j = 1, .., 6, \quad F_{j,1} := \omega x_1 D''_{1,j,1} + \varphi_1 D''_{6,j,1},$

$F_{j,l} := \omega(x_1 D''_{1,j,l} + x_l D_{1,j}) + \varphi_1 D''_{6,j,l} + \varphi_l D_{6,j}$ for $l = 2, \ldots, n-1,$

$F_{j,n} := \omega x_1 D'''_{1,j} + \varphi_1 D'''_{6,j} + \sum_{l=2}^n(\omega x_l D''_{1,j,l} + \varphi_l D''_{6,j,l}),$

$\boldsymbol{f} := (F_{1,1}, \ldots, F_{1,n}, \ldots, F_{6,1}, \ldots, F_{6,n}) \in \mathbb{G}^{6n}, \quad$ return ct$_{\vec{x}} := \boldsymbol{f}.$

Conv(pk, ck $:= W$, ct$_{\vec{x}} := \boldsymbol{f}$) : $\quad \rho \xleftarrow{\mathsf{U}} \mathbb{F}_q, \quad \boldsymbol{y} \xleftarrow{\mathsf{U}} \mathrm{span}\langle \boldsymbol{d}_{5n+1}, \ldots, \boldsymbol{d}_{6n}\rangle,$

$\boldsymbol{c} := (\rho \boldsymbol{f} + \boldsymbol{y}) W^{-1}, \quad$ return CT$_{\vec{x}} := \boldsymbol{c}.$

Query(pk, tk$_{\vec{v}} := \boldsymbol{k}^*$, CT$_{\vec{x}} := \boldsymbol{c}$) :

if $e(\boldsymbol{c}, \boldsymbol{k}^*) = 1,$ return 1, otherwise, return 0.

Remark 4. A part of output of Setup$(1^\lambda, n)$, $\{D_{i,j}, D'_{i,j,2}, \ldots, D'_{i,j,n}, D''_{i,j,1}, \ldots,$ $D''_{i,j,n-1}, D'''_{i,j}\}_{i=1,6; j=1,\ldots6}$, can be identified with $\widehat{\mathbb{D}} := (\boldsymbol{d}_1, \ldots, \boldsymbol{d}_n, \boldsymbol{d}_{5n+1}, \ldots,$ $\boldsymbol{d}_{6n})$, while $\mathbb{D} := (\boldsymbol{d}_1, \ldots, \boldsymbol{d}_{6n})$ is identified with $\{D_{i,j}, D'_{i,j,2}, \ldots, D'_{i,j,n}, D''_{i,j,1},$ $\ldots, D''_{i,j,n-1}, D'''_{i,j}\}_{i,j=1,\ldots6}$ as in Remark 3. Also, $\{B^*_{i,j}, B'^*_{i,j,2}, \ldots, B'^*_{i,j,n}, B''^*_{i,j,1},$

Table 1. Comparison with pairing-based IPE schemes in [12, 17, 21], where $|\mathbb{G}|$ represents size of an element of $\mathbb{G}$. PH, AH, PK, SK, TK, CT, GSD, and C3DH stand for predicate-hiding, attribute-hiding, public key, secret key, token, ciphertext, general subgroup decision [1], and composite 3-party (decisional) Diffie-Hellman [21], respectively.

	KSW08 IPE [12]	OT12 IPE [17] (basic)	(variant)	Proposed IPE-CC (basic)	(variant)	SSW09 SIPE [21]	Proposed SIPE (basic)	(variant)
Setting	public key	public key		public key		secret key	secret key	
Security	selective & fully-AH	adaptive & fully-AH		adaptive & fully-secure (PH & AH)		selective & single-chal. PH & AH	adaptive & fully-secure (PH & AH)	
Order of $\mathbb{G}$	composite	prime		prime		composite	prime	
Assump.	2 variants of GSD	DLIN		DLIN		A variant of GSD, C3DH,DLIN	DLIN	
PK size	$O(n)|\mathbb{G}|$	$O(n^2)|\mathbb{G}|$	$O(n)|\mathbb{G}|$	$O(n^2)|\mathbb{G}|$	$O(n)|\mathbb{G}|$	–	–	–
SK size	$O(n)|\mathbb{G}|$	$O(n^2)|\mathbb{G}|$	$O(n)|\mathbb{G}|$	$O(n^2)|\mathbb{G}|$	$O(n)|\mathbb{G}|$	$O(n)|\mathbb{G}|$	$O(n^2)|\mathbb{G}|$	$O(n)|\mathbb{G}|$
TK size	$(2n+1)|\mathbb{G}|$	$(4n+1)|\mathbb{G}|$	$10|\mathbb{G}|$	$6n|\mathbb{G}|$		$(2n+2)|\mathbb{G}|$	$6n|\mathbb{G}|$	
CT size	$(2n+1)|\mathbb{G}|$	$(4n+1)|\mathbb{G}|$	$5n|\mathbb{G}|$	$6n|\mathbb{G}|$		$(2n+2)|\mathbb{G}|$	$6n|\mathbb{G}|$	

$\ldots, B_{i,j,n-1}''^*, B_{i,j}'''^*\}_{i=1,5;\ j=1,\ldots 6}$ can be identified with $\widehat{\mathbb{B}}^* := (\boldsymbol{b}_1^*, \ldots, \boldsymbol{b}_n^*, \boldsymbol{b}_{4n+1}^*, \ldots, \boldsymbol{b}_{5n}^*)$, while $\mathbb{B}^* := (\boldsymbol{b}_1^*, \ldots, \boldsymbol{b}_{6n}^*)$ is identified with $\{B_{i,j}^*, B_{i,j,2}'^*, \ldots, B_{i,j,n}'^*, B_{i,j,1}''^*, \ldots, B_{i,j,n-1}''^*, B_{i,j}'''^*\}_{i,j=1,\ldots 6}$ in Remark 3. In **Query**, $\boldsymbol{c}$ and $\boldsymbol{k}^*$ can be alternatively described as $\boldsymbol{c} = (\ \overbrace{\omega\vec{x}}^{n},\ \overbrace{0^{3n}}^{3n},\ \overbrace{0^n}^{n},\ \overbrace{\vec{\varphi}}^{n}\ )_{\mathbb{B}}$, $\boldsymbol{k}^* = (\ \overbrace{\sigma\vec{v}}^{n},\ \overbrace{0^{3n}}^{3n},\ \overbrace{\vec{\eta}}^{n},\ \overbrace{0^n}^{n}\ )_{\mathbb{B}^*}$, where $\vec{\varphi} := (\varphi_1, \ldots, \varphi_n), \vec{\eta} := (\eta_1, \ldots, \eta_n) \in \mathbb{F}_q^n$.

Theorem 3. *The proposed IPE-CC scheme (with short public and secret keys) is fully secure under the DLIN assumption.*

Theorem 3 is proven in a similar manner to Theorem 3 (and 4) in [16]. For achieving dual system encryption proof for IPE-CC with employing a sparse matrix, $X \xleftarrow{\mathsf{U}} \mathcal{L}(6, n, \mathbb{F}_q)$, for base change, the matrix set $\mathcal{L}(6, n, \mathbb{F}_q)$ should form a (matrix) group. (For the reason, refer to [16].) Therefore, proofs of Theorem 1 and Theorem 3 have the same high-level structure using the full matrix group $GL(6n, \mathbb{F}_q)$ and a subgroup $\mathcal{L}(6, n, \mathbb{F}_q)$ based on Lemma 4, respectively.

Lemma 4. $\mathcal{L}(6, n, \mathbb{F}_q)$ *is a subgroup of* $GL(6n, \mathbb{F}_q)$.

Lemma 4 is proven in a similar manner to Lemma 2 in the full version of [16].

7   Efficiency Comparisons

Table 1 compares the proposed IPE-CC schemes in Sections 4 and 6 with pairing-based attribute-hiding IPE schemes in [12, 17], and compares the proposed SIPE schemes in Sections 5 (and 6) with pairing-based predicate- and attribute-hiding SIPE scheme in [21].

Acknowledgments. The authors would like to thank anonymous reviewers for their valuable comments.

References

1. Bellare, M., Waters, B., Yilek, S.: Identity-based encryption secure against selective opening attack. In: Ishai (ed.) [11], pp. 235–252
2. Boneh, D., Boyen, X.: Efficient selective-ID secure identity-based encryption without random oracles. In: Cachin, C., Camenisch, J.L. (eds.) EUROCRYPT 2004. LNCS, vol. 3027, pp. 223–238. Springer, Heidelberg (2004)
3. Boneh, D., Boyen, X.: Secure identity based encryption without random oracles. In: Franklin, M. (ed.) CRYPTO 2004. LNCS, vol. 3152, pp. 443–459. Springer, Heidelberg (2004)
4. Boneh, D., Franklin, M.: Identity-based encryption from the weil pairing. In: Kilian, J. (ed.) CRYPTO 2001. LNCS, vol. 2139, pp. 213–229. Springer, Heidelberg (2001)
5. Boneh, D., Kushilevitz, E., Ostrovsky, R., Skeith III, W.E.: Public key encryption that allows PIR queries. In: Menezes, A. (ed.) CRYPTO 2007. LNCS, vol. 4622, pp. 50–67. Springer, Heidelberg (2007)
6. Boneh, D., Raghunathan, A., Segev, G.: Function-private identity-based encryption: Hiding the function in functional encryption. In: Canetti, R., Garay, J.A. (eds.) CRYPTO 2013, Part II. LNCS, vol. 8043, pp. 461–478. Springer, Heidelberg (2013)
7. Boneh, D., Raghunathan, A., Segev, G.: Function-private subspace-membership encryption and its applications. IACR Cryptology ePrint Archive 2013, 403 (2013)
8. Boneh, D., Sahai, A., Waters, B.: Functional encryption: Definitions and challenges. In: Ishai (ed.) [11], pp. 253–273
9. Boneh, D., Waters, B.: Conjunctive, subset, and range queries on encrypted data. In: Vadhan, S.P. (ed.) TCC 2007. LNCS, vol. 4392, pp. 535–554. Springer, Heidelberg (2007)
10. Cocks, C.: An identity based encryption scheme based on quadratic residues. In: Honary, B. (ed.) Cryptography and Coding 2001. LNCS, vol. 2260, pp. 360–363. Springer, Heidelberg (2001)
11. Ishai, Y. (ed.): TCC 2011. LNCS, vol. 6597. Springer, Heidelberg (2011)
12. Katz, J., Sahai, A., Waters, B.: Predicate encryption supporting disjunctions, polynomial equations, and inner products. In: Smart, N.P. (ed.) EUROCRYPT 2008. LNCS, vol. 4965, pp. 146–162. Springer, Heidelberg (2008)
13. Lewko, A.B., Okamoto, T., Sahai, A., Takashima, K., Waters, B.: Fully secure functional encryption: Attribute-based encryption and (hierarchical) inner product encryption. In: Gilbert, H. (ed.) EUROCRYPT 2010. LNCS, vol. 6110, pp. 62–91. Springer, Heidelberg (2010), Full version is available at http://eprint.iacr.org/2010/110
14. Okamoto, T., Takashima, K.: Hierarchical predicate encryption for inner-products. In: Matsui, M. (ed.) ASIACRYPT 2009. LNCS, vol. 5912, pp. 214–231. Springer, Heidelberg (2009)

15. Okamoto, T., Takashima, K.: Fully secure functional encryption with general relations from the decisional linear assumption. In: Rabin, T. (ed.) CRYPTO 2010. LNCS, vol. 6223, pp. 191–208. Springer, Heidelberg (2010), Full version is available at http://eprint.iacr.org/2010/563

16. Okamoto, T., Takashima, K.: Achieving short ciphertexts or short secret-keys for adaptively secure general inner-product encryption. In: Lin, D., Tsudik, G., Wang, X. (eds.) CANS 2011. LNCS, vol. 7092, pp. 138–159. Springer, Heidelberg (2011), Full version is available at http://eprint.iacr.org/2011/648

17. Okamoto, T., Takashima, K.: Adaptively attribute-hiding (hierarchical) inner product encryption. In: Pointcheval, D., Johansson, T. (eds.) EUROCRYPT 2012. LNCS, vol. 7237, pp. 591–608. Springer, Heidelberg (2012), Full version is available at http://eprint.iacr.org/2011/543

18. Okamoto, T., Takashima, K.: Fully secure unbounded inner-product and attribute-based encryption. In: Wang, X., Sako, K. (eds.) ASIACRYPT 2012. LNCS, vol. 7658, pp. 349–366. Springer, Heidelberg (2012), Full version is available at http://eprint.iacr.org/2012/671

19. Okamoto, T., Takashima, K.: Efficient (hierarchical) inner-product encryption tightly reduced from the decisional linear assumption. IEICE Transactions 96-A(1), 42–52 (2013)

20. Park, J.H.: Inner-product encryption under standard assumptions. Des. Codes Cryptography 58(3), 235–257 (2011)

21. Shen, E., Shi, E., Waters, B.: Predicate privacy in encryption systems. In: Reingold, O. (ed.) TCC 2009. LNCS, vol. 5444, pp. 457–473. Springer, Heidelberg (2009)

22. Shi, E., Bethencourt, J., Chan, H.T.H., Song, D.X., Perrig, A.: Multi-dimensional range query over encrypted data. In: IEEE Symposium on Security and Privacy, pp. 350–364. IEEE Computer Society (2007)

23. Yoshino, M., Kunihiro, N., Naganuma, K., Sato, H.: Symmetric inner-product predicate encryption based on three groups. In: Takagi, T., Wang, G., Qin, Z., Jiang, S., Yu, Y. (eds.) ProvSec 2012. LNCS, vol. 7496, pp. 215–234. Springer, Heidelberg (2012)

A   Proposed (Basic 2-Level) Hierarchical IPE-CC Scheme

We refer to Section 1.4 for notations on DPVS. For matrix $W := (w_{i,j})_{i,j=1,\dots,N} \in \mathbb{F}_q^{N \times N}$ and element $\boldsymbol{g} := (G_1, \dots, G_N)$ in N-dimensional $\mathbb{V}$, for notation $\boldsymbol{g}W$, refer to Section 4.1. The hierarchical IPE-CC (HIPE-CC) below is based on the (basic) construction idea given in [13], however, since the scheme has enough hidden subspace and randomness spaces, the security is proven from the DLIN assumption.

$\mathsf{Setup}(1^\lambda, (n_1, n_2))$: $n := n_1 + n_2,$

$$(\mathsf{param}_{\mathbb{V}}, \mathbb{B} := (\boldsymbol{b}_1, \dots, \boldsymbol{b}_{6n}), \mathbb{B}^* := (\boldsymbol{b}_1^*, \dots, \boldsymbol{b}_{6n}^*)) \xleftarrow{\mathsf{R}} \mathcal{G}_{\mathsf{ob}}^{\mathsf{IPE}}(1^\lambda, N := 6n),$$

$$W \xleftarrow{\mathsf{U}} GL(N, \mathbb{F}_q), \quad \boldsymbol{d}_i := \boldsymbol{b}_i W \text{ for } i = 1, \dots, 6n, \quad \mathbb{D} := (\boldsymbol{d}_1, \dots, \boldsymbol{d}_{6n}),$$

$$\widehat{\mathbb{D}} := (\boldsymbol{d}_1, \dots, \boldsymbol{d}_n, \boldsymbol{d}_{5n+1}, \dots, \boldsymbol{d}_{6n}), \quad \widehat{\mathbb{B}}^* := (\boldsymbol{b}_1^*, \dots, \boldsymbol{b}_n^*, \boldsymbol{b}_{4n+1}^*, \dots, \boldsymbol{b}_{5n}^*),$$

return $\mathsf{pk} := (1^\lambda, \mathsf{param}_{\mathbb{V}}, \widehat{\mathbb{D}}), \quad \mathsf{ck} := W, \quad \mathsf{sk} := \widehat{\mathbb{B}}^*.$

$\mathsf{TokenGen}(\mathsf{pk}, \mathsf{sk}, \vec{v}_1 \in \mathbb{F}_q^{n_1} \setminus \{\vec{0}\}) :\quad \sigma, \psi \xleftarrow{\mathsf{U}} \mathbb{F}_q, \ \vec{\eta}_0, \vec{\eta}_1, \ldots, \vec{\eta}_{n_2} \xleftarrow{\mathsf{U}} \mathbb{F}_q^n,$

$$
\begin{array}{llllll}
& \overbrace{\phantom{\sigma\vec{v}_1,\ 0^{n_2},}}^{n} & \overbrace{\phantom{0^{3n},}}^{3n} & \overbrace{\phantom{\vec{\eta}_0,}}^{n} & \overbrace{}^{n} & \\
\boldsymbol{k}_0^* := (& \sigma\vec{v}_1, \ 0^{n_2}, & 0^{3n}, & \vec{\eta}_0, & 0^n &)_{\mathbb{B}^*}, \\
\boldsymbol{k}_i^* := (& \sigma\vec{v}_1, \ \psi\vec{e}_i, & 0^{3n}, & \vec{\eta}_i, & 0^n &)_{\mathbb{B}^*} \ \text{for } i = 1, \ldots, n_2,
\end{array}
$$

$$\text{where } \vec{e}_i := (\ 0^{i-1}, \ 1, \ 0^{n_2-i}\ ),$$

$\quad$ return $\mathsf{tk}_{\vec{v}_1} := (\ \boldsymbol{k}_0^*, \ \boldsymbol{k}_1^*, \ldots, \boldsymbol{k}_{n_2}^*\ ).$

$\mathsf{Enc}(\mathsf{pk}, \ \vec{x}_1 \in \mathbb{F}_q^{n_1} \setminus \{\vec{0}\}, \ \vec{x}_2 \in \mathbb{F}_q^{n_2}) :\quad \tau_1, \tau_2 \xleftarrow{\mathsf{U}} \mathbb{F}_q, \ \vec{\xi} \xleftarrow{\mathsf{U}} \mathbb{F}_q^n,$

$\quad$ if $\vec{x}_2 = \vec{0}, \ \vec{x}_2' \xleftarrow{\mathsf{U}} \mathbb{F}_q^{n_2},$ else $\vec{x}_2' := \vec{x}_2,$

$$
\begin{array}{llllll}
& \overbrace{\phantom{\tau_1\vec{x}_1,\ \tau_2\vec{x}_2',}}^{n} & \overbrace{\phantom{0^{3n},}}^{3n} & \overbrace{}^{n} & \overbrace{\phantom{\vec{\xi}}}^{n} & \\
\boldsymbol{f} := (& \tau_1\vec{x}_1, \ \tau_2\vec{x}_2', & 0^{3n}, & 0^n, & \vec{\xi} &)_{\mathbb{D}}, \quad \text{return } \mathsf{ct}_{\vec{x}} := \boldsymbol{f}.
\end{array}
$$

$\mathsf{Conv}(\mathsf{pk}, \ \mathsf{ck} := W, \ \mathsf{ct}_{\vec{x}} := \boldsymbol{f}) :\quad \rho \xleftarrow{\mathsf{U}} \mathbb{F}_q, \ \boldsymbol{y} \xleftarrow{\mathsf{U}} \mathrm{span}\langle \boldsymbol{d}_{5n+1}, \ldots, \boldsymbol{d}_{6n}\rangle,$

$\quad \boldsymbol{c} := (\rho\boldsymbol{f} + \boldsymbol{y})\,W^{-1}, \quad \text{return } \mathsf{CT}_{\vec{x}} := \boldsymbol{c}.$

$\mathsf{Query}(\mathsf{pk}, \ \mathsf{tk} := \mathsf{tk}_{\vec{v}_1} \text{ or } \mathsf{tk}_{(\vec{v}_1,\vec{v}_2)}, \ \mathsf{CT}_{\vec{x}} := \boldsymbol{c}) :$

$\quad$ if $\mathsf{tk} = \mathsf{tk}_{\vec{v}_1} = (\ \boldsymbol{k}_0^*, \ \boldsymbol{k}_1^*, \ldots, \boldsymbol{k}_{n_2}^*\ ),$

$\qquad$ if $e(\boldsymbol{c}, \boldsymbol{k}_0^*) = 1,$ output 1, $\ $ otherwise, output 0.

$\quad$ if $\mathsf{tk} = \mathsf{tk}_{(\vec{v}_1,\vec{v}_2)} = \widetilde{\boldsymbol{k}}^*,$ if $e(\boldsymbol{c}, \widetilde{\boldsymbol{k}}^*) = 1,$ output 1, $\ $ otherwise, output 0.

$\mathsf{Delegate}(\mathsf{pk}, \ \mathsf{tk}_{\vec{v}_1} := (\ \boldsymbol{k}_0^*, \ \boldsymbol{k}_1^*, \ldots, \boldsymbol{k}_{n_2}^*\ ), \ \vec{v}_2 := (v_{2,1}, \ldots, v_{2,n_2}) \in \mathbb{F}_q^{n_2} \setminus \{\vec{0}\}) :$

$\quad \xi, \delta \xleftarrow{\mathsf{U}} \mathbb{F}_q, \ \vec{\eta}' := (\eta_1', \ldots, \eta_n') \xleftarrow{\mathsf{U}} \mathbb{F}_q^n,$

$\quad \widetilde{\boldsymbol{k}}^* := \xi\boldsymbol{k}_0^* + \delta(\sum_{i=1}^{n_2} v_{2,i}\boldsymbol{k}_i^*) + \sum_{i=1}^n \eta_i' \boldsymbol{b}_{4n+i}^*,$

$\quad$ return $\mathsf{tk}_{(\vec{v}_1,\vec{v}_2)}(= \mathsf{tk}_{\vec{v}_1 \wedge \vec{v}_2}) := \widetilde{\boldsymbol{k}}^*.$

The full security notion of IPE-CC is extended to that for (2-level) HIPE-CC schemes in a usual way. The proof of Theorem 4 is given in the full paper.

Theorem 4. *The proposed (2-level) HIPE-CC scheme is fully secure under the DLIN assumption.*

Remark:

1. While we present a 2-level HIPE-CC scheme here, clearly, the construction can be extended to an arbitrary level HIPE-CC scheme.
2. While the above basic HIPE-CC scheme is built based on [13], if we apply several techniques given in [15, 16], efficiency of the HIPE scheme is greatly improved.

B Definition of Symmetric-Key Inner Product Encryption (SIPE)

This section defines symmetric-key inner product encryption (SIPE) and its security.

An attribute (or plaintext) of inner product predicates is expressed as a vector $\vec{x} \in \mathbb{F}_q^n \setminus \{\vec{0}\}$ and a predicate $f_{\vec{v}}$ is associated with a vector $\vec{v}$, where $f_{\vec{v}}(\vec{x}) = 1$ iff $\vec{v} \cdot \vec{x} = 0$. Let $\Sigma := \mathbb{F}_q^n \setminus \{\vec{0}\}$, i.e., the set of the attributes, and $\mathcal{F} := \{f_{\vec{v}} | \vec{v} \in \mathbb{F}_q^n \setminus \{\vec{0}\}\}$ i.e., the set of the predicates.

Definition 5. *A symmetric-key inner product encryption scheme (SIPE) for predicates $\mathcal{F}$ and attributes Σ consists of probabilistic polynomial-time algorithms* Setup, TokenGen, Enc *and* Query. *They are given as follows:*

- Setup *takes as input security parameter 1^λ, and it outputs a secret key* sk.
- TokenGen *takes as input a secret key* sk, *and a predicate vector $\vec{v}$. It outputs a corresponding token* $\mathsf{tk}_{\vec{v}}$.
- Enc *takes as input a secret key* sk *and an attribute (or plaintext) vector $\vec{x}$. It returns a ciphertext* $\mathsf{ct}_{\vec{x}}$.
- Query *takes as input a token* $\mathsf{tk}_{\vec{v}}$ *and a ciphertext* $\mathsf{ct}_{\vec{x}}$. *It outputs either 0 or 1, indicating the value of the predicate $f_{\vec{v}}$ evaluated on the underlying attribute $\vec{x}$.*

An SIPE scheme should have the following correctness property: for all $\mathsf{sk} \xleftarrow{\mathsf{R}}$ Setup$(1^\lambda, n)$, all $f_{\vec{v}} \in \mathcal{F}$ and $\vec{x} \in \Sigma$, all $\mathsf{tk}_{\vec{v}} \xleftarrow{\mathsf{R}}$ TokenGen$(\mathsf{sk}, \vec{v})$, all ciphertext $\mathsf{ct}_{\vec{x}} \xleftarrow{\mathsf{R}}$ Enc$(\mathsf{sk}, \vec{x})$, it holds that $1 = $ Query$(\mathsf{tk}_{\vec{v}}, \mathsf{ct}_{\vec{x}})$ if $f_{\vec{v}}(\vec{x}) = 1$. Otherwise, it holds with negligible probability.

We then define the *full* security notion of SIPE, which is the same as that given by Shen, Shi, and Waters [21].

Definition 6 (Full Security of SIPE). *The model for defining the full security of SIPE against adversary $\mathcal{A}$ is given as follows:*

1. *The challenger runs* Setup *to generate secret key* sk, *and picks a random bit b.*
2. *$\mathcal{A}$ may adaptively make a polynomial number of queries, where each query is one of two types:*
   - *On the ℓ-th ciphertext query, $\mathcal{A}$ outputs two attribute vectors $(\vec{x}_\ell^{(0)}, \vec{x}_\ell^{(1)})$. The challenger responds with $\mathsf{ct}_\ell \xleftarrow{\mathsf{R}}$ Enc$(\mathsf{sk}, \vec{x}_\ell^{(b)})$.*
   - *On the h-th token query, $\mathcal{A}$ outputs two predicate vectors, $(\vec{v}_h^{(0)}, \vec{v}_h^{(1)})$. The challenger responds with $\mathsf{tk}_h \xleftarrow{\mathsf{R}}$ TokenGen$(\mathsf{sk}, \vec{v}_h^{(b)})$.*
   $\mathcal{A}$'s queries are subject to the restriction that, for all ciphertext queries $(\vec{x}_\ell^{(0)}, \vec{x}_\ell^{(1)})$ and all token queries $(\vec{v}_h^{(0)}, \vec{v}_h^{(1)})$, $f_{\vec{v}_h^{(0)}}(\vec{x}_\ell^{(0)}) = f_{\vec{v}_h^{(1)}}(\vec{x}_\ell^{(1)})$.
3. *$\mathcal{A}$ outputs a guess b' of b.*

The success experiment in the above game, i.e., $b' = b$, is denoted by $\mathsf{Succ}_\mathcal{A}(\lambda)$, and the advantage of $\mathcal{A}$ is defined as $\mathsf{Adv}_\mathcal{A}^{\mathsf{SIPE}}(\lambda) := \Pr[\mathsf{Succ}_\mathcal{A}(\lambda)] - 1/2$ for any security parameter λ. An SIPE scheme is fully secure *if all probabilistic polynomial-time adversaries $\mathcal{A}$ have at most negligible advantage in the above game.*

Fast Symmetric Pairing Revisited

Xusheng Zhang[1,*] and Kunpeng Wang[2,**]

[1] Institute of Software, Chinese Academy of Sciences, Beijing
xszhang.is@gmail.com
[2] Institute of Information Engineering, Chinese Academy of Sciences, Beijing
kunpengwang@263.net

Abstract. During the past decade pairing-based cryptosystems have been through a huge development, and the implementation of bilinear pairings has been improved greatly. Two pairing models, namely symmetric and asymmetric pairings, are widely used and have common cryptographic properties in most cryptosystems. Symmetric pairings are more convenient to construct cryptographic schemes, but asymmetric pairings are more efficient and suitable for implementation due to their flexible embedding degrees. In this paper we revisit symmetric pairings on supersingular elliptic curves over large characteristic fields. We show that a special family of supersingular elliptic curves with embedding degree 3 admits a kind of fast symmetric pairings, whose computational costs might be twice the costs for the current fastest asymmetric pairings.

Keywords: Supersingular Elliptic Curve, Verschiebung Isogeny, Symmetric Pairing.

1 Introduction

In pairing-based cryptography, the symmetric pairing $e : G_1 \times G_1 \rightarrow G_3$ can be used to simplify cryptographic schemes; however, from the point of view of the implementation, the asymmetric pairing $e : G_1 \times G_2 \rightarrow G_3$ can greatly improve the efficiency. The key reason is that symmetric pairings are only constructed on supersingular (hyper-)elliptic curves with bounded embedding degrees, but asymmetric pairings can be derived on ordinary curves with flexible embedding degrees. Hence, many significant improvements have been proposed to speed up asymmetric pairing computations and optimise ordinary pairing-friendly curve constructions.

As far as we know, η_T pairings [7] derived on supersingular curves over binary and ternary fields, are the well-known fast symmetric pairings, and have some computational advantages for hardware implementation. But with the research going on, the computational advantage in hardware of symmetric pairing may be

---

* The majority of this work was done while the first author was doing his Ph.D research in Institute of Software, Chinese Academy of Sciences during 2012.
** Supported by the National Natural Science Foundation of China No.61272040 and the Strategic Research Program of Chinese Academy of Sciences No.XDA06010702.

Z. Cao and F. Zhang (Eds.): Pairing 2013, LNCS 8365, pp. 131–148, 2014.

less obvious than ever thought before. For example, at the 128-bit security level, the η_T pairing [9] on supersingular elliptic curve over $\mathbb{F}_{2^{1223}}$ can be computed in 0.19ms in hardware [19]. The currently fastest asymmetric pairing, namely the optimal ate pairing [36] on Barreto-Naehrig (BN) curves [9], can be computed in 0.37ms in hardware [20,37]. Besides, the software optimizations for symmetric pairings are relatively rare and only focused on the η_T pairing over binary field [14,5]. Also, at the 128-bit security level, the optimal ate pairing on the BN curve [4] can be computed in 0.52ms, which is at least three times faster than the parallel implementation of the η_T pairing on supersingular elliptic curve over $\mathbb{F}_{2^{1223}}$ [5]. Moreover, at higher security levels (e.g. the 192/256-bit security levels) the symmetric pairing computations would be much more expensive than the asymmetric cases and seem inconvenient in practice.

Very recently, Joux [26] presented a new DLP algorithm in $\mathbb{F}_{q^n}$ with a running time of $L[1/4 + o(1)]$ when q and n are balanced in the sense that $q \approx m$ where $n = 2m$. Later, Barbulescu, Gaudry, Joux and Thomé [6] presented another new DLP algorithm in $\mathbb{F}_{q^n}$ that is asymptotically faster than all previous algorithms. Specifically, when $n = 2m$, $q \approx m$ and $m \leq q+2$, the discrete logarithm problem can be solved in quasi-polynomial time $(\log Q)^{O(\log \log Q)}$ where $Q = q^n = q^{2m}$. Then, Adj, Menezes, Oliveira and Rodríguez-Henríquez [1] combined the new algorithms by Joux and Barbulescu et al. to solve the DLP in $\mathbb{F}_{3^{6 \cdot 509}}$ in $2^{73.7}$ time. So, these major breakthroughs in computing discrete logarithms in finite fields of small and medium characteristic, greatly weaken the security of pairing-based cryptosystems that use pairings derived from supersingular (hyper)elliptic curves over finite fields of characteristic 2 or 3.

In this paper, we revisit fast symmetric pairings by studying pairings derived from supersingular elliptic curves over large characteristic fields, in order to explore efficient and secure symmetric pairings. Concretely, we give a method to generate special supersingular curves over large characteristic extension fields, and then develop new fast symmetric pairings on these curves.

This paper is organized as follows: Section 2 provides basics of elliptic curve pairings. In Section 3, we first formulated the Verschiebung isogeny $\hat{\pi}_p$ and endomorphism $[p]$ on supersingular elliptic curves over extension fields $\mathbb{F}_{p^n}$, and then study two special supersingular curves of the pairing-friendly forms $y^2 = x^3 + ax$ and $y^2 = x^3 + b$ over large characteristic fields $\mathbb{F}_{p^n}$. We present our main results (Theorem 4) in Section 4, that is the construction of new symmetric pairing on supersingular elliptic curves with embedding degrees 3 over extension fields $\mathbb{F}_{p^{2m}}$ where $p > 3$. Furthermore, we develop an algorithm (Theorem 5) to generate a special family of supersingular elliptic curves, and provide suggested curves at the 80/128/192-bit security levels to accelerate the computation of our new symmetric pairings. Especially at the 80-bit security level, our algorithm can generate more suitable curves over the extension of optimal prime fields, that fits for fast Montgomery modular reduction (multiplication).

To speed up the computation of our new pairing, we develop a modified multi-Miller's algorithm, and utilize the Miller's formulas for curves $y^2 = x^3 + b$ with only cubic twist in [38] and refine these formulas for the case of square element *b*. Then we show that theoretically the cost of our new symmetric pairing for the 80-bit security is close to the recommended fast asymmetric pairing (the Tate pairing on MNT curve); and the costs of our new symmetric pairings for the 128/192-bit securities are nearly twice the costs for the current fastest asymmetric pairings (i.e. the optimal ate pairing on BN curve and the ate pairing on BLS12 curve).

2   Background

Let E be an elliptic curve over a field $\mathbb{F}_q$, where q is a power of prime p and $\mathcal{O}$ is the neutral element of the group E. From the Hasse's theorem, $\#E(\mathbb{F}_q) = q - t + 1$, where t is the Frobenius trace. Let $\pi_q(x, y) = (x^q, y^q)$ be the (q-th power) Frobenius endomorphism which is purely inseparable, and $\widehat{\pi}_q$ denotes the dual Frobenius endomorphism of π_q (also called Verschiebung endomorphism). $E/\mathbb{F}_q$ is called supersingular if $p \mid t$, or the Verschiebung endomorphism $\widehat{\pi}_q$ is purely inseparable; otherwise, $E/\mathbb{F}_q$ is called ordinary. Let r be the subgroup order of $E(\mathbb{F}_q)$ which is coprime to q. If $k > 1$ is the smallest integer such that $r \mid q^k - 1$, then k is called the embedding degree with respect to r. For supersingular elliptic curves, the embedding degrees are 2, 3, 4, and 6 (refer to [29]). Specially when $p > 3$, the largest embedding degree of supersingular elliptic curves is three.

For $P, Q \in E[r]$, there exist rational functions f_P and f_Q with divisor $\text{div}(f_{r,P}) = r(P) - r(\mathcal{O})$ and $\text{div}(f_{r,Q}) = r(Q) - r(\mathcal{O})$. Let $\mu_r \subset \mathbb{F}_{q^k}^*$ denote the group of r-th roots of unity. The reduced Tate pairing [8] is given as[1]

$$t_r : E(\mathbb{F}_q)[r] \times E(\mathbb{F}_{q^k})[r] \to \mu_r, \quad (P, Q) \mapsto f_{r,P}(Q)^{(q^k - 1)/r}.$$

The rational function $f_{n,R} \in \mathbb{F}_{q^k}(E)$ with divisor $\text{div}(f_{n,R}) = n(R) - ([n]R) - (n - 1)(\mathcal{O})$ can be computed by Miller's algorithm [30,31] with the property $f_{i_1+i_2,P} = f_{i_1,P} \cdot f_{i_2,P} \cdot l_{[i_1]P,[i_2]P}/v_{[i_1+i_2]P}$, where $l_{[i_1]P,[i_2]P}$ is the line passing through $[i_1]P$, $[i_2]P$, and $v_{[i_1+i_2]P}$ is the vertical line passing through $[i_1 + i_2]P$.

For supersingular curves, there exists distortion map ψ that maps a point of $E(\mathbb{F}_q)[r]$ to a distinct subgroup of $E(\mathbb{F}_{q^k})[r]$. By using the distortion map, the symmetric Tate pairing can be simplified as

$$t_r : E(\mathbb{F}_q)[r] \times E(\mathbb{F}_q)[r] \to \mu_r, \quad (P, P') \mapsto f_{r,P}(\psi(P'))^{(q^k - 1)/r}.$$

In a significant breakthrough, Barreto *et al.* [7] proposed the truncated pairing on supersingular curves with shorter Miller's loop length, namely η_T pairing (Theorem 1), and specifically optimized their η_T pairings on supersingular elliptic curves over $\mathbb{F}_{2^m}$ and $\mathbb{F}_{3^m}$.

Theorem 1. ([7], η_T pairing) *Let E be a supersingular elliptic curve over $\mathbb{F}_q$ with distortion map ψ and embedding degree $k > 1$. Let P and P' be non-neutral*

---

[1] In fact, Tate pairing is defined on $E(\mathbb{F}_q)[r] \times E(\mathbb{F}_{q^k})/rE(\mathbb{F}_{q^k})$, and an hypothesis is missing here. In [15], for a supersingular elliptic curve over $\mathbb{F}_q$, if $r > 4\sqrt{q}$, then $E(\mathbb{F}_{q^k})[r] \cap rE(\mathbb{F}_{q^k}) = \{\mathcal{O}\}$. Thus $E(\mathbb{F}_{q^k})[r]$ is isomorphic to $E(\mathbb{F}_{q^k})/rE(\mathbb{F}_{q^k})$.

points on $E(\mathbb{F}_q)$ with order r. Suppose T is such that: 1. $T \equiv q \pmod{r}$; 2. $\gamma(P) = [T]P$, where $\gamma \in \mathrm{Aut}(E)$ is defined over $\mathbb{F}_q$; 3. $\gamma \circ \psi^{(q)} = \psi$, where $\psi^{(q)}$ means the function obtained by applying the q-power Frobenius map to the coefficients of ψ. Then

$$\eta_T : E(\mathbb{F}_q)[r] \times E(\mathbb{F}_q)[r] \to \mu_r, \ (P, P') \mapsto f_{T,P}\big(\psi(P')\big)^{(q^k-1)/r}$$

defines a pairing , which is non-degenerate if and only if $T^k \not\equiv 1 \pmod{r^2}$.

3   Supersingular Elliptic Curves over Large Characteristic Fields

The results in [7] have shown good properties of special supersingular elliptic curves over $\mathbb{F}_2$ and $\mathbb{F}_3$ fitting for pairing computation. In this section we study properties of supersingular curves $E : y^2 = x^3 + ax + b$ over large characteristic fields $\mathbb{F}_q$ with $p = \mathrm{char}(\mathbb{F}_q) > 3$ and $q = p^n$.

3.1   Verschiebung Isogeny $\widehat{\pi}_p$ and Endomorphism $[p]$

Let $E^{(p^i)}$ denote the curve of the form $y^2 = x^3 + a^{p^i}x + b^{p^i}$ over $\mathbb{F}_{p^n}$. When the curve E is supersingular, both the endomorphism $[p]$ and the p-th power Verschiebung isogeny $\widehat{\pi}_p \in \mathrm{Hom}(E^{(p)}, E)$ are purely inseparable, and therefore there exists a decomposition $\widehat{\pi}_p = \phi \circ \pi_p$ where $\phi \in \mathrm{Hom}(E^{(p^2)}, E)$ is an isomorphism. Since $E^{(p^2)}$ and E are isomorphic it follows that $a^{3p^2} \cdot b^2 = a^3 \cdot b^{2p^2}$. Concretely, we formulate the p^i-th power Verschiebung isogeny $\widehat{\pi}_{p^i} \in \mathrm{Hom}(E^{(p^i)}, E)$ and the endomorphism $[p^i] \in \mathrm{End}(E)$ in the following proposition.

Besides, we recall an important necessary and sufficient condition ensuring elliptic curve $y^2 = x^3 + ax + b$ is supersingular, that is the coefficient of term x^{p-1} in $(x^3 + ax + b)^{(p-1)/2}$ is zero ([35]). Thus, for the case of $a = 0$, the condition is equivalent to $p \equiv 5 \pmod 6$; for the case of $b = 0$, the condition is equivalent to $p \equiv 3 \pmod 4$.

Proposition 1. *Let E be a supersingular curve of the form $y^2 = x^3 + ax + b$ over $\mathbb{F}_{p^n}$ with characteristic $p > 3$, and j-invariant $j(E) \in \mathbb{F}_p$. If $a \cdot b \neq 0$, then $\widehat{\pi}_{p^i}(x, y) = (x^{p^i}/a^{(p^{2i}-1)/2}, (-1)^i y^{p^i}/b^{(p^{2i}-1)/2})$ and $[p^i](x, y) = (x^{p^{2i}}/a^{(p^{2i}-1)/2}, (-1)^i y^{p^{2i}}/b^{(p^{2i}-1)/2})$. Especially, if $b = 0$, then $\widehat{\pi}_{p^i}(x, y) = (x^{p^i}/a^{(p^{2i}-1)/2}, (-1)^i y^{p^i}/a^{3(p^{2i}-1)/4})$. If $a = 0$, then $\widehat{\pi}_{p^i}(x, y) = (x^{p^i}/b^{(p^{2i}-1)/3}, (-1)^i y^{p^i}/b^{(p^{2i}-1)/2})$.*

Proof. Case: $a \cdot b \neq 0$. Since $j(E) \in \mathbb{F}_p$, then $j(E) = j(E^{(p)})$, i.e. $E \cong E^p$, and therefore $a^{3p} \cdot b^2 = a^3 \cdot b^{2p}$, i.e. $a^{3(p-1)} = b^{2(p-1)}$. Since $p + 1$ is even it follows that $a^{3(p^2-1)/2} = b^{(p^2-1)}$. Then it is easy to verify that $\phi_1(x, y) = (x/a^{(p^2-1)/2}, y/b^{(p^2-1)/2}) \in \mathrm{Hom}(E^{(p^2)}, E)$ is an isomorphism. Since $\#\mathrm{Aut}(E) = 2$, then the isomorphism ϕ satisfying $\widehat{\pi}_p = \phi \circ \pi_p$ equals ϕ_1 or $-\phi_1$.

Suppose $\phi = \phi_1$, then $[p] = \phi \circ \pi_p \circ \pi_p = (x^{p^2}/a^{(p^2-1)/2}, y^{p^2}/b^{(p^2-1)/2})$. Let $\psi(x,y) = (x^p/a^{(p-1)/2}, y^p/b^{(p-1)/2}) \in \text{End}(E)$ defined over $\mathbb{F}_{p^n}$, we can deduce $\psi^2 = [p]$ and $\widehat{\psi} = \psi$. From the theory of endomorphism rings (refer to [35]), when $\widehat{\psi} = \psi$, then ψ is a scalar multiplication. But this contradicts that p is prime. Thus we have $\phi = -\phi_1$, and therefore $\widehat{\pi}_p(x,y) = (x^p/a^{(p^2-1)/2}, -y^p/b^{(p^2-1)/2})$ and $[p](x,y) = (x^{p^2}/a^{(p^2-1)/2}, -y^{p^2}/b^{(p^2-1)/2})$. By induction, assume that $\widehat{\pi}_{p^{i-1}}(x,y) = (x^{p^{i-1}}/a^{(p^{2(i-1)}-1)/2}, (-1)^{i-1}y^{p^{i-1}}/b^{(p^{2(i-1)}-1)/2})$. Then, for $\widehat{\pi}_p^{(i)}(x,y) = (x^p/a^{p^{i-1}(p^2-1)/2}, -y^p/b^{p^{i-1}(p^2-1)/2}) \in \text{Hom}(E^{(p^i)}, E^{(p^{i-1})})$, we have $\widehat{\pi}_{p^i}(x,y) = \widehat{\pi}_{p^{i-1}} \circ \widehat{\pi}_p^{(i)}(x,y) = (x^{p^i}/a^{(p^{2i}-1)/2}, (-1)^i y^{p^i}/b^{(p^{2i}-1)/2})$.

Case: $b = 0$. It is easy to verify $\phi_1(x,y) = (x/a^{(p^2-1)/2}, y/a^{3(p^2-1)/4})$ is an isomorphism between $E^{(p^2)}$ and E. Since $\#\text{Aut}(E) = 4$, then the isomorphism ϕ satisfying $\widehat{\pi}_p = \phi \circ \pi_p$ may have four choices. If $\phi(x,y) = (\zeta_4^2 x/a^{(p^2-1)/2}, \zeta_4^3 y/a^{3(p^2-1)/4})$ where ζ_4 is a primitive 4-th root of unity, since $p \equiv 3 \pmod 4$ and $\zeta_4^p = -\zeta_4$ it follows that $\pi_p \circ [p] = -[p]^{(p)} \circ \pi_p$, where $[p]^{(p)}$ denotes the p-multiplication on $E^{(p)}$. But this contradicts the commutativity of scalar multiplication. Similarly, if $\phi = \phi_1$, we take an endomorphism $\psi(x,y) = (x^p/a^{(p-1)/2}, y^p/a^{3(p-1)/4})$ satisfying $\psi^2 = [p]$ to give another contradiction. So, the only available choice for ϕ is $-\phi_1$, then $\widehat{\pi}_{p^i}(x,y) = (x^{p^i}/a^{(p^{2i}-1)/2}, (-1)^i y^{p^i}/a^{3(p^{2i}-1)/4})$ by using the similar analysis above.

Case: $a = 0$. Similarly, since $\phi_1(x,y) = (x/b^{(p^2-1)/3}, y/b^{(p^2-1)/2})$ is an isomorphism between $E^{(p^2)}$ and E, and $\#\text{Aut}(E) = 6$, then the isomorphism ϕ may have six choices. If $\phi(x,y) = (\zeta_6^2 x/a^{(p^2-1)/2}, \zeta_6^3 y/a^{3(p^2-1)/4})$, where ζ_6 is a primitive 6-th root of unity. Since $p \equiv 5 \pmod 6$ and $\zeta_6^{2p} = \zeta_6^4$, then $\pi_p \circ [p] \neq [p]^{(p)} \circ \pi_p$, which contradicts the commutativity of scalar multiplication. Then we can also deduce a contradiction for the case of $\phi = \phi_1$. Thus we only have $\phi = -\phi_1$, and then $\widehat{\pi}_{p^i}(x,y) = (x^{p^i}/b^{(p^{2i}-1)/3}, (-1)^i y^{p^i}/b^{(p^{2i}-1)/2})$. $\square$

3.2   Special Supersingular Elliptic Curves

As with the constructions of pairing-friendly ordinary elliptic curves, we study two attractive forms of pairing-friendly curves $y^2 = x^3 + ax$ and $y^2 = x^3 + b$ in the supersingular case, by characterizing the relations between their curve's orders and their equations.

Theorem 2. *Let $p > 3$ be prime and let $E : y^2 = x^3 + ax$ be a supersingular elliptic curve where $a \in \mathbb{F}_{p^n}^*$. Then $\#E(\mathbb{F}_{p^n})$ satisfies one of the following conditions*

1. $\#E(\mathbb{F}_{p^n}) = p^n + 1$, *if and only if, n is odd, or n is even and a is not a square;*
2. $\#E(\mathbb{F}_{p^{2m}}) = (p^m - 1)^2$, *if and only if, m is even and a is a quartic residue, or m is odd and a is a square but not quartic residue;*
3. $\#E(\mathbb{F}_{p^{2m}}) = (p^m + 1)^2$, *if and only if, m is even and a is a square but not quartic residue, or m is odd and a is a quartic residue.*

Proof. When n is odd, $p^n \equiv 3 \pmod 4$, then $a^{(p^{2n}-1)/2} = a^{3(p^{2n}-1)/4} = 1$, thus $\widehat{\pi}_{p^n}(x,y) = (x^{p^n}, (-1)^n y^{p^n}) = -\pi_{p^n}(x,y)$ from Proposition 1, i.e. $tr(\pi_{p^n}) = 0$. When $n = 2m$, $p^{2m} \equiv 1 \pmod 4$, then $a^{(p^{4m}-1)/2} = 1$ and $a^{3(p^{4m}-1)/4} = \pm 1$, thus $\pi_{p^{2m}} = \widehat{\pi}_{p^{2m}}$ or $\pi_{p^{2m}} = -\widehat{\pi}_{p^{2m}}$, i.e. $tr(\pi_{p^{2m}}) = 0$ or $\pm 2p^m$. If a is not a square, since $a^{(p^{4m}-1)/2} = 1$ and $a^{3(p^{4m}-1)/4} = -1$, then $\widehat{\pi}_{p^{2m}}(x,y) = (x^{p^{2m}}, -y^{p^{2m}}) = -\pi_{p^{2m}}(x,y)$, i.e $tr(\pi_{p^n}) = 0$. If a is a square, we have $a^{(p^{4m}-1)/2} = a^{3(p^{4m}-1)/4} = 1$, then deduce $\widehat{\pi}_{p^{2m}} = \pi_{p^{2m}}$. Furthermore, since $[p^m](x,y) = (x^{p^{2m}}/a^{(p^{2m}-1)/2}, (-1)^m y^{p^{2m}}/a^{3(p^{2m}-1)/4})$, and if a is a quartic residue, then $[p^m](x,y) = (x^{p^{2m}}, (-1)^m y^{p^{2m}})$. Thus, we deduce that $tr(\pi_{p^n}) = 2p^m$ when m is even, or $tr(\pi_{p^{2m}}) = -2p^m$ when m is odd. If a is a quartic non-residue, then $[p^m](x,y) = (x^{p^{2m}}, (-1)^{m+1} y^{p^{2m}})$, and therefore we have $tr(\pi_{p^n}) = 2p^m$ when m is odd, or $tr(\pi_{p^n}) = -2p^m$ when m is odd.   □

Theorem 3. *Let $p > 3$ be prime and let $E : y^2 = x^3 + b$ be a supersingular elliptic curve where $b \in \mathbb{F}_{p^n}^*$. Then $\#E(\mathbb{F}_{p^n})$ satisfies one of the following conditions*

1. $\#E(\mathbb{F}_{p^n}) = p^n + 1$, if and only if, n is odd.
2. $\#E(\mathbb{F}_{p^{2m}}) = (p^m - 1)^2$, if and only if, m is odd and b is a cube but not square, or m is even and b is a cube and square;
3. $\#E(\mathbb{F}_{p^{2m}}) = (p^m + 1)^2$, if and only if, m is even and b is a cube but not square, or m is odd and b is a cube and square.
4. $\#E(\mathbb{F}_{p^{2m}}) = p^{2m} - p^m + 1$, if and only if, m is odd and b is a square but not cube, or m is even and b is not a square nor cube;
5. $\#E(\mathbb{F}_{p^{2m}}) = p^{2m} + p^m + 1$, if and only if, m is even and b is a square but not cube, or m is odd and b is not a square nor cube;

Proof. When n is odd, $p^n \equiv 2 \pmod 3$, then $b^{(p^{2n}-1)/2} = b^{(p^{2n}-1)/3} = 1$, thus $\widehat{\pi}_{p^n}(x,y) = (x^{p^n}, (-1)^n y^{p^n}) = -\pi_{p^n}(x,y)$ from Proposition 1, i.e. $tr(\pi_{p^n}) = 0$. When $n = 2m$ is even, $tr(\pi_{p^n})$ may equals 0, $\pm p$, or $\pm 2p$. Then we discuss each case as follows.

If b is a cube, then $\widehat{\pi}_{p^{2m}}(x,y) = (x^{p^{2m}}/b^{(p^{4m}-1)/3}, y^{p^{2m}}/b^{(p^{4m}-1)/2}) = (x^{p^{2m}}, y^{p^{2m}}) = \pi_{p^{2m}}(x,y)$. Furthermore, $[p^m](x,y) = (x^{p^{2m}}/b^{(p^{2m}-1)/3}, (-1)^m y^{p^{2m}}/b^{(p^{2m}-1)/2}) = (x^{p^{2m}}, (-1)^m y^{p^{2m}}/b^{(p^{2m}-1)/2})$. Thus, we deduce that $tr(\pi_{p^{2m}}) = 2p^m$ when m is even and b is a square, or m is odd and b is not a square; or, $tr(\pi_{p^{2m}}) = -2p^m$ when m is odd and b is a square, or m is even and b is not a square.

If b is not a cube, since $p^{2m} \equiv 1 \pmod 3$, then $\zeta_3 = b^{(p^{4m}-1)/3}$ is a primitive 3rd root of unity, and therefore $\zeta_3^2 = b^{2(p^{2m+1})(p^{2m}-1)/3} = b^{(p^{2m}-1)/3}$. From Proposition 1, we have $\widehat{\pi}_{p^{2m}}(x,y) = (x^{p^{2m}}/\zeta_3, y^{p^{2m}})$ and $[p^m](x,y) = (x^{p^{2m}}/\zeta_3^2, (-1)^m y^{p^{2m}}/b^{(p^{2m}-1)/2})$. Using the group law, we compute that $(\pi_{p^{2m}} + \widehat{\pi}_{p^{2m}})(x,y) = (x^{p^{2m}}/\zeta_3^2, -y^{p^{2m}})$, and then deduce that $\pi_{p^{2m}} + \widehat{\pi}_{p^{2m}} = p^{2m}$ when m is odd and b is a square, or m is even and b is not a square; or, $\pi_{p^{2m}} + \widehat{\pi}_{p^{2m}} = -p^{2m}$ when m is even and b is a square, or m is odd and b is not a square.   □

Remark 1. Note that when $\#E(\mathbb{F}_{p^{2m}}) = p^{2m} \pm p^m + 1$, E has the only form $y^2 = x^3 + b$ ($b \in \mathbb{F}_{p^{2m}}^*$). Suppose $a \cdot b \neq 0$, since $a^{(p^{4m}-1)/2} = b^{(p^{4m}-1)/2} = 1$, then $\pi_{p^{2m}} = \widehat{\pi}_{p^{2m}}$ and $tr(\pi_{p^{2m}}) = 2\pi_{p^{2m}} \neq \pm p^m$ from Proposition 1.

For the cases of embedding degree 2 and 3, the distortion maps ψ for supersingular curves $y^2 = x^3 + ax$ and $y^2 = x^3 + b$ can be constructed directly as with [15].

Embedding Degree 2 Case. Condition (1) in Theorem 2: when n is odd, let $\zeta_4^2 = -1$, $\psi_1(x,y) = \left(x, \frac{y}{\zeta_4}\right)$; when n is even, $\psi_2(x,y) = \left(\frac{x^p}{a^{(p-1)/2}}, \frac{y^p}{s_a{}^{3(p-1)/2}}\right)$ where $s_a \in \mathbb{F}_{p^{2n}}$ satisfies $s_a^2 = a$. Condition (1) in Theorem 3: let $\zeta_3^2 + \zeta_3 + 1 = 0$, $\psi_3(x,y) = \left(\frac{x}{\zeta_3}, y\right)$.

Embedding Degree 3 Case. Conditions (4), (5) in Theorem 3: $\psi_4(x,y) = \left(\frac{x^p}{s_b{}^{(p-1)}}, \frac{y^p}{b^{(p-1)/2}}\right)$ where $s_b \in \mathbb{F}_{p^{6m}}$ satisfies $s_b^3 = b$.

Proposition 2. *From the above constructions, distortion maps ψ_1, ψ_2, and ψ_4 satisfy the conditions in Theorem 1 (η_T pairing).*

Proof. Case 1: Since $p^n \equiv -1 \pmod{r}$, take the automorphism $\gamma = [-1]$. Since $p \equiv 3 \pmod 4$ and n is odd, then $p^n \equiv 3 \pmod 4$, and $\zeta_4^{p^n} = -\zeta_4$. Thus $\gamma \circ \psi_1^{(p^n)} = \psi_1$.

Case 2: Since a is not a square, then $s_a \notin \mathbb{F}_{p^n}$ and $s_a{}^{p^n} = -s_a$, and we have $(s_a{}^{3(p-1)/2})^{p^n} = (s_a{}^{p^n})^{3(p-1)/2} = (-1)^{3(p-1)/2} \cdot s_a{}^{3(p-1)/2}$. Since $p \equiv 3 \pmod 4$, then $3(p-1)/2$ is odd, and $(s_a{}^{3(p-1)/2})^{p^n} = -s_a{}^{3(p-1)/2}$, which is the key to prove that $\gamma \circ \psi_2^{(p^n)} = \psi_2$.

Case 3: Since b is not a cube and $s_b \notin \mathbb{F}_{p^{2m}}$, then $s_b{}^{p^{2m}} = \zeta_3 \cdot s_b$ where ζ_3 is a primitive 3rd root of unity. Since $p \equiv 2 \pmod 3$, then $p^{2m} - 1$ is divisible by 3 and $\zeta_3 = s_b{}^{p^{2m}-1} = b^{(p^{2m}-1)/3}$ is defined over $\mathbb{F}_{p^{2m}}$. Thus, we have $b^{(p^{4m}-1)/3} = \zeta_3{}^{p^{2m}+1} = \zeta_3{}^{-1}$. Also, $b^{(p^{4m}-1)/2} = (b^{(p^{2m}-1)})^{(p^{2m}+1)/2} = 1$. From Proposition 1, we then have $[p^{2m}](x,y) = (x^{p^{4m}}/b^{(p^{4m}-1)/3}, y^{p^{4m}}/b^{(p^{4m}-1)/2}) = (\zeta_3 \cdot x^{p^{4m}}, y^{p^{4m}}) = \gamma(x^{p^{4m}}, y^{p^{4m}})$, with the isomorphism $\gamma : (x,y) \mapsto (\zeta_3 \cdot x, y)$. Then, since $p - 1 \equiv 1 \pmod 3$ it is follows that $(s_b{}^{p-1})^{p^{2m}} = (s_b{}^{p^{2m}})^{p-1} = \zeta_3{}^{p-1} \cdot s_b{}^{p-1} = \zeta_3 \cdot s_b{}^{p-1}$. Thus we deduce that $\gamma \circ \psi_4^{(p^{2m})} = \psi_4$. $\square$

Remark that the distortion map ψ_3 does not satisfy the conditions in Theorem 1, but in this case the η_T pairing can be defined as a trivial variant of the Tate pairing by taking $T = p^n$. To construct fast symmetric pairing, we prefer supersingular elliptic curves with embedding degree 3, which has shorter Miller's loop length.

4 Fast Symmetric Pairing over Large Characteristic Field

In this section we develop a fast variant of the η_T pairing for embedding degree 3, and give a strategy for generating supersingular elliptic curves with embedding degree 3 admitting our fast pairing variants.

4.1   Fast Variant of Eta Pairing for Embedding Degree 3

For the supersingular curve $E : y^2 = x^3 + b$ over $\mathbb{F}_{p^{2m}}$ with embedding degree 3 satisfying $\#E(\mathbb{F}_{p^{2m}}) = p^{2m} - p^m + 1$, its η_T pairing is given as

$$\eta_T(P, P') = f_{p^m-1,P}\big(\psi_4(P')\big)^{(p^{6m}-1)/r}$$

$$= \left(f_{p^m,P}\big(\psi_4(P')\big) \cdot \frac{v_{[p^m]P}(\psi_4(P'))}{l_{[p^m-1]P,P}(\psi_4(P'))} \right)^{(p^{6m}-1)/r}.$$

Since the Miller function can be transformed as $f_{p^m,P} = \prod_{i=0}^{m-1} f_{p,[p^i]P}^{p^{(m-i-1)}}$, and each $[p^i]$ is purely inseparable, then $f_{p,[p^i]P} \circ [p^i] = f_{p,P}^{p^{2i}}$. Therefore η_T can be modified as

$$\eta_T(P, P') = \left(\prod_{i=0}^{m-1} f_{p,P}\big(\psi_4([p^{-i}]P')\big)^{p^{(m+i-1)}} \cdot \frac{v_{[p^m]P}(\psi_4(P'))}{l_{[p^m-1]P,P}(\psi_4(P'))} \right)^{(p^{6m}-1)/r}.$$

Then we consider a new pairing

$$\eta(P, P') = \eta_T(P, [p^{m-1}]P') = \left(\prod_{i=0}^{m-1} f_{p,P}\big(\psi_4([p^i]P')\big)^{p^{2(m-1)-i}} \cdot \right.$$

$$\left. \frac{v_{[p^m]P}(\psi_4([p^{m-1}]P'))}{l_{[p^m-1]P,P}(\psi_4([p^{m-1}]P'))} \right)^{(p^{6m}-1)/r}.$$

Let $d \equiv p \pmod{r}$, i.e. $p = d + cr$ for some integer c, then $[p^i]P' = [d^i]P'$, and we have

$$f_{p,P}\big(\psi_4([p^i]P')\big)^{(p^{6m}-1)/r} = f_{d+cr,P}\big(\psi_4([p^i]P')\big)^{(p^{6m}-1)/r}$$

$$= \left(f_{d,P}\big(\psi_4([p^i]P')\big) f_{r,P}\big(\psi_4([p^i]P')\big)^c \right)^{(p^{6m}-1)/r}$$

$$= f_{d,P}\big(\psi_4([p^i]P')\big)^{(p^{6m}-1)/r} \cdot t_r(P, P')^{cp^i}.$$

Thus we can separate a fixed pairing power $t_r(P, P')^{mcp^{2(m-1)}}$ from $\eta(P, P')$ to obtain a new truncated pairing in the following theorem.

Theorem 4. *Assume the curve $E : y^2 = x^3 + b$ over $\mathbb{F}_{p^{2m}}$ satisfies the condition 4 in Theorem 3. Let r be a prime dividing $p^{2m} - p^m + 1$, and let $d \equiv p \pmod{r}$. For $P, P' \in E(\mathbb{F}_{p^{2m}})[r]$, take $P_i' = \psi_4([p^i]P')$, then the following defines a pairing*

$$\eta_d(P, P') = \left(\prod_{i=0}^{m-1} f_{d,P}\big(P_i'\big)^{p^{2(m-1)-i}} \cdot \frac{v_{[p^m]P}(P_{m-1}')}{l_{[p^m-1]P,P}(P_{m-1}')} \right)^{(p^{6m}-1)/r}.$$

Remark 2. For the sake of fast computation, $\frac{v_{[p^m]P}(P_{m-1}')}{l_{[p^m-1]P,P}(P_{m-1}')}$ can be represented as $\frac{v_{[-p^m]P}(P_{m-1}')}{l_{[-p^m]P,P}(P_{m-1}')}$.

Usually an exponentiation of the characteristic power is efficient than a finite field multiplication. As with the method of [39], when $m > 1$ the computation of $\eta_d(P, P')$ can be speeded up further by using the multi-pairing technique, which is presented in Appendix A.

To speed up the final exponentiation, the final exponent is decomposed into easy part $(q^k - 1)/\Phi_k(q)$ and hard part $\Phi_k(q)/r$. Scott et al. [34] obtained a faster hard part that could be expressed to the base q by using an optimal addition chain case by case. Later, Fuentes-Castañeda et al. [18] showed that each pairing friendly curve admits an "optimal" expression to the base q by using the lattice-based method, whose complexity is nearly $O\left(\frac{\varphi(k)-1}{\varphi(k)} \log_2 r\right)$. For the curves $E/\mathbb{F}_{p^{2m}}$ generated by Theorem 5, we can use the following Corollary to give an optimal expression of $\Phi_3(p^{2m})/r$ to the base p without an addition chain, whose coefficients are polynomials of d with coefficients $\{\pm c, h\}$. When c and h are small, then the performance of the hard part has the complexity $O\left(\frac{2m-1}{\varphi(6m)} \log_2 r\right)$.

Corollary 1. *Let* $p = d + c \cdot r$, *and* r *satisfy* $h \cdot r = \Phi_6(d^m)$ *for some integer* h. *Then the final exponent of* η_d *can be expanded as* $(p^{6m} - 1)/r = (p^{2m} - 1)(p^{2m} + p^m + 1)f$, *where* $f = c(p^m + d^m - 1)(\sum_{i=0}^{m-1} d^{m-1-i}p^i) + h$.

Proof. Directly verify that

$$r \cdot f = r\left(c(p^m + d^m - 1)(p^{m-1} + \cdots + d^{m-2}p + d^{m-1}) + h\right)$$
$$= (p^m + d^m - 1)(p - d)(p^{m-1} + \cdots + d^{m-2}p + d^{m-1}) + (d^{2m} - d^m + 1)$$
$$= (p^m + d^m - 1)(p^m - d^m) + (d^{2m} - d^m + 1) = p^{2m} - p^m + 1.$$

$\square$

4.2   Supersingular Elliptic Curve with Embedding Degree 3

Compared with the recommended supersingular curves over $\mathbb{F}_{2^n}$ or $\mathbb{F}_{3^n}$ in [7], it is more flexible to generate supersingular curves over large characteristic fields containing smaller subgroup (but large enough to ensure the ECDLP is hard). For generating suitable supersingular elliptic curves with embedding degree 3, we can construct $\mathbb{F}_{p^{2m}}$ as pairing-friendly fields or towering-friendly fields. Note that the new pairing in Theorem 4 can be computed efficiently when d is relatively small. As with the analysis in [24], since $x - d$ belongs to the lattice $I = \{h(x) + (x^n - 1)\mathbb{Z}[x] \mid h(p) \equiv 0 \pmod{r}\}$, then the lower bound of $|d|$ is close to $\lceil r^{1/\varphi(6m)} \rceil$, and therefore the lower bound of the Miller's loop of η_d is $\lceil \log_2(r)/\varphi(6m) \rceil$ by using the multi-pairing technique. But, the new pairing η_d in Theorem 4 can not be rewriten in an optimal pairing form (or a pairing lattice form). Thus, our method to construct the pairing η_d with multi-Miller's loop length $\lceil \log_2(r)/\varphi(6m) \rceil$, is to generate special supersingular elliptic curve satisfying $d \approx r^{1/\varphi(6m)}$ directly.

Theorem 5. *Fix a positive integer* m *and a security parameter* λ. *Execute the following steps.*

1. *Pick an integer d of $\lceil \frac{2\lambda}{\varphi(6m)} \rceil$-bit such that $\Phi_{6m}(d)$ has a large prime factor r satisfying $(\frac{-3}{r}) = 1$, where Φ_{6m} is the $6m$-th cyclotomic polynomial.*
2. *Pick $p = d + c \cdot r$ such that p is prime and $p \equiv 5 \pmod{6}$.*
3. *If m is even, pick $b \in \mathbb{F}^*_{p^{2m}}$ as a non-square nor non-cube; if m is odd, pick $b \in \mathbb{F}^*_{p^{2m}}$ as a square but non-cube.*

Then $y^2 = x^3 + b$ is a supersingular curve over $\mathbb{F}_{p^{2m}}$ with an order-r subgroup, and embedding degree $k = 3$, and $\rho = 2m$, where both p and r are nearly 2λ-bit primes.

In Theorem 5 it is easy to generate supersingular elliptic curve with embedding degree three and a relatively small order subgroup, which can fit the gap between ECC security and MOV security. When generating such curve, one can pick an integer d of low hamming weight, small positive integers c and $h = (d^{2m} - d^m + 1)/r$, which could produce a fast Miller iteration and fast final exponentiation for the pairing η_d.

However, for elliptic curves E over extension fields $\mathbb{F}_q$ ($q = p^n$), there are two security issues: minimal embedding field and Weil decent (or GHS) attack. The first issue shown by Hitt [25], is that the minimal finite field ensuring the ECDLP of $E(\mathbb{F}_q)[r]$ secure is $\mathbb{F}_{p^{\mathrm{ord}_r(p)}} = \mathbb{F}_{q^{\mathrm{ord}_r(p)/n}}$, named the minimal embedding field, rather than $\mathbb{F}_{q^k}$. Later, Benger *et al.* [10] proved that the minimal embedding field of E with respect to r is $\mathbb{F}_{p^k}$ if and only if $r \mid \Phi_k(p)$. In our situation, when $\#E(\mathbb{F}_q) = q - q^{1/2} + 1$ and $q = p^{2m}$ the minimal embedding field is $\mathbb{F}_{q^3}$. On the other hand, our new supersingular curves could resist the Weil decent (or GHS) attack since the attack complexity $O(p^{2-1/m})$ is also more expensive than the generic attack complexity $O(p^{1/2})$.

We provide suggested parameters p and r, and the corresponding supersingular elliptic curves with embedding degree three at the $80/128/192$-bit security levels.

Example 1. **SS3$_{80}$ Curve** for 80-bit security. We take $m = 1$ such that the prime p has the form $p = d^2 + 1$. Then we pick $d = d_0 \cdot 2^{m_0}$ where d_0 is a small odd integer. Thus $p = d_0^2 \cdot 2^{2d_0} + 1$ can be used to define so-called optimal prime fields (OPFs) [23], which allow for the efficient Montgomery modular reduction with only linear complexity [40].

Here we suggest $d = 131 \cdot 2^{80} = (2^7 + 2 + 1)2^{80}$ such that $p = 17161 \cdot 2^{160} + 1$ is a prime of 175-bit. Then the tower extension can be constructed as $\mathbb{F}_{p^2} = \mathbb{F}_p[u]/(u^2 - 3)$ and $\mathbb{F}_{p^6} = \mathbb{F}_{p^2}[v]/(v^3 - 1 - u)$. And the curve equation is $y^2 = x^3 + 1 + u$ where $1 + u$ is a square in $\mathbb{F}_{p^2}$ and the group of rational points has a prime subgroup order $r = (p - d)/3$ of 173-bit

$$r = 8360276532745208326431145085291616843599678827834027.$$

Then we can define the new pairing as

$$\eta_d(P, P') = \left(f_{d,P}\big(\psi(P')\big) \cdot \frac{v_{[-p]P}\big(\psi(P')\big)}{l_{[-p]P,P}\big(\psi(P')\big)} \right)^{(p^6 - 1)/r}$$

where $(p^6 - 1)/r = (p^2 - 1)(p^2 + p + 1)(3(p + d - 1) + 3)$.

Example 2. **SS3$_{128}$ Curve** for 128-bit security. We take $m = 2$ and $p = cd^4 - cd^2 + d + c$. With searching in practice, it is impossible to choose d and c such that $(d^{2m} - d^m + 1)$ is nearly a prime and p is a prime. Here we provide suggested parameters $d = 2^{63} + 2^{40} + 2^{19}$, $c = 3$ and $h = 1$, which ensure p a 254-bit prime and r a 253-bit prime

$$p = 21711027084623094535976745886940615635977899645372382 81716$$
$$4688279661760217091,$$
$$r = 72370090282076981786589152956468718786592998817907942 72385$$
$$154968841797763073.$$

Then we construct the tower extension fields $\mathbb{F}_{p^2} = \mathbb{F}_p[u]/(u^2 + 1)$, $\mathbb{F}_{p^4} = \mathbb{F}_{p^2}[v]/(v^2 - 3 - u)$ and $\mathbb{F}_{p^{12}} = \mathbb{F}_{p^4}[w]/(w^3 - v)$, and the curve equation $y^2 = x^3 + v$, where v is a nonsquare in $\mathbb{F}_{p^4}$. The new pairing is given as

$$\eta_d(P, P') = \left(f_{d,P}\big(\psi([p]P')\big)^p f_{d,P}\big(\psi(P')\big)^{p^2} \cdot \frac{v_{[-p^2]P}(\psi([p]P'))}{l_{[-p^2]P,P}(\psi([p]P'))} \right)^{(p^{12}-1)/r}$$

where $(p^{12} - 1)/r = (p^4 - 1)(p^4 + p^2 + 1)(3(p^2 + d^2 - 1)(p + d) + 1)$.

Example 3. **SS3$_{192}$ Curve** for 192-bit security. Similarly as the case of the 128-bit security, we take $m = 4$ and choose parameters $d = 2^{47} + 2^{30} + 2^{21}$, $c = 27$ and $h = 1$, which ensure p a 381-bit prime and r a 377-bit prime

$$p = 41559344858201957346018435367042040286527537234685509 44995$$
$$92401118046970017574235664589393740780353451624959993 4491,$$
$$r = 15392349947482206424451272358163718624639828605439077 57405$$
$$89778191869248154657124320218293978066797569463371694081.$$

Then we construct the tower extension fields $\mathbb{F}_{p^2} = \mathbb{F}_p[u]/(u^2 + 1)$, $\mathbb{F}_{p^8} = \mathbb{F}_{p^2}[v]/(v^4 - 3 - u)$ and $\mathbb{F}_{p^{24}} = \mathbb{F}_{p^8}[w]/(w^3 - v)$, and the curve equation $y^2 = x^3 + v$, where v is a nonsquare in $\mathbb{F}_{p^8}$. The new pairing is given as

$$\eta_d(P, P') = \left(\prod_{i=0}^{3} f_{d,P}\big(\psi_i(P')\big)^{p^{6-i}} \cdot \frac{v_{[-p^4]P}(\psi_3(P'))}{l_{[-p^4]P,P}(\psi_3(P'))} \right)^{(p^{24}-1)/r}$$

where $(p^{24} - 1)/r = (p^8 - 1)(p^8 + p^4 + 1)(27(p^4 + d^4 - 1)(p^3 + dp^2 + d^2p + d^3) + 1)$.

5   Pairing Computation

5.1   Miller's Formulas and Main Loop

Recently, Zhang and Lin [38], Le and Tan [28], respectively proposed fast affine Miller's formulas for computing ate-like pairing on the curve $y^2 = x^3 + b$ with only cubic twist. Zhang and Lin also gave the faster projective formulas than the formulas in [17], costing $k\mathbf{M}_1 + 3\mathbf{M}_{k/3} + 9\mathbf{S}_{k/3} + \mathbf{M}_{(3b)}$ in a doubling step and $k\mathbf{M}_1 + 12\mathbf{M}_{k/3} + 5\mathbf{S}_{k/3}$ in a mixed addition step, where $\mathbf{M}_i$ and $\mathbf{S}_i$ denote multiplication and squaring in field $\mathbb{F}_{q^i}$, and $\mathbf{M}_{(c)}$ denotes multiplication by a constant c in $\mathbb{F}_{p^{k/3}}$. In our case of $k = 3$, the doubling step and mixed addition step respectively cost $1\mathbf{S}_3 + 1\mathbf{M}_3 + 6\mathbf{M}_1 + 9\mathbf{S}_1 + 1\mathbf{M}_{(3b)}$ and $1\mathbf{M}_3 + 15\mathbf{M}_1 + 5\mathbf{S}_1$, where $q = p^{2m}$.

As shown in [16,17], Miller's formulas could be improved due to the fast point doubling formulas when b is a square. Similarly, we can improve the ate-like Miller's formulas in [38] for a square b. With the notations in [16], let $b = c^2$ and the curve $E : y^2 = cx^3 + 1$. For $P' = (x_P\omega^2, y_P\omega^3, 1) \in E(\mathbb{F}_{q^k})$ with $x_P, y_P \in \mathbb{F}_q$, and $R_1 = (X_1, Y_1, Z_1) \in E(\mathbb{F}_{q^{k/3}})$, point doubling $(X_3, Y_3, Z_3) = [2](X_1, Y_1, Z_1)$ can be performed as $X_3 = 2X_1Y_1(Y_1^2 - 9Z_1^2)$, $Y_3 = (Y_1 - Z_1)(Y_1 + 3Z_1)^3 - 8Y_1^3Z_1$, $Z_3 = 8Y_1^3Z_1$. Then we can compute the point doubling and line formula $F_{DBL(R_1)}(P') = X_3^2 + 12X_1^2Y_1^2(Y_3 - Z_3y_P\omega^3) + 2X_3Z_3(\frac{x_P}{2}\omega^2) + Z_3^2(x_P\omega^4)$ in the coordinates $(X, Y, Z, T, U) = (X, Y, Z, X^2, Z^2)$ and the $\mathbb{F}_{p^{k/3}}$-basis $\{1, \omega, \omega^2\}$ of $\mathbb{F}_{p^k}$ as follows.

$$A = Y_1^2,\ B = (X_1 + Y_1)^2 - T_1 - A,\ C = (Y_1 + Z_1)^2 - A - U_1,\ Z_3 = 4A \cdot C,$$
$$X_3 = C \cdot (A - 9U_1),\ Y_3 = (A - 3U_1 + C)(A + 9U_1 + 3C) - Z_3,\ T_3 = X_3^2,$$
$$U_3 = Z_3^2,\ D = (X_3 + Z_3)^2 - T_3 - U_3,\ E = 3B^2,\ F = Z_3 \cdot y_P\omega^3,$$
$$L_0 = E \cdot (Y_3 - F) + T_3,\ L_1 = D \cdot (x_P/2),\ L_2 = U_3 \cdot (x_P^2).$$

Thus the point doubling with line computation needs $k\mathbf{M}_1 + 4\mathbf{M}_{k/3} + 7\mathbf{S}_{k/3}$. On the other hand, for $R_2 = (X_2, Y_2, Z_2) \in E(\mathbb{F}_{q^{k/3}})$, we can modify the point addition formulas and line formula $F_{ADD(R_1,R_2)}(P') = X_3^2 - \frac{Z_1}{c}(Z_1X_2 - X_1)^2(Z_1Y_2 - Y_1)(Y_3 - Z_3y_P\omega^3) + 2X_3Z_3(\frac{x_P}{2}\omega^2) + Z_3^2(x_P^2\omega^4)$ and perform these operations as follows, which costing $k\mathbf{M}_1 + 12\mathbf{M}_{k/3} + 4\mathbf{S}_{k/3} + 1\mathbf{M}_{(c^{-1})}$.

$$A = X_1 - Z_1 \cdot X_2,\ B = A^2,\ C = A \cdot B,\ D = X_1 \cdot B,\ E = 2D - C,\ F = D + E,$$
$$G = Y_1 - Z_1 \cdot Y_2,\ H = G \cdot Z_1 \cdot c^{-1},\ I = G \cdot H,\ X_3 = A \cdot (I - E),$$
$$Y_3 = G \cdot (F - I) - Y_1 \cdot C,\ Z_3 = Z_1 \cdot C,\ T_3 = X_3^2,\ U_3 = Z_3^2,$$
$$J = (X_3 + Z_3)^2 - T_3 - U_3,\ K = H \cdot B,\ L = Y_3 - Z_3 \cdot y_P\omega^3,\ L_0 = T_3 + K \cdot L,$$
$$L_1 = J \cdot (x_P/2),\ L_2 = U_3 \cdot (x_P^2).$$

In our case of $k = 3$ and $b = c^2$, the above doubling steps and mixed addition steps cost $1\mathbf{S}_3 + 1\mathbf{M}_3 + 7\mathbf{M}_1 + 7\mathbf{S}_1$ and $1\mathbf{M}_3 + 15\mathbf{M}_1 + 4\mathbf{S}_1 + 1\mathbf{M}_{(c^{-1})}$ respectively, which are faster compared with the formulas in [38].

We modify the multi-Miller's algorithm [22] in Appendix A to compute $\eta_d(P, P')$ in Theorem 4 with the precomputation of each $\psi_4([p^i]P')$. Since many common operations can be shared in doubling steps and addition steps for computing each $f_{d,P}(\psi_4([p^i]P'))$ $(0 \le i \le m-1)$, then the multi-doubling step costs $1\mathbf{S}_3 + m(\mathbf{M}_3 + 4\mathbf{M}_1) + 2\mathbf{M}_1 + 9\mathbf{S}_1 + 1\mathbf{M}_{(3b)}$ or $1\mathbf{S}_3 + m(\mathbf{M}_3 + 4\mathbf{M}_1) + 3\mathbf{M}_1 + 7\mathbf{S}_1$, and the multi-addition step $m(\mathbf{M}_3 + 4\mathbf{M}_1) + 11\mathbf{M}_1 + 5\mathbf{S}_1$ or $m(\mathbf{M}_3 + 4\mathbf{M}_1) + 11\mathbf{M}_1 + 4\mathbf{S}_1 + 1\mathbf{M}_{(c^{-1})}$.

5.2   Final Steps

When computing $\eta_d(P, P')$, the final steps involve the multiplication of the linear part $v_{[-p^m]P}(Q)/l_{[-p^m]P,P}(Q)$, where $P = (x_P, y_P)$, $[-p^m]P = (x_1, y_1)$, and $Q = \psi_4([p^{m-1}]P') = (x_Q\alpha, y_Q)$ with $\alpha = b^{2/3} \in \mathbb{F}_{p^{6m}}$. With the subfield elimination technique, $v_{[-p^m]P}(Q)/l_{[-p^m]P,P}(Q)$ can be transformed as

$$(x_P - x_1)^{-1}\frac{v_{[-p^m]P}(Q)}{l_{[-p^m]P,P}(Q)} = \frac{(x_P - x_1)^{-1}(x_Q\alpha - x_1)}{(y_Q - y_1) - (x_Q\alpha - x_1)(y_P - y_1)/(x_P - x_1)}$$

$$= \frac{x_Q\alpha - x_1}{(y_Q - y_1)(x_P - x_1) - (x_Q\alpha - x_1)(y_P - y_1)}$$

$$= \frac{x_Q\alpha - x_1}{\beta_0 - \beta_1 x_Q\alpha},$$

where $\beta_0 = (y_Q - y_1)(x_P - x_1) + x_1(y_P - y_1)$ and $\beta_1 = (y_P - y_1)$. Then the denominator $(\beta_0 - \beta_1 x_Q\alpha)$ can be transformed as $(\beta_0^3 - \beta_1^3 x_Q^3\alpha^3)/(\beta_0^2 + \beta_0\beta_1 x_Q\alpha + \beta_1^2 x_Q^2\alpha^2)$ such that the new denominator $(\beta_0^3 - \beta_1^3 x_Q^3\alpha^3)$ is omitted. Thus we only need to compute

$$(x_Q\alpha - x_1)(\beta_0^2 + \beta_0\beta_1 x_Q\alpha + \beta_1^2 x_Q^2\alpha^2)$$
$$= (\beta_0\beta_1 - \beta_1^2 x_1)x_Q^2\alpha^2 + (\beta_0^2 - \beta_0\beta_1 x_1)x_Q\alpha + (\beta_1^2 x_Q^3\alpha^3 - \beta_0^2 x_1)$$

with the following operations, which costing $10\mathbf{M}_1 + 2\mathbf{S}_1$ by precomputing x_Q^2 and $x_Q b^2$.

$$A = (y_Q - y_1)(x_P - x_1), \ B = x_1(y_P - y_1), \ C = A + B, \ E = A \cdot B, \ F = C^2,$$
$$G = (y_P - y_1)^2, \ H = F \cdot x_Q^2 \cdot x_Q b^2, \ I = E \cdot x_1, \ J = D \cdot x_1, \ K = F \cdot x_1,$$
$$L_0 = G - H, \ L_1 = x_Q(A - I), \ L_2 = x_Q^2(C - J).$$

5.3   Final Exponentiation

As we shown in §4.1, for the curve $E/\mathbb{F}_{p^{2m}}$ generated by Theorem 5, the performance of the hard part has the complexity $O\left(\frac{2m-1}{\varphi(6m)}\log_2 r\right)$. When $p^m \equiv 1 \pmod 6$, we can apply fast squaring technique in cyclotomic subgroups $G_{\Phi_6(p^m)}$ to accelerate the final exponentiation. When $m = 2^a \cdot 3^b$, Granger and Scott's squaring [21] needs $1\mathbf{S}_{6m} = (6^b \cdot 3^a \cdot 6)\mathbf{M}_1$, and Karabina's squaring [27] needs $1\mathbf{S}_{6m} = (6^b \cdot 3^a \cdot 4)\mathbf{M}_1$ and extra decompression cost $1\mathbf{I}_m + (6^b \cdot 3^a \cdot 5)\mathbf{M}_1$. Thus, the final exponentiation of our new symmetric pairings can be speeded up as the asymmetric case when m is even, e.g. the curves in the 128-bit and 192-bit security cases.

5.4   Exponentiation by p

For our new pairing (4), a few exponentiations of the characteristic p need to be computed in each Miller's iteration and the final exponentiation. Due to the special field extension, the exponentiations of the characteristic could be computed very efficient. For example, when the characteristic satisfies $p \equiv 19 \pmod{24}$, the field extension of $\mathbb{F}_{p^{2m}}$ with $m = 2^i 3^j$ can be constructed as $\mathbb{F}_{p^{2m}} = \mathbb{F}_{p^2}[x]/(x^m - (1 + \sqrt{-1}))$ according to [10]. Thus the exponentiation by p is fast by costing $m - 1$ modular reductions.

In our case, since $p \equiv 2 \pmod{3}$ it follows that the above field extension is feasible when $m = 2^i$ and $p \equiv 3 \pmod{8}$. Regarding the field $\mathbb{F}_{p^{6m}}$ with $m = 2^i$, we recommend the field extension $\mathbb{F}_{p^{2m}} = \mathbb{F}_{p^2}[x]/(x^m - (1 + \sqrt{-1}))$ and $\mathbb{F}_{p^{6m}} = \mathbb{F}_{p^{2m}}[y]/(y^3 - (a + bx))$ for our suggested curves SS3$_{128}$ and SS3$_{192}$. Then the exponentiation of p in field $\mathbb{F}_{p^{6m}}$ needs two (constant) multiplications in field $\mathbb{F}_{p^{2m}}$ and several modular reductions, whose cost is at most one half of the cost for the squaring in field $\mathbb{F}_{p^{6m}}$.

Besides, for the curve SS3$_{80}$, we have $p \equiv 1 \pmod{4}$ since the field $\mathbb{F}_p$ is an optimal prime field. Then the exponentiation of p in field $\mathbb{F}_{p^6}$ needs two (constant) multiplications in field $\mathbb{F}_{p^2}$, three (constant) multiplications in field $\mathbb{F}_p$ and several modular reductions.

5.5   Special Modular Reduction

The modular arithmetic in a generic finite field would be costly when its characteristic is large. The Montgomery reduction usually has better computational complexity than the classical method by a constant factor. Moreover, the lazy reduction and the residue number system are proposed for further optimizations. In practical public key cryptography, however, it is recommended to use primes of special forms (e.g. Mersenne and NIST primes). Unluckily, it is hard to utilize these special primes in fast pairing computation. But in our suggested examples, the curve SS3$_{80}$ can be specially defined over an quadratic extension of an optimal prime field, which admits fast Montgomery modular reduction (multiplication).

5.6   Cost Estimation

At different levels of the 80/128/192-bit securities, we give the rough estimations and comparisons of the computational costs for our new symmetric pairings and the currently recommended symmetric and asymmetric pairings listed in Table 1.

From the comparisons in Table 2, we can assume that for software computation our new symmetric pairings at the 80/128-bit security levels can be more efficient than the recommended η_T pairings. Moreover, compared with the recommended asymmetric pairings in Table 1, our new symmetric pairings might shorten the efficiency gap between symmetric pairings and asymmetric pairings within two times for the 80/128/192-bit securities. Specially, due to the fast modular reduction in our new pairing computation at the 80 security level, our new pairing might have faster performance compared with the Tate pairing on the MNT curve.

Table 1. Different recommended pairing-friendly curves at different security levels

Security	Curve	Equation	Field	Pairing
80-bit	Supersingular $k = 4$ [13]	$y^2 + y = x^3 + x + 1$	$\mathbb{F}_{2^{457}}$	η_T
	Supersingular $k = 6$ [13]	$y^2 = x^3 - x - 1$	$\mathbb{F}_{3^{239}}$	η_T
	MNT ($k = 6$) [33]	$y^2 = x^3 - 3x + b$	$\mathbb{F}_{p_{mnt}}$	Tate
	SS3$_{80}$ (Example 1)	$y^2 = x^3 + 1 + u$	$\mathbb{F}_{p^2}$	η_d
	$b = 1948567758854590258311056860286339287536660625487$			
	$p_{mnt} = 8672585233075186470871826201273162781791221963 39$			
128-bit	Supersingular $k = 4$ [19]	$y^2 + y = x^3 + x + 1$	$\mathbb{F}_{2^{1223}}$	η_T
	Supersingular $k = 6$ [2]	$y^2 = x^3 - x + 1$	$\mathbb{F}_{3^{509}}$	η_T
	BN ($k = 12$) [32]	$y^2 = x^3 + 2$	$\mathbb{F}_{p_{bn}}$	opt-ate
	SS3$_{128}$ (Example 2)	$y^2 = x^3 + 2 + v$	$\mathbb{F}_{p^4}$	η_d
	$p_{bn} = 36z_1^4 + 36z_1^3 + 24z_1^2 + 6z_1 + 1,\ z_1 = -2^{62} - 2^{55} - 1$			
192-bit	BLS12 ($k = 12$) [3]	$y^2 = x^3 + 4$	$\mathbb{F}_{p_{bls}}$	ate
	SS3$_{192}$ (Example 3)	$y^2 = x^3 + 1 + 3v$	$\mathbb{F}_{p^8}$	η_d
	$p_{bls} = (z_2 - 1)^2(z_2^8 - z_2^4 + 1)/3 + z_2,\ z_2 = -2^{107} + 2^{105} + 2^{93} + 2^5$			

Table 2. Comparisons of pairing computations at the 80/128/192-bit security levels

Security	Pairing	ML+FS Cost	FE Cost	Total Cost
80-bit	SS4, η_T [11] (*Alg1*)	$1599m_{2457} + 458s_{2457}$ $+456r_{2457}$	$i_{2457} + 26m_{2457}$ $+932s_{2457}$	$i_{2457} + 1625m_{2457}$ $+1390s_{2457} + 456r_{2457}$
	SS6, η_T [12] (*Alg5*)	$1495m_{3239} + 1311c_{3239}$	$i_{3239} + 73m_{3239}$ $+720c_{3239}$	$i_{3239} + 1568m_{3239}$ $+2031c_{3239}$
	MNT, Tate [33]	$4733m_{160}$	$i_{160} + 1076m_{160}$	$i_{160} + 5809m_{160}$
	SS3$_{80}$, η_d (*this work*)	$5843m_{173}$	$i_{173} + 674m_{173}$	$i_{173} + 6517m_{173}$
128-bit	SS4, η_T [11] (*Alg1*)	$4280m_{21223} + 1224s_{21223}$ $+1222r_{21223}$	$i_{21223} + 26m_{21223}$ $+2455s_{21223}$	$i_{21223} + 4306m_{21223} +$ $3679s_{21223} + 1222r_{21223}$
	SS6, η_T [12] (*Alg5*)	$3181m_{3509} + 2797c_{3509}$	$i_{3509} + 73m_{3509}$ $+1530c_{3509}$	$i_{3509} + 3254m_{3509}$ $+4327c_{3509}$
	BN, opt-ate [4]	$6792m_{254}$	$4i_{254} + 3769m_{254}$	$4i_{254} + 10561m_{254}$
	SS3$_{128}$, η_d (*this work*)	$21168m_{254}$	$4i_{254} + 3417m_{254}$	$4i_{254} + 24585m_{254}$
192-bit	BLS12, ate [3]	$10865m_{638}$ $(\approx 29249m_{384})$	$6i_{638} + 8464m_{638}$ $(\approx 6i_{638} + 22785m_{384})$	$6i_{638} + 19329m_{638}$ $(\approx 6i_{638} + 52034m_{384})$
	SS3$_{192}$, η_d (*this work*)	$72144m_{381}$	$8i_{381} + 18283m_{381}$	$8i_{381} + 90427m_{381}$

6 Conclusion

We have constructed fast symmetric pairings on the supersingular curves $y^2 = x^3 + b$ over extension fields $\mathbb{F}_{p^{2m}}$ with embedding degree 3. In order to obtain fast performance, we have given some suggestions about choices of curve's parameters and introduced a new variant of the η_T pairing on our suggested supersingular curves. Moreover, we have recommended to use the multi-pairing technique to speed up our new pairing computation. At last, we have given the concrete formulas and estimated the rough costs for our pairing computations to illustrate that our new symmetric pairings could be efficient candidates in practice.

Acknowledgments. We are heartily grateful to Jérémie Detrey for reviewing the revised paper and helping us to remedy some proof shortcomings and improve the readability. We also thank the Pairing2013 reviewers for many helpful comments and suggestions, and particularly for directing us to the breakthrough papers of Joux and Barbulescu *et al.* and Adj *et al.*.

References

1. Adj, G., Menezes, A., Oliveira, T., Rodríguez-Henríquez, F.: Weakness of $\mathbb{F}_{3^{6*509}}$ for discrete logarithm cryptography. IACR ePrint Archive Report 2013/446

2. Ahmadi, O., Hankerson, D., Menezes, A.: Software implementation of arithmetic in $\mathbb{F}_{3^m}$. In: Carlet, C., Sunar, B. (eds.) WAIFI 2007. LNCS, vol. 4547, pp. 85–102. Springer, Heidelberg (2007)

3. Aranha, D.F., Fuentes-Castañeda, L., Knapp, E., Menezes, A., Rodríguez-Henríquez, F.: Implementing Pairings at the 192-Bit Security Level. In: Abdalla, M., Lange, T. (eds.) Pairing 2012. LNCS, vol. 7708, pp. 177–195. Springer, Heidelberg (2013)

4. Aranha, D., Karabina, K., Longa, P., Gebotys, C., López, J.: Faster explicit formulas for computing pairings over ordinary curves. In: Paterson, K.G. (ed.) EUROCRYPT 2011. LNCS, vol. 6632, pp. 48–68. Springer, Heidelberg (2011)

5. Aranha, D.F., López, J., Hankerson, D.: High-Speed Parallel Software Implementation of the η_T Pairing. In: Pieprzyk, J. (ed.) CT-RSA 2010. LNCS, vol. 5985, pp. 89–105. Springer, Heidelberg (2010)

6. Barbulescu, R., Gaudry, P., Joux, A., Thomé, E.: A quasi-polynomial algorithm for discrete logarithm in finite fields of small characteristic. IACR ePrint Archive Report 2013/400

7. Barreto, P., Galbraith, S., hÉigeartaigh, C.Ó., Scott, M.: Efficient pairing computation on supersingular abelian varieties. Designs, Codes and Cryptography 42(3), 239–271 (2007)

8. Barreto, P.S.L.M., Kim, H.Y., Lynn, B., Scott, M.: Efficient Algorithms for Pairing-Based Cryptosystems. In: Yung, M. (ed.) CRYPTO 2002. LNCS, vol. 2442, pp. 354–369. Springer, Heidelberg (2002)

9. Barreto, P., Naehrig, M.: Pairing-friendly elliptic curves of prime order. In: Preneel, B., Tavares, S. (eds.) SAC 2005. LNCS, vol. 3897, pp. 319–331. Springer, Heidelberg (2006)

10. Benger, N., Scott, M.: Constructing tower extensions of finite fields for implementation of pairing-based cryptography. In: Hasan, M.A., Helleseth, T. (eds.) WAIFI 2010. LNCS, vol. 6087, pp. 180–195. Springer, Heidelberg (2010)

11. Beuchat, J.-L., Brisebarre, N., Detrey, J., Okamoto, E., Rodríguez-Henríquez, F.: A Comparison between Hardware Accelerators for the Modified Tate Pairing over F_{2^m} and F_{3^m}. In: Galbraith, S.D., Paterson, K.G. (eds.) Pairing 2008. LNCS, vol. 5209, pp. 297–315. Springer, Heidelberg (2008)

12. Beuchat, J.L., Brisebarre, N., Detrey, J., Okamoto, E., Shirase, M., Takagi, T.: Algorithms and Arithmetic Operators for Computing the η_T Pairing in Characteristic Three. IEEE Transactions on Computers 57(11), 1454–1468 (2008)

13. Beuchat, J.L., Detrey, J., Estibals, N., Okamoto, E., Rodríguez-Henríquez, F.: Fast Architectures for the η_T Pairing over Small-Characteristic Supersingular Elliptic Curves. IEEE Transactions on Computers 60(2), 266–281 (2011)

14. Beuchat, J.-L., López-Trejo, E., Martínez-Ramos, L., Mitsunari, S., Rodríguez-Henríquez, F.: Multi-core Implementation of the Tate Pairing over Supersingular Elliptic Curves. In: Garay, J.A., Miyaji, A., Otsuka, A. (eds.) CANS 2009. LNCS, vol. 5888, pp. 413–432. Springer, Heidelberg (2009)
15. Blake, I., Seroussi, G., Smart, N.: Advances in Elliptic Curve Cryptography. LMS Lecture Note Series, vol. 317. Cambridge University Press (2005)
16. Costello, C., Hisil, H., Boyd, C., Gonzalez Nieto, J., Wong, K.K.-H.: Faster Pairings on Special Weierstrass Curves. In: Shacham, H., Waters, B. (eds.) Pairing 2009. LNCS, vol. 5671, pp. 89–101. Springer, Heidelberg (2009)
17. Costello, C., Lange, T., Naehrig, M.: Faster pairing computations on curves with high-degree twists. In: Nguyen, P.Q., Pointcheval, D. (eds.) PKC 2010. LNCS, vol. 6056, pp. 224–242. Springer, Heidelberg (2010)
18. Fuentes-Castañeda, L., Knapp, E., Rodríguez-Henríquez, F.: Faster Hashing to $\mathbb{G}_2$. In: Miri, A., Vaudenay, S. (eds.) SAC 2011. LNCS, vol. 7118, pp. 412–430. Springer, Heidelberg (2012)
19. Ghosh, S., Roychowdhury, D., Das, A.: High Speed Cryptoprocessor for η_T Pairing on 128-bit Secure Supersingular Elliptic Curves over Characteristic Two Fields. In: Preneel, B., Takagi, T. (eds.) CHES 2011. LNCS, vol. 6917, pp. 442–458. Springer, Heidelberg (2011)
20. Ghosh, S., Verbauwhede, I., Roychowdhury, D.: Core Based Architecture to Speed Up Optimal Ate Pairing on FPGA Platform. In: Abdalla, M., Lange, T. (eds.) Pairing 2012. LNCS, vol. 7708, pp. 141–159. Springer, Heidelberg (2013)
21. Granger, R., Scott, M.: Faster squaring in the cyclotomic subgroup of sixth degree extensions. In: Nguyen, P.Q., Pointcheval, D. (eds.) PKC 2010. LNCS, vol. 6056, pp. 209–223. Springer, Heidelberg (2010)
22. Granger, R., Smart, N.: On computing products of pairings. IACR ePrint Archive Report 2006/172
23. Großschädl, J.: TinySA: A security architecture for wireless sensor networks. In: CoNEXT 2006, pp. 288–289. ACM Press (2006)
24. Hess, F.: Pairing lattices. In: Galbraith, S.D., Paterson, K.G. (eds.) Pairing 2008. LNCS, vol. 5209, pp. 18–38. Springer, Heidelberg (2008)
25. Hitt, L.: On the minimal embedding field. In: Takagi, T., Okamoto, T., Okamoto, E., Okamoto, T. (eds.) Pairing 2007. LNCS, vol. 4575, pp. 294–301. Springer, Heidelberg (2007)
26. Joux, A.: A new index calculus algorithm with complexity L(1/4 + o(1)) in very small characteristic. IACR ePrint Archive Report 2013/095
27. Karabina, K.: Squaring in cyclotomic subgroups. Mathematics of Computation 82(281), 555–579 (2013)
28. Le, D.-P., Tan, C.H.: Speeding up ate pairing computation in affine coordinates. In: Kwon, T., Lee, M.-K., Kwon, D. (eds.) ICISC 2012. LNCS, vol. 7839, pp. 262–277. Springer, Heidelberg (2013)
29. Menezes, A., Okamoto, T., Vanstone, S.: Reducing Elliptic Curve Logarithms to Logarithms in a Finite Field. IEEE Transactions on Information Theory 39(5), 1639–1646 (1993)
30. Miller, V.: Short programs for functions on curves (1986) (unpublished manuscript)
31. Miller, V.: The Weil pairing, and its efficient calculation. Journal of Cryptology 17(4), 235–261 (2004)
32. Pereira, G., Simplício, M., Naehrig, M., Barreto, P.: A family of implementation-friendly BN elliptic curves. Journal of Systems and Software 84, 1319–1326 (2011)
33. Scott, M., Barreto, P.: Generating More MNT Elliptic Curves. Designs, Codes and Cryptography 38, 209–217 (2006)

34. Scott, M., Benger, N., Charlemagne, M., Dominguez Perez, L.J., Kachisa, E.J.: On the final exponentiation for calculating pairings on ordinary elliptic curves. In: Shacham, H., Waters, B. (eds.) Pairing 2009. LNCS, vol. 5671, pp. 78–88. Springer, Heidelberg (2009)
35. Silverman, J.: The Arithmetic of Elliptic Curves. GTM, vol. 106. Springer (2009)
36. Vercauteren, F.: Optimal Pairings. IEEE Transactions on Information Theory 56(1), 455–461 (2010)
37. Yao, G.X., Fan, J., Cheung, R.C.C., Verbauwhede, I.: Faster Pairing Coprocessor Architecture. In: Abdalla, M., Lange, T. (eds.) Pairing 2012. LNCS, vol. 7708, pp. 160–176. Springer, Heidelberg (2013)
38. Zhang, X., Lin, D.: Analysis of Optimum Pairing Products at High Security Levels. In: Galbraith, S., Nandi, M. (eds.) INDOCRYPT 2012. LNCS, vol. 7668, pp. 412–430. Springer, Heidelberg (2012)
39. Zhang, X., Wang, K., Lin, D.: On Efficient Pairings on Elliptic Curves over Extension Fields. In: Abdalla, M., Lange, T. (eds.) Pairing 2012. LNCS, vol. 7708, pp. 1–18. Springer, Heidelberg (2013)
40. Zhang, Y., Großschädl, J.: Efficient Prime-Field Arithmetic for Elliptic Curve Cryptography on Wireless Sensor Nodes. In: ICCSNT 2011, pp. 459–466. IEEE (2011)

A   Modified Multi-miller's Algorithm for Computing $\eta_d(P, P')$

Input: $d = \sum_{i=0}^{l} d_i \cdot 2^i$, $d_i \in \{0, 1\}$, $d_l = 1$; $P, P' \in G_1$; $h = (p^{2m} - p^m + 1)/r$;
Output: $\eta_d(P, P')$;

1:    **for** $i = m - 1$ to 0 **do**
2:        $P_i' \leftarrow \psi_4([p^{m-i-1}]P')$;
3:    **end for**
4:    $R \leftarrow P$;
5:    **for** $j = l - 1$ to 0 **do**
6:        $f \leftarrow f^2$; $R \leftarrow [2]R$; $F \leftarrow F_{DBL(R)}$;
7:        **for** $i = m - 1$ to 0 **do**
8:            $f \leftarrow f \cdot F(P_i')^{p^i}$;
9:        **end for**
10:        **if** $d_j = 1$ **then**
11:            $R \leftarrow R + P$; $F \leftarrow F_{ADD(R,P)}$;
12:            **for** $i = m - 1$ to 0 **do**
13:                $f \leftarrow f \cdot F(P_i')^{p^i}$;
14:            **end for**
15:        **end if**
16:    **end for**
17:    $f \leftarrow f^{p^{(m-1)}}$;
18:    $R' \leftarrow [-p^m]P$;
19:    $f \leftarrow f \cdot v_{R'}(P_0')/l_{P,R'}(P_0')$;
20:    **return** $f^{(p^{3m}-1)(p^m+1)h}$;

Efficient Leakage-Resilient Identity-Based Encryption with CCA Security

Shi-Feng Sun, Dawu Gu*, and Shengli Liu

Department of Computer Science and Engineering,
Shanghai Jiao Tong University, Shanghai 200240, China
{crypto99,dwgu,slliu}@sjtu.edu.cn

Abstract. Due to the proliferation of side-channel attacks, lots of efforts have been made to construct cryptographic systems that are still secure even if part of the secret information is leaked to the adversary. Recently, many identity-based encryption (IBE) schemes have been proposed in this context, almost all of which, however, are only proved CPA secure. As far as we know, the IBE scheme presented by Alwen et al. is the unique CCA secure and the most practical one in the standard model. Unfortunately, this scheme suffers from an undesirable shortcoming that the leakage parameter λ and the message length m are subject to $\lambda + m \leq \log p - \omega(\log \kappa)$, where κ is the security parameter and p is the prime order of the underlying group. To overcome this drawback, we designed a new IBE scheme based on Gentry's IBE in this paper, which is λ-leakage resilient CCA2 secure in the standard model where $\lambda \leq \log p - \omega(\log \kappa)$. In contrast, the leakage parameter λ in our proposal is independent of the size of the message space. Moreover, our scheme is quite practical and almost as efficient as the original scheme. To the best of our knowledge, it is the first practical leakage-resilient fully CCA2 secure IBE scheme in the standard model, tolerating up to $(\log p - \omega(\log \kappa))$-bit leakage of the private key, the leakage parameter of which is independent of the message length.

Keywords: Identity-Based Encryption, Leakage-Resilient, Bounded Memory Leakage, Chosen Ciphertext Security.

1 Introduction

The right and reasonable definition of security models is crucial to provably secure cryptography. Traditionally, the security of cryptographic systems is analyzed in an idealized model, where the secret states are assumed to be generated using perfectly random bits and completely hidden from the adversary. That is, an adversary in this setting only can see the specified input and output behaviors of one system, but has no any other access to the internal secret states. However, it has been observed that the assumption above does not hold in the real world.

---

* Corresponding author.

Z. Cao and F. Zhang (Eds.): Pairing 2013, LNCS 8365, pp. 149–167, 2014.

Actually, the potential attackers may exploit the variously physical character-istics, such as computation-time, power-consumption, electro-magnetic radiation etc, of the execution of a cryptographic device to learn some partial information of the secret states, which are usually called side-channel attacks [24,5,23,3,18]. What's more, another kind of attack called cold-boot attack is presented by Halderman et al. in 2008 [21], where an attacker is allowed to learn information about the contents of a machine, even after the machine is powered down. Under many such attacks, many systems proved secure in the traditional security mod-els, without key leakage, may become completely insecure, even if the attacker leaks only a small amount of information about the secret states.

To take account of these attacks in the security proof, leakage-resilient cryp-tography has been initiated by the cryptographic community, with the goal of constructing stronger secure cryptographic systems that remain provably se-cure even in the presence of some key leakage attacks. Recently, many excellent works, such as [13,15,22,17,28,2,27,14], have been proposed in this new setting, and they are proved secure in several different leakage models, such as the only computation leakage model and auxiliary input leakage model. In this work, we focus on a simple and general leakage model, called bounded memory-leakage model (or sometimes relative leakage model), where the attacker is allowed to learn arbitrary information about the secret key, with the only restriction that the number of leakage bits is bounded by some parameter λ. In recent years, the bounded memory-leakage model has received considerable attentions.

1.1   Related Work

To capture the cold-boot attack, bounded memory-leakage model was first intro-duced by Akavia et al. [1], who also proposed CPA secure PKE and IBE schemes in this leakage model based on the learning with errors (LWE) assumption. Sub-sequently, Naor and Segev [28] gave a general construction of CPA secure leakage resilient PKE derived from hash proof system [12], and they presented two ef-ficient concrete constructions in this framework under the DDH and K-Linear assumptions, the leakage-ratio (leakage bits/secret key bits) of which are almost to approach 1. Moreover, in the same work they considered how to achieve CCA secure leakage resilient PKE, and showed that given any CPA leakage resilient PKE, the corresponding CCA leakage resilient PKE can be obtained by leverag-ing Naor-Yung paradigm [29]. Except this inefficiently general method, they still gave two efficient CCA secure leakage resilient constructions based on the practi-cal Cramer-Shoup cryptosystem [11], one CCA1 and the other CCA2. However, these schemes suffer from one undesirable shortcoming that the leakage param-eter λ is dependent to the message length m. The relationship between them is $\lambda + m \leq \log q - \omega(\log \kappa)$, where κ is the security parameter and q is the prime order of the underlying group. In order to solve this problem, Liu et al.[26] gave a new leakage resilient PKE based on Cramer-Shoup cryptosystem, in which the number of leakage bits $\lambda \leq \log q - \omega(\log \kappa)$.

Furthermore, Alwen et al.[2] generalized hash proof system in [12] to the identity-based setting and referred to it as identity-based hash proof system, based on which they showed how to construct leakage resilient IBE schemes. In particular, they presented three instantiations based on Boneh et al.' IBE [6], Gentry et al.' IBE [20] and Gentry's IBE [19], respectively. In addition, based on the framework presented by Alwen et al., the work of [10] gave three new leakage-resilient IBE schemes, which were constructed from Waters's IBE [30], Lewko et al.' IBE [25] and Boneh et al.' IBE [4], and Chen et al. [8] also present a new IBE in this new setting. Different from these works, Yuen et. al.[32] put forward a novel IBE scheme in the auxiliary input model, which can tolerate a more general form of leakage. Among all these leakage resilient IBE schemes, those presented in [10,32] are all proved secure in the standard model, in contrast to the others most of which are proposed in the random oracle model. However, all these leakage resilient IBE schemes are only proved CPA secure, except the only one presented in the work [2]. Unfortunately, this unique CCA secure scheme also suffers from the undesirable drawback that the leakage parameter λ and the message length m are subject to $\lambda + m \leq \log q - \omega(\log \kappa)$, where κ is the security parameter and q is the prime order of the underlying group. In this case, when the message length m approaches to $\log q$, the number of leakage bits approaches to 0, vice verse. Hence, it is natural to ask whether there exists one IBE scheme that can achieve CCA security in the context of leakage resilience, and does not suffer from this inherent drawback.

In this work, we present a new leakage resilient IBE based on Gentry's IBE, which not only has almost the same efficiency as the original one, but also can achieve CCA2 security in the standard model, simultaneously without suffering from the undesirable drawback as in [2].

1.2 Organization

The rest paper is organized as follows. Section 2 describes some preliminaries, including some basic notations, definitions and security models. The concrete construction and the security analysis will be presented in section 3 and 4, respectively. Section 5 gives a detailed performance analysis. And at last, we end this work with a brief conclusion.

2   Preliminaries

In the following, we first give some notations, definitions and assumptions used in our work, and then review the security model of IBE in the bounded memory leakage setting.

2.1   Notations

Let κ denote the security parameter. For a set S, we write $s \leftarrow S$ to denote sampling s uniformly at random from S, and $|S|$ the cardinality of the set S; if S is a random variable or distribution, it denotes sampling a random s according to S. For a randomized algorithm $A(\cdot)$, $a \leftarrow A(\cdot)$ denotes running the algorithm and obtaining a as an output, which is distributed over the internal random coins of A. PPT and $negl(\kappa)$ denote probabilistic polynomial time and a negligible function of κ, respectively.

2.2   Bilinear Maps and Complexity Assumption

Let G and G_T be two multiplicative cyclic groups of prime order p. We assume that the discrete logarithm problems in both G and G_T are intractable. Let $e : G \times G \to G_T$ be a bilinear map with the following properties:

(1) Bilinear: $e(P^a, Q^b) = e(P, Q)^{ab}$, for all $P, Q \in G$, and $a, b \in Z_p^*$.
(2) Non-degenerate: There exists $P \in G$ such that $e(P, P) \neq 1_{G_T}$.
(3) Computable: There exists an efficient algorithm to compute $e(P, Q)$ for any $P, Q \in G$.

Definition 1 (Complexity Assumption [19]). Let G and G_T be two multiplicative cyclic groups of order p, which are determined by some security parameter κ. The complexity assumption used in our scheme is a truncated version of the decisional q-augmented bilinear Diffie-Hellman exponent assumption (q-ABDHE). That is, the ensembles $\mathcal{P}_{ABDHE} = \{(G, g', (g')^{\alpha^{q+2}}, g, g^\alpha, \ldots, g^{\alpha^q}, e(g, g')^{\alpha^{q+1}})\}$ and $\mathcal{R}_{ABDHE} = \{(G, g', (g')^{\alpha^{q+2}}, g, g^\alpha, \ldots, g^{\alpha^q}, Z)\}$ are computationally indistinguishable, where the elements $g, g' \in G$, $Z \in G_T$ and $\alpha \in Z_p$ are chosen independently and uniformly at random.

2.3   Entropy and Randomness Extractors

Definition 2 (Average Min-entropy [16]). Let $X \in \mathcal{X}$ and $Z \in \mathcal{Z}$ be two random variables, the min-entropy of X denoted by $\mathbf{H}_\infty(X)$, is defined as $\mathbf{H}_\infty(X) = \min_{x \in \mathcal{X}}\{-\log(Pr[X = x])\} = -\log(\max_{x \in \mathcal{X}} Pr[X = x])$. Given a (correlated) random variable Z, the average min-entropy of X conditioned on Z, is defined as

$$\tilde{\mathbf{H}}_\infty(X|Z) = -\log(\mathbb{E}_{z \in \mathcal{Z}}[\max_{x \in \mathcal{X}} Pr[X = x|Z = z]]) = -\log(\mathbb{E}_{z \in \mathcal{Z}}[2^{-\mathbf{H}_\infty(X|Z=z)}]).$$

This notion of average min-entropy measures the optimal probability of guessing X for an adversary who may observe the knowledge of Z.

Lemma 1 [16]. Let X, Y, Z be arbitrarily correlated random variables where Y takes at most 2^l possible values, then $\tilde{\mathbf{H}}_\infty(X|(Y, Z)) \geq \tilde{\mathbf{H}}_\infty(X|Z) - l$. In particular, $\tilde{\mathbf{H}}_\infty(X|Y) \geq \mathbf{H}_\infty(X) - l$.

Definition 3 (Statistical Distance and Extractors [9,16]). Let X, Y be two random variables with the same range $\mathcal{U}$, the statistical distance between random variable X and Y, denoted by $SD(X, Y)$, is defined as $SD(X, Y) = \frac{1}{2} \sum_{u \in \mathcal{U}} |Pr[X = u] - Pr[Y = u]|$. A function $Ext : \mathcal{U} \times \mathcal{R} \to \mathcal{V}$ is an average-case (l, δ)-extractor if for all random variables X, Z such that $X \in \mathcal{U}$ and

$\tilde{\mathbf{H}}_\infty(X|Z) \geq l$, we have $SD((Ext(X,R),R,Z),(V,R,Z)) \leq \delta$, where R and V are distributed uniformly and independently over their domain $\mathcal{R}$ and $\mathcal{V}$, respectively.

Definition 4 (Universal Hash [31,7]). A family $\mathcal{H}$ of hash functions $\mathcal{H} = \{h_k : \mathcal{X} \to \mathcal{Y}\}_{k \in \mathcal{K}}$ is called universal if, for every $x_1, x_2 \in \mathcal{X}$ with $x_1 \neq x_2$,

$$Pr_{k \in \mathcal{K}}[h_k(x_1) = h_k(x_2)] \leq \frac{1}{|\mathcal{Y}|}.$$

Two specific examples of universal hash are given as follows:

- the family $\mathcal{H}$ of functions $\{h_{k_1,k_2,\cdots,k_t} : \mathcal{X} \to \mathcal{Y}\}_{k_i \in Z_p, i=1,2,\cdots,t}$ is universal, where $h_{k_1,k_2,\cdots,k_t}(x_0, x_1, \cdots, x_t) = x_0 + x_1 k_1 + \cdots + x_t k_t$, all the operations are in the prime field F_p.
- the family $\mathcal{H}$ of functions $\{h_{k_1,k_2,\cdots,k_t} : \mathcal{G}^{t+1} \to \mathcal{G}\}_{k_i \in Z_p, i=1,2,\cdots,t}$ is universal, where $\mathcal{G}$ is a multiplicative group of prime order p with a generator g, and $h_{k_1,k_2,\cdots,k_t}(g_0, g_1, \cdots, g_t) = g_0 \cdot g_1^{k_1} \cdots \cdots g_t^{k_t} (= g^{x_0 + x_1 k_1 + \cdots + x_t k_t})$, with $g_i = g^{x_i}$ for $i = 0, 1, \cdots, t$.

Actually, the second family of universal hash is derived from the fact that the multiplicative group $(\mathcal{G}, \cdot)$ of prime order p is isomorphic to $(Z_p, +)$.

Lemma 2 (Leftover Hash Lemma and Its Generalization [16]). Assume that $\mathcal{H} = \{h_k : \mathcal{X} \to \mathcal{Y}\}_{k \in \mathcal{K}}$ is a family of universal hash functions, then for arbitrarily random variables $X \in \mathcal{X}, K \in \mathcal{K}$ and Z, we have $SD((h_K(X), K), (U_{\mathcal{Y}}, K))$ $\leq \frac{1}{2}\sqrt{2^{-\mathbf{H}_\infty(X)}|\mathcal{Y}|}$, and $SD((h_K(X), K, Z), (U_{\mathcal{Y}}, K, Z)) \leq \frac{1}{2}\sqrt{2^{-\tilde{\mathbf{H}}_\infty(X|Z)}|\mathcal{Y}|}$.

The leftover hash lemma stats that a family of universal hash functions gives an average-case (l, δ)-extractor $Ext : \mathcal{X} \times \mathcal{K} \to \mathcal{Y}$, with $\log|\mathcal{Y}| \leq l - 2\log(1/\delta) + 2$.

2.4 CCA2 Security of Leakage Resilient IBE

Similar to previous works [4,10,2], an IBE system $\mathcal{E}$ consists of four algorithms: *Setup, KeyGen, Encrypt,* and *Decrypt. Setup* algorithm takes as input a security parameter κ, and establishes PKG's public parameters *params* and the master secret key *msk. KeyGen* takes the master secret key *msk* and an identity ID as input, and generates the private key for the identity ID. On input a message, an identity ID and *params, Encrypt* algorithm outputs a ciphertext for ID. Receiving a ciphertext, the recipient with identity ID decrypts the ciphertext using algorithm *Decrypt*, with the ciphertext and her private key as input.

In this work, we use the bounded memory-leakage model, which is simple and general, and used in many PKE and IBE settings. The CCA2 security of leakage resilient IBE is defined via the following game, which is refined from the definition in [2]. Consistent with the work of [10,2], our security definition also only allows leakage attacks against the private keys of the various identities, but not the master secret key. Additionally, just as noted by [28,2,1], we also only allow the adversary to make leakage queries *before* seeing the challenge ciphertext.

Setup: The challenger generates $(params, msk) \leftarrow Setup(1^\kappa)$, and sends $params$ to the adversary $\mathcal{A}$.

Phase 1: In this phase, the adversary $\mathcal{A}$ can adaptively make the following three kinds of queries.

- Key generation queries: On input identity ID, the challenger runs $KeyGen$ on ID and replies with the resulting private key sk_{ID}.
- Leakage queries: On input ID and a PPT leakage function $f_i : \{0,1\}^* \to \{0,1\}^{\lambda_i}$, the challenger replies with $f_i(sk_{ID})$, if $\sum_{k=1}^{i} \lambda_k \leq \lambda$; Otherwise, outputs $\perp$.
- Decryption queries: On input the ciphertext (ID, C), the challenger first runs $KeyGen$ on ID, and then decrypts C using the resulting private key.

Challenge: The adversary submits two messages m_0, m_1 and a challenge identity ID^*, which never appeared in a key generation query and appeared in leakage queries with at most λ bits leakage. The challenger selects a random bit $b \in \{0,1\}$, and sends $C^* \leftarrow Encrypt(params, ID^*, m_b)$ to the adversary as the challenge ciphertext.

Phase 2: This Phase is almost the same as Phase 1, with the restriction that neither key generation queries on ID^* nor decryption queries on (ID^*, C^*) are allowed to make. Also, as mentioned above, no leakage query is allowed to make in this phase.

Guess: Finally, the adversary outputs a guess $b' \in \{0,1\}$. The adversary wins the game if $b' = b$.

We call an adversary $\mathcal{A}$ in the above game a IND-KL-ID-CCA2 adversary. The advantage of $\mathcal{A}$ is defined by $Adv_{IBE,\mathcal{A}}^{LR-CCA2-IBE}(\kappa, \lambda) = |Pr[\mathcal{A} \text{ wins }] - \frac{1}{2}|$.

Definition 5 (λ-LR-CCA2-IBE). An IBE scheme $\mathcal{E} = (Setup, KeyGen, Encrypt, Decrypt)$ is λ-leakage resilient CCA2 secure if for any probabilistic polynomial time IND-LR-ID-CCA2 adversary $\mathcal{A}$, it holds that $Adv_{IBE,\mathcal{A}}^{LR-CCA2-IBE}(\kappa, \lambda) \leq negl(\kappa)$.

3   Concrete Construction

The proposed leakage-resilient identity-based encryption scheme consists of four algorithms, each of which is described as follows:

- **Setup(1^κ):** On input the security parameter κ, PKG chooses random generators $g, h_1, h_2, h_3 \in G$, a random $\alpha \in Z_p$, and a hash function H from a universal one-way hash function family $\mathcal{H}$. Then the public parameters $params$ and the master secret key msk are set to be:

$$params = \{G, g, g_1 = g^\alpha, h_1, h_2, h_3, H\}, msk = \alpha.$$

- **KeyGen(ID, msk):** To generate a private key for identity $ID \in Z_p$, PKG randomly chooses $r_{ID,i} \in Z_p$ for $i \in \{1, 2, 3\}$, and outputs the corresponding private key sk_{ID} for ID:

$$sk_{ID} = \{(r_{ID,i}, h_{ID,i})\}, \text{ where } h_{ID,i} = (h_i g^{-r_{ID,i}})^{1/(\alpha - ID)}.$$

If $ID = \alpha$, PKG aborts. We require that PKG always uses the same values $r_{ID,i}, i \in \{1, 2, 3\}$ for the same ID.

- **Encrypt**($params, m$): To encrypt a message $m \in G_T$ for ID, the sender picks $r, s \in Z_p$ at random, and outputs the ciphertext $C = (u, v, w, r, y)$, where $u = g_1^s g^{-s \cdot ID}, v = e(g, g)^s, w = m \cdot e(g, h_3 h_1^r)^{-s}, y = e(g, h_2 h_3^\beta)^s$, and $\beta = H(u, v, w, r)$.

- **Decrypt**(sk_{ID}, C): To decrypt a ciphertext $C = (u, v, w, r, y)$, the recipient with identity ID computes $\beta = H(u, v, w, r)$ and check whether

$$y = e(u, h_{ID,2} h_{ID,3}^\beta) v^{(r_{ID,2} + r_{ID,3} \cdot \beta)}.$$

If the check fails, outputs $\perp$. Otherwise, outputs

$$m = w \cdot e(u, h_{ID,3} h_{ID,1}^r) v^{(r_{ID,3} + r_{ID,1} \cdot r)}.$$

4 Security and Correctness Analysis

4.1 Correctness

Assuming the ciphertext $C = (u, v, w, r, y)$ received by the recipient with ID is well-formed, we have:

$$e(u, h_{ID,2} h_{ID,3}^\beta) v^{(r_{ID,2} + r_{ID,3} \cdot \beta)}$$
$$= e(g^{s(\alpha - ID)}, (h_2 h_3^\beta)^{1/(\alpha - ID)} g^{-(r_{ID,2} + r_{ID,3} \cdot \beta)/(\alpha - ID)}) e(g, g)^{s(r_{ID,2} + r_{ID,3} \cdot \beta)}$$
$$= e(g, h_2 h_3^\beta)^s,$$

where $\beta = H(u, v, w, r)$, and

$$e(u, h_{ID,3} h_{ID,1}^r) v^{(r_{ID,3} + r_{ID,1} \cdot r)}$$
$$= e(g^{s(\alpha - ID)}, (h_3 h_1^r)^{1/(\alpha - ID)} g^{-(r_{ID,3} + r_{ID,1} \cdot r)/(\alpha - ID)}) e(g, g)^{s(r_{ID,3} + r_{ID,1} \cdot r)}$$
$$= e(g, h_3 h_1^r)^s.$$

4.2 Security Analysis

In this section, we prove that the proposed scheme is semantically secure against λ-bounded memory leakage and chosen-ciphertext attacks (λ-leakage resilient CCA2 secure), based on the truncated decision q-$ABDHE$ assumption.

Theorem 1. Under the hardness assumption of the truncated decision q-$ABDHE$ problem, where $q = q_{ID} + 2$, the above IBE scheme is $(\log p - \omega(\log \kappa))$-leakage resilient CCA2 secure, where q_{ID} is the maximum number of key generation queries made by the adversary, p is the prime order of the underlying group, and κ denotes the security parameter.

Proof. Suppose that there exists an adversary $\mathcal{A}$ that, making at most q_{ID} key generation queries and q_C decryption queries, breaks the λ-LR-CCA2 security of the presented IBE scheme above. Then, we can use $\mathcal{A}$ as a subroutine to construct an algorithm $\mathcal{B}$, which can solve the truncated decision q-$ABDHE$ assumption. On input a random truncated decision q-$ABDHE$ instance $(G, g', (g')^{\alpha^{q+2}}, g, g^\alpha, \ldots, g^{\alpha^q}, Z)$, where Z is either $e(g, g')^{\alpha^{q+1}}$ or a random element of G_T, the algorithm $\mathcal{B}$ proceeds as follows:

Setup: $\mathcal{B}$ randomly generates $f_i(x) \in Z_p[x]$ of degree q for $i \in \{1, 2, 3\}$, and sets $h_i = g^{f_i(\alpha)}$, which can be computed from $(g, g^\alpha, \ldots, g^{\alpha^q})$. Then the public parameters are published as $params = \{G, g, g_1, h_1, h_2, h_3, H\}$, where H is chosen at random from one universal one-way hash function family $\mathcal{H}$ and g_1 set to be g^α.

Phase 1: In this phase, the adversary $\mathcal{A}$ can adaptively make the following queries.

- Key generation queries: On input $ID \in Z_p$, if $ID = \alpha$, $\mathcal{B}$ uses α to solve the truncated decision q-$ABDHE$ immediately. Else, let $F_{ID,i}(x) = (f_i(x) - f_i(ID))/(x - ID)$, then sets $sk_{ID} = (r_{ID,i}, h_{ID,i}) = (f_i(ID), g^{F_{ID,i}(\alpha)})$. This is a valid private key for ID, since $g^{F_{ID,i}(\alpha)} = g^{\frac{f_i(\alpha) - f_i(ID)}{\alpha - ID}} = (g^{f_i(\alpha)}g^{-f_i(ID)})^{\frac{1}{\alpha-ID}} = (h_i g^{-r_{ID,i}})^{\frac{1}{\alpha-ID}}$, as required.

- Leakage queries: On input a leakage function $L_i : \{0,1\}^* \to \{0,1\}^{\lambda_i}$ for ID, if $ID = \alpha$, $\mathcal{B}$ uses α to solve the truncated decision q-$ABDHE$ immediately. Else, $\mathcal{B}$ replies with $L_i(sk_{ID})$, if $\sum_{k=1}^i \lambda_k \le \lambda$; Otherwise, outputs $\perp$.

- Decryption queries: On input the ciphertext (ID, C) for ID, $\mathcal{B}$ first generates a private key for ID as above, and then decrypts C by performing the usual *Decrypt* algorithm with this private key, and eventually sends the result to the adversary.

Challenge: $\mathcal{A}$ outputs two messages m_0, m_1, and the challenge identity ID^*. If $ID^* = \alpha$, $\mathcal{B}$ uses α to solve the truncated decision q-$ABDHE$ immediately. Else, $\mathcal{B}$ generates $b \in \{0, 1\}$ and computes a private key $sk_{ID^*} = (r_{ID^*,i}, h_{ID^*,i})$ for ID^* as in Phase 1. Let $f_4(x) = x^{q+2}$ and $F_{4,ID^*}(x) = (f_4(x) - f_4(ID^*))/(x - ID^*)$, which is a polynomial of degree $q + 1$. $\mathcal{B}$ sets $u^* = g'^{f_4(\alpha) - f_4(ID^*)}$, $v^* = Z \cdot e(g', \prod_{i=0}^q g^{F_{4,ID^*,i} \cdot \alpha^i})$, $w^* = m_b / e(u^*, h_{ID^*,3} h_{ID^*,1}^{r^*}) v^{*(r_{ID^*,3} + r_{ID^*,1} \cdot r^*)}$, where $F_{4,ID^*,i}$ is the coefficient of x^i in $F_{4,ID^*}(x)$, and r^* is chosen randomly from Z_p. After setting $\beta^* = H(u^*, v^*, w^*, r^*)$, $\mathcal{B}$ sets $y^* = e(u^*, h_{ID^*,2} h_{ID^*,3}^{\beta^*}) v^{*(r_{ID^*,2} + r_{ID^*,3} \cdot \beta^*)}$, and sends $C^* = (u^*, v^*, w^*, r^*, y^*)$ as the challenge ciphertext to the adversary.

Phase 2: This Phase is almost the same as Phase 1, with the restriction that no leakage queries, and neither key generation queries on ID^* nor decryption queries on (ID^*, C^*) are allowed to make.

Guess: Finally, $\mathcal{A}$ outputs a guess $b' \in \{0, 1\}$. If $b' = b$, $\mathcal{B}$ outputs 0 (indicating that $Z = e(g, g')^{\alpha^{q+1}}$); otherwise, returns 1.

Lemma 3. If $\mathcal{B}$'s input is sampled according to $\mathcal{P}_{ABDHE}$, $\mathcal{A}$'s view is identical to the actual attack.

Proof. It is clear that the public parameters in the simulation, from the adversary's view of point, have an identical distribution to the actual construction. This is because g, α, and $f_i(x)$ for $i \in \{1, 2, 3\}$ are all chosen uniformly at random, and so h_1, h_2 and h_3 are uniformly random.

As to the challenge ciphertext, it also has the correct distribution in the case of $\mathcal{B}$'s input sampled according to $\mathcal{P}_{ABDHE}$, i.e., $Z = e(g, g')^{\alpha^{q+1}}$. Indeed, in this case $u^* = g^{s^*(\alpha - ID^*)}$, $v^* = e(g, g)^{s^*}$, $m_b/w^* = e(g, h_3 h_1^{r^*})^{s^*}$, and $y^* = e(g, h_2 h_3^{\beta^*})^{s^*}$, where s^* is implicitly set to be $(\log_g g') \cdot F_{4,ID^*}(\alpha)$; thus, $(u^*, v^*, w^*, r^*, y^*)$ is a valid ciphertext for (ID^*, m_b) under randomness s^* and r^*. Since $\log_g g'$ is uniformly random, s^* is uniformly random. Besides, r^* is uniformly random, so $(u^*, v^*, w^*, r^*, y^*)$ is a valid and appropriately-distributed challenge to the adversary $\mathcal{A}$.

At last, with similar analysis to [19], it is easy to show that, from $\mathcal{A}$'s view, the private keys issued by $\mathcal{B}$ in the simulation are appropriately distributed, which follows from the fact that $f_i(x) \in Z_p[x]$ for $i \in \{1, 2, 3\}$ are uniformly random polynomials of degree q.

Lemma 4. If $\mathcal{B}$'s input is sampled according to $\mathcal{R}_{ABDHE}$, $\mathcal{A}$ has only a negligible advantage in outputting the correct bit b.

The *Lemma* follows from the following two claims. In later parts, we say a ciphertext $C' = (u', v', w', r', y')$ for ID is "invalid" if $v' \neq e(u', g)^{1/(\alpha - ID)}$.

Claim 1. If the decryption oracle rejects all invalid ciphertexts, then $\mathcal{A}$ has only a negligible advantage in outputting the correct bit b.

Proof. If all the invalid ciphertexts queried by $\mathcal{A}$ are rejected by the decryption oracle, $\mathcal{A}$ cannot gain any more information about the private key from it. The only information regarding the private key, known by $\mathcal{A}$, relates to the evaluations of $(f_1(x), f_2(x), f_3(x))$ at α (from the public key components), q_{ID} identities (from its key generation queries), the λ-bit leakage on the private key, and the challenge ciphertext $C^* = (u^*, v^*, w^*, r^*, y^*, ID^*)$. The information gained from the public key components and the key generation queries can be represented as follows:

$$\begin{cases} f_1(ID_i) = r_{ID_i,1}, for \ i \in \{1, 2, \cdots, q_{ID}\} \\ g^{f_1(\alpha)} = h_1 \\ f_2(ID_i) = r_{ID_i,2}, for \ i \in \{1, 2, \cdots, q_{ID}\} \\ g^{f_2(\alpha)} = h_2 \\ f_3(ID_i) = r_{ID_i,3}, for \ i \in \{1, 2, \cdots, q_{ID}\} \\ g^{f_3(\alpha)} = h_3 \end{cases} \tag{1}$$

Hence, the secret vector $\vec{f} = (f_{1,0}, f_{1,1}, \cdots, f_{1,q}, f_{2,0}, f_{2,1}, \cdots, f_{2,q}, f_{3,0}, f_{3,1},$ $\cdots, f_{3,q})$, where $f_{i,j}$ denotes the coefficient of x^j in $f_i(x)$, satisfies the following matrix product:

$$
\vec{f}
\begin{pmatrix}
1 & \cdots & 1 & 1 & 0 & \cdots & 0 & 0 & 0 & \cdots & 0 & 0 \\
ID_1 & \cdots & ID_{q_{ID}} & \alpha & 0 & \cdots & 0 & 0 & 0 & \cdots & 0 & 0 \\
\vdots & \ddots & \vdots & \vdots & \vdots & \ddots & \vdots & \vdots & \vdots & \ddots & \vdots & \vdots \\
ID_1^q & \cdots & ID_{q_{ID}}^q & \alpha^q & 0 & \cdots & 0 & 0 & 0 & \cdots & 0 & 0 \\
0 & \cdots & 0 & 0 & 1 & \cdots & 1 & 1 & 0 & \cdots & 0 & 0 \\
0 & \cdots & 0 & 0 & ID_1 & \cdots & ID_{q_{ID}} & \alpha & 0 & \cdots & 0 & 0 \\
\vdots & \ddots & \vdots & \vdots & \vdots & \ddots & \vdots & \vdots & \vdots & \ddots & \vdots & \vdots \\
0 & \cdots & 0 & 0 & ID_1^q & \cdots & ID_{q_{ID}}^q & \alpha^q & 0 & \cdots & 0 & 0 \\
0 & \cdots & 0 & 0 & 0 & \cdots & 0 & 0 & 1 & \cdots & 1 & 1 \\
0 & \cdots & 0 & 0 & 0 & \cdots & 0 & 0 & ID_1 & \cdots & ID_{q_{ID}} & \alpha \\
\vdots & \ddots & \vdots & \vdots & \vdots & \ddots & \vdots & \vdots & \vdots & \ddots & \vdots & \vdots \\
0 & \cdots & 0 & 0 & 0 & \cdots & 0 & 0 & ID_1^q & \cdots & ID_{q_{ID}}^q & \alpha^q
\end{pmatrix}
=
\begin{pmatrix}
r_{ID_1,1} \\
\vdots \\
r_{ID_{q_{ID}},1} \\
\log_g h_1 \\
r_{ID_1,2} \\
\vdots \\
r_{ID_{q_{ID}},2} \\
\log_g h_2 \\
r_{ID_1,3} \\
\vdots \\
r_{ID_{q_{ID}},3} \\
\log_g h_3
\end{pmatrix}^{\mathsf{T}}
$$

where "T" denotes matrix transposition.

In addition, from the challenger ciphertext $C^* = (u^*, v^*, w^*, r^*, y^*)$ we have:

$$
\begin{cases}
e(u^*, h_{ID^*,3}) v^{*r_{ID^*,3}} = A \\
e(u^*, h_{ID^*,1}) v^{*r_{ID^*,1}} = B \\
e(u^*, h_{ID^*,2} h_{ID^*,3}^{\beta^*}) v^{*(r_{ID^*,2}+r_{ID^*,3}\cdot\beta^*)} = y^*
\end{cases}
\tag{2}
$$

which equation system is equal to:

$$
\begin{cases}
a_{u^*} \log_g h_{ID^*,3} + a_{v^*} r_{ID^*,3} = \log_{e(g,g)} A \\
a_{u^*} \log_g h_{ID^*,1} + a_{v^*} r_{ID^*,1} = \log_{e(g,g)} B \\
a_{u^*}(\log_g h_{ID^*,2} + \beta^* \log_g h_{ID^*,3}) + \\
\quad a_{v^*}(r_{ID^*,2} + \beta^* \cdot r_{ID^*,3}) = a_{y^*}
\end{cases}
\tag{3}
$$

where $a_{u^*} = \log_g u^*$, $a_{v^*} = \log_{e(g,g)} v^*$ and $a_{y^*} = \log_{e(g,g)} y^*$.

Combining the following equations (4) got by the construction of the private key,

$$
\begin{cases}
\log_g h_1 = (\alpha - ID^*) \cdot \log_g h_{ID^*,1} + r_{ID^*,1} \\
\log_g h_2 = (\alpha - ID^*) \cdot \log_g h_{ID^*,2} + r_{ID^*,2} \\
\log_g h_3 = (\alpha - ID^*) \cdot \log_g h_{ID^*,3} + r_{ID^*,3}
\end{cases}
\tag{4}
$$

equations (3) can be rephrased as:

$$
\begin{cases}
\frac{a_{u^*}}{\alpha-ID^*} \log_g h_3 + (a_{v^*} - \frac{a_{u^*}}{\alpha-ID^*}) r_{ID^*,3} = \log_{e(g,g)} A \\
\frac{a_{u^*}}{\alpha-ID^*} \log_g h_1 + (a_{v^*} - \frac{a_{u^*}}{\alpha-ID^*}) r_{ID^*,1} = \log_{e(g,g)} B \\
\frac{a_{u^*}}{\alpha-ID^*}(\log_g h_2 + \beta^* \log_g h_3) + \\
\quad (a_{v^*} - \frac{a_{u^*}}{\alpha-ID^*})(r_{ID^*,2} + \beta^* \cdot r_{ID^*,3}) = a_{y^*}
\end{cases}
\tag{5}
$$

from which we know that the secret vector $\overrightarrow{f}$ also satisfies the following matrix product:

$$\overrightarrow{f}\begin{pmatrix} 0 & 1 & 0 \\ 0 & ID^* & 0 \\ \vdots & \vdots & \vdots \\ 0 & ID^{*q} & 0 \\ 0 & 0 & 1 \\ 0 & 0 & ID^* \\ \vdots & \vdots & \vdots \\ 0 & 0 & ID^{*q} \\ 1 & 0 & \beta^* \\ ID^* & 0 & \beta^* ID^* \\ \vdots & \vdots & \vdots \\ ID^{*q} & 0 & \beta^* ID^{*q} \end{pmatrix} = \begin{pmatrix} \dfrac{\log_{e(g,g)} A - \frac{a_{y^*}}{\alpha - ID^*} \log_g h_3}{a_{v^*} - \frac{a_{y^*}}{\alpha - ID^*}} \\[2mm] \dfrac{\log_{e(g,g)} B - \frac{a_{y^*}}{\alpha - ID^*} \log_g h_1}{a_{v^*} - \frac{a_{y^*}}{\alpha - ID^*}} \\[2mm] \dfrac{a_{y^*} - \frac{a_{y^*}}{\alpha - ID^*}(\log_g h_2 + \beta^* \log_g h_3)}{a_{v^*} - \frac{a_{y^*}}{\alpha - ID^*}} \end{pmatrix}^{\mathsf{T}}$$

where "T" denotes matrix transposition.

In what follows we will show that m_b/w^* is in fact the output of a $(2\log p - \lambda, \delta)$ extractor, with $A = e(u^*, h_{ID^*,3})v^{*^{r_{ID^*},3}}$ and $B = e(u^*, h_{ID^*,1})v^{*^{r_{ID^*},1}}$ as input.

By the matrix products derived from the equation systems (1) and (5), we can obtain the following coefficient matrix:

$$\begin{pmatrix} 1 & \cdots & 1 & 1 & 0 & \cdots & 0 & 0 & 0 & \cdots & 0 & 0 & 0 & 1 & 0 \\ ID_1 & \cdots & ID_{q_{ID}} & \alpha & 0 & \cdots & 0 & 0 & 0 & \cdots & 0 & 0 & 0 & ID^* & 0 \\ \vdots & \ddots & \vdots & \vdots & \vdots & \ddots & \vdots & \vdots & \vdots & \ddots & \vdots & \vdots & \vdots & \vdots & \vdots \\ ID_1^q & \cdots & ID_{q_{ID}}^q & \alpha^q & 0 & \cdots & 0 & 0 & 0 & \cdots & 0 & 0 & 0 & ID^{*q} & 0 \\ 0 & \cdots & 0 & 0 & 1 & \cdots & 1 & 1 & 0 & \cdots & 0 & 0 & 0 & 0 & 1 \\ 0 & \cdots & 0 & 0 & ID_1 & \cdots & ID_{q_{ID}} & \alpha & 0 & \cdots & 0 & 0 & 0 & 0 & ID^* \\ \vdots & \ddots & \vdots & \vdots & \vdots & \vdots & \ddots & \vdots & \vdots & \ddots & \vdots & \vdots & \vdots & \vdots & \vdots \\ 0 & \cdots & 0 & 0 & ID_1^q & \cdots & ID_{q_{ID}}^q & \alpha^q & 0 & \cdots & 0 & 0 & 0 & 0 & ID^{*q} \\ 0 & \cdots & 0 & 0 & 0 & \cdots & 0 & 0 & 1 & \cdots & 1 & 1 & 1 & 0 & \beta^* \\ 0 & \cdots & 0 & 0 & 0 & \cdots & 0 & 0 & ID_1 & \cdots & ID_{q_{ID}} & \alpha & ID^* & 0 & \beta^* ID^* \\ \vdots & \ddots & \vdots & \vdots & \vdots & \ddots & \vdots & \vdots & \vdots & \ddots & \vdots & \vdots & \vdots & \vdots & \vdots \\ 0 & \cdots & 0 & 0 & 0 & \cdots & 0 & 0 & ID_1^q & \cdots & ID_{q_{ID}}^q & \alpha^q & ID^{*q} & 0 & \beta^* ID^{*q} \end{pmatrix}$$

It is easy to prove that the columns of the $(3q + 3) \times (3q)$ coefficient matrix above denoted by M are linearly independent, where $q = q_{ID} + 2$. Specifically, let $\overrightarrow{v_1}, \overrightarrow{v_2}, \cdots, \overrightarrow{v_{3q}}$ be the $3q$ columns of M. Suppose that they are linearly dependent, then there must exist integers $a_1, a_2, \cdots, a_{3q}$, not all zero, such that $a_1 \overrightarrow{v_1} + a_2 \overrightarrow{v_2} + \cdots + a_{3q} \overrightarrow{v_{3q}} = 0$. From this equation, we have $a_1 \overrightarrow{v_1}' + a_2 \overrightarrow{v_2}' + \cdots + a_{q-1} \overrightarrow{v_{q-1}}' + a_{3q-1} \overrightarrow{v_{3q-1}}' = 0$, where $\overrightarrow{v_i}'$ denotes the first $q + 1$ coordinates of the column $\overrightarrow{v_i}$ for $i \in \{1, 2, \cdots, q - 1, 3q - 1\}$. Since all the columns $\overrightarrow{v_1}', \overrightarrow{v_2}', \cdots, \overrightarrow{v_{q-1}}', \overrightarrow{v_{3q-1}}'$ constitute a Vandermonde matrix, we get that $a_1 = a_2 = \cdots = a_{q-1} = a_{3q-1} =$

0. Similarly, we can obtain $a_q = a_{q+1} = \cdots = a_{2q-2} = a_{3q} = 0$ and $a_{2q-1} = a_{2q} = \cdots = a_{3q-3} = (a_{3q-2} + \beta^* a_{3q}) = 0$. Through these equations, it is easy to get that $a_1 = a_2 = \cdots = a_{3q} = 0$. Thus, this forms a contradiction.

Then, according to the equation system $\overrightarrow{f} \cdot M = \overrightarrow{v}$ got from (1) and (5), where $\overrightarrow{v} = (r_{ID_1,1}, \cdots, r_{ID_{q_{ID}},1}, \log_g h_1, r_{ID_1,2}, \cdots, r_{ID_{q_{ID}},2}, \log_g h_2, r_{ID_1,3}, \cdots,$ $r_{ID_{q_{ID}},3}, \log_g h_3, (\log_{e(g,g)} A - \frac{a_{u^*}}{\alpha - ID^*} \log_g h_3)/(a_{v^*} - \frac{a_{u^*}}{\alpha - ID^*}), (\log_{e(g,g)} B - \frac{a_{u^*}}{\alpha - ID^*}$ $\log_g h_1)/(a_{v^*} - \frac{a_{u^*}}{\alpha - ID^*}), (a_{y^*} - \frac{a_{u^*}}{\alpha - ID^*}(\log_g h_2 + \beta^* \log_g h_3))/(a_{v^*} - \frac{a_{u^*}}{\alpha - ID^*}))$, we get that for each $(A, B) \in G_T \times G_T$, the equation system has a three-dimensional solution space for $\overrightarrow{f}$, and that, even given $(h_1, h_2, h_3, (sk_1, sk_2, \cdots, sk_{q_{ID}}), y^*)$, (A, B) is still uniformly distributed over $G_T \times G_T$. Hence, we obtain:

$$\tilde{H}_\infty((A, B)|h_1, h_2, h_3, (sk_1, sk_2, \cdots, sk_{q_{ID}}), y^*) = 2 \log p.$$

Besides the knowledge above, the adversary also obtains at most λ-bit leakage on the private key. Thus, from the point of the adversary's view, we have:

$$\tilde{H}_\infty((A, B)|h_1, h_2, h_3, (sk_1, sk_2, \cdots, sk_{q_{ID}}), y^*, \lambda\text{-bit leakage}) \geq 2 \log p - \lambda,$$

where the inequality is obtained from the *Lemma 1*.

Moreover, from the construction of the ciphertext $C^* = (u^*, v^*, w^*, r^*, y^*)$, we have:

$$\begin{aligned} m_b/w^* &= e(u^*, h_{ID^*,3} h_{ID^*,1}^{r^*}) v^{*(r_{ID^*,3} + r_{ID^*,1} \cdot r^*)} \\ &= e(u^*, h_{ID^*,3}) v^{*r_{ID^*,3}}[e(u^*, h_{ID^*,1}) v^{*r_{ID^*,1}}]^{r^*} \\ &= h_{r^*}(A, B). \end{aligned}$$

By the definition of universal hash function (see, the example 2, with $t=1$), we know that m_b/w^* is the output of the universal hash $h_{r^*}(A, B) = A \cdot B^{r^*}$, with A and B as input.

According to the generalized leftover hash lemma, the statical distance between w^* and w chosen uniformly at random from G_T is given by $SD(w^*, w) \leq \frac{1}{2}\sqrt{p \cdot \frac{2^\lambda}{p^2}} = \frac{2^{\lambda/2-1}}{\sqrt{p}} = \delta$.

The strong extractor then guarantees that the part of challenge ciphertext w^* that depends on b is δ-close to the uniform on G_T, given the adversary's view, where δ is negligible.

From the condition $\log |\mathcal{Y}| \leq l - 2\log(1/\delta) + 2$ satisfied by the (l, δ)-extractor $Ext : \mathcal{X} \times \mathcal{K} \to \mathcal{Y}$, we can obtain that $\lambda \leq \log p - 2\log(1/\delta) + 2$.

Claim 2. The decryption oracle rejects all invalid ciphertexts, except with a negligible probability.

Proof. Suppose that the adversary $\mathcal{A}$ submits an invalid ciphertext (u', v', w', r', y') for unqueried identity ID, where $(u', v', w', r', y', ID) \neq (u^*, v^*, w^*, r^*, y^*, ID^*)$. Let $\{(r_{ID,i}, h_{ID,i}) : i \in \{1, 2, 3\}\}$ be the private key for ID. For the invalid ciphertext to be accepted, it must satisfy $y' = e(u', h_{ID,2} h_{ID,3}^{\beta'}) v'^{(r_{ID,2} + r_{ID,3} \cdot \beta')}$, which is equal to :

$$a_{y'} = a_{u'}(\log_g h_{ID,2} + \beta' \log_g h_{ID,3}) + a_{v'}(r_{ID,2} + \beta' \cdot r_{ID,3}) \quad (6)$$

where $\beta' = H(u', v', w', r')$, $a_{u'} = \log_g u'$, $a_{v'} = \log_{e(g,g)} v'$ and $a_{y'} = \log_{e(g,g)} y'$.

To compute the probability that $\mathcal{A}$ can generate such a y', we consider the distribution of $\{(r_{ID,i}, h_{ID,i}) : i \in \{1, 2, 3\}\}$ from the point of the adversary's view.

By the construction of the private key, $\mathcal{A}$ knows that $\{(r_{ID,i}, h_{ID,i}) : i \in \{1, 2, 3\}\}$ satisfy the following equations:

$$\begin{cases} \log_g h_1 = (\alpha - ID) \cdot \log_g h_{ID,1} + r_{ID,1} \\ \log_g h_2 = (\alpha - ID) \cdot \log_g h_{ID,2} + r_{ID,2} \\ \log_g h_3 = (\alpha - ID) \cdot \log_g h_{ID,3} + r_{ID,3} \end{cases} \tag{7}$$

Combined with the above equations (7), equation (6) can be rephrased as follows:

$$a_{y'} = \frac{a_{u'}}{\alpha - ID}(\log_g h_2 + \beta' \log_g h_3) + (a_{v'} - \frac{a_{u'}}{\alpha - ID})(r_{ID,2} + \beta' \cdot r_{ID,3}) \tag{8}$$

where $a_{v'} - \frac{a_{u'}}{\alpha - ID} \neq 0$, because the ciphertext (u', v', w', r', y') is invalid.

It is known to us that $r_{ID,i}$ is generated by computing $f_i(ID)$ for each identity in the simulation, in contrast to its generation in the actual construction where each $r_{ID,i}$ is chosen uniformly at random and independently. Therefore, $\mathcal{A}$ could conceivably gain some information regarding $(r_{ID,1}, r_{ID,2}, r_{ID,3})$ from its information regarding $f_1(x), f_2(x)$ and $f_3(x)$.

In the following, we denote the simulator's secret vector $(f_{1,0}, f_{1,1}, \cdots, f_{1,q}, f_{2,0}, f_{2,1}, \cdots, f_{2,q}, f_{3,0}, f_{3,1}, \cdots, f_{3,q})$ by $\overrightarrow{f}$ and the identity vector $(1, ID, ID^2, \cdots, ID^q)$ by $\overrightarrow{\gamma}_{ID}$, where $f_{i,j}$ is the coefficient of x^j in $f_i(x)$. Then we rephrase the equation (8) and obtain the following version:

$$a_{y'} = \frac{a_{u'}}{\alpha - ID}(\log_g h_2 + \beta' \log_g h_3) + (a_{v'} - \frac{a_{u'}}{\alpha - ID})(\overrightarrow{f} \cdot \overrightarrow{0} \parallel \overrightarrow{\gamma}_{ID} \parallel \beta' \overrightarrow{\gamma}_{ID}) \tag{9}$$

where "$\cdot$" denotes the dot product and "$\parallel$" denotes the concatenation of the coordinates of $\overrightarrow{\gamma}_{ID}$ and $\beta' \overrightarrow{\gamma}_{ID}$.

Prior to submitting the first invalid ciphertext, $\mathcal{A}$ is given the public parameters $(G, g, g_1, h_1, h_2, h_3, H)$, the challenge ciphertext $(u^*, v^*, w^*, r^*, y^*)$ for ID^*, the answers $\{(r_{ID_{i,j}}, h_{ID_{i,j}}) : i \in \{1, 2, \cdots, q_{ID}\}, j \in \{1, 2, 3\}\}$ to the q_{ID} key generation queries on identities $(ID_1, \cdots, ID_{q_{ID}})$, the λ-bit leakage on the private key, and the answers to the decryption queries on the valid ciphertexts. It could gain the information regarding $(f_1(x), f_2(x), f_3(x))$ from the evaluations of these values, but except the valid ciphertext queries. In fact, by submitting a valid ciphertext to the decryption oracle the adversary only learns the linear combinations of $\log_g h_1, \log_g h_2$ and $\log_g h_3$, which are already known from the public parameters. Ignoring the λ-bit leakage for now, the knowledge gained by $\mathcal{A}$ can be represented as follows:

$$\begin{cases} f_1(ID_i) = r_{ID_i,1}, for \ i \in \{1,2,\cdots,q_{ID}\} \\ g^{f_1(\alpha)} = h_1 \\ f_2(ID_i) = r_{ID_i,2}, for \ i \in \{1,2,\cdots,q_{ID}\} \\ g^{f_2(\alpha)} = h_2 \\ f_3(ID_i) = r_{ID_i,3}, for \ i \in \{1,2,\cdots,q_{ID}\} \\ g^{f_3(\alpha)} = h_3 \\ e(u^*, h_{ID^*,2} h_{ID^*,3}^{\beta^*}) v^{*(r_{ID^*,2}+r_{ID^*,3}\cdot\beta^*)} = y^* \\ e(u^*, h_{ID^*,3} h_{ID^*,1}^{r^*}) v^{*(r_{ID^*,3}+r_{ID^*,1}\cdot r^*)} = m_b/w^* \end{cases} \tag{10}$$

From the above, it is easy to get the coefficient matrix V of the matrix product corresponding to the equation system (10):

$$\begin{pmatrix}
1 & \cdots & 1 & 1 & 0 & \cdots & 0 & 0 & 0 & \cdots & 0 & 0 & 0 & r^* \\
ID_1 & \cdots & ID_{q_{ID}} & \alpha & 0 & \cdots & 0 & 0 & 0 & \cdots & 0 & 0 & 0 & r^*ID^* \\
\vdots & \ddots & \vdots & \vdots & \vdots & \ddots & \vdots & \vdots & \vdots & \ddots & \vdots & \vdots & \vdots & \vdots \\
ID_1^q & \cdots & ID_{q_{ID}}^q & \alpha^q & 0 & \cdots & 0 & 0 & 0 & \cdots & 0 & 0 & 0 & r^*ID^{*q} \\
0 & \cdots & 0 & 0 & 1 & \cdots & 1 & 1 & 0 & \cdots & 0 & 0 & 1 & 0 \\
0 & \cdots & 0 & 0 & ID_1 & \cdots & ID_{q_{ID}} & \alpha & 0 & \cdots & 0 & 0 & ID^* & 0 \\
\vdots & \ddots & \vdots & \vdots & \vdots & \ddots & \vdots & \vdots & \vdots & \ddots & \vdots & \vdots & \vdots & \vdots \\
0 & \cdots & 0 & 0 & ID_1^q & \cdots & ID_{q_{ID}}^q & \alpha^q & 0 & \cdots & 0 & 0 & ID^{*q} & 0 \\
0 & \cdots & 0 & 0 & 0 & \cdots & 0 & 0 & 1 & \cdots & 1 & 1 & \beta^* & 1 \\
0 & \cdots & 0 & 0 & 0 & \cdots & 0 & 0 & ID_1 & \cdots & ID_{q_{ID}} & \alpha & \beta^*ID^* & ID^* \\
\vdots & \ddots & \vdots & \vdots & \vdots & \ddots & \vdots & \vdots & \vdots & \ddots & \vdots & \vdots & \vdots & \vdots \\
0 & \cdots & 0 & 0 & 0 & \cdots & 0 & 0 & ID_1^q & \cdots & ID_{q_{ID}}^q & \alpha^q & \beta^*ID^{*q} & ID^{*q}
\end{pmatrix}$$

where the first $3q_{ID}+3$ columns of V correspond to the public terms h_1, h_2, h_3 and q_{ID} key generation queries made by $\mathcal{A}$, and the last two columns correspond to the challenge ciphertext for ID^*. In particular, from the challenge ciphertext $(u^*, v^*, w^*, r^*, y^*)$ we know that

$$\begin{cases} e(u^*, h_{ID^*,2} h_{ID^*,3}^{\beta^*}) v^{*(r_{ID^*,2}+r_{ID^*,3}\cdot\beta^*)} = y^* \\ e(u^*, h_{ID^*,3} h_{ID^*,1}^{r^*}) v^{*(r_{ID^*,3}+r_{ID^*,1}\cdot r^*)} = m_b/w^* \end{cases} \tag{11}$$

Combining with the following equations derived from the constructions of the private key for ID^*,

$$\begin{cases} \log_g h_1 = (\alpha - ID^*) \cdot \log_g h_{ID^*,1} + r_{ID^*,1} \\ \log_g h_2 = (\alpha - ID^*) \cdot \log_g h_{ID^*,2} + r_{ID^*,2} \\ \log_g h_3 = (\alpha - ID^*) \cdot \log_g h_{ID^*,3} + r_{ID^*,3} \end{cases} \tag{12}$$

they can be rephrased as:

$$\begin{cases} \frac{a_{u^*}}{\alpha-ID^*}(\log_g h_2 + \beta^* \log_g h_3) + \\ \quad (a_{v^*} - \frac{a_{u^*}}{\alpha-ID^*})(r_{ID^*,2} + \beta^* \cdot r_{ID^*,3}) = a_{y^*} \\ \frac{a_{u^*}}{\alpha-ID^*}(r^* \log_g h_1 + \log_g h_3) + \\ \quad (a_{v^*} - \frac{a_{u^*}}{\alpha-ID^*})(r^* \cdot r_{ID^*,1} + r_{ID^*,3}) = \log_{e(g,g)} m_b/w^* \end{cases} \tag{13}$$

where $a_{u^*} = \log_g u^*$, $a_{v^*} = \log_{e(g,g)} v^*$ and $a_{y^*} = \log_{e(g,g)} y^*$, from which the last two columns of V are obtained.

Beyond that, the adversary learns at most λ-bit leakage on the private key. Now, there are 3 cases to consider:

1. $(u', v', w', r') = (u^*, v^*, w^*, r^*)$: In this case, $\beta' = \beta^*$. If $ID = ID^*$ but $y' \neq y^*$, the decryption oracle certainly rejects the ciphertext. If $ID \neq ID^*$, for the invalid ciphertext to be accepted by the decryption oracle, $\mathcal{A}$ must generate a y' that satisfies equation (9). However, it is easy to know that the vector $(\overrightarrow{0} \parallel \overrightarrow{\gamma}_{ID} \parallel \beta'\overrightarrow{\gamma}_{ID})^\top$ corresponding to equation (9) and the columns of V in $Z_p^{3(q+1)}$ are linearly independent, where "$\top$" denotes matrix transposition. That is, the new matrix $V' = (V, (\overrightarrow{0} \parallel \overrightarrow{\gamma}_{ID} \parallel \beta'\overrightarrow{\gamma}_{ID})^\top)$ is column full rank. Thus, for each $y' \in G_T$ the equation system with the coefficient matrix V', obtained by combining (9) with (10), has a three-dimensional solution space for $\overrightarrow{f}$, and y' is uniformly distributed over G_T, conditioned on the adversary's view except the λ-bit leakage. Hence, ignoring the leakage on the private key for the time being, the adversary can guess a correct y' with probability $1/p$, even given the public parameters $params$, key generation queries on $(ID_1, \cdots, ID_{q_{ID}})$, and the challenge ciphertext $(u^*, v^*, w^*, r^*, y^*)$ for ID^*. Now, taking the λ-bit leakage in account, we have $\tilde{H}_\infty(y'|\text{view}) \geq \log p - \lambda$, where view denotes the view of the adversary prior to submitting the first invalid ciphertext. In particular, by the definition of the average min-entropy, it implies that the probability of $\mathcal{A}$ in generating a correct y' is at most $2^{\tilde{H}_\infty(y'|\text{view})} \leq 2^\lambda/p$. Thus, the first invalid ciphertext is accepted by the decryption oracle with probability at most $2^\lambda/p$. An almost identical argument holds for all the subsequent invalid ciphertext queries. The decryption oracle accepts the i-th invalid ciphertext with probability at most $2^\lambda/(p - i + 1) \leq 2^\lambda/(p - q_c)$, where q_c is total number of decryption queries. Therefore, the probability that at least one of the invalid ciphertexts can be accepted is at most $2^\lambda q_c/(p - q_c)$, which is negligible. This follows from the fact that q_c is a polynomial, and from the restriction $\lambda \leq \log p - \omega(\log \kappa)$.

2. $(u', v', w', r') \neq (u^*, v^*, w^*, r^*)$ and $\beta' = \beta^*$: This violates the universal one-wayness of the hash function H. An argument can be made, analogously to that in Cramer-Shoup cryptosystem [11].

3. $(u', v', w', r') \neq (u^*, v^*, w^*, r^*)$ and $\beta' \neq \beta^*$: In this case, to pass the decryption algorithm, $\mathcal{A}$ must generate such a y' for ID that satisfies the equation (9). When $ID \neq ID^*$, $\mathcal{A}$ just can do this with a negligible probability, the reason for which is essentially the same as that discussed in *Case 1*. If $ID = ID^*$, then $(\overrightarrow{0} \parallel \overrightarrow{\gamma}_{ID} \parallel \beta'\overrightarrow{\gamma}_{ID})^\top$ and the columns of V are also linearly independent because of $\beta' \neq \beta^*$. Similar to the analysis in *Case 1*, the adversary $\mathcal{A}$ can guess y' correctly in this case with only a negligible probability.

Note. Due to the underlying design rationale, we can also obtain some other variants of our proposal, such as $w = m \cdot e(g, h_2)^{-s} e(g, h_1)^{-sr}$, $y = e(g, h_2)^s e(g, h_3)^{s\beta}$ and $w = m \cdot e(g, h_2 h_3)^{-s} e(g, h_1)^{-sr}$, $y = e(g, h_1 h_2)^s e(g, h_3)^{s\beta}$.

5   Performance Analysis

In this part, we will give a comparison of our work with the original scheme proposed by Gentry et. al. [19] and the leakage-resilient version presented in [2], in terms of the message space, leakage size, computation cost, and so on. The results are shown in the following tables (cf. Table 1 & 2).

From Table 1, it is easy to see that our scheme gives a larger message space than that in Alwen et.al.'s scheme [2] and can tolerate a larger amount of leakage. In particular, the message space in our work is the group G, which is exactly the same as that in the original scheme [19]. Moreover, in our scheme it is independent of the bit-size λ of leakage. However, in Alwen et. al.'s work the length m of the encrypted message is limited by $\log p - \lambda - \omega(\log \kappa)$, which is due to the fact that the length m of the plaintext and the leakage bits λ in [2] need to satisfy the relation $\lambda + m \leq \log p - \omega(\log \kappa)$. That is, the size of the message space in [2] is limited by $p/2^{\lambda}$, i.e., $2^m < p/2^{\lambda}$. Thus, our proposal can encrypt a longer message and tolerate a larger amount of leakage simultaneously.

Table 1. Comparison of leakage resilience

Scheme	$|\mathcal{M}|$	Leakage λ^*	Ratio
Gentry et.al.[19]	p	–	–
Alwen et.al.[2]	2^m	$(\log p - m - \omega(\log \kappa))$	1/6
Our Scheme	p	$(\log p - \omega(\log \kappa))$	1/6

$|\mathcal{M}|$: the size of message space $\mathcal{M}$; Ratio: the fraction of leakage, i.e., the size of leakage permitted / the size of private key; *: the upper bound of the bit-size of leakage allowed.

Table 2. Computational efficiency comparison

Scheme	KeyGen	Encryption	Decryption	Ciphertext
Gentry et.al.[19]	6Exp	6Exp	2P+3Exp	$1G+3G_T$
Alwen et.al.[2]	6Exp	6Exp+1Ext	2P+3Exp+1Ext	$1G+2G_T+(m+d)$-bit
Our Scheme	6Exp	7Exp	2P+4Exp	$1G+3G_T+\log p$-bit

m: the bit-size of the encrypted message; P: a pairing operation; Exp: a group exponentiation in G or G_T; Ext: an evaluation of $Ext: G_T \times \{0,1\}^d \to \{0,1\}^m$.

As to the computational efficiency, it is shown in Table 2 that our proposal is quite practical, which is comparable to the original scheme [19]. Specifically, Gentry et. al.'s scheme is a little more efficient than ours, but it cannot tolerate any leakage. For the scheme in [2], when it is used to encrypt $\log p$-bit message, our proposal has almost the same efficiency as [2] and can still tolerate $\log p - \omega(\log \kappa)$ bits of leakage. In contrast, the scheme in [2] almost disallows any key leakage, as in this case the leakage parameter λ is approaching to 0. Furthermore, when the scheme is deployed in the environments where the key leakage occurs with a large amount, assuming it approaching to $\log p - \omega(\log \kappa)$, our proposal will be significantly more efficient than the scheme in [2], since in this case the length of the encrypted message in [2] is approaching to 0. Overall, our proposal is quite practical, and has almost the same efficiency as the original scheme and a much better performance than [2].

6   Conclusion

As an important primitive, IBE has attracted much attention in the context of leakage resilience in recent years. However, almost all of the existing leakage-resilient IBE schemes only achieve CPA security in this new setting, except that one proposed by Alwen et al.. Unfortunately, this CCA secure scheme suffers from an undesirable shortcoming that the leakage parameter λ and the message length m are subject to $\lambda + m \leq \log p - \omega(\log \kappa)$. In this paper, we put forward a new IBE scheme, which is proved λ-leakage resilient CCA2 secure in the standard model under the truncated decision q-ABDHE assumption. Compared with the existing CCA secure IBE scheme, the leakage parameter in our proposal, $\lambda \leq \log p - \omega(\log \kappa)$, is independent of the size of the message space. As far as we know, it is the most practical and the first leakage-resilient fully CCA2 secure IBE scheme in the standard model, whose leakage parameter is independent of the message length. Although we overcome this undesirable drawback in this work, the leakage ratio (cf. Table 1) here is still approximately equal to $1/6$. In the future work, we will try to give some new proposal with higher leakage ratio.

Acknowledgements. The authors are grateful to all anonymous reviewers for valuable suggestions and comments. The authors Shi-Feng Sun and Dawu Gu are supported by the Major State Basic Research Development Program (973 Plan)(No. 2013CB338004), and the Doctoral Fund of Ministry of Education of China (No. 20120073110094). And the author Shengli Liu is supported by the Natural Science Foundation of China (No. 61170229, 61373153), and the Scientific Innovation Project of Shanghai Municipal Education Commission (No. 12ZZ021).

References

1. Akavia, A., Goldwasser, S., Vaikuntanathan, V.: Simultaneous hardcore bits and cryptography against memory attacks. In: Reingold, O. (ed.) TCC 2009. LNCS, vol. 5444, pp. 474–495. Springer, Heidelberg (2009)
2. Alwen, J., Dodis, Y., Naor, M., Segev, G., Walfish, S., Wichs, D.: Public-key encryption in the bounded-retrieval model. In: Gilbert, H. (ed.) EUROCRYPT 2010. LNCS, vol. 6110, pp. 113–134. Springer, Heidelberg (2010)
3. Biham, E., Shamir, A.: Differential fault analysis of secret key cryptosystems. In: Kaliski Jr., B.S. (ed.) CRYPTO 1997. LNCS, vol. 1294, pp. 513–525. Springer, Heidelberg (1997)
4. Boneh, D., Boyen, X.: Efficient selective-ID secure identity-based encryption without random oracles. In: Cachin, C., Camenisch, J.L. (eds.) EUROCRYPT 2004. LNCS, vol. 3027, pp. 223–238. Springer, Heidelberg (2004)
5. Boneh, D., DeMillo, R.A., Lipton, R.J.: On the importance of checking cryptographic protocols for faults (extended abstract). In: Fumy, W. (ed.) EUROCRYPT 1997. LNCS, vol. 1233, pp. 37–51. Springer, Heidelberg (1997)
6. Boneh, D., Gentry, C., Hamburg, M.: Space-efficient identity based encryption without pairings. In: FOCS, pp. 647–657 (2007)
7. Carter, L., Wegman, M.N.: Universal classes of hash functions (extended abstract). In: STOC, pp. 106–112 (1977)

8. Chen, Y., Luo, S., Chen, Z.: A new leakage-resilient IBE scheme in the relative leakage model. In: Li, Y. (ed.) DBSec 2011. LNCS, vol. 6818, pp. 263–270. Springer, Heidelberg (2011)

9. Chor, B., Goldreich, O.: Unbiased bits from sources of weak randomness and probabilistic communication complexity. SIAM J. Comput. 17(2), 230–261 (1988)

10. Chow, S.S.M., Dodis, Y., Rouselakis, Y., Waters, B.: Practical leakage-resilient identity-based encryption from simple assumptions. In: ACM Conference on Computer and Communications Security, pp. 152–161 (2010)

11. Cramer, R., Shoup, V.: A practical public key cryptosystem provably secure against adaptive chosen ciphertext attack. In: Krawczyk, H. (ed.) CRYPTO 1998. LNCS, vol. 1462, pp. 13–25. Springer, Heidelberg (1998)

12. Cramer, R., Shoup, V.: Universal hash proofs and a paradigm for adaptive chosen ciphertext secure public-key encryption. In: Knudsen, L.R. (ed.) EUROCRYPT 2002. LNCS, vol. 2332, pp. 45–64. Springer, Heidelberg (2002)

13. Dodis, Y., Goldwasser, S., Kalai, Y.T., Peikert, C., Vaikuntanathan, V.: Public-key encryption schemes with auxiliary inputs. In: Micciancio, D. (ed.) TCC 2010. LNCS, vol. 5978, pp. 361–381. Springer, Heidelberg (2010)

14. Dodis, Y., Haralambiev, K., López-Alt, A., Wichs, D.: Efficient public-key cryptography in the presence of key leakage. In: Abe, M. (ed.) ASIACRYPT 2010. LNCS, vol. 6477, pp. 613–631. Springer, Heidelberg (2010)

15. Dodis, Y., Kalai, Y.T., Lovett, S.: On cryptography with auxiliary input. In: STOC, pp. 621–630 (2009)

16. Dodis, Y., Ostrovsky, R., Reyzin, L., Smith, A.: Fuzzy extractors: How to generate strong keys from biometrics and other noisy data. SIAM J. Comput. 38(1), 97–139 (2008)

17. Dziembowski, S., Pietrzak, K.: Leakage-resilient cryptography. In: FOCS, pp. 293–302 (2008)

18. Gandolfi, K., Mourtel, C., Olivier, F.: Electromagnetic analysis: Concrete results. In: Koç, Ç.K., Naccache, D., Paar, C. (eds.) CHES 2001. LNCS, vol. 2162, pp. 251–261. Springer, Heidelberg (2001)

19. Gentry, C.: Practical identity-based encryption without random oracles. In: Vaudenay, S. (ed.) EUROCRYPT 2006. LNCS, vol. 4004, pp. 445–464. Springer, Heidelberg (2006)

20. Gentry, C., Peikert, C., Vaikuntanathan, V.: Trapdoors for hard lattices and new cryptographic constructions. In: STOC, pp. 197–206 (2008)

21. Halderman, J.A., Schoen, S.D., Heninger, N., Clarkson, W., Paul, W., Calandrino, J.A., Feldman, A.J., Appelbaum, J., Felten, E.W.: Lest we remember: Cold boot attacks on encryption keys. In: USENIX Security Symposium, pp. 45–60 (2008)

22. Juma, A., Vahlis, Y., Yung, M.: Multi-location leakage resilient cryptography. In: Fischlin, M., Buchmann, J., Manulis, M. (eds.) PKC 2012. LNCS, vol. 7293, pp. 504–521. Springer, Heidelberg (2012)

23. Kocher, P.C.: Timing attacks on implementations of diffie-hellman, RSA, DSS, and other systems. In: Koblitz, N. (ed.) CRYPTO 1996. LNCS, vol. 1109, pp. 104–113. Springer, Heidelberg (1996)

24. Kocher, P.C., Jaffe, J., Jun, B.: Differential power analysis. In: Wiener, M. (ed.) CRYPTO 1999. LNCS, vol. 1666, pp. 388–397. Springer, Heidelberg (1999)

25. Lewko, A., Waters, B.: New techniques for dual system encryption and fully secure HIBE with short ciphertexts. In: Micciancio, D. (ed.) TCC 2010. LNCS, vol. 5978, pp. 455–479. Springer, Heidelberg (2010)

26. Liu, S., Weng, J., Zhao, Y.: Efficient public key cryptosystem resilient to key leakage chosen ciphertext attacks. In: Dawson, E. (ed.) CT-RSA 2013. LNCS, vol. 7779, pp. 84–100. Springer, Heidelberg (2013)
27. Micali, S., Reyzin, L.: Physically observable cryptography (extended abstract). In: Naor, M. (ed.) TCC 2004. LNCS, vol. 2951, pp. 278–296. Springer, Heidelberg (2004)
28. Naor, M., Segev, G.: Public-key cryptosystems resilient to key leakage. In: Halevi, S. (ed.) CRYPTO 2009. LNCS, vol. 5677, pp. 18–35. Springer, Heidelberg (2009)
29. Naor, M., Yung, M.: Public-key cryptosystems provably secure against chosen ciphertext attacks. In: STOC, pp. 427–437 (1990)
30. Waters, B.: Efficient identity-based encryption without random oracles. In: Cramer, R. (ed.) EUROCRYPT 2005. LNCS, vol. 3494, pp. 114–127. Springer, Heidelberg (2005)
31. Wegman, M.N., Carter, L.: New hash functions and their use in authentication and set equality. J. Comput. Syst. Sci. 22(3), 265–279 (1981)
32. Yuen, T.H., Chow, S.S.M., Zhang, Y., Yiu, S.M.: Identity-based encryption resilient to continual auxiliary leakage. In: Pointcheval, D., Johansson, T. (eds.) EUROCRYPT 2012. LNCS, vol. 7237, pp. 117–134. Springer, Heidelberg (2012)

Revocable IBE Systems
with Almost Constant-Size Key Update

Le Su, Hoon Wei Lim, San Ling, and Huaxiong Wang

Division of Mathematical Sciences
School of Physical and Mathematical Sciences
Nanyang Technological University, Singapore
lsu1@e.ntu.edu.sg, {hoonwei,lingsan,hxwang}@ntu.edu.sg

Abstract. Identity-based encryption (IBE) has been regarded as an attractive alternative to more conventional certificate-based public key systems. It has recently attracted not only considerable research from the academic community, but also interest from the industry and standardization bodies. However, while key revocation is a fundamental requirement to any public key systems, not much work has been done in the identity-based setting. In this paper, we continue the study of *revocable* IBE (RIBE) initiated by Boldyreva, Goyal, and Kumar. Their proposal of a selective secure RIBE scheme, and a subsequent construction by Libert and Vergnaud in a stronger adaptive security model are based on a binary tree approach, such that their key update size is *logarithmic* in the number of users. In this paper, we show that the key update size could be further reduced to constant with some small amount of auxiliary information, through a novel combination of the Lewko and Waters IBE scheme and the Camenisch, Kohlweiss, and Soriente pairing-based dynamic accumulator.

Keywords: public-key cryptography, identity-based encryption, revocation, accumulator, adaptive security.

1 Introduction

It is sometimes necessary to remove keying material from use prior to the end of its normal cryptoperiod (or key lifetime) for reasons that include key compromise, removal of an entity from an organization, and so on. This process is known as *key revocation* and is used to explicitly revoke a symmetric key or the public key of a key pair, although the private key associated with the public key is also revoked [5]. Public key revocation in a conventional, certificate-based public key infrastructure (PKI) has been well studied and understood. A widely deployed revocation mechanism is through the use of a Certificate Revocation List (CRL) [21]. Alternatively, an Internet protocol called the Online Certificate Status Protocol (OCSP) is used to check if a certificate has been revoked [26].

In this paper, we study public key revocation in an *identity-based encryption* (IBE) system. The idea of using an identity (or identifier) as a public key was

Z. Cao and F. Zhang (Eds.): Pairing 2013, LNCS 8365, pp. 168–185, 2014.
© Springer International Publishing Switzerland 2014

originally conceived by Shamir [32], and subsequently realized by Cocks [15] using quadratic residues, and Boneh and Franklin [10] using pairings on elliptic curves. One very appealing property of IBE is that it alleviates cumbersome certificate management in a traditional PKI. To securely send a message to an intended receiver, the sender no longer needs to look up for the public key certificate associated with the receiver, but simply encrypts the message directly using a common set of public system parameters and the receiver's identifier, such as email address. Over the past decade, pairing-based IBE has not only received considerable attention from academic researchers, but also attracted commercial interest from Mitsubishi, Noretech, Trend Micro, Voltage Security, and Gemplus [18], for example. Moreover, identity-based cryptographic techniques using pairings are currently undergoing standardization through the IEEE 1363.3 and the IETF S/MIME working groups. However, very few studies, for example [7, 14, 25, 31], have been devoted to key revocation thus far.

1.1 Motivation

Unlike a certificate-based public key, which is simply a random-looking string, a public key in the IBE setting is a user's identity. This hinders "explicit" revocation of an identity-based public key using conventional revocation mechanisms. Instead, one typically adopts a more "implicit" approach by periodically updating the corresponding private key after a pre-defined validity period, while letting the old private key expire automatically and keeping the public key (identity) unchanged. One trivial way of achieving this is by encoding a current time period into an identity during encryption. This forces a decryptor to regularly obtain her private key (corresponding to the current time period) from a key authority [10]. However, such an approach does not scale well because the key authority has to generate new keys for all the remaining non-revoked users at the beginning of each time period. Further, distribution of private keys requires establishment of secure channels between the key authority and the users. This may not be always feasible for every user.

A more desirable approach is to let the key authority broadcast some *public* information, from which the users can perform key update themselves without interacting with the key authority. Clearly, we must ensure that the broadcast information is useful only to non-revoked users, but meaningless to those who have been revoked. Hanaoka et al. [20] proposed one of the first IBE schemes that supports a *non-interactive* key revocation approach. However, their scheme requires each user to posses a special tamper-resistant hardware device that stores a secret helper key used for key update—a requirement that is likely to hinder practical deployment of the scheme.

Subsequently, Boldyreva et al. [7] proposed a scheme that obviates the need for special devices and significantly reduces the complexity of key update information from linear to *logarithmic* in the number users. They cleverly combined fuzzy IBE (FIBE) [30] with binary tree structure, which has previously been used to improve the efficiency of certificate revocation in a traditional PKI [1, 27]. By making use of the concept of FIBE, Boldyreva et al. gave a construction they called revocable IBE (RIBE), in which a message is encrypted under two attributes, namely identity id and time t. Correspondingly, the associated decryption key comprises two components, of which the identity part is fixed (also called a long-term private key), while the time part is updated after each time period (or epoch). In order to revoke a user, the key authority simply stops issuing key update for that user in the next time period. Without the latest key update, a revoked user will no longer be able to decrypt any ciphertext generated beyond the current (expiring) time period. As with [1, 27], a binary tree can then be used to more efficiently (logarithmically) represent all the remaining non-revoked users than simply listing all the revoked or non-revoked users. In Boldyreva et al.'s RIBE scheme, each user's id is assigned to a leaf node in the binary tree and her long-term private key is generated according to the key material on each node along the path from the user's leaf node to the root. To decrypt a message encrypted under id and t, the user needs an updated decryption key (associated with t) that can be derived from the key material associated with any one of the nodes along the path from her id leaf node to the root. Hence, if a user has been revoked, such key material will not be made available in the key update broadcast by the key authority.

However, Boldyreva et al.'s scheme was proven secure in a *selective* security model, which is widely accepted as a weaker model in comparison with an *adaptive* security model. The former requires the adversary to announce the target identity and time at the beginning of a security game simulated in the model, while the latter has no such restriction. Nevertheless, Libert and Vergnaud [25] showed that adaptive security is possible. They proposed an RIBE scheme which has key update size that is also logarithmic using a similar binary tree technique, while proving their scheme to be adaptively secure. However, they achieved this at the expense of increasing the size of public parameters from constant to linear in the number of users.

The goal of this paper is then to study whether or not we could further reduce the key update size while retaining the adaptive security requirement. We give an affirmative answer and provide a concrete construction which relies on only constant-size of key update material along with some auxiliary information, through a novel approach that combines IBE with the concept of a cryptographic *accumulator*.

1.2   Our Approach

The key component in our approach that enables efficient key revocation and update is a pairing-based cryptographic accumulator by Camenisch et al. [13]. An accumulator, originally introduced by Benaloh and de Mare [6] as an alternative to digital signatures for secure decentralized and distributed protocols, is an algorithm that "compresses" a large set of values into a single, short value with the following two basic properties:

– For each accumulated value, it is possible to compute a *witness* that can be used to prove that a given value was indeed incorporated into the accumulator;

– Whenever a value is added or removed from the accumulator, all witnesses correspond to all the remaining values in the updated accumulator need to be re-computed as well.

The accumulator proposed by Camenisch et al. [13] is designed to address the problem of revocation of *anonymous credentials*—to efficiently prove that a hidden value has been accumulated. By making use of techniques from broadcast encryption developed by Boneh et al. [11], Camenisch et al.'s accumulator has a very nice property that allows update of witnesses to be performed very efficiently. Only one multiplication is required for addition or deletion of a value from the accumulator. Further, update of witnesses can be delegated to an untrusted entities without compromising the security of an anonymous credential system.

In this work, we take a different approach from that of [13] when considering public key revocation in the IBE setting. We combine Lewko and Waters' IBE scheme [23] with Camenisch et al.'s accumulator [13] in a particular way. Conventionally, an accumulator is used for revocation of credentials or keys in an anonymous authentication system that is based on concepts such as, group signatures or anonymous e-cash. Also, a witness is independent of the authentication system, in the sense that it is not directly used for authentication, but rather is typically used to convince a verifier that a user has or has not been revoked through a zero-knowledge proof. On the other hand, in our approach, we integrate an accumulator with a public key encryption scheme, such that the accumulator is associated with ciphertexts, while witnesses are associated with decryption keys. Particularly, our encryption algorithm takes as input a message, an identity, and an up-to-date accumulator for current time period t, such that a target recipient is able to decrypt the resulting ciphertext using an up-to-date witness. That is, the decryption would succeed only if the recipient has not already been revoked at time t. Here, a user's decryption key comprises an identity-based key and a witness. During decryption, both the witness and the ciphertext component containing the accumulator are required to cancel out a blinding factor of the message.

Our approach of combining the IBE scheme of [23] and the accumulator of [13] requires a careful treatment. As described, one of the basic properties of an accumulator is that a witness can be used to prove that an associated value has been accumulated. Translating this into our design of RIBE, it turns out that a *collusion attack* is possible if a decryption key comprising a witness and an identity-based key is formed in a naïve manner. This is because a revoked user can collude with a non-revoked user, such that a valid witness (of the non-revoked user) can be used by the revoked user (together with her own identity-based key) to decrypt ciphertexts that she no longer has authorized access. To address this, for each user, we introduce a new secret component[1] that is associated with the accumulator and a witness, such that the secret component must be used to cancel out the blinding factor. We then bind the secret component to the user's

---

[1] Coincidentally, the secret component we adopt here is also used as a user private key in Boneh et al.'s broadcast encryption scheme [11].

identity-based key. Since the identity-based key is randomized for each user, two users will no longer be able to collude to share one of their witnesses to perform decryption.

Our key update method (to be performed by the key authority) through an accumulator differs in two aspects from that of existing RIBE schemes [7, 25] which make use of a binary tree. First, we simply update an accumulator according to the updated revocation list at a new time period t', generate a new witness associated with t', and create a signature over the updated accumulator. (We note that we also add t' into the accumulator to ensure that the accumulated value for each time period is always distinct even if there is no change in the revocation list between two successive time periods.) However, in the binary tree method, they first need to identify the minimal set of nodes (in the tree) for which key update needs to be published so that only non-revoked users are able to decrypt ciphertexts generated at time t'. For each node in the identified set, they then generate some key material required to update a decryption key. Second, in terms of communication overhead, our key update material comprises just a (short) accumulator, a witness, and a signature. Hence, the complexity of the size of our key update improves significantly from $O(\log(n))$ in the binary tree approach for n users to $O(1)$ with some relatively small amount of bookkeeping information by using accumulator. (We provide further details on the efficiency of our scheme in Section 3.4.).

In our security analysis, we adopt the Waters dual system encryption methodology [34]. As with that of [7, 25], we consider two types of adversaries: Type I adversaries that are *not* allowed to request for the private key of a target identity throughout the entire security game; and Type II adversaries that are allowed to make a query on the private key of a target identity, provided that the queried identity must subsequently be revoked before the challenge time. However, we show that our accumulator-based approach has simpler and tighter security proofs than those of a binary-tree method. To simulate a security game in the latter setting, extra care needs to be taken in order to appropriately answer any private key query that is associated with a node in the tree. Particularly, to achieve adaptive security, the simulator has to guess the position of the target identity-time pair in the tree beforehand. This causes some loss of reduction in their security proofs. Such concerns do not exist in our proofs.

1.3   Other Related Work

After the work by Boldyreva et al. [7] and Libert and Vergnaud [25], there have been proposals on various instances of functional encryption (generalization of IBE) schemes that support revocation, such as *revocable attribute-based encryption* (RABE) and *revocable predicate encryption* (RPE) [2, 3, 19]. We note that the revocation method in the schemes of [3, 19] is different from that of existing RIBE schemes. In the RABE schemes, the users themselves are the ones who enforce key revocation instead of the key authority. This is known as *sender-local revocation* and is achieved by taking as input a revocation list during encryption. A receiver's private key can decrypt a ciphertext only if her identity has not been included in the revocation list. This way, the users are not required to perform any private key update as with that in [7]. In [2], a key revocation system combining both approaches from [7] and [3] was proposed.

Moreover, there exist proposals on revocable IBE schemes with *mediators* [4, 9,17,24]. Here, a mediator is a semi-trusted authority that helps users to decrypt ciphertexts. If a user has been revoked, the mediator simply stops decrypting for the user. Such an approach, while interesting, does not seem to be satisfactory as it requires interactions between the mediator and the users for decryption of each ciphertext.

Seo and Emura [31] gave a pairing-based RIBE construction and proved that it is secure under a new security model, which considers not only exposure of long-term private keys, but also *exposure of decryption keys*[2] (associated to each time period). We further discuss this in Section 4.2. Recently, Chen et al. [14] proposed an RIBE scheme based on *lattices* under a similar security model as [7].

1.4 Outline

The paper is organized as follow: Section 2 introduces some background on bilinear maps and assumptions used in our security analysis. It also describes the definitions for RIBE. In Section 3, we present our RIBE construction and its security proofs. In Section 4, we discuss and sketch some extensions to our scheme. We conclude the paper in Section 5.

2 Preliminaries

2.1 Composite Order Bilinear Groups

Composite order bilinear groups, originally introduced in [12], are defined by a group generator $\mathcal{G}$ which takes as input a security parameter λ and outputs the description of a bilinear map G. This includes (N, G, G_T, e), where $N = p_1 p_2 p_3$ and p_1, p_2, p_3 are distinct primes, G and G_T are cyclic groups of order N, and $e : G \times G \to G_T$ is a bilinear map such that:

- (Bilinear) $\forall g, h \in G, a, b, \in \mathbb{Z}_N, e(g^a, h^b) = e(g, h)^{ab}$
- (Non-degenerate) $\exists g \in G$ such that $e(g, g)$ has order N in G_T.

In addition to the above properties, we also require that the group operations in G and G_T, together with the bilinear map e, are polynomial time computable with respect to the security parameter λ. We also assume that the group descriptions of G and G_T include the group generators. For ease of exposition, we let $G_{p_1}, G_{p_2}, G_{p_3}$ denote the subgroups of order p_1, p_2 and p_3 in G respectively. We also note the orthogonality property of our bilinear map: that is, $e(h_i, h_j)$ is the identity element in G_T whenever $h_i \in G_{p_i}$ and $h_j \in G_{p_j}$ for $i \neq j$. This property of the three subgroups will be a principal tool in our construction and proofs.

---

[2] In the security model of [31], an adversary is allowed to make decryption key queries, in addition to the conventional private key queries allowed in [7].

2.2   Complexity Assumptions

Our construction and security proofs relies on four complexity assumptions. The first three assumptions are the same as those used by Lewko and Waters in [23]. They are static (not dependent on the number of queries made by an adversary) and can be proved using the theorem introduced by Katz, Sakai and Waters [22]. The fourth assumption is called the Oracle Bilinear Diffie Hellman Exponent (OBDHE) assumption, which was used in [28] to prove the security of a broadcast encryption scheme. It is a modified version of the standard decisional BDHE problem such that it provides the adversary with an additional query oracle. In the assumptions below, we let $G_{p_i p_j}$ denote the subgroup of order $p_i p_j$ in G.

Assumption 1. *(Subgroup decisional problem for 3 primes)* *Given a group generator $\mathcal{G}$, we define the following distribution:*

$$\mathbb{G} = (N = p_1 p_2 p_3, G, G_T, e) \xleftarrow{R} \mathcal{G},$$
$$g \xleftarrow{R} G_{p_1}, \; X_3 \xleftarrow{R} G_{p_3},$$
$$D = (\mathbb{G}, g, X_3),$$
$$T_1 \xleftarrow{R} G_{p_1 p_2}, \; T_2 \xleftarrow{R} G_{p_1}.$$

We define the advantage of an algorithm $\mathcal{A}$ in breaking Assumption 1 to be:

$$Adv1_{\mathcal{G},\mathcal{A}}(\lambda) := |Pr[\mathcal{A}(D, T_1) = 1] - Pr[\mathcal{A}(D, T_2) = 1]|.$$

Definition 1. *We say that $\mathcal{G}$ satisfies Assumption 1 if $Adv1_{\mathcal{G},\mathcal{A}}(\lambda)$ is a negligible function of λ for any polynomial time algorithm $\mathcal{A}$.*

Assumption 2. *Given a group generator $\mathcal{G}$, we define the following distribution:*

$$\mathbb{G} = (N = p_1 p_2 p_3, G, G_T, e) \xleftarrow{R} \mathcal{G},$$
$$g, X_1 \xleftarrow{R} G_{p_1}, X_2, Y_2 \xleftarrow{R} G_{p_2}, X_3, Y_3 \xleftarrow{R} G_{p_3},$$
$$D = (\mathbb{G}, g, X_1 X_2, X_3, Y_2 Y_3),$$
$$T_1 \xleftarrow{R} G, T_2 \xleftarrow{R} G_{p_1 p_3}.$$

We define the advantage of an algorithm $\mathcal{A}$ in breaking Assumption 2 to be:

$$Adv2_{\mathcal{G},\mathcal{A}}(\lambda) := |Pr[\mathcal{A}(D, T_1) = 1] - Pr[\mathcal{A}(D, T_2) = 1]|.$$

Definition 2. *We say that $\mathcal{G}$ satisfies Assumption 2 if $Adv2_{\mathcal{G},\mathcal{A}}(\lambda)$ is a negligible function of λ for any polynomial time algorithm $\mathcal{A}$.*

Assumption 3. *Given a group generator $\mathcal{G}$, we define the following distribution:*

$$\mathbb{G} = (N = p_1 p_2 p_3, G, G_T, e) \xleftarrow{R} \mathcal{G}, \alpha, s \xleftarrow{R} \mathbb{Z}_N,$$
$$g \xleftarrow{R} G_{p_1}, X_2, Y_2, Z_2 \xleftarrow{R} G_{p_2}, X_3 \xleftarrow{R} G_{p_3},$$
$$D = (\mathbb{G}, g, g^\alpha X_2, X_3, g^s Y_2, Z_2),$$
$$T_1 = e(g, g)^{\alpha s}, T_2 \xleftarrow{R} G_T.$$

We define the advantage of an algorithm $\mathcal{A}$ in breaking Assumption 3 to be:

$$Adv3_{\mathcal{G},\mathcal{A}}(\lambda) := |Pr[\mathcal{A}(D, T_1) = 1] - Pr[\mathcal{A}(D, T_2) = 1]|.$$

Definition 3. *We say that $\mathcal{G}$ satisfies Assumption 3 if $Adv3_{\mathcal{G},\mathcal{A}}(\lambda)$ is a negligible function of λ for any polynomial time algorithm $\mathcal{A}$.*

We now define the Diffie-Hellman computation oracle required for the OBDHE assumption.

Definition 4. *The Diffie Hellman computation oracle $\mathcal{O}_{g,e}^{DH}$ takes as inputs $u, v \in \mathbb{G}$ and outputs $w \in \mathbb{G}$ such that $e(u, v) = e(g, w)$.*

We let prime p_1 be the group order of G and define the OBDHE assumption as follow:

Assumption 4. *(Oracle Bilinear Diffie-Hellman Exponent) Given a group generator $\mathcal{G}$, we define the following distribution:*

$$\mathbb{G} = (G, G_T, e) \xleftarrow{R} \mathcal{G}, \alpha \xleftarrow{R} \mathbb{Z}_N,$$
$$g, f \xleftarrow{R} G,$$
$$D = (\mathbb{G}, f, g, g^\alpha, g^{\alpha^2}, \ldots, g^{\alpha^\ell}, g^{\alpha^{\ell+2}}, \ldots, g^{\alpha^{2\ell}})$$
$$T_1 = e(g^{\alpha^{\ell+1}}, f), T_2 \xleftarrow{R} G_T.$$

We define the advantage of an algorithm $\mathcal{A}$ in breaking Assumption 4 to be:

$$Adv4_{\mathcal{G},\mathcal{A}}(\lambda) := |Pr[\mathcal{A}(D, T_1) = 1] - Pr[\mathcal{A}(D, T_2) = 1]|$$

given that $\mathcal{A}$ has access to the $\mathcal{O}_{g,e}^{DH}$ oracle.

Definition 5. *We say that $\mathcal{G}$ satisfies Assumption 4 if $Adv4_{\mathcal{G},\mathcal{A}}(\lambda)$ is a negligible function of λ for any polynomial time algorithm $\mathcal{A}$.*

2.3   Revocable Identity-Based Encryption

We are now ready to define RIBE [7]. Let $\mathcal{M}$ denote a message space, $\mathcal{I}$ denote an identity space, and $\mathcal{T}$ denote a time space. Assume that the sizes of $\mathcal{M}, \mathcal{I}, \mathcal{T}$ are all polynomial in the security parameter. Each algorithm within RIBE is run by either one of three types of parties—key authority, sender or receiver. The key authority maintains a revocation list RL and state ST. An algorithm is called stateful if it updates RL or ST. We treat time as discrete as opposed to continuous.

Definition 6 (RIBE). *An identity-based encryption scheme with efficient revocation or simply revocable IBE (RIBE) scheme has seven PPT algorithms as follows:*

- Setup$(1^k, n) \to$ (PP, MK, RL, ST) The setup algorithm takes as input a security parameter k and a maximal number of users n. It outputs a public parameters PP, a master key MK, a revocation list RL (initially empty), and a state ST. (This is run by the key authority.)

- PriKeyGen(PP, MK, id, ST) $\rightarrow$ (SK$_{id}$, ST) The private key generation algorithm takes as input the public parameters PP, the master key MK, an identity $id \in \mathcal{I}$, and the state ST. It outputs a private key SK$_{id}$ and an updated state ST. (This is stateful and run by the key authority.)
- KeyUpd(PP, MK, t, RL, ST) $\rightarrow$ KU$_t$ The key update algorithm takes as input the public parameters PP, the master key MK, a key update time $t \in \mathcal{T}$, the revocation list RL, and the state ST. It outputs a key update KU$_t$. (This is run by the key authority.)
- DecKeyGen(SK$_{id}$, KU$_t$) $\rightarrow$ DK$_{id,t}$ The decryption key generation takes as input a private key SK$_{id}$ and key update KU$_t$. It outputs a decryption key DK$_{id,t}$ or a special symbol $\perp$ indicating that id was revoked. (This is run by the receiver.)
- Enc(PP, id, t, M) $\rightarrow$ CT$_{id,t}$ The encryption algorithm takes as input the public parameters PP, an identity id, an encryption time t, and a message $M \in \mathcal{M}$. It outputs a ciphertext CT$_{id,t}$. (This is run by the sender. For simplicity and without loss of generality, we assume that id, t are efficiently computable from CT$_{id,t}$.)
- Dec(PP, DK$_{id,t}$, CT$_{id,t}$) $\rightarrow$ M The decryption algorithm takes as input the public parameters PP, a decryption key DK$_{id,t}$, and a ciphertext CT$_{id,t}$. It outputs a message M. (This is deterministic and run by the receiver.)
- KeyRev(id, t, RL, ST) $\rightarrow$ RL The key revocation algorithm takes as input an identity to be revoked id, a revocation time t, the revocation list RL, and the state ST. It outputs an updated revocation list RL. (This is stateful and run by the key authority.)

The consistency condition requires that for all $k \in \mathbb{N}$ and polynomials (in k) n, all PP and MK output by setup algorithm Setup, all $M \in \mathcal{M}, id \in \mathcal{I}, t \in \mathcal{T}$ and all possible valid states ST and revocation lists RL, we then have Dec(PP, DK$_{id,t}$, CT$_{id,t}$) $= M$ with probability 1 if identity id was not revoked before or at time t.

Next, we define the security of RIBE in the form of a security game played between an adversary and a challenger.

- Setup: It is run to generate some public parameters PP, a master key MK, a revocation list RL (initially empty), and a state ST. Then PP is given to $\mathcal{A}$.
- Query: $\mathcal{A}$ may adaptively make a polynomial number of queries of the following oracles (which share state information):
  - The private key generation oracle PriKeyGen($\cdot$) takes as input an identity id and runs PriKeyGen(PP, MK, id, ST) to return a private key SK$_{id}$.
  - The key update generation oracle KeyUpd($\cdot$) takes as input time t and runs KeyUpd(PP, MK, t, RL, ST) to return key update KU$_t$.
  - The revocation oracle KeyRev($\cdot$, $\cdot$) takes as input an identity id and time t, and runs KeyRev(id, t, RL, ST) to update RL.
- Challenge: $\mathcal{A}$ outputs the target ID-time pair (id^*, t^*) and two messages M_0, M_1. The challenger flips a random bit d and returns the output of

Enc(PP, id^*, t^*, M_d) to $\mathcal{A}$. After that, the adversary may continue to make queries to the oracles as with in the Query phase.
- Guess: At the end of the game, the adversary outputs a bit d', and succeeds if $d' = d$.

The following restrictions must always hold:

1. $M_0, M_1 \in \mathcal{M}$ and $|M_0| = |M_1|$.
2. KeyUpd($\cdot$) and KeyRev($\cdot, \cdot$) can be queried on a time which is greater than or equal to all the previously queried times, i.e., the adversary is allowed to query only in non-decreasing order of time. Also, the oracle KeyRev($\cdot, \cdot$) cannot be queried at time t if KeyUpd($\cdot$) was queried on t.
3. If PriKeyGen($\cdot$) was queried on identity id^*, then KeyRev($\cdot, \cdot$) must be queried on (id^*, t) for some $t \leq t^*$.

If the adversary's output d' equals to d, we set return = 1, otherwise return = 0. We define the adversary's advantage as

$$Adv_{\mathcal{A}}^{RIBE}(\lambda) := |Pr[\text{return} = 1] - \frac{1}{2}|.$$

An RIBE scheme is adaptive-ID secure if for all PPT adversaries $\mathcal{A}$ the function $Adv_{\mathcal{A}}^{RIBE}(\lambda)$ is negligible.

3 Our Construction

3.1 Intuition

Our RIBE scheme is based on the Lewko and Waters IBE scheme [23]. In our scheme, however, the decryption key of each user has two components: one is fixed (long-term) and is associated with her identity id; while the other is updated at the beginning of each time period (epoch) and corresponds to t. Particularly, the key component associated with id is essentially a normal identity-based key (in the IBE setting) combined with a secret value[3] that is associated with an accumulator, while the key component associated with t is a witness in the context of an accumulator.

All non-revoked users' identities are captured through an accumulator. At the beginning of each time period t, the key authority adds t to the accumulator and generates the corresponding witness (i.e., the values contained in the up-to-date accumulator are current time period and the identities of all legitimate users under this period). The key authority then broadcasts the updated accumulator and witness (with respect to t) to all users, who will then update their respective existing witnesses. We note here that the integrity of the accumulator is protected through a standard signature. To encrypt a message intended for id at time t, the encryptor makes use of the updated accumulator as part of the ciphertext. To

---

[3] As described in Section 1.2, this is needed to circumvent a possible collusion attack.

decrypt a ciphertext, on the other hand, the decryptor must possess the correct identity-based key associated with id and updated witness corresponds to t. To revoke a user, the key authority simply removes the identity of the user from the accumulator. A revoked user would not be able to update his witness and therefore, would not be able to decrypt any ciphertext generated beyond the current epoch.

3.2   Construction

In addition to the Lewko and Waters IBE scheme [23], our RIBE construction makes use of two other building blocks: Camenisch et al.'s accumulator [13], and any standard public key signatures scheme PKS with three algorithms: the key generation algorithm PKSGen, the signing algorithm PKSSig and the verification algorithm PKSVer.

Let ϕ denote a one-to-one map from a string (id or t) to an index i. Our RIBE construction is described as follows:

- Setup($1^k, n$) $\rightarrow$ (PP, MK, RL, ST$_\emptyset$) The setup algorithm first chooses a bilinear group G of order $N = p_1 p_2 p_3$ (with 3 distinct primes), random exponents $\alpha, \gamma \in \mathbb{Z}_N$, and random group elements $u, g, h \in G_{p_1}$. It also computes $e(g,g)^\alpha$, where $e : G \times G \rightarrow G_T$ is a bilinear map.

  From the parameters $\langle N, G, G_T, e, g \rangle$, the algorithm performs the following steps:

  1. run the PKSGen algorithm to generate a private-public key pair (sk, pk);
  2. calculate $\mathsf{z} = e(g,g)^{(\gamma^{n+1})} \in G_T$ and $P_i = g^{(\gamma^i)} \in G_{p_1}$ for $i = 1, 2, \ldots, n, n+2, \ldots, 2n$, where γ is randomly chosen from $\mathbb{Z}_N$;
  3. choose a random $\beta \in \mathbb{Z}_N$ and compute $g^\beta \in G_{p_1}$.

  Let U be the bookkeeping information of all the elements that have ever been added into the accumulator (but not necessarily contained in the current accumulator), and at the point of system setup, $U = \emptyset$. The Setup algorithm then sets the accumulator AC$_\emptyset = 1$ and state ST$_\emptyset = \{U, P_1, \ldots, P_n, P_{n+2}, \ldots, P_{2n}\}$. The revocation list RL is initially empty. The public parameters PP are $\langle N, u, g, h, g^\beta, e(g,g)^\alpha, \mathsf{z}, pk, \mathsf{AC}_\emptyset, P_1, \ldots, P_n, P_{n+2}, \ldots, P_{2n} \rangle$. The master secrete key MK is $\langle \alpha, \beta, \gamma, sk \rangle$ and a generator of G_{p_3}.

- PriKeyGen(PP, MK, id, ST$_U$) $\rightarrow$ (SK$_{id}$, ST$_{U \cup \{i\}}$) Let V denotes the bookkeeping information of the values that have currently been accumulated (so V is a subset of U). Given $i = \phi(id) \in [n]$, the private key generation algorithm performs the following steps:

  1. compute $w_i = \prod_{j \in V, j \neq i} P_{n+1-j+i}$;
  2. update the accumulator and state such that

$$\mathsf{AC}_{V \cup \{i\}} = \mathsf{AC}_V \cdot P_{n+1-i} \text{ and}$$
$$\mathsf{ST}_{U \cup \{i\}} = \{U \cup \{i\}, P_1, \ldots, P_n, P_{n+2}, \ldots, P_{2n}\}.$$

The PriKeyGen algorithm then chooses a random $r \in \mathbb{Z}_N$, and random elements $R_3, R'_3 \in G_{p_3}$. The private key SK_{id} is then:

$$\langle K_1 = g^r R_3, \; K_2 = g^\alpha (u^{id} h)^r P_i^\beta R'_3, \; K_3 = w_i \rangle.$$

The PriKeyGen algorithm also prepares a set V_w, which denotes the values contained in the accumulator when a witness w_i was created (so V_w is fixed for each user and it is also a subset of U). This set V_w is given to the user along with his private key SK_{id}.

- KeyUpd($\mathsf{PP}, \mathsf{MK}, t, \mathsf{RL}, \mathsf{ST}_U$) $\to \mathsf{KU}_t$ At the start of each new time period t, the key update algorithm first updates the accumulator by performing the following steps:
  1. remove $l' = \phi(t')$ associated with the just expired time period t' from V;
  2. remove all $i = \phi(id)$ that corresponds to t' in RL from V;
  3. update the accumulator, that is $\mathsf{AC}_V = \prod_{i' \in V} P_{n+1-i'}$ for all i' in the updated V.

The KeyUpd algorithm then adds the new time period $l = \phi(t) \in [n]$ following the same steps as before (in PriKeyGen) to obtain the latest accumulator $\mathsf{AC}_{V \cup \{l\}}$. It then generates a signature σ_l on $\mathsf{AC}_{V \cup \{l\}}$. The algorithm also prepares a set ΔV, which contains a list of recently joined and revoked users' identities within the last (just expired) epoch. Then the KeyUpd algorithm broadcasts $\mathsf{KU}_t = \langle \mathsf{AC}_{V \cup \{l\}}, \sigma_l, w_l \rangle$, together with the set ΔV, to all users.

- DecKeyGen($\mathsf{SK}_{id}, \mathsf{KU}_t$) $\to \mathsf{DK}_{id,t}$ The decryption key generation algorithm first checks if:
  1. $i = \phi(id), l = \phi(t) \in V$;
  2. σ_l is a valid signature associated with AC_V using the PKSVer algorithm and pk;
  3. $e(P_l, \mathsf{AC}_V)/e(g, w_l) = z$ to ensure the correctness of AC_V.

We set a Boolean flag denoted by DecKeyChk to 0 if any of the above three checks fails. If all the three conditions are satisfied, we set DecKeyChk $= 1$. If DecKeyChk $= 0$, then the DecKeyGen algorithm outputs a special symbol $\perp$. Otherwise, DecKeyGen replaces the existing accumulator with an up-to-date one. It then updates the witness and computes the decryption key as follows:
  1. if $i \in V$ and $V \cup V_w \subset U$, compute

$$w'_i = w_i \cdot \frac{\prod_{j \in V \setminus V_w} P_{n+1-j+i}}{\prod_{j \in V_w \setminus V} P_{n+1-j+i}};$$

  2. otherwise, output $\perp$.

Set the decryption key $\mathsf{DK}_{id,t}$ to be

$$\langle K_1 = g^r R_3, \; K_2 = g^\alpha (u^{id} h)^r P_i^\beta R'_3, \; K_3 = w'_i \rangle.$$

- Enc($\mathsf{PP}, M, id, \mathsf{AC}_V$) $\to \mathsf{CT}_{id,t}$ Given a message M and an up-to-date accumulator AC_V containing current time t, the encryption algorithm chooses $s \in \mathbb{Z}_N$ randomly, and set the ciphertext $\mathsf{CT}_{id,t}$ to be

$$C = M \frac{e(g,g)^{\alpha s}}{\mathsf{z}^s}, \; C_0 = g^s, \; C_1 = (u^{id} h)^s, \; C_2 = (g^\beta \mathsf{AC}_V)^s.$$

- $\mathsf{Dec}(\mathsf{PP}, \mathsf{DK}_{id,t}, \mathsf{CT}_{id,t}) \to M$ The decryption algorithm computes

$$\frac{e(C_0, K_2 K_3)}{e(C_1, K_1) e(P_{\phi(id)}, C_2)} = \frac{e(g, g)^{\alpha s}}{\mathsf{z}^s}.$$

The message M can be recovered by dividing C by the computed term.

- $\mathsf{KeyRev}(id, t, \mathsf{RL}, \mathsf{ST}_U) \to \mathsf{RL}$ The key revocation algorithm adds (id, t) to the revocation list RL if $i = \phi(id) \in \mathsf{ST}_U$.

CORRECTNESS. We now verify that the decryption algorithm works correctly. First we notice that a correct accumulator is always in the form of $\mathsf{AC}_V = \prod_{j \in V} P_{n+1-j}$, and the witness w_i for each $i \in V$ always has a value $w_i = \prod_{j \in V, j \neq i} P_{n+1-j+i}$. Hence, the following equation always holds:

$$\frac{e(P_i, \mathsf{AC}_V)}{e(g, w_i)} = \frac{e(g, g)^{\sum_{j \in V}(\gamma^{n+1-j+i})}}{e(g, g)^{\sum_{j \in V, j \neq i}(\gamma^{n+1-j+i})}} = e(g, g)^{(\gamma^{n+1})} = \mathsf{z}.$$

Thus we have

$$
\begin{aligned}
\frac{e(C_0, K_2 K_3)}{e(C_1, K_1) e(P_{\phi(id)}, C_2)} &= \frac{e(g^s, g^{\alpha}(u^{id}h)^r P_{\phi(id)}^{\beta} R_3' \cdot w_{\phi(id)})}{e((u^{id}h)^s, g^r R_3) e(P_{\phi(id)}, (g^{\beta} \mathsf{AC}_V)^s)} \\
&= \frac{e(g^s, g^{\alpha}(u^{id}h)^r R_3')}{e((u^{id}h)^s, g^r R_3)} \cdot \frac{e(g^s, P_{\phi(id)}^{\beta} w_{\phi(id)})}{e(P_{\phi(id)}, (g^{\beta} \mathsf{AC}_V)^s)} \\
&= \frac{e(g, g)^{\alpha s} e(g, u^{id}h)^{rs}}{e(u^{id}h, g)^{rs}} \cdot \frac{e(g, P_{\phi(id)})^{\beta s} e(g, w_{\phi(id)})^s}{e(P_{\phi(id)}, g)^{\beta s} e(P_{\phi(id)}, \mathsf{AC}_V)^s} \\
&= \frac{e(g, g)^{\alpha s}}{\mathsf{z}^s}.
\end{aligned}
$$

REMARK. In comparison with the Lewko and Waters IBE scheme, our identity-based private key component K_2 has an additional secret value P_i^{β}. Moreover, our ciphertexts are different in two aspects: the blinding factor of our ciphertext component C has an additional term z^{-s}, and we have an additional ciphertext component C_2.

It is also worth stressing again that our scheme enforces key revocation through decryption (at the recipient), that is, a ciphertext recipient can decrypt properly only if he uses an updated decryption key. An encryptor may or may not know the set V (which is associated with a revocation list),[4] and hence, may not always know if a target recipient has been revoked.

3.3   Security Analysis

Overview. In our security analysis, we consider the following two types of adversaries:

---

[4] Recall that in IBE, anyone can encrypt to an identity using the appropriate public parameters (even without having a decryption key).

- Type I adversaries that never make a private key query on the target identity id^* at any time throughout the game.
- Type II adversaries that are allowed to make a private key query on the target identity id^* at some point of the game, provided that the queried identity must subsequently be revoked before the challenge time t^*.

We then prove the security of our RIBE scheme by adopting the dual system encryption technique by Waters [34]. In our proofs, private keys and ciphertexts take two forms: normal or semi-functional. A normal private key could decrypt a ciphertext, which in turn, is either normal or semi-functional; while a semi-functional private key can only decrypt a normal ciphertext. When using a semi-functional key to decrypt a semi-functional ciphertext, the decryption will fail. We then use a hybrid argument through a sequence of games to prove the security of our scheme. We first change the challenge ciphertext to semi-functional, then gradually change the private keys into semi-functional one by one. At the very last step, we change the semi-functional ciphertext into an encryption of a random message, in which the adversary has no advantage at all. Particularly, we prove that neither Type I nor Type II adversary learns any useful information about the chosen message from the challenge ciphertext, even when they are provided some information on the associated blinding factor.

Theorem 1. *If Assumptions 1, 2, 3, and 4 hold, then our RIBE scheme is secure.*

Due to space constraints, please refer to [33] for the full security proof.

3.4 Efficiency

We now compare the efficiency of our construction against existing pairing-based RIBE schemes. We let $\tilde{n}$ denote the number of users in the system, $\hat{n}$ denote the size of identity space representing $\tilde{n}$ many users, r denote the number of revoked users, and $r' = |\Delta V|$, where ΔV is as defined in Section 3.2. Also, we let PP, DK, CT, KUp, Dec, SM and Group denote public parameters, decryption key, ciphertext, key update, decryption, security model and underlying bilinear group, respectively. The sizes for PP, DK, CT, and KUp are measured in the number of group elements; Dec is measured as the number of pairing operations; SM is either selective or adaptive and Group is either prime or composite.

From Table 1, we see that all RIBE schemes, including ours, have comparable DK and CT sizes, and the computational overhead of Dec. However, our scheme has a clear advantage of having constant size KUp. As illustrated in the scheme, our core key update material only consists of three group elements.

We note that during key update, the key authority of all the above considered schemes also broadcasts some auxiliary information with respect to non-revoked/revoked user identities. As shown in the analysis of the key update algorithm in [7], the binary tree approach is most advantageous when $r \leq \frac{\tilde{n}}{2}$, in which case the complexity of key update is $O(r \log(\frac{\tilde{n}}{r}))$. (For the case of $r > \frac{\tilde{n}}{2}$, we simply assume that the scheme can be "reset" to retain the efficiency of key

Table 1. A comparison between existing and our RIBE schemes

	PP size	DK size	CT size	KUp size	Dec	SM	Group
BGK [7]	$O(1)$	4	4	$O(\log(\hat{n}))$	4	select.	prime
LV [25]	$O(\hat{n})$	4	5	$O(\log(\hat{n}))$	3	adapt.	prime
SE [31]	$O(\hat{n})$	3	4	$O(\log(\hat{n}))$	3	adapt.	prime
Ours	$O(\tilde{n})$	3	4	$O(1)$	3	adapt.	composite

update.) By considering only the case of $r \leq \frac{\tilde{n}}{2}$, we have $\frac{\tilde{n}}{r} \geq 2$ and $\log(\frac{\tilde{n}}{r}) \geq 1$, and thus we have $O(r \log(\frac{\tilde{n}}{r})) \geq O(r)$. In the BGK, LV, SE schemes, therefore, the auxiliary information required during key update has complexity of $O(r)$, while ours has complexity of $O(r')$. In reality, we have $r' < r$, or even $r' \ll r$. Consider a concrete example by letting $r' = |\Delta V| = 100$ and assuming a user identity is of 32-bits, our bookkeeping information during key update consumes only 400 bytes.

4 Extension

4.1 Supporting More Than n Users

Our scheme presented in Section 3.2 supports up to only n users. However, as shown by Phan et al. [28] in their dynamic broadcast encryption scheme, our scheme similarly can handle polynomially many more than n users (but still bounded) and remains secure under a generalization [16, 28] of the decisional bilinear Diffie-Hellman Exponent (BDHE) assumption [8].

4.2 Forward-Secure Decryption Keys

Our security model, as with that of Boldyreva et al.'s [7], considers exposure of only long-term private keys, but not decryption keys. However, if the adversary is also allowed access to the decryption key of any user, such as that in a security model recently considered by Seo and Emura [31], we then require the decryption keys to be forward-secure. Nevertheless, our RIBE scheme can naturally be extended to achieve forward-secure decryption keys using a 2-level Lewko and Waters HIBE scheme [23]. Particularly, we let level 1 keys be users' long-term private keys (associated with identities), and let level 2 keys be decryption keys (associated with times). For each time period, a user "delegates" a new, fully randomized decryption key with her long-term private key. As shown in [31], re-randomization of decryption keys is sufficient to achieve the forward-secure property.

4.3 Revocable Attribute-Based Encryption

Boldyreva et al. [7] sketched a construction of revocable KP-ABE using the binary tree method. Subsequently Sahai et al. [29] extended their idea and gave a complete construction with a security proof. Similarly, our accumulator-based revocation technique can be extended to the KP-ABE setting. Intuitively, we rely on an accumulator to capture all valid (non-revoked) attributes such that they can be represented with a single group element. Without loss of generality, we assume that an attribute can be a user identity. This way, we can revoke not only a common attribute shared among multiple users, but also a unique identity attribute to revoke a user. We also believe that similar techniques can be applied to obtain a revocable ciphertext-policy ABE (CP-ABE) scheme, another variant of ABE that reverses the properties of KP-ABE.

Further details of the above extensions and their security proofs will be provided in a full version of this paper.

5   Conclusions

In this paper, we proposed a very efficient and adaptively secure RIBE scheme based on an accumulator. Our scheme enjoys constant-size key update, a major improvement from all previous RIBE schemes.

One immediate open problem would be to achieve adaptive security under more standard assumptions. Also, it would be interesting to investigate if our accumulator-based key update technique can be applied to revocable storage ABE proposed by Sahai et al. [29] and other variants of functional encryption.

Acknowledgment. The first author is supported by the A*STAR Graduate Scholarship. The other three authors are supported by the Singapore Ministry of Education Research Grant MOE2013-T2-1-041 and National Research Foundation of Singapore Research Grant NRF-CRP22007-03. The authors are thankful to the very useful comments from the anonymous reviewers.

References

1. Aiello, W., Lodha, S., Ostrovsky, R.: Fast digital identity revocation. In: Krawczyk, H. (ed.) CRYPTO 1998. LNCS, vol. 1462, pp. 137–152. Springer, Heidelberg (1998)
2. Attrapadung, N., Imai, H.: Attribute-based encryption supporting direct/indirect revocation modes. In: Parker, M.G. (ed.) Cryptography and Coding 2009. LNCS, vol. 5921, pp. 278–300. Springer, Heidelberg (2009)
3. Attrapadung, N., Imai, H.: Conjunctive broadcast and attribute-based encryption. In: Shacham, H., Waters, B. (eds.) Pairing 2009. LNCS, vol. 5671, pp. 248–265. Springer, Heidelberg (2009)
4. Baek, J., Zheng, Y.: Identity-based threshold decryption. In: Bao, F., Deng, R., Zhou, J. (eds.) PKC 2004. LNCS, vol. 2947, pp. 262–276. Springer, Heidelberg (2004)
5. Barker, E., Barker, W., Burr, W., Polk, W., Smid, M.: Recommendation for key management – part 1: General (revision 3). In: NIST Special Publication 800-57 (2012)

6. Benaloh, J.C., de Mare, M.: One-way accumulators: A decentralized alternative to digital signatures. In: Helleseth, T. (ed.) EUROCRYPT 1993. LNCS, vol. 765, pp. 274–285. Springer, Heidelberg (1994)
7. Boldyreva, A., Goyal, V., Kumar, V.: Identity-based encryption with efficient revocation. In: ACM Conference on Computer and Communications Security, pp. 417–426. ACM (2008)
8. Boneh, D., Boyen, X., Goh, E.-J.: Hierarchical identity based encryption with constant size ciphertext. In: Cramer, R. (ed.) EUROCRYPT 2005. LNCS, vol. 3494, pp. 440–456. Springer, Heidelberg (2005)
9. Boneh, D., Ding, X., Tsudik, G., Wong, C.M.: A method for fast revocation of public key certificates and security capabilities. In: USENIX, p. 22. USENIX Association (2001)
10. Boneh, D., Franklin, M.: Identity-based encryption from the weil pairing. In: Kilian, J. (ed.) CRYPTO 2001. LNCS, vol. 2139, pp. 213–229. Springer, Heidelberg (2001)
11. Boneh, D., Gentry, C., Waters, B.: Collusion resistant broadcast encryption with short ciphertexts and private keys. In: Shoup, V. (ed.) CRYPTO 2005. LNCS, vol. 3621, pp. 258–275. Springer, Heidelberg (2005)
12. Boneh, D., Goh, E.-J., Nissim, K.: Evaluating 2-DNF formulas on ciphertexts. In: Kilian, J. (ed.) TCC 2005. LNCS, vol. 3378, pp. 325–341. Springer, Heidelberg (2005)
13. Camenisch, J., Kohlweiss, M., Soriente, C.: An accumulator based on bilinear maps and efficient revocation for anonymous credentials. In: Jarecki, S., Tsudik, G. (eds.) PKC 2009. LNCS, vol. 5443, pp. 481–500. Springer, Heidelberg (2009)
14. Chen, J., Lim, H.W., Ling, S., Wang, H., Nguyen, K.: Revocable identity-based encryption from lattices. In: Susilo, W., Mu, Y., Seberry, J. (eds.) ACISP 2012. LNCS, vol. 7372, pp. 390–403. Springer, Heidelberg (2012)
15. Cocks, C.: An identity based encryption scheme based on quadratic residues. In: Honary, B. (ed.) Cryptography and Coding 2001. LNCS, vol. 2260, pp. 360–363. Springer, Heidelberg (2001)
16. Delerablée, C., Paillier, P., Pointcheval, D.: Fully collusion secure dynamic broadcast encryption with constant-size ciphertexts or decryption keys. In: Takagi, T., Okamoto, T., Okamoto, E., Okamoto, T. (eds.) Pairing 2007. LNCS, vol. 4575, pp. 39–59. Springer, Heidelberg (2007)
17. Ding, X., Tsudik, G.: Simple identity-based cryptography with mediated RSA. In: Joye, M. (ed.) CT-RSA 2003. LNCS, vol. 2612, pp. 193–210. Springer, Heidelberg (2003)
18. Franklin, M.: An introduction to identity-based encryption. In: NIST Identity-based Encryption Workshop (2008)
19. González-Nieto, J.M., Manulis, M., Sun, D.: Fully private revocable predicate encryption. In: Susilo, W., Mu, Y., Seberry, J. (eds.) ACISP 2012. LNCS, vol. 7372, pp. 350–363. Springer, Heidelberg (2012)
20. Hanaoka, Y., Hanaoka, G., Shikata, J., Imai, H.: Identity-based hierarchical strongly key-insulated encryption and its application. In: Roy, B. (ed.) ASIACRYPT 2005. LNCS, vol. 3788, pp. 495–514. Springer, Heidelberg (2005)
21. Housley, R., Polk, W., Ford, W., Solo, D.: Internet X.509 public key infrastructure certificate and certificate revocation list (CRL) profile (2002)
22. Katz, J., Sahai, A., Waters, B.: Predicate encryption supporting disjunctions, polynomial equations, and inner products. In: Smart, N.P. (ed.) EUROCRYPT 2008. LNCS, vol. 4965, pp. 146–162. Springer, Heidelberg (2008)

23. Lewko, A., Waters, B.: New techniques for dual system encryption and fully secure HIBE with short ciphertexts. In: Micciancio, D. (ed.) TCC 2010. LNCS, vol. 5978, pp. 455–479. Springer, Heidelberg (2010)
24. Libert, B., Quisquater, J.-J.: Efficient revocation and threshold pairing based cryptosystems. In: Proceedings of the 22nd Annual Symposium on Principles of Distributed Computing, pp. 163–171. ACM (2003)
25. Libert, B., Vergnaud, D.: Adaptive-ID secure revocable identity-based encryption. In: Fischlin, M. (ed.) CT-RSA 2009. LNCS, vol. 5473, pp. 1–15. Springer, Heidelberg (2009)
26. Myers, M., Ankney, R., Malpani, A., Galperin, S., Adams, C.: X.509 internet public key infrastructure online certificate status protocol-OCSP. Technical report (1999)
27. Naor, M., Nissim, K.: Certificate revocation and certificate update. In: USENIX, p. 17. USENIX Association (1998)
28. Phan, D.-H., Pointcheval, D., Shahandashti, S.F., Strefler, M.: Adaptive CCA broadcast encryption with constant-size secret keys and ciphertexts. In: Susilo, W., Mu, Y., Seberry, J. (eds.) ACISP 2012. LNCS, vol. 7372, pp. 308–321. Springer, Heidelberg (2012)
29. Sahai, A., Seyalioglu, H., Waters, B.: Dynamic credentials and ciphertext delegation for attribute-based encryption. In: Safavi-Naini, R., Canetti, R. (eds.) CRYPTO 2012. LNCS, vol. 7417, pp. 199–217. Springer, Heidelberg (2012)
30. Sahai, A., Waters, B.: Fuzzy identity-based encryption. In: Cramer, R. (ed.) EUROCRYPT 2005. LNCS, vol. 3494, pp. 457–473. Springer, Heidelberg (2005)
31. Seo, J.H., Emura, K.: Revocable identity-based encryption revisited: Security model and construction. In: Kurosawa, K., Hanaoka, G. (eds.) PKC 2013. LNCS, vol. 7778, pp. 216–234. Springer, Heidelberg (2013)
32. Shamir, A.: Identity-based cryptosystems and signature schemes. In: Blakely, G.R., Chaum, D. (eds.) CRYPTO 1984. LNCS, vol. 196, pp. 47–53. Springer, Heidelberg (1985)
33. Su, L., Lim, H.W., Ling, S., Wang, H.: Revocable IBE systems with almost constant-size key update. Cryptology ePrint Archive, Report 2013/495 (2013), http://eprint.iacr.org/
34. Waters, B.: Dual system encryption: Realizing fully secure IBE and HIBE under simple assumptions. In: Halevi, S. (ed.) CRYPTO 2009. LNCS, vol. 5677, pp. 619–636. Springer, Heidelberg (2009)

Pseudo 8–Sparse Multiplication for Efficient Ate–Based Pairing on Barreto–Naehrig Curve

Yuki Mori[1], Shoichi Akagi[1], Yasuyuki Nogami[1], and Masaaki Shirase[2]

[1] Graduate School of Natural Science and Technology, Okayama University
3-1-1, Tsushima-naka, Okayama, Okayama 700-8530, Japan
[2] Future University Hakodate, Japan
yasuyuki.nogami@okayama-u.ac.jp

Abstract. According to some recent implementation reports on Ate–based pairings such as optimal ate pairing with Barreto–Naehrig curve whose embedding degree is 12, *sparse multiplication* accelerates Miller's loop calculation in a pairing calculation. Especially, 7–sparse multiplication is available when the implementation uses affine coordinates, where 7–sparse means that the multiplicand or multiplier has 7 zeros among 12 coefficients. This paper extends it to *pseudo 8–sparse multiplication*. Then, some experimental results together with theoretic calculation costs are shown in order to evaluate its efficiency.

Keywords: sparse multiplication, pairing, Barreto–Naehrig curve.

1 Introduction

Recent Ate–based pairings such as R–ate [1], Optimal ate [2] and Xate [3] on Barreto–Naehrig (BN) curve have received much attention since they achieve quite efficient pairing calculations. Then, many researchers have tried to implement these Ate–based pairings as thoroughly efficient programs using mathematic and programmatic techniques such as Montgomery reduction (Montgomery representation), lazy reduction, Projective/Jacobian coordinates, sparse multiplication, and final exponentiation with Gröbner basis. Among these techniques, this paper focuses on *sparse multiplication*. Note here that pairings on BN curve are defined over $\mathbb{F}_{q^{12}}$ since the embedding degree of BN curve is 12, where q denotes the field characteristic throughout this paper.

Aranha et al. [4] and Grewal et al. [5] have well introduced the preceding techniques. According to their works, 6–sparse multiplication[1] with *projective coordinates* accelerates Miller's loop calculation that is a major calculation part together with *final exponentiation*. They have also introduced 7–sparse multiplication with *affine coordinates*. It seems that, from the viewpoint of efficiency, 7–sparse multiplication is better than 6–sparse multiplication though the difference of the adapted coordinates should be carefully taken into account. This paper proposes a more efficient sparse multiplication.

---

[1] It means that the multiplier/multiplicand has 6 *zeros* among 12 vector coefficients.

Z. Cao and F. Zhang (Eds.): Pairing 2013, LNCS 8365, pp. 186–198, 2014.
© Springer International Publishing Switzerland 2014

This paper first focuses on the fact that multiplying/dividing the result of Miller's loop calculation by an arbitrary non–zero element in $\mathbb{F}_q$ does not change the result of the pairing because of the following *final exponentiation*. Based on this fact, this paper achieves *pseudo 8–sparse multiplication* by dividing one of non–zero coefficients of the preceding 7–sparse multiplier with affine coordinates. According to the division, one of 5 non–zero coefficients becomes one and thus it contributes to a calculation efficiency. After that, in order to cancel the calculation overhead caused from the division, this paper applies *isomorphic* twist with a quadratic and cubic residue in $\mathbb{F}_q$, where note that *sextic* twist with a quadratic and cubic *non* residue in $\mathbb{F}_{q^2}$ is available for BN curves. Then, in order to evaluate the efficiency of *pseudo 8–sparse multiplication*, this paper shows some experimental results together with theoretic calculation costs.

Throughout this paper, $\mathbb{F}_q$ and $\mathbb{F}_{q^m}$ denote a prime field of characteristic q and its m–th extension field, respectively.

2   Preliminaries

This section briefly reviews Barreto–Naehrig (BN) curve [6], towering extension field with irreducible binomials [4], sextic twist [3], Ate pairing, and sparse multiplication (7–sparse multiplication) appeared in Miller's loop [4].

2.1   Barreto–Naehrig Curve

Barreto–Naehrig curve [7] that is well known to realize an efficient *asymmetric* pairing is defined in the form of

$$E : y^2 = x^3 + b, \quad b \in \mathbb{F}_q, \tag{1}$$

together with the following parameter settings,

$$q(\chi) = 36\chi^4 - 36\chi^3 + 24\chi^2 - 6\chi + 1, \tag{2a}$$
$$r(\chi) = 36\chi^4 - 36\chi^3 + 18\chi^2 - 6\chi + 1, \tag{2b}$$
$$t(\chi) = 6\chi^2 + 1, \tag{2c}$$

where χ is a certain integer[2]. This paper focuses on recent efficient Ate–based pairings such as optimal ate [2], R–ate [1], and Xate [3] pairings on BN curve.

Towering Extension Field with Irreducible Binomials $\mathbb{F}_{((q^2)^3)^2}$
In what follows, let $q - 1$ be divisible by 4 and c be a cubic and quadratic non residue in $\mathbb{F}_q$. Then, $\mathbb{F}_{q^{12}}$ is constructed as a tower field in the following representations.

---

[2] There are some conditions such as q to be a prime number for defining $\mathbb{F}_q$.

$$\begin{cases} \mathbb{F}_{q^2} = \mathbb{F}_q[i]/(i^2 - \beta), \text{ where } \beta = c. \\ \mathbb{F}_{q^6} = \mathbb{F}_{q^2}[v]/(v^3 - \xi), \text{ where } \xi = i. \\ \mathbb{F}_{q^{12}} = \mathbb{F}_{q^6}[w]/(w^2 - v). \end{cases} \quad (3)$$

According to most of previous works such as Aranha et al. [4], the above v is used for the following *sextic twist* of BN curve.

Sextic Twist. For BN curve E defined above, *sextic twisted curve E'* together with a certain quadratic and cubic non residue $z \in \mathbb{F}_{q^2}$ and an isomorphic mapping ψ_6 are given as follows [3].

$$\begin{aligned} E' &: y^2 = x^3 + bz, \\ \psi_6 &: E'(\mathbb{F}_{q^2})[r] \longmapsto E(\mathbb{F}_{q^{12}})[r] \cap \text{Ker}(\pi_q - [q]), \\ (x, y) &\longmapsto (z^{-1/3}x, z^{-1/2}y). \end{aligned} \quad (4)$$

where $\text{Ker}(\cdot)$ and π_q respectively denote the kernel of the mapping $\cdot$ and Frobenius mapping for rational point as

$$\pi_q : (x, y) \longmapsto (x^q, y^q). \quad (5)$$

In addition, its order $\#E'(\mathbb{F}_{q^2})$ is also divisible by r that is the order of BN curve E over $\mathbb{F}_q$. Thus, some efficient pairings [4] have made the best use of the sextic twisted *subfield* curve $E'(\mathbb{F}_{q^2})$ based on the isomorphic twist. In this paper, $E'(\mathbb{F}_{q^2})[r]$ shown in Eq. (4) is denoted by $\mathbb{G}'_2$ such as shown in Alg. 1.

When $\hat{z}$ is a Quadratic and Cubic Residue in $\mathbb{F}_q$
Consider the following curve $\hat{E}(\mathbb{F}_q)$ and mapping.

$$\begin{aligned} \hat{E} &: y^2 = x^3 + b\hat{z}, \\ \hat{E}(\mathbb{F}_q)[r] &\longmapsto E(\mathbb{F}_q)[r], \\ (x, y) &\longmapsto (\hat{z}^{-1/3}x, \hat{z}^{-1/2}y), \\ &\text{where } \hat{z}, \hat{z}^{-1/2}, \hat{z}^{-1/3} \in \mathbb{F}_q. \end{aligned} \quad (6)$$

Throughout this paper, it should be carefully noted that $E(\mathbb{F}_q)$ and $\hat{E}(\mathbb{F}_q)$ are isomorphic[3] since $\hat{z}$ is a quadratic and cubic *residue* in $\mathbb{F}_q$.

---

[3] $E(\mathbb{F}_{q^2})$ and $\hat{E}(\mathbb{F}_{q^2})$ furthermore $E(\mathbb{F}_{q^{12}})$ and $\hat{E}(\mathbb{F}_{q^{12}})$ are also isomorphic.

2.2 Pairings

In what follows, let the embedding degree be k. For example, $k = 12$ in the case of BN curve. As previously introduced, this paper focuses on Ate–based pairings.

Ate Pairing. Suppose the following two groups and Ate pairing notation.

$$\mathbb{G}_1 = E(\mathbb{F}_{q^k})[r] \cap \mathrm{Ker}(\pi_q - [1]),$$
$$\mathbb{G}_2 = E(\mathbb{F}_{q^k})[r] \cap \mathrm{Ker}(\pi_q - [q]),$$

$$\alpha: \ \mathbb{G}_2 \times \mathbb{G}_1 \to \mathbb{F}_{q^k}^* / (\mathbb{F}_{q^k}^*)^r. \tag{7}$$

In the case of BN curve, the above $\mathbb{G}_1$ is just $E(\mathbb{F}_q)$. Then, let $P \in \mathbb{G}_1$ and $Q \in \mathbb{G}_2$, Ate pairing $\alpha(Q, P)$ is given as follows.

$$\alpha(Q, P) = f_{t-1,Q}(P)^{\frac{q^k-1}{r}}, \tag{8}$$

where $f_{t-1,Q}(P)$ is the output of Miller's algorithm. After calculating the *final exponentiation*, the bilinearity of Ate pairing holds.

In the case of Xate pairing $\zeta(Q, P)$ on BN curve defined by

$$\zeta(Q, P) = \Big\{ f_{\chi,Q}(P)^{(1+q^3)(1+q^{10})} \cdot l_{\chi Q, \pi_q^3(\chi Q)}(P)$$
$$\cdot l_{\chi Q + \pi_q^3(\chi Q), \pi_q^{10}(\chi Q + \pi_q^3(\chi Q))}(P) \Big\}^{\frac{q^k-1}{r}}. \tag{9}$$

where χ is the setting integer parameter shown at Eqs. (2), the calculation procedure becomes as shown in Alg. 1. In what follows, the calculation steps from 1 to 6 shown in Alg. 1 is called Miller's loop. In addition, it is found that steps 3 and 5 in Alg. 1 are key to accelerating a pairing calculation. As one of such accelerating techniques, *sparse multiplication* has been introduced and thus a lot of related works have been reported [4], [5].

7–sparse Multiplication in Miller's Loop on Affine Coordinates

According to Grewal et al.'s work [5], in the case of adapting affine coordinates for representing rational points, the *doubling* phase (step 3) and *addition* phase (step 5) in Miller's loop are efficiently carried out by the following calculations. In what follows, let $P = (x_P, y_P) \in E(\mathbb{F}_q)$, $T = (x, y)$, and $Q = (x_2, y_2) \in E'(\mathbb{F}_{q^2})$ be given in affine coordinates, and let $T + Q = (x_3, y_3)$ be the sum of T and Q.

Doubling phase (when $T = Q$)

$$A = \frac{1}{2y}, \ B = 3x^2, \ C = AB, \ D = 2x, \ x_3 = C^2 - D,$$

$$E = Cx - y, \ y_3 = E - Cx_3, \ F = C\bar{x}_P,$$

$$l_{T,T}(P) = y_P + Fw + Ew^3 = y_P - Cx_Pw + Ew^3, \tag{10a}$$

where $\bar{x}_P = -x_P$ will be precomputed.   □

Algorithm 1. Xate pairing on BN curves (generalized for $\chi < 0$)

Input: $P \in \mathbb{G}_1$, $Q \in \mathbb{G}_2'$, χ
Output: $\zeta(Q, P)$
1 $T \leftarrow Q, f \leftarrow 1$
2 **for** $i = \lfloor \log_2(|\chi|) \rfloor - 1$ **downto** 0 **do**
3 | $f \leftarrow f^2 \cdot l_{T,T}(P)$, $T \leftarrow 2T$;   (*see* Doubling phase Eq. (10a))
4 | **if** $|\chi|_i = 1$ **then**
5 | | $f \leftarrow f \cdot l_{T,Q}(P)$, $T \leftarrow T + Q$;   (*see* Addition phase Eq. (10b))
6 | **if** $|\chi|_i = -1$ **then**
7 | | $f \leftarrow f \cdot l_{T,-Q}(P)$, $T \leftarrow T - Q$;   (*see* Addition phase Eq. (10b))

8 **end for**
9 **if** $\chi < 0$ **then**
10 | $T \leftarrow -T, f \leftarrow f^{-1}$
11 $f \leftarrow f \cdot \pi_q^3(f)$, $Q_1 \leftarrow \pi_q^3(T)$
12 $f \leftarrow f \cdot l_{T,Q_1}(P)$, $Q_2 \leftarrow T + Q_1$
13 $f \leftarrow f \cdot \pi_q^{10}(f)$, $T \leftarrow \pi_q^{10}(Q_2)$
14 $f \leftarrow f \cdot l_{T,Q_2}(P)$
15 $f \leftarrow \text{FinalExp}(f)(= f \leftarrow f^{(q^k-1)/r})$
16 **return** f

Addition phase (when $T \neq Q$)

$$A = \frac{1}{x_2 - x}, \; B = y_2 - y, \; C = AB, \; D = x + x_2, \; x_3 = C^2 - D,$$

$$E = Cx - y, \; y_3 = E - Cx_3, \; F = C\bar{x}_P,$$

$$l_{T,Q}(P) = y_P + Fw + Ew^3 = y_P - Cx_Pw + Ew^3, \tag{10b}$$

where $\bar{x}_P = -x_P$ will be precomputed.   □

As shown in Eqs. (10), since 1, w, and $w^3 = vw$ are basis elements of $\mathbb{F}_{q^{12}}$ for $\mathbb{F}_{q^2}$ as previously introduced, it is found that 7 coefficients among 12 of the vector representation of $l_{\psi_6(T),\psi_6(T)}(P) \in \mathbb{F}_{q^{12}}$ are equal to zero at least. In other words, only 5 coefficients $y_P \in \mathbb{F}_q$, $Cx_P \in \mathbb{F}_{q^2}$, and $E \in \mathbb{F}_{q^2}$ are possible to be non-zero. $l_{\psi_6(T),\psi_6(Q)}(P)$ also has the same property. Thus, the calculation of multiplying $l_{\psi_6(T),\psi_6(T)}(P)$ or $l_{\psi_6(T),\psi_6(Q)}(P)$ is called *sparse multiplication*, in this case especially 7–sparse multiplication, that accelerates Miller's loop calculation as shown in Alg. 1. This paper proposes *pseudo* 8–sparse multiplication.

3   Main Proposal

This paper proposes the following two ideas in order to realize an efficient 8–sparse multiplication for Ate–based pairing on BN curve such as Ate, optimal ate [2], R–ate [1], and Xate [3] pairings.

1. As shown in Eqs. (10), one of non–zero coefficients is $y_P \in \mathbb{F}_q$. This coefficient does not change through Miller's loop calculation. Thus, dividing both sides of those equations by y_p, the coefficient becomes 1. It leads to a more efficient sparse multiplication by $l_{\psi_6(T), \psi_6(T)}(P)$ or $l_{\psi_6(T), \psi_6(Q)}(P)$. In this paper, it is called *pseudo 8–sparse multiplication*.

2. The above division by y_P causes a little more calculation cost for the other non–zero coefficients in the Miller's loop as it is. Applying the map introduced in Eqs. (6), such an additional cost in Miller's loop is canceled.

As shown in Eq. (10a) and Eq. (10b), they are basically the same. Thus, using Eq. (10a) in what follows, these ideas are introduced in detail.

3.1   Pseudo 8–Sparse Multiplication

Note that y_P shown in Eq. (10a) is an non–zero[4] element in $\mathbb{F}_q$. Thus, dividing both sides of Eq. (10a) by y_P,

$$y_P^{-1} l_{T,T}(P) = 1 - C(x_P y_P^{-1})w + E y_P^{-1} w^3. \tag{11}$$

Even if replacing $l_{T,T}(P)$ by the above $y_P^{-1} l_{T,T}(P)$, the calculation result of the pairing does not change because *final exponentiation* cancels $y_P^{-1} \in \mathbb{F}_p$. Then, as shown above, one of the non–zero coefficients becomes 1 and it realizes more efficient vector multiplications in Miller's loop. This paper calls it *pseudo 8–sparse multiplication*. The detailed calculation procedure of pseudo 8–sparse multiplication is introduced in **App. A**.

3.2   Line Evaluation in Miller's Loop

Comparing the line evaluations Eq. (10a) and Eq. (11), it is found that the latter needs a little more calculation cost for $E y_P^{-1}$ even though $x_P y_P^{-1}$ and y_P^{-1} can be precomputed. In what follows, an approach to cancel $x_P y_P^{-1}$ is introduced.

   In brief, based on $P(x_P, y_P)$, the map introduced in Eqs. (6) can find a certain isomorphic rational point $\hat{P}(x_{\hat{P}}, y_{\hat{P}}) \in \hat{E}(\mathbb{F}_q)$ such that

$$x_{\hat{P}} y_{\hat{P}}^{-1} = 1 \tag{12}$$

by letting the twist parameter z of Eq. (4) be $\hat{z} = (x_P y_P^{-1})^6$ of Eqs. (6), where $\hat{E}$ denotes the BN curve defined by Eqs. (6). Of course, this $\hat{z}$ is a quadratic and

---

[4] $P(x_P, y_P) \in E(\mathbb{F}_q)$ for pairing on BN curve is selected such that $x_P \neq 0$ and $y_P \neq 0$.

cubic residue in $\mathbb{F}_p$ and thus it yields the map. According to Eq. (4), such z is obtained by solving the following equation from the input $P(x_P, y_P)$.

$$z^{1/3} x_P = z^{1/2} y_P. \tag{13}$$

Then, $\hat{P}(x_{\hat{P}}, y_{\hat{P}}) \in \hat{E}(\mathbb{F}_q)$ is given by

$$\hat{P}(x_{\hat{P}}, y_{\hat{P}}) = (x_P^3 y_P^{-2}, x_P^3 y_P^{-2}). \tag{14}$$

Since the x and y coordinates of $\hat{P}$ are the same, $x_{\hat{P}} y_{\hat{P}}^{-1} = 1$. Therefore, corresponding to the the map introduced in Eqs. (6), first mapping not only P to $\hat{P}$ shown above but also Q to $\hat{Q}$ shown below,

$$\hat{Q}(x_{\hat{Q}}, y_{\hat{Q}}) = (x_P^2 y_P^{-2} x_Q, x_P^3 y_P^{-3} y_Q). \tag{15}$$

the line evaluations Eq. (10a) becomes

$$\hat{l}_{\hat{T}, \hat{T}}(\hat{P}) = y_{\hat{P}}^{-1} l_{\hat{T}, \hat{T}}(\hat{P}) = 1 - C(x_{\hat{P}} y_{\hat{P}}^{-1}) w + E y_{\hat{P}}^{-1} w^3$$
$$= 1 - Cw + E(x_P^{-3} y_P^2) w^3. \tag{16}$$

Eq. (10b) becomes the same. Compared to Eq. (11), the second term of the right–hand side has become simple because $x_{\hat{P}} y_{\hat{P}}^{-1} = 1$.

Computing $\hat{P}$, $\hat{Q}$, and $x_P^{-3} y_P^2$ using x_P^{-1} and y_P^{-1} will be an overhead; however, Miller's loop calculation becomes efficient together with pseudo 8–sparse multiplication. Alg. 2 shows the proposed algorithm for which x_P^{-1} and y_P^{-1} thus need to be once calculated[5].

4   Cost Evaluation and Experimental Result

In order to show the efficiency of the proposal, this section shows some experimental results with evaluating the calculation costs.

In what follows, "Grewal's work" means optimal ate pairing with affine coordinates and 7–sparse multiplication (*see* the detail [5]). "This work" means Xate pairing with affine coordinates and 8–sparse multiplication.

4.1   Parameter Settings and Computational Environment

This paper has set the following parameters (*see* Sec. 2.1).

$$\chi = -4611686018425225214, \tag{17a}$$
$$= -2^{62} + 2^{21} + 2^{16} + 2,$$
$$\text{where } r(\chi) \text{ becomes a 254–bit prime,}$$
$$b = c = 2, \tag{17b}$$
$$z = i^{-1}. \tag{17c}$$

---

[5] They are obtained by one $\mathbb{F}_q$–inversion using Montgomery trick.

Algorithm 2. Proposed Xate pairing on BN curves (generalized for $\chi < 0$)

Input: $P(x_P, y_P) \in \mathbb{G}_1,\ Q(x_Q, y_Q) \in \mathbb{G}'_2,\ \chi$

Output: $\zeta(Q, P)$

1 Compute x_P^{-1} and y_P^{-1} ;   (they are used at steps 3 and 4)

2 Compute $x_P^{-3} y_P^{2}$;   (it is used at steps 7 and 9 with Eq. (16))

3 $\hat{P} \leftarrow \text{Mapping}(P)$;   (*see* Eq. (14))

4 $\hat{Q} \leftarrow \text{Mapping}(Q)$;   (*see* Eq. (15))

5 $\hat{T} \leftarrow \hat{Q}, f \leftarrow 1$

6 **for** $i = \lfloor \log_2(|\chi|) \rfloor - 1$ **downto** 0 **do**

7     $f \leftarrow f^2 \cdot \hat{l}_{\hat{T},\hat{T}}(\hat{P}), \hat{T} \leftarrow 2\hat{T}$;   (*see* Eq. (16))

8   **if** $|\chi|_i = 1$ **then**

9         $f \leftarrow f \cdot \hat{l}_{\hat{T},\hat{Q}}(\hat{P}),\ \hat{T} \leftarrow \hat{T} + \hat{Q}$;   (*see* Eq. (16))

10   **if** $|\chi|_i = -1$ **then**

11       $f \leftarrow f \cdot \hat{l}_{\hat{T},-\hat{Q}}(\hat{P}),\ \hat{T} \leftarrow \hat{T} - \hat{Q}$;   (*see* Eq. (16))

12 **end for**

13 **if** $\chi < 0$ **then**

14    $\hat{T} \leftarrow -\hat{T},\ f \leftarrow f^{-1}$

15 $f \leftarrow f \cdot \pi_q^3(f),\ \hat{Q}_1 \leftarrow \pi_q^3(\hat{T})$

16 $f \leftarrow f \cdot \hat{l}_{\hat{T},\hat{Q}_1}(\hat{P}),\ \hat{Q}_2 \leftarrow \hat{T} + \hat{Q}_1$;   (*see* Eq. (16))

17 $f \leftarrow f \cdot \pi_q^{10}(f),\ \hat{T} \leftarrow \pi_q^{10}(\hat{Q}_2)$

18 $f \leftarrow f \cdot \hat{l}_{\hat{T},\hat{Q}_2}(\hat{P})$;   (*see* Eq. (16))

19 $f \leftarrow \text{FinalExp}(f)(= f \leftarrow f^{(q^k-1)/r})$

20 **return** f

Table 1 shows the computational environments.

Table 1. Computing environment

	PC	iPad2	iPhone5
CPU	Core 2 Duo* E8135 2.66GHz	Apple A5* 1.0GHz	Apple A6* 1.3GHz
OS	Mac OS X 10.7.2	iOS 6.1.3	iOS 6.1.4
Library	GMP 5.1.2	gmp4osx (GMP 5.0.5)	gmp4osx (GMP 5.0.5)
Compiler	g++ 4.2.1	g++ 4.2.1	g++ 4.2.1
Programming Language	C++	C++ and Objective-C	C++ and Objective-C

* Only single core is used though it has two cores.

4.2   Cost Evaluation

In the same manner of Aranha et al. [4] and Grewal et al. [5], this paper uses the following notations for evaluating the calculation costs. Thus, the following paragraph is almost the same of that of Grewal et al.'s [5].

Notation and Definitions (*see also* Grewal et al.'s instruction [5])
Throughout this paper, lower case variables denote single–precision integers, upper case variables denote double–precision integers. The operation $+$ represents addition without reduction, and $\oplus$ represents addition with reduction (*see* Alg. alg:sparse). The quantities m, s, a, i and r denote the times for multiplication, squaring, addition, inversion, and modular reduction in $\mathbb{F}_q$, respectively. Likewise, $\tilde{m}, \tilde{s}, \tilde{a}, \tilde{i}$ and $\tilde{r}$ denote the times for multiplication, squaring, addition, inversion, and reduction in $\mathbb{F}_{q^2}$, respectively, and $m_u, s_u, \tilde{m}_u$ and $\tilde{s}_u$ denote the times for multiplication and squaring without reduction in the corresponding fields. Finally, m_β and m_ξ m_v denote the times for multiplication by the quantities β and ξ, respectively (*see* the preceding *towering extension field*).

First, Table 2 shows the calculation costs for the arithmetics in $E'(\mathbb{F}_{q^2})$, $\mathbb{F}_{q^2}$, and $\mathbb{F}_{q^{12}}$. Since their constructions are slightly different though both are based on *towering extension field* technique, the calculation costs are slightly different. Basically, the number of multiplications such as m and $\tilde{m}_u$ are the same though those of additions such as a and $\tilde{a}$ are different; however, 7–sparse multiplication and *pseudo* 8–sparse multiplication have the difference of $6m_u$. It leads to the main contribution of this paper.

Based on these fundamental arithmetics, Table 3 shows the calculation costs for pairings by Grewal et al.'s work and this paper in which that of final exponentiation is excluded[6]. Instead of 7–sparse multiplication, pseudo 8–sparse multiplication is applied 66 times in Xate pairing calculation excluding final exponentiation. Thus, as shown in Table 3, the difference of $66 \times 6m_u = 396m_u$ has occurred between the pairings excluding final exponentiation. According to the calculation costs of pairings, it is found that pseudo 8–sparse multiplication has reduced a few hundreds of m_u's. For iPad 2 and iPhone 5, since the relation of $69\tilde{i} + 204a + s + 2i \leq 178\tilde{m}_u + 326\tilde{s} + 229\tilde{r} + 2056\tilde{a} + 131m$, This work is faster than the Xate pairing using projective coordinates.

4.3   Experimental Result

Table 4 shows the calculation times of Xate pairing including(excluding) final exponentiation. They are the averages of 100,000 and 9,000 iterations of pairing on PC and iOS devices (iPad 2 and iPhone 5), respectively. According to the experimental results, pseudo 8–sparse multiplication contributes to a few percent acceleration of Previous work, which the Xate pairing uses affine coordinates and uses 7–sparse multiplication. It seems to be very small but makes the recent marvelous implementations of pairing [4], [5] a little more efficient.

---

[6] Because the calculation cost of final exponentiation is almost the same.

Table 2. Operation counts for 254-bit prime fields

$E'(\mathbb{F}_{q^2})$ Arithmetics	Grewal's work [5]	This work
Doubling/Line Evaluation	$\tilde{i} + 3\tilde{m}_u + 2\tilde{s}_u + 5\tilde{r} + 7\tilde{a} + 2m$	$\tilde{i} + 3\tilde{m}_u + 2\tilde{s}_u + 5\tilde{r} + 7\tilde{a} + 2m$
Addition/Line Evaluation	$\tilde{i} + 3\tilde{m}_u + 1\tilde{s}_u + 4\tilde{r} + 6\tilde{a} + 2m$	$\tilde{i} + 3\tilde{m}_u + 1\tilde{s}_u + 4\tilde{r} + 6\tilde{a} + 2m$
q–power Frobenius	$2\tilde{m} + 2a$	–
q^2–power Frobenius	$4m$	–
q^3–power Frobenius	–	$4a + 2m$
q^{10}–power Frobenius	–	$2a + 2m$

$\mathbb{F}_{q^2}$ Arithmetics	Grewal's work [5]	This work
Add/Subtr./Nega.	$\tilde{a} = 2a$	$\tilde{a} = 2a$
Multiplication	$\tilde{m} = 3m_u + 2r + 8a$	$\tilde{m} = 3m_u + 2r + 8a$
Squaring	$\tilde{s} = 2m_u + 2r + 3a$	$\tilde{s} = 2m_u + 2r + 6a$
Multiplication by β	$m_\beta = a$	$m_\beta = a$
Multiplication by ξ	$m_\xi = 2a$	$m_\xi = a$

$\mathbb{F}_{q^{12}}$ Arithmetics	Grewal's work [5]	This work
Multiplication	$18\tilde{m}_u + 6\tilde{r} + 110\tilde{a}$	$18\tilde{m}_u + 6\tilde{r} + 96\tilde{a} + a$
7–sparse Mult.	$10\tilde{m}_u + 6\tilde{r} + 47\tilde{a} + 6m_u + a$	–
Pseudo 8–sparse Mult.	–	$10\tilde{m}_u + 6\tilde{r} + 37\tilde{a} + 3a$
Squaring	$12\tilde{m}_u + 6\tilde{r} + 73\tilde{a}$	$12\tilde{m}_u + 6\tilde{r} + 63\tilde{a}$
q–power Frobenius	$5\tilde{m}_u + 6a$	$a + 10m$
q^2–power Frobenius	$10\tilde{m}_u + 2\tilde{a}$	$2a + 8m$
q^3–power Frobenius	–	$3a + 6m$
q^6–power Frobenius	–	$3\tilde{a}$
q^{10}–power Frobenius	–	$2a + 8m$

* : Add./Subtr./Nega./Mult. denote Addition/Subtraction/Negation/Multiplication.

Table 3. Calculation cost of pairings excluding final exponentiation

Method	Calculation cost*
Projective	$1835\tilde{m}_u + 458\tilde{s}_u + 1359\tilde{r} + 9118\tilde{a} + 25a + 308m$
Grewal's work [5]	$70\tilde{i} + 1628\tilde{m}_u + 135\tilde{s}_u + 1120\tilde{r} + 7618\tilde{a} + 69a + 144m + \mathbf{396m_u}$
This work	$69\tilde{i} + 1657\tilde{m}_u + 132\tilde{s}_u + 1130\tilde{r} + 7062\tilde{a} + 229a + 177m + s + 2i$

* : "Projective" means that the Xate pairing uses projective coordinates,
and thus 6–sparse multiplication is only available in its Miller's loop.

Table 4. Calculation time of Xate pairing

Method	Calculation time of Xate pairing* [ms]		
	PC	iPad 2	iPhone 5
Previous work	1.48(0.9)	12.3(7.4)	9.97(5.8)
This work	1.46(0.89)	12.1(7.2)	9.84(5.7)

* : In the parenthesis, the calculation time excluding *final exponentiation* is shown.
In other words, it is the calculation time for steps 1 to 15 on Alg. 2.
** : "Previous" means that the Xate pairing uses 7–sparse multiplication and
affine coordinates.

Table 5. Calculation time of multi–Xate pairing

# pairings	Calculation time of multi–pairing on PC [ms]		
	PC		
	This work	Previous work*	Projective**
1	1.46	1.48	1.31
2	1.86	1.92	1.78
3	2.25	2.30	2.28
4	2.65	2.70	2.75
5	3.02	3.12	3.24
6	3.40	3.51	3.70
7	3.82	3.89	4.18
8	4.18	4.29	4.64
9	4.62	4.71	5.12
10	4.96	5.09	5.58

# pairings	Calculation time of multi–pairing on iPhone 5 [ms]		
	This work	Previous work*	Projective**
1	9.83	9.97	9.91
2	13.0	13.4	13.9
3	16.1	16.8	17.7
4	19.2	20.1	21.5
5	22.5	23.4	25.3
6	25.5	26.7	29.1
7	28.7	30.1	32.9
8	31.8	33.4	36.6
9	34.8	36.7	40.5
10	38.1	40.0	44.3

* : "Projective" means that the Xate pairing uses projective coordinates, and thus 6–sparse multiplication is only available in its Miller's loop.

** : "Previous" means that the Xate pairing uses 7–sparse multiplication and affine coordinates.

By the way, the proposed pseudo 8–sparse multiplication is not able to accelerate *final exponentiation*. Thus, it yields a greater effect for *multi–pairing* than a single pairing because *multi–pairing* can combine the final exponentiations as

$$\prod_{i=1}^{N} \alpha(Q_i, P_i) = \prod_{i=1}^{N} (f_{t-1,Q_i}(P_i))^{(p^k-1)/r}$$

$$= \left(\prod_{i=1}^{N} f_{t-1,Q_i}(P_i)\right)^{(p^k-1)/r}. \tag{18}$$

In addition, squarings at step 6 in Alg. 2, for example, can also be combined. Table 5 shows the calculation time for N multi–pairing. They are the averages of 12,500 and 4,500 iterations of N multi–pairing on PC and iOS devices (iPad 2 and iPhone 5), respectively. Compared to the case with 6–sparse multiplication and projective coordinates, that with pseudo 8–sparse multiplication and affine coordinates becomes more efficient as the number N becomes larger.

5   Conclusion and Future Works

This paper has proposed *pseudo* 8–sparse multiplication for accelerating Ate–based pairing with affine coordinates on Barreto–Naehrig (BN) curve. According to the calculation costs and experimental results shown in this paper, the proposal made recent efficient pairings such as optimal ate and Xate pairings more efficient, especially together with multi–pairing technique.

As a future work, it should be considered to apply such a sparse multiplication for the other pairings together with some twist techniques.

Acknowledgement. This research was supported by KAKENHI Grant–in–Aid for Scientific Research (B) Number 25280047.

References

1. Lee, E., Lee, H.-S., Park, C.-M.: Efficient and generalized pairing computation on abelian varieties. IEEE Transactions on Information Theory 55(4), 1793–1803 (2009)
2. Vercauteren, F.: Optimal pairings. IEEE Transactions on Information Theory 56(1), 455–461 (2010)
3. Nogami, Y., Sakemi, Y., Kato, H., Akane, M., Morikawa, Y.: Integer Variable χ-based Cross Twisted Ate Pairing and Its Optimization for Barreto-Naehrig Curve. IEICE Transactions on Fundamentals of Electronics 2009(8), 1859–1867 (2009)
4. Aranha, D.F., Karabina, K., Longa, P., Gebotys, C.H., López, J.: Faster explicit formulas for computing pairings over ordinary curves. In: Paterson, K.G. (ed.) EUROCRYPT 2011. LNCS, vol. 6632, pp. 48–68. Springer, Heidelberg (2011)
5. Grewal, G., Azarderakhsh, R., Longa, P., Hu, S., Jao, D.: Efficient Implementation of Bilinear Pairings on ARM Processors. Cryptology ePrint Archive, Vol. 2012:408 (2012)
6. Barreto, P.S.L.M., Naehrig, M.: Pairing-Friendly Elliptic Curves of Prime Order. In: Preneel, B., Tavares, S. (eds.) SAC 2005. LNCS, vol. 3897, pp. 319–331. Springer, Heidelberg (2006)
7. Freeman, D., Scott, M., Teske, E.: A Taxonomy of Pairing-Friendly Elliptic Curves. Journal of Cryptology 23, 224–280 (2006)

A   Pseudo 8–Sparse Multiplication

The calculation procedure of pseudo 8–sparse multiplication becomes as follows.

Algorithm 3. Pseudo 8–sparse multiplication

Input: $a, b \in \mathbb{F}_{q^{12}}$,

$a = (a_0 + a_1 v + a_2 v^2) + (a_3 + a_4 v + a_5 v^2)w$, $b = 1 + (b_3 + b_4 v)w$,

where $a_j, b_k \in \mathbb{F}_{q^2} (j = 0, \cdots, 5, k = 3, 4)$,

Output: $c = ab = (c_0 + c_1 v + c_2 v^2) + (c_3 + c_4 v + c_5 v^2)w \in \mathbb{F}_{q^{12}}$

1	$D_0 \leftarrow a_3 \times b_3, D_1 \leftarrow a_4 \times b_4, S_0 \leftarrow a_5 \times b_3$;	$(3\tilde{m}_u)$
2	$T_0 \leftarrow S_0 + D_1$;	$(2\tilde{a})$
3	$T_1 \leftarrow T_0 \times i$;	(m_ξ)
4	$c_0 \leftarrow \text{MontRed}(T_1)$;	$(\tilde{r})$
5	$T_0 \leftarrow a_5 \times b_4$;	$(\tilde{m}_u)$
6	$S_0 \leftarrow S_0 + T_0$;	$(2\tilde{a})$
7	$T_1 \leftarrow T_0 \times i$;	(m_ξ)
8	$c_0 \leftarrow c_0 \oplus a_0$;	$(\tilde{a})$
9	$T_1 \leftarrow T_1 + D_0$;	$(2\tilde{a})$
10	$c_1 \leftarrow \text{MontRed}(T_1)$;	$(\tilde{r})$
11	$t_0 \leftarrow a_3 + a_4, s_0 \leftarrow b_4 + b_3$;	$(2\tilde{a})$
12	$T_1 \leftarrow t_0 \times s_0$;	$(\tilde{m}_u)$
13	$c_1 \leftarrow c_1 \oplus a_1$;	$(\tilde{a})$
14	$T_1 \leftarrow T_1 - D_0 - D_1$;	$(4\tilde{a})$
15	$c_2 \leftarrow \text{MontRed}(T_1)$;	$(\tilde{r})$
16	$T_0 \leftarrow a_2 \times b_4$;	$(\tilde{m}_u)$
17	$c_2 \leftarrow c_2 \oplus a_2$;	$(\tilde{a})$
18	$S_0 \leftarrow S_0 + T_0$;	$(2\tilde{a})$
19	$T_1 \leftarrow T_0 \times i$;	(m_ξ)
20	$t_0 \leftarrow a_0 + a_3, t_{1,0} \leftarrow b_{3,0} + 1, t_{1,1} \leftarrow b_{3,1}$;	$(\tilde{a} + a)$
21	$T_0 \leftarrow t_0 \times t_1$;	$(\tilde{m}_u)$
22	$T_0 \leftarrow T_0 - D_0$;	$(2\tilde{a})$
23	$T_1 \leftarrow T_1 + T_0$;	$(2\tilde{a})$
24	$c_3 \leftarrow \text{MontRed}(T_1)$;	$(\tilde{r})$
25	$T_1 \leftarrow a_1 \times b_3$;	$(\tilde{m}_u)$
26	$S_0 \leftarrow S_0 + T_1$;	$(2\tilde{a})$
27	$c_3 \leftarrow c_3 - a_0, t_0 \leftarrow a_0 + a_4$;	$(2\tilde{a})$
28	$t_{1,0} \leftarrow b_{4,0} + 1, t_{1,1} \leftarrow b_{4,1}$;	(a)
29	$T_0 \leftarrow t_0 \times t_1$;	$(\tilde{m}_u)$
30	$T_0 \leftarrow T_0 - D_1$;	$(2\tilde{a})$
31	$T_1 \leftarrow T_1 + T_0$;	$(2\tilde{a})$
32	$c_4 \leftarrow \text{MontRed}(T_1)$;	$(\tilde{r})$
33	$t_0 \leftarrow a_1 + a_2, s_{0,0} \leftarrow s_{0,0} + 1$;	$(\tilde{a} + a)$
34	$t_0 \leftarrow t_0 + a_5$;	$(\tilde{a})$
35	$T_1 \leftarrow s_0 \times t_0$;	$(\tilde{m}_u)$
36	$T_1 \leftarrow T_1 - S_0$;	$(2\tilde{a})$
37	$c_5 \leftarrow \text{MontRed}(T_1)$;	$(\tilde{r})$
38	$t_0 \leftarrow a_1 \oplus a_2$;	$(\tilde{a})$
39	$c_4 \leftarrow c_4 - a_0$;	$(\tilde{a})$
40	$c_5 \leftarrow c_5 - t_0$;	$(\tilde{a})$
41	Return $c = (c_0 + c_1 v + c_2 v^2) + (c_3 + c_4 v + c_5 v^2)w$	

Adaptable Ciphertext-Policy Attribute-Based Encryption

Junzuo Lai[1,2], Robert H. Deng[2], Yanjiang Yang[3], and Jian Weng[1,2]

[1] Department of Computer Science, Jinan University, China
[2] School of Information Systems, Singapore Management University, Singapore
{junzuolai,robertdeng,jianweng}@smu.edu.sg
[3] Institute for Infocomm Research, Singapore
yyang@i2r.a-star.edu.sg

Abstract. In this paper, we introduce a new cryptographic primitive, called adaptable ciphertext-policy attribute-based encryption (CP-ABE). Adaptable CP-ABE extends the traditional CP-ABE by allowing a semi-trusted proxy to modify a ciphertext under one access policy into ciphertexts of the same plaintext under *any* other access policies; the proxy, however, learns nothing about the underlying plaintext. With such "adaptability" possessed by the proxy, adaptable CP-ABE has many real world applications, such as handling policy changes in CP-ABE encryption of cloud data and outsourcing of CP-ABE encryption.

Specifically, we first specify a formal model of adaptable CP-ABE; then, based on the CP-ABE scheme by Waters, we propose a concrete adaptable CP-ABE scheme and further prove its security under our security model.

Keywords: ciphertext-policy attribute-based encryption, adaptability, policy change.

1   Introduction

Attribute-based encryption (ABE), e.g., [25,9,3], has thus far received enormous attention, due to its ability in enforcing encryption/decryption capabilities defined over descriptive attributes. Unlike standard public key encryption, where encryption is performed under a public key and the ciphertext can be decrypted by a single private key, ABE is a one-to-many public key encryption primitive, allowing data to be encrypted with certain access policy/attributes while each decryption key is associated with certain attributes/policy; only when the attributes satisfy the access policy can a key decrypt the ciphertext successfully.

Two types of ABE are distinguished in the literature: ciphertext-policy ABE (CP-ABE) such as [3], and key-policy ABE (KP-ABE) such as [9]. The difference lies in that in the former, a ciphertext is generated under an access policy (also called access structure), and decryption keys are associated with attributes; while the latter is the other way around. While it is often possible to transform one type of ABE into the other [8], CP-ABE appears more aligned with practice

Z. Cao and F. Zhang (Eds.): Pairing 2013, LNCS 8365, pp. 199–214, 2014.

where the encryptor directly specifies the access policy under which a ciphertext can be decrypted.

In reality, a user's access privileges are often granted based on the functional role he/she assumes in an organization, where a role reduces to no more than a set of attributes. In this regard, CP-ABE enables a kind of cryptographic access control over data with respect to functional roles, rather than the usual notion of individuals inherent to the standard public key encryption. Thus CP-ABE represents a practically promising encryption primitive, and it has been an active research field in the past few years. Existing research on CP-ABE in the literature generally follows several lines. For example, since the earlier CP-ABE scheme [3] can only attain security in the generic group model, one direction of research is to propose CP-ABE constructions with security under a more solid ground (e.g., in the standard model) [5]. Another line of efforts is to enable CP-ABE schemes to accommodate more expressive and complex access policies [14,27,16,6,7]. Still, there are also many attempts to pursue more privacy-wise CP-ABE or variants that hide the associated access policies, besides encryption of the payload data [22,17,12,13,11,26,23,24].

In this work, we propose yet another new variant of CP-ABE, namely *adaptable CP-ABE*. We introduce a semi-trusted party, called *proxy*, into the setting of CP-ABE. Given a *trapdoor*, the proxy is entitled to transform a ciphertext under one access policy into ciphertexts of the same plaintext under any other access policies. The proxy, however, learns nothing about the plaintext during the process of transformation. We first formulate a model for adaptable CP-ABE, and then present a concrete construction. In fact, we can use the similar method to obtain adaptable KP-ABE. Due to space limitations, we do not discuss adaptable KP-ABE in this paper.

Comparison with PRE. To better understand the concept of adaptable CP-ABE, it is conducive to outline the distinctions between adaptable CP-ABE and proxy re-encryption (PRE), or more precisely ciphertext-policy attribute-based PRE (CP-ABPRE) [19,20,18]. PRE is a public key encryption primitive also incorporating a semi-trusted proxy which is capable of converting ciphertexts (Please refer to Section 2 for more details on the concept of PRE). Particularly, in CP-ABPRE [19,20,18], the proxy given a trapdoor (called re-encryption key in PRE) issued for a set S of attributes and an access policy $\mathbb{B}$, can transform a ciphertext under access policy $\mathbb{A}$ to a ciphertext under another access policy $\mathbb{B}$, if S satisfies $\mathbb{A}$.

The major differences between our adaptable CP-ABE and CP-ABPRE [19,20,18] can be summarized as follows. First, in adaptable CP-ABE the proxy is not restricted in its ability in converting ciphertexts, in that with a single trapdoor it can transform ciphertexts under any access policies and to the ones under any other policies. In comparison, each re-encryption key held by the proxy in CP-ABPRE is bound to a set of attributes and a destination access policy, and it is applicable only to the source ciphertexts whose access policies are satisfied by the set of attributes. Second, in adaptable CP-ABE the proxy's trapdoor is generated in a "centralized" manner by a trusted authority who is responsible for establishing system parameters. In contrast, re-encryption keys in CP-ABPRE are generated in a "distributed" manner by individual users each holding a private key associated with a set of attributes. Lastly, in CP-ABPRE, a source ciphertext and its transformed version have different formats; the transformed ciphertext usually expands in size, compared to the ciphertext in the "source format" under the same access policy. This is not the case for adaptable CP-ABE, in which no discrepancy exists between "source format" and "destination format", and thus there is no ciphertext size expansion.

1.1 Applications of Adaptable CP-ABE

Recall that, in CP-ABPRE, a proxy with a re-encryption key generated by a user, only can transform the ciphertexts whose access policies are satisfied by the user's attributes set. In some applications, the access polices associated with the ciphertexts *across many users* need to be modified; in these cases, CP-ABPRE is cumbersome to fulfill if not impossible and adaptable CP-ABE will show its capabilities. Below we give examples of applications that demonstrate the genuine applicability of adaptable CP-ABE. In view of the fact that cloud computing has been well accepted as a powerful platform for data sharing, we especially choose to consider the scenario where CP-ABE is used to encrypt the data outsourced to the cloud storage, to achieve confidentiality against the cloud.

Handling Policy Changes in CP-ABE Encryption of Cloud Data. Indeed, cloud computing enables users to outsource their data to the cloud, where massive storage capacity is available. However, a major concern over this data outsourcing paradigm is that the data owner who outsources his data (e.g., a company) may not want the cloud to see the data in cleartext. It is now basically accepted that in data critical applications, a user should only outsource encrypted data in order to ensure confidentiality against the cloud.

In practice, data accessing is often obliged to enforce fine-grained access control rules. For example, imagine that a hospital moves patient data to the cloud. Access control rules must guarantee that a patient's information is only allowed to be accessed by appropriate doctors/nurses from appropriate departments. Undoubtedly, CP-ABE is a nice tool for achieving this type of fine-grained cryptographic access control over cloud data.

In such applications where CP-ABE is used for encryption of cloud data, changes of access policies are not a rare phenomenon. For example, specifications on a new product might be only allowed access by the engineering department during the design and testing stage. As the product is ready to be launched in the market, access of the product specifications will need to be transferred from the engineering department to the marketing and sales departments. A straightforward application of CP-ABE would involve the data owner downloading the encrypted data from the cloud, decrypting it to obtain the original data, re-encrypting the data under the new access policies and uploading again. This is a daunting task if the quantity of data involved is massive.

Adaptable CP-ABE offers an effective solution by delegating the task of data re-encryption to the cloud. More specifically, the cloud is trusted as the proxy and is given the trapdoor for data transformation. As a result, the data owner simply needs to instruct the cloud to re-encrypt the data by providing the new access policies, while retaining data confidentiality against the cloud. We should point out that it is also possible to apply CP-ABPRE to accomplish the same task, but at a much higher price: for each old/new policy pair, the data owner must provide a seperate re-encryption key.

Outsourcing of CP-ABE Encryption. Consider again the above scenario of encryption of cloud data using CP-ABE, but now we focus on the situation where the data owner uses a resource-constrained device (e.g., tablet or smart phone) to do the data outsourcing. This is in accord with the current trend of growing use of such low-powered devices in our daily life. An example is that a user encrypts the photos taken with his smart phone, and uploads them to his personal account over the cloud for sharing with his friends.

We observe that in the existing CP-ABE schemes in the literature, the encryption function cannot be deemed efficient, and an encryption operation normally involves $\mathcal{O}(n)$ scalar exponentiations, where n is the number of attributes involved in the access policy. This is quite a burden for resource-limited devices. Adaptable CP-ABE would provide a good solution to this problem, inflicting fixed computation on the weak devices by delegating the majority of the computation to the cloud.

The basic idea is as follows. We first extend the original attributes of the system with an additional single-valued dummy attribute, but no one will be issued a private key corresponding to this dummy attribute. To generate the ciphertext for data to be outsourced to cloud, the data owner encrypts the data under a single-attribute access policy involving only the dummy attribute (i.e., only the dummy attribute satisfies the policy). The computation overhead for this is thus constant. The data owner then sends the ciphertext together with the intended access policy to the cloud, who then does the ciphertext conversion, generating the desired ciphertext. It goes without saying that using CP-ABPRE would require the data owner to provide a re-encryption key from the dummy attribute to each intended access policy.

1.2   Organization

This paper is organized as follows. In Section 2, we provide an overview of related work. In Section 3, some standard notations and cryptographic definitions are highlighted. In Section 4, we describe the formal model for adaptable CP-ABE, followed by a concrete construction together with its security analysis. Concluding remarks are contained in Section 5.

2   Related Work

ABE and proxy re-encryption (PRE) are of obvious relevance to our work, and we next give an overview of them, respectively.

ABE. The notion of ABE is introduced by Sahai and Waters as an application of their fuzzy identity-based encryption (IBE) scheme [25], where both ciphertexts and secrete keys are associated with sets of attributes. The decryption of a ciphertext is enabled if and only if the set of attributes for the ciphertext and the set of attributes for the secret key overlap by at least a fixed threshold value d. Goyal et al. [9] formulate two complementary forms of ABE: KP-ABE and CP-ABE. Our focus in this work is CP-ABE. In a CP-ABE scheme, decryption keys are associated with sets of attributes and ciphertexts are associated with access policies.

The first CP-ABE construction proposed by Bethencourt et al. [3] is proven secure under the generic group model. Later, Cheung and Newport [5] present a CP-ABE scheme that is secure under the standard model; however, the access policies in that scheme are restricted to be in the form of a AND combination of different attributes. Recently, secure and more expressive CP-ABE schemes [27,14,16,6,7] are proposed. In virtually all existing CP-ABE schemes, the size of a ciphertext in a CP-ABE scheme is proportional to the size of its associated access policy, and the decryption time is proportional to the number of attributes that have been used for decryption. This has motivated some work [1,10] to design CP-ABE schemes with faster decryption algorithms. Müller et al. [21] and Lewko et al. [15] led another line of research, considering CP-ABE schemes with multiple authorities, in an attempt to meet the need of a more general framework where data are shared according to policies defined over attributes or credentials issued across different trust domains and organizations.

Proxy Re-Encryption (PRE). Proxy re-encryption (PRE), first introduced in [4], involves a set of users (each holding a public/private key pair for standard public-key encryption), and a semi-trusted proxy. Let pk_A and pk_B be the public keys of Alice and Bob, respectively. The proxy is given a re-encryption key $rk_{A \to B}$ from Alice to Bob, and can transform ciphertexts under Alice's public key into ciphertexts under Bob's public key, where the procedure is intuitively depicted as $Enc(pk_A, m) \xrightarrow{rk_{A \to B}} Enc(pk_B, m)$. The proxy does not learn anything about the messages m encrypted under either key.

Later, the concept of conditional proxy re-encryption(CPRE) [28] emerged, which strengthens PRE in such a way that a ciphertext under Alice's public key is generated under a condition $\mathbb{C}$, and the re-encryption key from Alice to Bob is associated with certain properties $\mathbb{P}$ (denoted as $rk_{A \xrightarrow{\mathbb{P}} B}$). A ciphertext for Alice can be transferred to one for Bob, if and only if $\mathbb{P}$ satisfies $\mathbb{C}$. Intuitively, the procedure is $Enc(pk_A, m, \mathbb{C}) \xrightarrow{rk_{A \xrightarrow{\mathbb{P}} B}} Enc(pk_B, m)$. Most of the existing CPRE schemes such as [28,29] can only handle keyword-based conditions, where both $\mathbb{C}$ and $\mathbb{P}$ are a keyword. The scheme in [30] is an exception, and it manages to process attribute-based conditions.

To implement PRE in the attribute-based cryptographic setting, Liang et al. [19] introduce ciphertext-policy attribute-based PRE (CP-ABPRE), in which a proxy is allowed to transform a ciphertext under a source access policy into another ciphertext under a destination policy. At the mean time, CP-ABPRE has the flavor of CPRE, in the sense that a re-encryption key is bounded with a set S of attributes as well as a destination access policy, and ciphertext transformation is *conditioned* upon the satisfaction of S to the source access policy. Liang et al. [19] propose a concrete construction of CP-ABPRE based on a CP-ABE scheme [5] in which access policy is only represented as AND gates on positive and negative attributes. Luo et al. [20] propose a CP-ABPRE scheme which supports AND gates on multi-valued and negative attributes. Recently, Liang et al. [18] present a CP-ABPRE scheme supporting any monotonic access policy.

Adaptable CP-ABE is similar to CP-ABPRE, in terms of the concept of ciphertext transformation among source/destination access policies, but they also differ in delicate ways as shown earlier. Adaptable CP-ABE has no implication of "conditional" transformation, and the trapdoor for ciphertext conversion is independent of specific attributes and access policies, and entitles to transform ciphertext under any source access policy and to any destination policy.

3   Preliminaries

If S is a set, then $s \xleftarrow{\$} S$ denotes the operation of picking an element s uniformly at random from S. Let $z \leftarrow \mathsf{A}(x, y, \ldots)$ denote the operation of running an algorithm A with inputs $(x, y, \ldots)$ and output z. A function $f(\lambda)$ is *negligible* if for every $c > 0$ there exists a λ_c such that $f(\lambda) < 1/\lambda^c$ for all $\lambda > \lambda_c$.

3.1   Access Structures

Definition 1 (Access Structure [2]). *Let* $\{P_1, \ldots, P_n\}$ *be a set of parties. A collection* $\mathbb{A} \subseteq 2^{\{P_1, \ldots, P_n\}}$ *is monotone for* $\forall B$ *and* C, *if* $B \in \mathbb{A}, B \subseteq C$, *then* $C \in \mathbb{A}$. *An access structure (respectively, monotone access structure) is a collection (respectively, monotone collection)* $\mathbb{A}$ *of non-empty subsets of* $\{P_1, \ldots, P_n\}$, *i.e.,* $\mathbb{A} \subseteq 2^{\{P_1, \ldots, P_n\}} \backslash \{\emptyset\}$. *The sets in* $\mathbb{A}$ *are called authorized sets, and the sets not in* $\mathbb{A}$ *are called unauthorized sets.*

In our context, attributes play the role of parties and we restrict our attention to monotone access structures. It is possible to (inefficiently) realize general access structures using our techniques by treating the negation of an attribute as a separate attribute.

3.2   Linear Secret Sharing Schemes

Our construction will employ linear secret-sharing schemes. We use the definition adapted from [2].

Definition 2 (Linear Secret-Sharing Schemes (LSSS)). *A secret sharing scheme* Π *over a set of parties* $\mathcal{P}$ *is called linear (over* $\mathbb{Z}_p$*) if*

1. *The shares for each party form a vector over* $\mathbb{Z}_p$.

2. *There exists a matrix $\mathbf{A}$ with ℓ rows and n columns called the share-generating matrix for Π. For all $i = 1, \ldots, \ell$, the ith row of $\mathbf{A}$ is labeled by a party $\rho(i)$ (ρ is a function from $\{1, \ldots, \ell\}$ to $\mathcal{P}$). When we consider the column vector $v = (s, r_2, \ldots, r_n)$, where $s \in \mathbb{Z}_p$ is the secret to be shared, and $r_2, \ldots, r_n \in \mathbb{Z}_p$ are randomly chosen, then $\mathbf{A}v$ is the vector of ℓ shares of the secret s according to Π. The share $(\mathbf{A}v)_i$ belongs to party $\rho(i)$.*

It is shown in [2] that every linear secret-sharing scheme according to the above definition also enjoys the linear reconstruction property, defined as follows. Suppose that Π is an LSSS for the access structure $\mathbb{A}$. Let $S \in \mathbb{A}$ be any authorized set, and let $I \subset \{1, \ldots, \ell\}$ be defined as $I = \{i | \rho(i) \in S\}$. Then there exist constants $\{\omega_i \in \mathbb{Z}_p\}_{i \in I}$ such that, if $\{\lambda_i\}$ are valid shares of any secret s according to Π, then $\sum_{i \in I} \omega_i \lambda_i = s$. Let A_i denotes the ith row of $\mathbb{A}$, we have $\sum_{i \in I} \omega_i A_i = (1, 0, \ldots, 0)$. These constants $\{\omega_i\}$ can be found in time polynomial in the size of the share-generation matrix $\mathbf{A}$ [2]. Note that, for unauthorized sets, no such constants $\{\omega_i\}$ exist.

Boolean Formulas. Access structures might also be described in terms of monotonic boolean formulas. Using standard techniques one can convert any monotonic boolean formula into an LSSS representation. We can represent the boolean formula as an access tree. An access tree of ℓ nodes will result in an LSSS matrix of ℓ rows. We refer the reader to the appendix of [15] for a discussion on how to perform this conversion.

3.3 Bilinear Groups

Let $\mathcal{G}$ be an algorithm that takes as input a security parameter λ and outputs a tuple $(p, \mathbb{G}, \mathbb{G}_T, e)$, where $\mathbb{G}$ and $\mathbb{G}_T$ are multiplicative cyclic groups of prime order p, and $e : \mathbb{G} \times \mathbb{G} \to \mathbb{G}_T$ is a map such that:

1. **Bilinearity:** $e(g^a, h^b) = e(g, h)^{ab}$ for all $g, h \in \mathbb{G}$ and $a, b \in \mathbb{Z}_p^*$.
2. **Non-degeneracy:** $e(g, h) \neq 1$ whenever $g, h \neq 1_{\mathbb{G}}$.
3. **Computable:** efficient computability for any input pair.

We refer to the tuple $(p, \mathbb{G}, \mathbb{G}_T, e)$ as a bilinear group.

3.4 Complexity Assumption

Definition 3 (DBDH Problem). *Given a group $\mathbb{G}$ of prime order p with generator g and elements $g^a, g^b, g^c \in \mathbb{G}$, $e(g, g)^z \in \mathbb{G}_T$ where a, b, c, z are selected uniformly at random from $\mathbb{Z}_p^*$. A fair binary coin $\beta \in \{0, 1\}$ is flipped. If $\beta = 1$, it outputs the tuple $(g, g^a, g^b, g^c, T = e(g, g)^{abc})$. If $\beta = 0$, it outputs the tuple $(g, g^a, g^b, g^c, T = e(g, g)^z)$. The Decisional Bilinear Diffie-Hellman (DBDH) problem is to guess the value of β.*

The advantage of an adversary $\mathcal{A}$ in solving the DBDH problem is defined as

$$|\Pr[\mathcal{A}(g, g^a, g^b, g^c, T = e(g, g)^{abc}) = 1]$$
$$-\Pr[\mathcal{A}(g, g^a, g^b, g^c, T = e(g, g)^z) = 1]|$$

where the probability is over the randomly chosen a, b, c, z and the random bits consumed by $\mathcal{A}$. We refer to the distribution on the left-hand size as $\mathcal{P}_{BDH}$ and the one on the right as $\mathcal{R}_{BDH}$.

Definition 4 (DBDH assumption). *We say that DBDH assumption holds if all probabilistic polynomial time (PPT) adversaries have at most a negligible advantage in solving the DBDH problem.*

4   Adaptable Ciphertext-Policy Attribute-Based Encryption

In this section, we give the formal definition of adaptable CP-ABE firstly. Then, we present the formal security model for adaptable CP-ABE. Finally, drawing on the CP-ABE scheme proposed by Waters [27], we propose a concrete construction of adaptable CP-ABE and prove that it is secure in our security model.

4.1   Formal Definition of Adaptable CP-ABE

Besides Setup, KeyGen, Encrypt and Decrypt algorithms as in a traditional CP-ABE scheme, an adaptable CP-ABE scheme also includes two additional algorithms: TrapdoorGen and PolicyAdp. The authority runs the algorithm TrapdoorGen to generate a trapdoor. Given the trapdoor, a proxy can transform a ciphertext under an access policy into another ciphertext of the same plaintext under *any* access policy using the algorithm PolicyAdp.

Formally, an adaptable CP-ABE scheme consists of the following six algorithms:

Setup(λ, U) takes as input a security parameter λ and an attribute universe description U. It outputs the public parameters PK and a master secret key MSK. This algorithm is run by a trusted authority.

KeyGen(PK, MSK, S) takes as input the public parameters PK, the master secret key MSK and a set of attributes S. It outputs a private key SK_S corresponding to S. This algorithm is run by a trusted authority.

TrapdoorGen(PK, MSK) takes as input the public parameters PK and the master secret key MSK. It outputs a trapdoor TK. This algorithm is run by a trusted authority and the trapdoor TK is sent to a semi-trusted proxy.

Encrypt$(PK, M, \mathbb{A})$ takes as input the public parameters PK, a message M and an access structure $\mathbb{A}$. It outputs a ciphertext CT.

PolicyAdp$(PK, TK, CT, \mathbb{A}')$ takes as input the public parameters PK, a trapdoor TK, a ciphertext CT which contains an access policy $\mathbb{A}$, and a new access policy $\mathbb{A}'$. It outputs a new ciphertext CT' associated with the access policy $\mathbb{A}'$, without changing the underlying plaintext message of CT. This algorithm is run by a semi-trusted proxy.

Decrypt(PK, SK_S, CT) takes as input the public parameters PK, a private key SK_S, and a ciphertext CT associated with an access policy $\mathbb{A}$. If the set S of attributes satisfies the access structure $\mathbb{A}$, then the algorithm will decrypt the ciphertext and return a message M; otherwise, it outputs $\bot$.

Let $(PK, MSK) \leftarrow Setup(\lambda, U)$, $SK_S \leftarrow KeyGen(PK, MSK, S)$, TK $\leftarrow$ TrapdoorGen(PK, MSK), $CT \leftarrow Encrypt(PK, M, \mathbb{A})$ and $CT' \leftarrow$ PolicyAdp $(PK, TK, CT, \mathbb{A}')$. For correctness, we require the following to hold:

1. If the set S of attributes satisfies the access structure $\mathbb{A}$, then $M \leftarrow$ Decrypt(PK, SK_S, CT);
2. The distributions of CT' and Encrypt(PK, $M, \mathbb{A}'$) are identical.

4.2 Security Model for Adaptable CP-ABE

Given the formal definition for adaptable CP-ABE, we are now in a position to define its security specification. We consider two types of adversaries. Type 1 adversaries who are allowed to query for any private keys that cannot be used to decrypt the challenge ciphertext, model adversaries in a traditional CP-ABE scheme. We also want to consider Type 2 adversaries who are equipped with a transformation trapdoor, in order to model security against an eavesdropping proxy. We assume that the proxy in an adaptable CP-ABE scheme is semi-trusted. That is to say, the proxy does not collude with any user. Thus, Type 2 adversaries are not allowed to query for any private keys.

We now give the security model against Type 1 adversaries for adaptable CP-ABE, described as a security game between a challenger and a Type 1 adversary. The game proceeds as follows:

Setup. The challenger runs Setup to obtain the public parameters PK and a master secret key MSK. It gives the public parameters PK to the adversary and keeps MSK to itself.

Query Phase 1. The adversary adaptively queries the challenger for secret keys corresponding to sets of attributes $S_1, \ldots, S_q$. In response, the challenger runs $SK_{S_i} \leftarrow KeyGen(PK, MSK, S_i)$ and gives the secret key SK_{S_i} to the adversary, for $1 \leq i \leq q$.

Challenge. The adversary submits two (equal length) messages M_0, M_1 and an access structures $\mathbb{A}$, subject to the restriction that $\mathbb{A}$ cannot be satisfied by any of the queried sets of attributes in Query phase 1. The challenger selects a random bit $\beta \in \{0, 1\}$, sets $CT = Encrypt(PK, M_\beta, \mathbb{A})$ and sends CT to the adversary as the challenge ciphertext.

Query Phase 2. The adversary continues to adaptively query the challenger for secret keys corresponding to sets of attributes with the restriction that none of these satisfies $\mathbb{A}$.

Guess. The adversary outputs its guess $\beta' \in \{0, 1\}$ for β.

The advantage of the Type 1 adversary in this game is defined as $|Pr[\beta = \beta'] - \frac{1}{2}|$ where the probability is taken over the random bits used by the challenger and the Type 1 adversary.

Note that, a Type 1 adversary of adaptable CP-ABE can see the transformed ciphertexts CT' of the challenge ciphertext $CT \leftarrow Encrypt(PK, M_\beta, \mathbb{A})$. The challenger does not provide the information for the adversary in the above game, since CT' does not leak any additional information about M_β.

We give a brief explanation. One can easily prove that, if $C \leftarrow \mathsf{Encrypt}(\mathsf{PK}, M, \mathbb{A})$, $C' \leftarrow \mathsf{Encrypt}(\mathsf{PK}, M, \mathbb{A}')$ are the ciphertexts of a secure CP-ABE, then given $C \| C'$ simultaneously, the adversary also can not obtain any information about M. On the other hand, adaptable CP-ABE requires that the distributions of CT' and $\mathsf{Encrypt}(\mathsf{PK}, M_\beta, \mathbb{A}')$ should be identical, hence CT' does not leak any additional information about M_β.

Definition 5. *An adaptable CP-ABE scheme is secure against Type 1 adversaries if all PPT adversaries have at most a negligible advantage in the above game.*

We say that an adaptable CP-ABE scheme is *selectively* secure against Type 1 adversaries if we add an **Init** stage before **Setup** where the adversary commits to the challenge access structure $\mathbb{A}$.

The security model against Type 2 adversaries for adaptable CP-ABE is also described as a security game between a challenger and a Type 2 adversary. The game proceeds as follows:

Setup. The challenger runs Setup to generate a public parameters/master secret key pair $(\mathsf{PK}, \mathsf{MSK})$ firstly. Then, it runs $\mathsf{TrapdoorGen}(\mathsf{PK}, \mathsf{MSK})$ to obtain a trapdoor TK. Finally, it sends $(\mathsf{PK}, \mathsf{TK})$ to the adversary and keeps MSK to itself.

Challenge. The adversary submits two (equal length) messages M_0, M_1 and an access structures $\mathbb{A}$. The challenger selects a random bit $\beta \in \{0, 1\}$, sets $CT = \mathsf{Encrypt}(\mathsf{PK}, M_\beta, \mathbb{A})$ and sends CT to the adversary as the challenge ciphertext.

Guess. The adversary outputs its guess $\beta' \in \{0, 1\}$ for β.

The advantage of the Type 2 adversary in this game is defined as $|\Pr[\beta = \beta'] - \frac{1}{2}|$ where the probability is taken over the random bits used by the challenger and the Type 2 adversary.

Definition 6. *An adaptable CP-ABE scheme is secure against Type 2 adversaries if all PPT adversaries have at most a negligible advantage in the above game.*

4.3   Proposed Adaptable CP-ABE Scheme

Based on the CP-ABE scheme proposed by Waters [27], we propose a concrete construction of adaptable CP-ABE scheme. Inheriting from the underlying Waters CP-ABE scheme [27], our proposed adaptable CP-ABE is only *selectively* secure against Type 1 adversaries and the size of the public parameters is linear in the number of attributes in the universe.

Recently, the first CP-ABE scheme that achieved full security was proposed by Lewko et al. [14]. Since the underlying structure of the CP-ABE scheme presented by Lewko et al. [14] is almost identical to the underlying Waters CP-ABE scheme [27] we use, one can adapt our construction techniques to the

CP-ABE scheme proposed in [14] to achieve a new adaptable CP-ABE scheme, which is (*fully*) secure against Type 1 adversaries. On the other hand, it is also possible to adapt our techniques to obtain a large universe construction. In a large universe construction, we could use all elements of $\mathbb{Z}_p$ as attributes. To obtain a large universe construction, we could replace the group elements h_i associated with attribute i with a function $h : \mathbb{Z}_p \to \mathbb{G}$ based on a polynomial, as shown in [27].

Concretely, the proposed adaptable CP-ABE scheme is as follows:

Setup(λ, U) The setup algorithm takes as input a security parameter λ and a small universe description $U = \{1, 2, \ldots, |U|\}$. It first runs $\mathcal{G}(\lambda)$ to obtain a bilinear group $(p, \mathbb{G}, \mathbb{G}_T, e)$, where $\mathbb{G}$ and $\mathbb{G}_T$ are cyclic groups of prime order p. It then chooses $g, h_1, \ldots, h_{|U|} \in \mathbb{G}$, and $\alpha, \beta \in \mathbb{Z}_p$ uniformly at random. The public parameters are published as $\mathsf{PK} = (\mathbb{G}, \mathbb{G}_T, e, g, g^\beta, e(g, g)^\alpha, h_1, \ldots, h_{|U|})$. The master secret key is $\mathsf{MSK} = (\alpha, \beta)$.

KeyGen($\mathsf{PK}, \mathsf{MSK}, S$) The key generation algorithm takes as input the public parameters, the master secret key and a set S of attributes. The algorithm first randomly picks $t \in \mathbb{Z}_p$. Then, the secret key $\mathsf{SK}_S = (S, K, K_0, K_i)$ is computed as $K = g^\alpha g^{\beta t}$, $K_0 = g^t$, $K_i = h_i^t \; \forall i \in S$.

TrapdoorGen($\mathsf{PK}, \mathsf{MSK} = (\alpha, \beta)$) The trapdoor generation algorithm takes as input the public parameters and the master secret key. It creates the trapdoor as $\mathsf{TK} = \beta$.

Encrypt($\mathsf{PK}, M \in \mathbb{G}_T, \mathbb{A}$) The encryption algorithm takes as input the public parameters PK, a message $M \in \mathbb{G}_T$ to encrypt and an LSSS access structure $\mathbb{A} = (\mathbf{A}, \rho)$, where $\mathbf{A}$ is an $\ell \times n$ matrix and ρ is a map from each row A_i of $\mathbf{A}$ to an attribute $\rho(i)$.

The algorithm first chooses a random vector $\boldsymbol{v} = (s, v_2, \ldots, v_n) \in \mathbb{Z}_p^n$. These values will be used to share the encryption exponent s. Then, for each row A_i of $\mathbf{A}$, it chooses $r_i \in \mathbb{Z}_p$ uniformly at random. The ciphertext is $CT = ((\mathbf{A}, \rho), C, C', C_i, D_i)$, where $C = M \cdot e(g, g)^{\alpha s}$, $C' = g^s$, $C_i = g^{\beta A_i \cdot \boldsymbol{v}} h_{\rho(i)}^{-r_i}$, $D_i = g^{r_i} \; \forall i \in \{1, 2, \ldots, \ell\}$.

PolicyAdp($\mathsf{PK}, \mathsf{TK} = \beta, CT, \mathbb{A}' = (\mathbf{A}', \rho')$) The policy adaptation algorithm takes as input the public parameters PK, the trapdoor TK, a ciphertext $CT = (\mathbb{A} = (\mathbf{A}, \rho), C, C', C_i, D_i)$ and an access structure $\mathbb{A}' = (\mathbf{A}', \rho')$. With the help of the trapdoor TK, this algorithm transforms the ciphertext CT into a ciphertext CT' associated with the access structure $\mathbb{A}' = (\mathbf{A}', \rho')$, without changing the underlying message of CT.

Let $CT = ((\mathbf{A}, \rho), C = M \cdot e(g, g)^{\alpha s}, C' = g^s, C_i = g^{\beta A_i \cdot \boldsymbol{v}} h_{\rho(i)}^{-r_i}, D_i = g^{r_i} \; \forall i \in \{1, 2, \ldots, \ell\})$, where $\mathbf{A}$ is an $\ell \times n$ matrix and $\boldsymbol{v} = (s, v_2, \ldots, v_n) \in \mathbb{Z}_p^n$ is a random vector.

Let $\mathbf{A}'$ be an $\ell' \times n'$ matrix. The algorithm proceeds as follows. First choose a random vector $\tilde{\boldsymbol{v}} = (\tilde{s}, \tilde{v}_2, \ldots, \tilde{v}_{n'}) \in \mathbb{Z}_p^{n'}$. Then, for each row A_i' of $\mathbf{A}'$, choose $r_i' \in \mathbb{Z}_p$ uniformly at random. Let $\boldsymbol{v}' = (s', \tilde{v}_2, \ldots, \tilde{v}_{n'})$, where

$s' = s + \tilde{s}$. The new ciphertext $CT' = ((\mathbf{A}', \rho'), \ \tilde{C}, \tilde{C}', \tilde{C}_i, \tilde{D}_i)$ is computed as

$$CT' = ((\mathbf{A}', \rho'), \ \tilde{C} = C \cdot (e(g, g)^{\alpha})^{\tilde{s}} = M \cdot e(g, g)^{\alpha s'},$$
$$\tilde{C}' = C' \cdot g^{\tilde{s}} = g^{s + \tilde{s}} = g^{s'},$$
$$\forall i \in \{1, 2, \ldots, \ell'\} : \tilde{C}_i = g^{\beta A_i' \cdot \boldsymbol{v}'} h_{\rho'(i)}^{-r_i'}, \ \tilde{D}_i = g^{r_i'}).$$

It can see that the distribution of CT' is the same as that generated directly from $\mathsf{Encrypt}(\mathsf{PK}, M, \mathbb{A}' = (\mathbf{A}', \rho'))$.

Comment: Note that, although s is unknown, we show how exactly $\tilde{C}_i$ are computed. Let the row vector $A_i' = (a_{i,1}, \ldots, a_{i,n'})$. Then,

$$g^{\beta A_i' \cdot \boldsymbol{v}'} = g^{\beta(a_{i,1} s' + a_{i,2} \tilde{v}_2 + \cdots + a_{i,n'} \tilde{v}_{n'})}$$
$$= (g^{s'})^{\beta a_{i,1}} \cdot g^{\beta(a_{i,2} \tilde{v}_2 + \cdots + a_{i,n'} \tilde{v}_{n'})} = (\tilde{C}')^{\beta a_{i,1}} \cdot g^{\beta(a_{i,2} \tilde{v}_2 + \cdots + a_{i,n'} \tilde{v}_{n'})}.$$

Thus, $\tilde{C}_i$ can be computed from β, $\tilde{C}'$, the LSSS access structure $\mathbb{A}' = (\mathbf{A}', \rho')$, the randomness $\tilde{v}_2, \ldots, \tilde{v}_{n'}$ and r_i', and the public parameters.

$\mathsf{Decrypt}(\mathsf{PK}, \mathsf{SK}_S, CT)$ The decryption algorithm takes as input the public parameters PK, a private key $\mathsf{SK}_S = (S, \ K, \ K_0, K_i)$ for a set of attributes S and a ciphertext $CT = ((\mathbf{A}, \rho), \ C, C', C_i, D_i)$ for an access structure $\mathbb{A} = (\mathbf{A}, \rho)$, where $\mathbf{A}$ is an $\ell \times n$ matrix. If S does not satisfy the access structure $\mathbb{A}$, it outputs $\perp$. Suppose that S satisfies the access structure $\mathbb{A}$ and let $I \subset \{1, 2, \ldots, \ell\}$ be defined as $I = \{i : \rho(i) \in S\}$. It computes constant $\omega_i \in \mathbb{Z}_p$ such that $\sum_{i \in I} \omega_i A_i = (1, 0, \ldots, 0)$.

The decryption algorithm first computes:

$$\frac{e(C', K)}{\prod_{i \in I}(e(C_i, K_0) \cdot e(K_{\rho(i)}, D_i))^{\omega_i}} = \frac{e(g, g)^{\alpha s} e(g, g)^{\beta t s}}{\prod_{i \in I} e(g, g)^{\beta t A_i \cdot \boldsymbol{v} \cdot \omega_i}} = e(g, g)^{\alpha s}.$$

The decryption algorithm can then divide out this value from C and obtain the message M.

Obviously, the above scheme satisfies the correctness of adaptable CP-ABE. We now state the security theorems of our adaptable CP-ABE scheme.

Theorem 1. *If the CP-ABE scheme proposed in [27] is selectively secure, then our proposed adaptable CP-ABE scheme is selectively secure against Type 1 adversaries.*

Proof. Recall that, Type 1 adversaries in an adaptable CP-ABE scheme, which model adversaries in a traditional CP-ABE scheme, are allowed to possess any private keys that cannot be used to decrypt the challenge ciphertext. Observe that, the algorithms Setup, KeyGen, $\mathsf{Encrypt}$ and $\mathsf{Decrypt}$ constitute a traditional CP-ABE scheme, and the scheme is same as the CP-ABE scheme proposed by Waters [27]. Since Waters [27] has proved that the CP-ABE scheme is selectively secure, thus, our proposed adaptable CP-ABE scheme is also selectively secure against Type 1 adversaries. □

Theorem 2. *If DBDH assumption holds, then our proposed adaptable CP-ABE is secure against Type 2 adversaries.*

Proof. Suppose there exists a Type 2 adversary $\mathcal{A}$ against our proposed adaptable CP-ABE scheme with non-negligible advantage. We are going to construct another PPT $\mathcal{B}$ that makes use of $\mathcal{A}$ to solve the DBDH problem with non-negligible probability.

$\mathcal{B}$ is given as input a random 5-tuple (g, g^a, g^b, g^c, T) that is either sampled from $\mathcal{P}_{BDH}$ (where $T = e(g,g)^{abc}$) or from $\mathcal{R}_{BDH}$ (where T is uniform and independent in $\mathbb{G}_T$). Algorithm $\mathcal{B}$'s goal is to output 1 if $T = e(g,g)^{abc}$ and 0 otherwise. Algorithm $\mathcal{B}$, playing the role of challenger, runs $\mathcal{A}$ executing the following steps.

Setup. $\mathcal{B}$ chooses random exponents $\beta, \gamma_1, \ldots, \gamma_{|U|} \in \mathbb{Z}_p^*$. The public parameters $\mathsf{PK} = (\mathbb{G}, g, g^\beta, e(g^a, g^b), h_1 = g^{\gamma_1}, \ldots, h_{|U|} = g^{\gamma_{|U|}})$ and the trapdoor $\mathsf{TK} = \beta$ are passed to $\mathcal{A}$. It sets $\alpha = ab$ implicitly, which is unknown to $\mathcal{B}$.

Challenge. The adversary $\mathcal{A}$ outputs two equal-length messages (M_0, M_1) and an access structure $\mathbb{A} = (\mathbf{A}, \rho)$, where $\mathbf{A}$ is an $\ell \times n$ matrix and ρ is a map from each row A_i of $\mathbf{A}$ to an attribute $\rho(i)$.

$\mathcal{B}$ flips a fair coin $\sigma \in \{0, 1\}$ firstly. Then, for each row A_i of $\mathbf{A}$, $\mathcal{B}$ chooses $r_i \in \mathbb{Z}_p$ uniformly at random. $\mathcal{B}$ also chooses random $v_2, \ldots, v_n \in \mathbb{Z}_p$ and sets $\boldsymbol{v} = (c, v_2, \ldots, v_n)$. $\mathcal{B}$ computes the ciphertext CT as $((\mathbf{A}, \rho), C = M_\beta \cdot T, C' = g^c, C_i = g^{\beta A_i \cdot \boldsymbol{v}} h_{\rho(i)}^{-r_i}, D_i = g^{r_i} \ \forall i \in \{1, 2, \ldots, \ell\})$, Note that, although c is unknown to $\mathcal{B}$, it can compute C_i from g^c, β, the LSSS access structure $\mathbb{A} = (\mathbf{A}, \rho)$, the randomness $v_2, \ldots, v_n$ and r_i, and the public parameters, as in the PolicyAdp algorithm.

Finally, $\mathcal{B}$ sets CT as the challenge ciphertext and sends it to $\mathcal{A}$. Obviously, the challenge ciphertext is a valid encryption of M_β with the correct distribution whenever $T = e(g,g)^{abc} = e(g^a, g^b)^c = e(g,g)^{\alpha c}$ (as is the case when the input 5-tuple is sampled from $\mathcal{P}_{BDH}$). On the other hand, when T is uniform and independent in $\mathbb{G}_T$ (which occurs when the input 5-tuple is sampled from $\mathcal{R}_{BDH}$) the challenge ciphertext CT is independent of σ in the adversary's view.

Guess. The adversary $\mathcal{A}$ outputs a bit σ'. If $\sigma' = \sigma$ then $\mathcal{B}$ outputs 1 meaning $T = e(g,g)^{abc}$. Otherwise, it outputs 0 meaning $T \neq e(g,g)^{abc}$.

Observe that, when the input 5-tuple is sampled from $\mathcal{P}_{BDH}$ (where $T = e(g,g)^{abc}$) then $\mathcal{A}$'s view is identical to its view in a real attack game. On the other hand, when the input 5-tuple is sampled from $\mathcal{R}_{BDH}$ (where T is uniform in $\mathbb{G}_T$) then the value of σ is information-theoretically hidden from the adversary $\mathcal{A}$. Thus, if $\mathcal{A}$ breaks our proposed adaptable CP-ABE scheme with non-negligible advantage, then $\mathcal{B}$ will solve the DBDH problem with non-negligible probability. □

5 Conclusions

In this paper, we introduced a new cryptographic primitive, called adaptable CP-ABE, which enables a *semi-trusted* proxy, given a trapdoor, to transform a ciphertext under one access policy into ciphertexts under any other access policies. We showed that adaptable CP-ABE has many interesting real world applications. We gave the formal model of adaptable CP-ABE and proposed a concrete construction.

In our construction, since a proxy with the trapdoor can transform a ciphertext under one access policy into ciphertexts under *any* other access policies, then the proxy colluding with *any* user can decrypt all ciphertexts in the system. Hence, we require that the proxy should be *semi-trusted*, i.e., it does not collude with any user in the system. On the one hand, the assumption that a proxy is semi-trusted is reasonable and is used in many related works, such as PREs. On the other hand, a future research direction is to construct adaptable CP-ABE schemes, where the "adaptability" capability of the semi-trusted proxy could be controlled *flexibly*, called controlled adaptable CP-ABE. In a controlled adaptable CP-ABE, the semi-trusted proxy with a trapdoor only can transform a ciphertext associated with an access policy $\mathbb{A}_1 \in \mathcal{AS}_1$ into a ciphertext of the same plaintext under the access policy $\mathbb{A}_2 \in \mathcal{AS}_2$, where the access policies sets $\mathcal{AS}_1, \mathcal{AS}_2$ are specified by the trusted authority who setups the system and generates the trapdoor. Our proposed scheme can be viewed as of a special case of controlled adaptable CP-ABE, where $\mathcal{AS}_1, \mathcal{AS}_2$ are the sets of *all* access polices. Observe that, since the authority also can generate the re-encryption keys which is generated by the users in CP-ABPRE, one can easily construct a special case of controlled adaptable CP-ABE, which has the same functionality of CP-ABPRE.

Acknowledgment. The research effort of Robert H. Deng was funded through a research grant 13-C220-SMU-005 from Singapore MOE's AcRF Tier 1 funding support through Singapore Management University. The work of Junzuo Lai was supported by the National Natural Science Foundation of China (Nos. 61300226, 61272534, 61272453), the Research Fund for the Doctoral Program of Higher Education of China (No. 20134401120017), the Guangdong Provincial Natural Science Foundation (No. S2013040014826), and the Fundamental Research Funds for the Central Universities. The work of Jian Weng was supported by the National Natural Science Foundation of China under Grant Nos. 61272413, 61005049, 61373158, 61133014, 61070249, 61272415, the Fok Ying Tung Education Foundation under Grant No. 131066, the Program for New Century Excellent Talents in University under Grant No. NCET-12-0680, the Opening Project of Shanghai Key Laboratory of Integrate Administration Technologies for Information Security under Grand No. AGK2011003, and the R&D Foundation of Shenzhen Basic Research Project under Grant No. JC201105170617A.

References

1. Attrapadung, N., Herranz, J., Laguillaumie, F., Libert, B., de Panafieu, E., Ràfols, C.: Attribute-based encryption schemes with constant-size ciphertexts. Theor. Comput. Sci. 422, 15–38 (2012)

2. Beimel, A.: Secure Schemes for Secret Sharing and Key Distribution. PhD thesis, Israel Institute of Technology (1996)
3. Bethencourt, J., Sahai, A., Waters, B.: Ciphertext-policy attribute-based encryption. In: IEEE Symposium on Security and Privacy, pp. 321–334 (2007)
4. Blaze, M., Bleumer, G., Strauss, M.: Divertible protocols and atomic proxy cryptography. In: Nyberg, K. (ed.) EUROCRYPT 1998. LNCS, vol. 1403, pp. 127–144. Springer, Heidelberg (1998)
5. Cheung, L., Newport, C.C.: Provably secure ciphertext policy ABE. In: ACM Conference on Computer and Communications Security, pp. 456–465 (2007)
6. Garg, S., Gentry, C., Halevi, S., Sahai, A., Waters, B.: Attribute-based encryption for circuits from multilinear maps. IACR Cryptology ePrint Archive, 2013:128 (2013)
7. Gorbunov, S., Vaikuntanathan, V., Wee, H.: Attribute-based encryption for circuits. In: STOC, pp. 545–554 (2013)
8. Goyal, V., Jain, A., Pandey, O., Sahai, A.: Bounded Ciphertext Policy Attribute Based Encryption. In: Aceto, L., Damgård, I., Goldberg, L.A., Halldórsson, M.M., Ingólfsdóttir, A., Walukiewicz, I. (eds.) ICALP 2008, Part II. LNCS, vol. 5126, pp. 579–591. Springer, Heidelberg (2008)
9. Goyal, V., Pandey, O., Sahai, A., Waters, B.: Attribute-based encryption for fine-grained access control of encrypted data. In: ACM Conference on Computer and Communications Security, pp. 89–98 (2006)
10. Hohenberger, S., Waters, B.: Attribute-based encryption with fast decryption. In: Kurosawa, K., Hanaoka, G. (eds.) PKC 2013. LNCS, vol. 7778, pp. 162–179. Springer, Heidelberg (2013)
11. Katz, J., Sahai, A., Waters, B.: Predicate encryption supporting disjunctions, polynomial equations, and inner products. In: Smart, N.P. (ed.) EUROCRYPT 2008. LNCS, vol. 4965, pp. 146–162. Springer, Heidelberg (2008)
12. Lai, J., Deng, R.H., Li, Y.: Fully secure cipertext-policy hiding CP-ABE. In: Bao, F., Weng, J. (eds.) ISPEC 2011. LNCS, vol. 6672, pp. 24–39. Springer, Heidelberg (2011)
13. Lai, J., Deng, R.H., Li, Y.: Expressive cp-abe with partially hidden access structures. In: ASIACCS, pp. 18–19 (2012)
14. Lewko, A., Okamoto, T., Sahai, A., Takashima, K., Waters, B.: Fully secure functional encryption: Attribute-based encryption and (Hierarchical) inner product encryption. In: Gilbert, H. (ed.) EUROCRYPT 2010. LNCS, vol. 6110, pp. 62–91. Springer, Heidelberg (2010)
15. Lewko, A., Waters, B.: Decentralizing attribute-based encryption. In: Paterson, K.G. (ed.) EUROCRYPT 2011. LNCS, vol. 6632, pp. 568–588. Springer, Heidelberg (2011)
16. Lewko, A., Waters, B.: New proof methods for attribute-based encryption: Achieving full security through selective techniques. In: Safavi-Naini, R., Canetti, R. (eds.) CRYPTO 2012. LNCS, vol. 7417, pp. 180–198. Springer, Heidelberg (2012)
17. Li, J., Ren, K., Zhu, B., Wan, Z.: Privacy-aware attribute-based encryption with user accountability. In: Samarati, P., Yung, M., Martinelli, F., Ardagna, C.A. (eds.) ISC 2009. LNCS, vol. 5735, pp. 347–362. Springer, Heidelberg (2009)
18. Liang, K., Fang, L., Wong, D.S., Susilo, W.: A ciphertext-policy attribute-based proxy re-encryption with chosen-ciphertext security. IACR Cryptology ePrint Archive, 2013:236 (2013)
19. Liang, X., Cao, Z., Lin, H., Shao, J.: Attribute-based proxy re-encrytpion with delegating capabilities. In: ACM ASIACCS, pp. 276–286 (2009)

20. Luo, S., Hu, J., Chen, Z.: Ciphertext policy attribute-based proxy re-encryption. In: Soriano, M., Qing, S., López, J. (eds.) ICICS 2010. LNCS, vol. 6476, pp. 401–415. Springer, Heidelberg (2010)

21. Müller, S., Katzenbeisser, S., Eckert, C.: Distributed attribute-based encryption. In: Lee, P.J., Cheon, J.H. (eds.) ICISC 2008. LNCS, vol. 5461, pp. 20–36. Springer, Heidelberg (2009)

22. Nishide, T., Yoneyama, K., Ohta, K.: Attribute-based encryption with partially hidden encryptor-specified access structures. In: Bellovin, S.M., Gennaro, R., Keromytis, A.D., Yung, M. (eds.) ACNS 2008. LNCS, vol. 5037, pp. 111–129. Springer, Heidelberg (2008)

23. Okamoto, T., Takashima, K.: Hierarchical predicate encryption for inner-products. In: Matsui, M. (ed.) ASIACRYPT 2009. LNCS, vol. 5912, pp. 214–231. Springer, Heidelberg (2009)

24. Okamoto, T., Takashima, K.: Fully secure functional encryption with general relations from the decisional linear assumption. In: Rabin, T. (ed.) CRYPTO 2010. LNCS, vol. 6223, pp. 191–208. Springer, Heidelberg (2010)

25. Sahai, A., Waters, B.: Fuzzy identity-based encryption. In: Cramer, R. (ed.) EUROCRYPT 2005. LNCS, vol. 3494, pp. 457–473. Springer, Heidelberg (2005)

26. Shen, E., Shi, E., Waters, B.: Predicate privacy in encryption systems. In: Reingold, O. (ed.) TCC 2009. LNCS, vol. 5444, pp. 457–473. Springer, Heidelberg (2009)

27. Waters, B.: Ciphertext-policy attribute-based encryption: An expressive, efficient, and provably secure realization. In: Catalano, D., Fazio, N., Gennaro, R., Nicolosi, A. (eds.) PKC 2011. LNCS, vol. 6571, pp. 53–70. Springer, Heidelberg (2011)

28. Weng, J., Deng, R.H., Ding, X., Chu, C.K., Lai, J.: Conditional proxy re-encryption secure against chosen-ciphertext attack. In: ACM Symposium on Information, Computer and Communications Security, ASIACCS 2009, pp. 322–332 (2009)

29. Weng, J., Yang, Y., Tang, Q., Deng, R.H., Bao, F.: Efficient conditional proxy re-encryption with chosen-ciphertext security. In: Samarati, P., Yung, M., Martinelli, F., Ardagna, C.A. (eds.) ISC 2009. LNCS, vol. 5735, pp. 151–166. Springer, Heidelberg (2009)

30. Zhao, J., Feng, D., Zhang, Z.: Attribute-based conditional proxy re-encryption with chosen-ciphertext security. In: IEEE GLOBECOM 2010, pp. 1–6 (2010)

Algorithms for Pairing-Friendly Primes

Maciej Grześkowiak*

Adam Mickiewicz University,
Faculty of Mathematics and Computer Science,
Umultowska 87, 61-614 Poznań, Poland
maciejg@amu.edu.pl

Abstract. Given an integer $n > 1$ and a square-free $\Delta < 0$, we present a general method of generating primes p and q such that $q \mid \Phi_n(p)$ and $q \mid p + 1 - t$, where $|t| \leq 2\sqrt{p}$ and $4p - t^2 = -\Delta f^2$ for some integers f, t. Such primes can be used for implementing pairing-based cryptographic systems.

Keywords: pairing-based cryptography, embedding degree, pairing-friendly elliptic curves.

1 Introduction

Let E be an elliptic curve defined over finite field $\mathbb{F}_p$, where p is a prime. Let $|E(\mathbb{F}_p)|$ be the order of group of $\mathbb{F}_p$-rational points of E. Given E over $\mathbb{F}_p$, Hasse's theorem states $|E(\mathbb{F}_p)| = p + 1 - t$, where $|t| \leq 2\sqrt{p}$, and $t \in \mathbb{Z}$ [11], [21]. Let q be a divisor of $|E(\mathbb{F}_p)|$ such that q is prime to p. The embedding degree of E with respect to q is the smallest positive integer n such that $q \mid p^n - 1$, but q does not divide $p^d - 1$ for $d \mid n$ [15]. This condition is equivalent to $q > n$ divides $\Phi_n(p)$ [18, Lemma 2.4], where $\Phi_n(x)$ is the nth cyclotomic polynomial; this is a unique monic polynomial of degree $\varphi(n)$ whose roots are the complex primitive nth roots of unity, where φ is Euler's totient function. Elliptic curves that have large prime-order subgroups and small embedding degrees are commonly referred to as *pairing-friendly* [15].

Many new cryptographic protocols have been introduced in recent years which require generating pairing-friendly elliptic curves. For instance: one-round three-way key exchange [17], identity-based encryption [5], identity-based signature [10], and short signatures schemes [6]. From the security point of view it is essential to find a pairing-friendly curve E over $\mathbb{F}_p$ such that the discrete logarithm problems in the group $E(\mathbb{F}_p)$ and in the multiplicative group $\mathbb{F}_{p^n}^*$ both are computationally infeasible. To achieve security comparable to Advance Encryption Standard (AES-128), that is 128-bit security, we need to find a large prime q dividing $|E(\mathbb{F}_p)|$ having no less than 256 bits to make ECDLP Problem in subgroup of order q of $E(\mathbb{F}_p)$ intractable. Moreover, one should find a prime p such

---

* The author was partially supported by the grant no. N N201 605940 from National Science Centre.

that p^n has no less than 3248 bits to make the DLP Problem in $\mathbb{F}_{p^n}^*$ be computationally infeasible [15]. From the implementation point of view the ratio $\rho = \frac{\log p}{\log q}$ should be close to 1. Now, we introduce the following definition.

Definition 1. *Given $n \in \mathbb{N}$ and a square-free integer $\Delta < 0$. Primes p and q are pairing-friendly with respect to n and Δ if there exist integers f and t such that*

$$|t| \leq 2\sqrt{p}, \quad q \mid p + 1 - t, \quad q \mid \Phi_n(p), \quad 4p - t^2 = -\Delta f^2. \tag{1}$$

Given pairing-friendly primes p and q with respect to n, Δ and integers f, t as above, then there exists an ordinary elliptic curve E over $\mathbb{F}_p$ having cardinality $p + 1 - t$. The only known algorithm to find the equation of such an elliptic curve E over $\mathbb{F}_p$ is to use the *complex multiplication (CM) method* [2], [13]. Thus, if q is a large prime and n is a small positive integer, then a pairing-friendly elliptic curve E over $\mathbb{F}_p$ can be constructed. Constructing elliptic curves with CM method can be computationally very expensive. Let $\Delta < 0$ be a square-free integer, and let $K = \mathbb{Q}(\sqrt{\Delta})$ be quadratic field with the corresponding ring of integers $\mathcal{O}_K$. Let $\mathcal{O}_f = [1, f\omega]$ be an arbitrary order of conductor f of K, where $\omega = \frac{1+\sqrt{\Delta}}{2}$ for $\Delta \equiv 1 \pmod 4$ and $\omega = \sqrt{\Delta}$ for $\Delta \equiv 2, 3 \pmod 4$. The CM method constructs a curve with endomorphism ring isomorphic to a given order $\mathcal{O}_f \subseteq \mathcal{O}_K$. Let $D < 0$ be the discriminant of the order $\mathcal{O}_f$, so $D = f^2\Delta$ for $\Delta \equiv 1 \pmod 4$, and $D = 4f^2\Delta$ for $\Delta \equiv 2, 3 \pmod 4$. Then for any $\epsilon > 0$ the CM algorithm takes $O(|D|^{1+\epsilon})$ arithmetic operations [14]. In practice we can take $\mathcal{O}_f$ to be $\mathcal{O}_K$, which reduces the complexity of the CM method to $O(|\Delta|^{1+\epsilon})$. Given current computational power, the method can construct curves over $\mathbb{F}_p$ when $|D| \leq 10^{12}$ [22]. For this reason Δ defined in (10) should be sufficiently small to make the CM method work effectively in practice.

There are many approaches for generating pairing-friendly primes. Idea of most presented methods is based on the observation related to the factorization of polynomials [4], [9], [11], [13], [15], [19]. Another approach for generating pairing-friendly primes with respect n and Δ was introduced by Cocks and Pinch [11]. Unfortunately, their work has not been published. For the convenience of the reader, we remind the idea of the Cocks-Pinch algorithm [15]. Let $q \equiv 1 \pmod n$ be a prime, and let $\Delta < 0$ be a square-free integer such that Δ is a square modulo q. Determine a nth a primitive root of unity w_n modulo q. Set $t' \equiv w_n + 1 \pmod q$, and $f' \equiv (t' - 2)(\sqrt{\Delta})^{-1} \pmod q$. Find $t \equiv t' \pmod q$ and $f \equiv f' \pmod q$ such that $p = \frac{1}{4}(t^2 - \Delta f^2)$ is an integer and prime. Finally, find corresponding elliptic curve E over $\mathbb{F}_p$ using the complex multiplication method.

In this paper, we present a variant of the Cocks-Pinch method for generating pairing-friendly curves. Namely, we slightly change the form of the prime p in the above algorithm and we consider p depending on Δ modulo 4. We further generate a prime q which is of the same form as the prime p. Thanks to this approach our algorithm does not require calculation of square roots of Δ modulo q. Our method can also be used to construct pairing-friendly composite order groups with prescribed embedding degree associated with ordinary elliptic curves. However, in constructions in which the order of elliptic curves is divisible by N, where N is a product of distinct primes congruent to 1 modulo n, it is necessary that additional information about factorization N does not leak [7]. This is required in order for pairing-based cryptosystems using elliptic curves of composite order were secure [15]. Similarly to [7], a square root of Δ (mod N) leaks in our construction, but we do not know how to use this additional information to factor N.

Let $H(K)$ be the ideal class group of K, and let $h(K)$ be the number of elements in $H(K)$. Analysis of our algorithm shows that the Cocks-Pinch method is a special case of our construction for generating pairing-friendly primes when $h(K) = 1$ and $\Delta \equiv 2, 3$ (mod 4). For $\Delta \equiv 1$ (mod 4) our algorithm generates primes of the form $q = a^2 + ab + \frac{1-\Delta}{4}b^2$, $p = t^2 + tf + \frac{1-\Delta}{4}f^2$, where $a, b, t, f \in \mathbb{Z}$. Such primes have not been considered so far. Our variant of the Cocks-Pinch algorithm produced primes with $\rho \approx 2$.

The remaining part of the paper is organized as follows. In Section 2 we present the algorithm for generating pairing-friendly primes with respect to n and Δ. A detailed analysis of our algorithm is presented in Section 3. In Section 4 we construct paring-friendly elliptic curves E over $\mathbb{F}_p$ with embedding degree n with respect to N, where N divides $|E(\mathbb{F}_p)|$. A numerical example is given in Section 5.

2   The Main Algorithm

Throughout this paper, let n be a positive integer, and let $\Delta < 0$ be a square-free integer, $K = \mathbb{Q}(\sqrt{\Delta})$ is the quadratic field with the corresponding ring of integers $\mathcal{O}_K = \{a + b\omega : a, b \in \mathbb{Z}\}$, and $\mathcal{O}_f = [1, f\omega]$, $f \in \mathbb{Z}$ is any order of K, where $\omega = \frac{1+\sqrt{\Delta}}{2}$ when $\Delta \equiv 1$ (mod 4) and $\omega = \sqrt{\Delta}$ for $\Delta \equiv 2, 3$ (mod 4). By $N(\alpha) = \alpha\overline{\alpha} = (a + b\omega)(a + b\overline{\omega})$ we denote the norm of any element $\alpha = a + b\omega \in \mathcal{O}_K$ with respect to $\mathbb{Q}$. That is

$$N(\alpha) = a^2 + ab + \frac{1-\Delta}{4}b^2 \quad \text{if} \quad \Delta \equiv 1 \pmod 4,$$
$$N(\alpha) = a^2 - \Delta b^2 \qquad\qquad \text{if} \quad \Delta \equiv 2, 3 \pmod 4.$$

We describe the algorithm which generates pairing-friendly primes p and q with respect to n and Δ. The algorithm consists of the following two procedures.

Procedure. FINDPRIMEQ(n, Δ, γ). Given $n \in \mathbb{N}$, a square-free $\Delta \in \mathbb{Z}$, $\Delta < 0$. Fix $K = \mathbb{Q}(\sqrt{\Delta})$ with the corresponding ring of integers $\mathcal{O}_K$. Let $\gamma = f + g\omega \in \mathcal{O}_K$ be such that $|f|, |g| \leq n$, $N(\gamma) \equiv 1$ (mod n); this procedure finds $\alpha = a + b\omega \in \mathcal{O}_K$, $N(\alpha) \equiv 1$ (mod n), such that $N(\alpha) = q$ is a prime.

step 1. Choose u, v at random in $\mathbb{Z}$.
step 2. Compute $a = nu + f$ and $b = nv + g$.
step 3. Compute $q = N(a + b\omega)$.
step 4. If q is a prime, then terminate the procedure. Otherwise go to step 1.
step 5. Return $\alpha = a + b\omega$, q.

Procedure. FINDPRIMEP(α, q, Δ). Fix $K = \mathbb{Q}(\sqrt{\Delta})$ with the corresponding ring of integers $\mathcal{O}_K$. Given $\alpha = a + b\omega \in \mathcal{O}_K$ such that $q = N(\alpha) \equiv 1 \pmod{n}$ is a prime; this procedure finds $\beta \in \mathcal{O}_K$ such that $N(\beta) \equiv w_n \pmod{q}$, where w_n is a primitive nth root of unity modulo q, and $N(\beta)$ is a prime.

step 1. Compute a primitive nth root of unity w_n modulo q.
step 2. Compute $r \equiv a(-b)^{-1} \pmod{q}$.
step 3. Compute k and l modulo q.
   If $\Delta \equiv 1 \pmod 4$,

$$k \equiv (1 - (1 + \omega_n)r)(1 - 2r)^{-1} \pmod{q}, \quad l \equiv (\omega_n - 1)(1 - 2r)^{-1} \pmod{q}.$$

   If $\Delta \equiv 2, 3 \pmod 4$

$$k \equiv (1 - \omega_n)2^{-1} \pmod{q}, \quad l \equiv (1 + \omega_n)(2r)^{-1} \pmod{q}.$$

step 4. Choose s, t at random in $\mathbb{Z}$.
step 5. Compute $c = qs + k$ and $d = qt + l$.
step 6. Compute $p = N(c + d\omega)$. If p is a prime, then terminate the procedure.
   Otherwise go to step 3.
step 7. Return $\beta = c + d\omega$, p.

Remark 1. Computing w_n modulo q can be easily done with the randomized algorithm. The algorithm fails with probability $1/n$, and otherwise return w_n $\pmod q$. Its expected running time is $O(\log^4 q)$ bits operations.

We are now in a position to introduce our main algorithm.

Algorithm 1. (n, Δ, γ, w_n)

step 1. $\alpha, q := $ FINDPRIMEQ(n, Δ, γ).
step 2. $\beta, p := $ FINDPRIMEP(α, q, Δ).
step 3. Return p, q, α, β.

Theorem 1. *Given $n \in \mathbb{N}$, and a square-free integer $\Delta < 0$. Fix $K = \mathbb{Q}(\sqrt{\Delta})$ with the corresponding ring of integers $\mathcal{O}_K$. Then Algorithm 1 finds $\alpha, \beta \in \mathcal{O}_K$, $\beta = c + d\omega$ such that $N(\alpha) = q$, $N(\beta) = p$ are pairing-friendly primes with respect to n and Δ.*

3 Analysis of the Main Algorithm

3.1 Proof of Theorem 1

Lemma 1. *Let $\Delta < 0$ be a square-free integer. Fix $K = \mathbb{Q}(\sqrt{\Delta})$ with the corresponding ring of integers $\mathcal{O}_K$. Let $\alpha = a + b\omega \in \mathcal{O}_K$ be such that $q = N(\alpha)$ is a prime that does not divide Δ. Then there exists an integer $r \equiv \omega \pmod{(\alpha)}$. Further, the map*

$$\psi : \mathcal{O}_K / \alpha\mathcal{O}_K \longrightarrow \mathbb{Z}/q\mathbb{Z}$$

defined by

$$(e + f\omega) + \alpha\mathcal{O}_K \longmapsto (e + fr) + q\mathbb{Z}$$

is the ring isomorphism. Moreover, $r \equiv a(-b)^{-1} \pmod{q}$.

Proof. Since $q = N(\alpha)$ is a prime, the ideal $\alpha\mathcal{O}_K$ is a prime ideal, and $\mathcal{O}_K/\alpha\mathcal{O}_K$ is isomorphic to $\mathbb{Z}/q\mathbb{Z}$. Let

$$\phi_2 : \mathcal{O}_K \longrightarrow \mathcal{O}_K/\alpha\mathcal{O}_K$$

be a homomorphism. Let

$$\phi_1 : \mathcal{O}_K/\alpha\mathcal{O}_K \longrightarrow \mathbb{Z}/q\mathbb{Z}$$

be an isomorphism. Then

$$\phi = \phi_1 \circ \phi_2 : \mathcal{O}_K \longrightarrow \mathbb{Z}/q\mathbb{Z}$$

is a homomorphism with $\ker(\phi) = \alpha\mathcal{O}_K$. We show that there exists $r \in \mathbb{Z}$ such that $r \equiv \omega \pmod{(\alpha)}$. Consider a homomorphism

$$\phi_{/z} : \mathbb{Z} \longrightarrow \mathbb{Z}/q\mathbb{Z}.$$

Since $\alpha\mathcal{O}_K \cap \mathbb{Z} = q\mathbb{Z}$, so $\ker(\phi_{/z}) = q\mathbb{Z}$. Hence, $\mathbb{Z}/\ker(\phi_{/z})$ is isomorphic to $\mathbb{Z}/q\mathbb{Z}$ and the number of elements of $\mathrm{im}(\phi_{/z})$ is equal to q, so $\phi_{/z}$ is surjective. Therefore, there exists $r \in \mathbb{Z}$ such that

$$r + \alpha\mathcal{O}_K = \omega + \alpha\mathcal{O}_K \tag{2}$$

and r is uniquely modulo q. We show that $\phi_1 = \psi$. Let $\beta \in \mathcal{O}_K$, $\beta = e + f\omega$. We have

$$\phi_2(\beta) = \beta + \alpha\mathcal{O}_K,$$

so by (2)

$$\phi_1(\beta + \alpha\mathcal{O}_K) = \phi_1 \circ \phi_2(\beta) = \phi(\beta) = e + f\phi(\omega) =$$
$$= e + f\phi_1(\omega + \alpha\mathcal{O}_K) = e + f\phi_1(r + \alpha\mathcal{O}_K) =$$
$$= \phi_1((e + fr) + \alpha\mathcal{O}_K) = (e + fr) + q\mathbb{Z}.$$

Hence $\phi_1 = \psi$. We compute $r \pmod q$. Since α divides $r - \omega$, so there exists $\gamma = c + d\omega \in \mathcal{O}_K$ such that

$$\begin{array}{ll} \alpha\gamma = ac - \frac{1-\Delta}{4}bd + (bc + (a+b)d)\omega = r - \omega & \text{if } \Delta \equiv 1 \pmod 4, \\ \alpha\gamma = ac + \Delta bd + (bc + ad)\omega = r - \omega & \text{if } \Delta \equiv 2,3 \pmod 4. \end{array} \tag{3}$$

Let

$$M_\alpha = \begin{bmatrix} a & -\frac{1-\Delta}{4}b \\ b & a+b \end{bmatrix} \quad \text{if } \Delta \equiv 1 \pmod 4,$$

$$M_\alpha = \begin{bmatrix} a & \Delta b \\ b & a \end{bmatrix} \quad \text{if } \Delta \equiv 2,3 \pmod 4,$$

and let $B = [c, d]^T$, $C_r = [r, -1]^T$. We can write (3) as

$$M_\alpha B = C_r. \tag{4}$$

By Cramer's rule, (4) has a unique solution B, given by

$$c = \frac{\det A_1}{q}, \quad d = \frac{\det A_2}{q},$$

where A_k, $k = 1, 2$ is the matrix formed by replacing the kth column of M_α by C_r. Clearly,

$$c = \frac{r(a + b) - \frac{1-\Delta}{4}b}{q}, \quad d = \frac{-a - br}{q} \quad \text{if} \quad \Delta \equiv 1 \pmod 4,$$

$$c = \frac{ra + \Delta b}{q}, \quad d = \frac{-a - rb}{q} \quad \text{if} \quad \Delta \equiv 2, 3 \pmod 4.$$

Since $(a + b, q) = (a, q) = (b, q) = 1$ and $c, d \in \mathbb{Z}$, so

$$
\begin{aligned}
&r \equiv \tfrac{(1-\Delta)b}{4(a+b)} \pmod q, \quad r \equiv a(-b)^{-1} \pmod q \text{ if } \Delta \equiv 1 \pmod 4, \\
&r \equiv -\Delta b a^{-1} \pmod q, \, r \equiv a(-b)^{-1} \pmod q \text{ if } \Delta \equiv 2, 3 \pmod 4.
\end{aligned}
\tag{5}
$$

This finishes the proof.

Lemma 2. *Let $\Delta < 0$ be a square-free integer. Fix $K = \mathbb{Q}(\sqrt{\Delta})$ with the corresponding ring of integers $\mathcal{O}_K$. Let $\alpha = a + b\omega \in \mathcal{O}_K$, where $q = N(\alpha) \equiv 1$ (mod n) is a prime that does not divide Δ. Let w_n be a primitive nth root of unity modulo q, and let $r \equiv a(-b)^{-1}$ (mod q). Let k, l be the solution of the system of linear equations over $\mathbb{Z}/q\mathbb{Z}$*

$$
\begin{cases}
\psi(1 + \alpha\mathcal{O}_K)k + \psi(\omega + \alpha\mathcal{O}_K)l = 1 + q\mathbb{Z} \\
\psi(1 + \alpha\mathcal{O}_K)k + \psi(\overline{\omega} + \alpha\mathcal{O}_K)l = w_n + q\mathbb{Z},
\end{cases}
\tag{6}
$$

where ψ is defined in (2). Let $\delta = k + l\omega \in \mathcal{O}_K$, then $N(\delta) \equiv w_n$ (mod q). Moreover, $k \equiv (1 - (1+w_n)r)(1-2r)^{-1}$ (mod q), $l \equiv (w_n - 1)(1-2r)^{-1}$ (mod q) when $\Delta \equiv 1$ (mod 4), and $k \equiv (1 - w_n)2^{-1}$ (mod q) and $l \equiv (1 + w_n)(2r)^{-1}$ (mod q) if $\Delta \equiv 2, 3$ (mod 4).

Proof. Firstly, we show that (6) has a solution in $\mathbb{Z}/q\mathbb{Z}$. Since $\omega + \overline{\omega} = 1$ if $\Delta \equiv 1$ (mod 4), $\omega + \overline{\omega} = 0$ when $\Delta \equiv 2, 3$ (mod 4), so

$$
\det \begin{bmatrix} \psi(1 + \alpha\mathcal{O}_K) & \psi(\omega + \alpha\mathcal{O}_K) \\ \psi(1 + \alpha\mathcal{O}_K) & \psi(\overline{\omega} + \alpha\mathcal{O}_K) \end{bmatrix} = \begin{cases} (1 - 2r) + q\mathbb{Z} & \text{if} \quad \Delta \equiv 1 \pmod 4, \\ (-2r) + q\mathbb{Z} & \text{if} \quad \Delta \equiv 2, 3 \pmod 4. \end{cases}
$$

On the other hand, it is an elementary check that

$$
\overline{\omega} - \omega = \begin{cases} -\sqrt{\Delta} & \text{if} \quad \Delta \equiv 1 \pmod 4, \\ -2\sqrt{\Delta} & \text{if} \quad \Delta \equiv 2, 3 \pmod 4. \end{cases}
\tag{7}
$$

Moreover,

$$
\psi((\overline{\omega} - \omega) + \alpha\mathcal{O}_K) = \begin{cases} (1 - 2r) + q\mathbb{Z} & \text{if} \quad \Delta \equiv 1 \pmod 4, \\ (-2r) + q\mathbb{Z} & \text{if} \quad \Delta \equiv 2, 3 \pmod 4. \end{cases}
\tag{8}
$$

Since $(\Delta, q) = 1$, by (8), (7) we obtain

$$\begin{cases} (1 - 2r) + q\mathbb{Z} \neq 0 + q\mathbb{Z} & \text{if } \Delta \equiv 1 \pmod{4}, \\ (-2r) + q\mathbb{Z} \neq 0 + q\mathbb{Z} & \text{if } \Delta \equiv 2, 3 \pmod{4}. \end{cases}$$

Consequently, (6) has a unique solution in $\mathbb{Z}/q\mathbb{Z}$. By Cramer's rule, the solution of (6) are given by $k \equiv (1 - (1 + \omega_n)r)(1 - 2r)^{-1} \pmod{q}$, $l \equiv (\omega_n - 1)(1 - 2r)^{-1}$ (mod q) when $\Delta \equiv 1 \pmod{4}$, and $k \equiv (1 - \omega_n)2^{-1} \pmod{q}$ and $l \equiv (1 + \omega_n)(2r)^{-1} \pmod{q}$ if $\Delta \equiv 2, 3 \pmod{4}$. Let $\delta = k + l\omega$. We show that $N(\delta) \equiv \omega_n \pmod{q}$. By (6),

$$\psi((k + l\omega) + \alpha\mathcal{O}_K) = 1 + q\mathbb{Z},$$
$$\psi((k + l\overline{\omega}) + \alpha\mathcal{O}_K) = \omega_n + q\mathbb{Z},$$

so $\psi(N(k + l\omega) + \alpha\mathcal{O}_K) = \omega_n + q\mathbb{Z}$. This finishes the proof.

We are now in a position to prove Theorem 1

Proof. Let $p = N(\beta)$ be a prime computed in step 6 of procedure FINDPRIMEP, where $\beta = c + d\omega \in \mathcal{O}_K$ is computed in step 5. Let a prime $q = N(\alpha)$, be output from procedure FINDPRIMEQ. We show that primes p and q are pairing friendly with respect to n and Δ. Since β is the root of $x^2 - Tr(\beta)x + N(\beta)$, so

$$Tr(\beta)^2 - 4N(\beta) = d^2\Delta, \quad |Tr(\beta)| \leq 2\sqrt{p}.$$

We show that q divides $N(\beta) + 1 - Tr(\beta)$. Since $c \equiv k \pmod{q}$ and $d \equiv l \pmod{q}$, by (6)

$$\psi(\beta + \alpha\mathcal{O}_K) = \psi((c + d\omega) + \alpha\mathcal{O}_K) = (k + lr) + q\mathbb{Z} = 1 + q\mathbb{Z}.$$

Hence $\psi((\beta - 1) + \alpha\mathcal{O}_K) = 0 + q\mathbb{Z}$, so $\psi(N(\beta - 1) + \alpha\mathcal{O}_K) = 0 + q\mathbb{Z}$. On the other hand, it is an elementary check that $N(\beta - 1) = N(\beta) + 1 - Tr(\beta)$, so q divides $N(\beta) + 1 - Tr(\beta)$. Now, we show that q divides $\Phi_n(p)$. By (6),

$$\psi(\overline{\beta} + \alpha\mathcal{O}_K) = \psi((c + d\overline{\omega}) + \alpha\mathcal{O}_K) = \omega_n + q\mathbb{Z},$$

hence $\psi(N(\beta) + \alpha\mathcal{O}_K) = \omega_n + q\mathbb{Z}$, and so $\psi(\Phi_n(N(\beta)) + \alpha\mathcal{O}_K) = 0 + q\mathbb{Z}$. Consequently, p and q are pairing-friendly with respect to n and Δ. This finishes the proof.

Remark 2. Let $\Delta < 0$ be a square-free integer, and $n \in \mathbb{N}$. Let $q = N(\alpha)$, $p = N(\beta)$ be pairing-friendly primes with respect to n and Δ, where $\alpha, \beta \in \mathcal{O}_K$, $\beta = c + d\omega$. It is well known that for every $f \mid d$ there exists an elliptic curve E over $\mathbb{F}_p$ with complex multiplication by an order $\mathcal{O}_f = [1, f\omega] \subseteq K$ such that q divides

$$|E(\mathbb{F}_p)| = p + 1 - 2c - d \quad \text{if } \Delta \equiv 1 \pmod{4},$$
$$|E(\mathbb{F}_p)| = p + 1 - 2c \quad \text{if } \Delta \equiv 2, 3 \pmod{4}.$$

For more details we refer the reader to [11], [23]. Moreover, if $\Delta < 10^{12}$, then E over $\mathbb{F}_p$ can be effectively constructed via the CM method.

Remark 3. Fix $n \in \mathbb{N}$ and $K = Q(\sqrt{\Delta})$, $\Delta < 0$. Let $q = N(\alpha)$, $\alpha = a + b\omega \in \mathcal{O}_K$ be the output of procedure FINDPRIMEQ. The system of linear equations over $\mathbb{Z}/q\mathbb{Z}$

$$\begin{cases} \psi(1 + \alpha\mathcal{O}_K)u + \psi(\overline{\omega} + \alpha\mathcal{O}_K)v = 1 + q\mathbb{Z} \\ \psi(1 + \alpha\mathcal{O}_K)u + \psi(\omega + \alpha\mathcal{O}_K)v = w_n + q\mathbb{Z}, \end{cases}$$

has a solution u, v in $\mathbb{Z}/q\mathbb{Z}$, where ψ is defined in (2). Moreover, $u \equiv (r - (w_n(1 - r))(-1 + 2r)^{-1} \pmod{q}$, $v \equiv (w_n - 1)(-1 + 2r)^{-1} \pmod{q}$ if $\Delta \equiv 1 \pmod 4$, and $u \equiv (w_n + 1)2^{-1} \pmod{q}$, $v \equiv (w_n - 1)(2r)^{-1} \pmod{q}$ when $\Delta \equiv 2, 3 \pmod 4$, where $r \equiv a(-b)^{-1} \pmod{q}$. The proof is similar to that of Lemma 2. Let $\overline{\beta} = c + d\overline{\omega}$, where $c \equiv u \pmod{q}$, $d \equiv v \pmod{q}$ be such that $p = N(\overline{\beta})$ is a prime. Then p and q are pairing-friendly with respect to n and Δ. Indeed, $\psi(\overline{\beta} + \alpha\mathcal{O}_K) = 1 + q\mathbb{Z}$, $\psi(\beta + \alpha\mathcal{O}_K) = w_n + q\mathbb{Z}$, so $\psi(N(\overline{\beta} - 1) + \alpha\mathcal{O}_K) = 0 + q\mathbb{Z}$, and $\psi(N(\overline{\beta}) + \alpha\mathcal{O}_K) = w_n + q\mathbb{Z}$. Hence $\psi(\Phi_n(N(\overline{\beta})) + \alpha\mathcal{O}_K) = 0 + q\mathbb{Z}$. Moreover, q divides $|E(\mathbb{F}_p)| = N(\overline{\beta} - 1)$. Consequently, step 3 of procedure FINDPRIMEP can be constructed as follows.

step 3'. Compute k and l modulo q.
If $\Delta \equiv 1 \pmod 4$,

$$k' \equiv (r - (w_n(1 - r))(-1 + 2r)^{-1} \pmod{q}, \quad l' \equiv (w_n - 1)(-1 + 2r)^{-1} \pmod{q}.$$

If $\Delta \equiv 2, 3 \pmod 4$

$$k' \equiv (w_n + 1)2^{-1} \pmod{q}, \quad l' \equiv (w_n - 1)(2r)^{-1} \pmod{q}.$$

Remark 4. Note that, the primes generated by procedure FINDPRIMEP with **step 3'** instead of **step 3** correspond to the primes that are generated by the Cocks-Pinch method [15] for $\Delta \equiv 2, 3 \pmod 4$.

Remark 5. Let $H(K)$ be the ideal class group of $K = \mathbb{Q}(\sqrt{\Delta})$, where $\Delta < 0$, and let $h(K)$ be the number of elements in $H(K)$. Fix a class $X_0 \in H(K)$ containing principal ideals. Note that, procedure FINDPRIMEQ finds $\alpha \in \mathcal{O}_K$ that generates a prime ideal $\mathfrak{q} \in X_0$ such that $N(\mathfrak{q}) = q$. Now, let $h(K) = 1$. A prime $q \neq 2$ which does not divide Δ is of the form

$$\begin{array}{ll} a^2 + ab + \frac{1-\Delta}{4}b^2 & \text{if} \quad \Delta \equiv 1 \pmod 4, \\ a^2 - \Delta b^2 & \text{if} \quad \Delta \equiv 2, 3 \pmod 4 \end{array} \tag{9}$$

for some $a, b \in \mathbb{Z}$ if and only if $\left(\frac{\Delta}{q}\right) = 1$ (see, [16, Theorem 1.25, page 185]). Assume that $q \equiv 1 \pmod n$ is of the form (9). There exist $a + b\omega \in \mathcal{O}_K$ such that $N(a + b\omega) = q$. Moreover, there exist $e + f\omega \in \mathcal{O}_K$ such that $N(a + b\omega) \equiv N(e + f\omega) \pmod n$, where $a \equiv e \pmod n$, $b \equiv f \pmod n$, $|e| \leq n$, $|f| \leq n$. By the above, if $h(K) = 1$ every set of parameters output by the Cocks-Pinch method is also output by our algorithm. It is known that for square-free $\Delta < 0$, $h(K) = 1$ for the nine values $\Delta = -1, -2, -3, -7, -11, -19, -47, -67, -163$.

Remark 6. Remarks 4 and 5 shows that the Cocks-Pinch method [15] is a special case of our construction when $h(K) = 1$ and $\Delta \equiv 2, 3 \pmod 4$. When $h(K) > 1$ then the Cocks-Pinch method generates a larger set of primes q than our method does. On the other hand, if $q \equiv 1 \pmod n$ and $(\frac{\Delta}{q}) = 1$, then $r \equiv \sqrt{\Delta} \pmod q$, where $\Delta \equiv 2, 3 \pmod 4$ (or $r \equiv (1 + \sqrt{\Delta})/2 \pmod q$, when $\Delta \equiv 1 \pmod 4$) can be computed in step 1 of procedure FINDPRIMEP. For this reason , every such a prime q can be input to procedure FINDPRIMEP. Remark 3 shows that the Cocks-Pinch algorithm is a special of our method in this case. However, in the Cocks-Pinch method is easier to choose a prime q that have low Hamming weight or a prime q that satisfy other security properties.

Remark 7. The Cocks-Pinch method finds a prime p that lie in the proper order $\mathbb{Z}[\sqrt{\Delta}] \subset \mathcal{O}_K$ when $\Delta \equiv 1 \pmod 4$. In our method, a prime p is obtained as a norm of an algebraic integer $\beta \in \mathcal{O}_K$ that need not lie in $\mathbb{Z}[\sqrt{\Delta}]$. For this reason, procedure FINDPRIMEP reaches a slightly larger set of primes p when $h(K) = 1$.

4   Composite Order Elliptic Curves

Let N be a composite positive integer. In [7], the Cocks-Pinch method was generalized by Boneh, Rubin and Silverberg. The authors constructed an algorithm which generates an ordinary elliptic curve E over a finite field $\mathbb{F}_p$ such that N divides $|E(\mathbb{F}_p)|$ and embedding degree of E with respect to N is n. Our method can be used for finding such curves too. We begin with the following definition.

Definition 2. *Given $n \in \mathbb{N}$ and a square-free integer $\Delta < 0$. A prime p and a positive integer N are pairing-friendly with respect to n and Δ if there exist integers f and t such that*

$$|t| \leq 2\sqrt{p}, \quad N \mid p + 1 - t, \quad N \mid \Phi_n(p), \quad 4p - t^2 = -\Delta f^2. \tag{10}$$

Our algorithm utilizes the following procedure.

Procedure. FINDPRIMEP'$(\alpha_i, q_i, \Delta, m)$. Fix $K = \mathbb{Q}(\sqrt{\Delta})$ with the corresponding ring of integers $\mathcal{O}_K$. Given $\alpha_i = a_i + b_i\omega \in \mathcal{O}_K$ such that $q_i = N(\alpha_i) \equiv 1 \pmod n$ is a prime; this procedure finds $\beta \in \mathcal{O}_K$ such that $N(\beta) \equiv w_n \pmod N$, and $N(\beta)$ is a prime, where $N = \prod_{i=1}^m q_i$, $w_n \equiv w_{n_i} \pmod{q_i}$, where w_{n_i} is a primitive nth root of unity modulo q_i, $i = 1, \dots, m$.

step 1. Compute a primitive nth root of unity w_{n_i} modulo q_i for $i = 1, \dots, m$.
step 2. For $1, \dots, m$ compute $r_i \equiv a_i(-b_i)^{-1} \pmod{q_i}$.
step 3. Apply the Chinese Remainder Theorem to find $r \pmod N$ a solution of the system of linear equations $r \equiv r_i \pmod{q_i}$, $1 \leq i \leq m$.
step 4. For $1, \dots, m$ find a primitive nth root of unity $w_{n_i} \pmod{q_i}$ for $1 \leq i \leq k$.
step 5. Apply the Chinese Remainder Theorem to find $w_n \pmod N$ a solution of the system of linear equations $w_n \equiv w_{n_i} \pmod{q_i}$, $1 \leq i \leq m$.

step 6. Compute k and l modulo N,
If $\Delta \equiv 1 \pmod 4$,

$$k \equiv (1 - (1 + \omega_n)r)(1 - 2r)^{-1} \pmod N, \, l \equiv (\omega_n - 1)(1 - 2r)^{-1} \pmod N.$$

If $\Delta \equiv 2, 3 \pmod 4$

$$k \equiv (1 - \omega_n)2^{-1} \pmod N, \quad l \equiv (1 + \omega_n)(2r)^{-1} \pmod N.$$

step 7. Choose s, t at random in $\mathbb{Z}$, and compute $\beta = c + d\omega$, where $c = Ns + k$ and $d = Nt + l$.
step 8. Compute $p = N(\beta)$. If p is a prime, then terminate the procedure. Otherwise go to step 6.
step 9. Return $\beta = c + d\omega$, p, N.

Algorithm 2. (n, m, Δ, γ)

step 1. For $1, \ldots, m$ using procedure FINDPRIMEQ(n, Δ, γ) find $\alpha_i = a_i + b_i \omega \in \mathcal{O}_K$ such that $N(\alpha_i) = q_i$, $N(\alpha_i) \equiv 1 \pmod n$, where q_i are distinct primes.
step 2. FINDPRIMEP'$(\alpha_i, q_i, \Delta, m)$.
step 3. Return $\beta = c + d\omega$, p, N.

Theorem 2. *Given $n, m \in \mathbb{N}$, and a square-free integer $\Delta < 0$. Fix $K = \mathbb{Q}(\sqrt{\Delta})$ with the corresponding ring of integers $\mathcal{O}_K$. Then Algorithm 2 finds $\alpha_i, \beta \in \mathcal{O}_K$, $N(\alpha_i)$ is a prime, $1 \leq i \leq m$, and $\beta = c + d\omega$ such that $p = N(\beta)$, $N = \prod_{i=1}^m N(\alpha_i)$ are pairing-friendly with respect to n and Δ.*

Proof. Let $p = N(\beta)$ be a prime computed in step 8 of procedure FINDPRIMEP', where $\beta = c + d\omega \in \mathcal{O}_K$ is computed in step 7. Let $q_i = N(\alpha_i)$, $i = 1, \ldots, m$ be outputs from procedure FINDPRIMEQ. Let $N = \prod_{i=1}^m q_i$. We show that a prime p and a positive integer N are pairing friendly with respect to n and Δ. Since β is the root of $x^2 - Tr(\beta)x + N(\beta)$, so

$$Tr(\beta)^2 - 4N(\beta) = d^2\Delta, \quad |Tr(\beta)| \leq 2\sqrt{p}.$$

We show that N divides $N(\beta - 1) = N(\beta) + 1 - Tr(\beta)$. Since $q_i \neq q_j$, $i \neq j$, by the Chinese Remainder Theorem and Lemma 1 we have an isomorphism of rings

$$\mathcal{O}_K / (\prod_{i=1}^m \alpha_i)\mathcal{O}_K \simeq \bigoplus_{i=1}^m \mathcal{O}_K/(\alpha_i \mathcal{O}_K) \simeq \bigoplus_{i=1}^m \mathbb{Z}/(q_i\mathbb{Z}) \simeq \mathbb{Z}/(N\mathbb{Z}). \tag{11}$$

Let $r \pmod N$ and $w_n \pmod N$ be computed in step 3 and step 5 of procedure FINDPRIMEP' respectively. Let $k \pmod N$ and $l \pmod N$ be computed in step 6 of procedure FINDPRIMEP'. By Lemma 2, $k_i \equiv k \pmod{q_i}$ and $l_i \equiv l \pmod{q_i}$ are the solution of the system of linear equations over $\mathbb{Z}/q_i\mathbb{Z}$

$$\begin{cases} \psi(1 + \alpha_i\mathcal{O}_K)k_i + \psi(\omega + \alpha_i\mathcal{O}_K)l_i = 1 + q_i\mathbb{Z} \\ \psi(1 + \alpha_i\mathcal{O}_K)k_i + \psi(\overline{\omega} + \alpha_i\mathcal{O}_K)l_i = w_{n_i} + q_i\mathbb{Z}, \end{cases} \tag{12}$$

for $1 \le i \le m$. Hence, by (11), (12)

$$\beta + (\prod_{i=1}^{m} \alpha_i)\mathcal{O}_K = c + d\omega + (\prod_{i=1}^{m} \alpha_i)\mathcal{O}_K \mapsto$$
$$\mapsto ((c + d\omega) + \alpha_1\mathcal{O}_K, \ldots, (c + d\omega) + \alpha_m\mathcal{O}_K) \mapsto$$
$$\mapsto ((c + dr_1) + q_1\mathbb{Z}, \ldots, (c + dr_m) + q_m\mathbb{Z}) =$$
$$= ((k_1 + l_1 r_1) + q_1\mathbb{Z}, \ldots, (k_m + l_m r_m) + q_m\mathbb{Z}) =$$
$$= (1 + q_1\mathbb{Z}, \ldots, 1 + q_m\mathbb{Z}) \mapsto 1 + N\mathbb{Z}.$$

Hence $(\beta - 1) + (\prod_{i=1}^{m} \alpha_i)\mathcal{O}_K$ maps to $0 + N\mathbb{Z}$ under (11), and consequently N divides $N(\beta - 1)$. Now, we show that N divides $\Phi_n(N(\beta))$. By (11), (12),

$$\overline{\beta} + (\prod_{i=1}^{m} \alpha_i)\mathcal{O}_K = c + d\overline{\omega} + (\prod_{i=1}^{m} \alpha_i)\mathcal{O}_K \mapsto$$
$$\mapsto ((c + d\overline{\omega}) + \alpha_1\mathcal{O}_K, \ldots, (c + d\overline{\omega}) + \alpha_m\mathcal{O}_K) \mapsto$$
$$\mapsto ((c + d\psi(\overline{\omega} + \alpha_1\mathcal{O}_K)) + q_1\mathbb{Z}, \ldots, (c + d\psi(\overline{\omega} + \alpha_m\mathcal{O}_K)) + q_m\mathbb{Z}) =$$
$$= ((k_1 + l_1\psi(\overline{\omega} + \alpha_1\mathcal{O}_K)) + q_1\mathbb{Z}, \ldots, (k_m + l_m\psi(\overline{\omega} + \alpha_m\mathcal{O}_K)) + q_m\mathbb{Z}) =$$
$$= (w_{n_1} + q_1\mathbb{Z}, \ldots, w_{n_m} + q_m\mathbb{Z}) \mapsto w_n + N\mathbb{Z}.$$

Hence $N(\beta) + (\prod_{i=1}^{m} \alpha_i)\mathcal{O}_K$ maps to $w_n + N\mathbb{Z}$ under (11), $\Phi_n(N(\beta)) + (\prod_{i=1}^{m} \alpha_i)\mathcal{O}_K$ maps to $0 + N\mathbb{Z}$ under (11), so N divides $\Phi_n(N(\beta))$. Consequently, p and N are pairing-friendly with respect to n and Δ. This finishes the proof.

Remark 8. Given pairing-friendly integers p and N with respect to n, Δ and $\beta \in \mathcal{O}_K$, an elliptic curve E over $\mathbb{F}_p$ with embedding degree n such that N divides $|E(\mathbb{F}_p)| = p + 1 - Tr(\beta)$ can be constructed using the CM method for $K = \mathbb{Q}(\sqrt{\Delta})$.

Remark 9. As pointed out in [7], every construction of pairing-friendly curves will leak $w_n \pmod{N}$ a nth root of unity modulo N, by the definition of embedding degree and the existence of efficient point counting algorithms. Anyone can compute c, d and $k, l \mod N$ from p, N and E using Cornacchia's algorithm. In this way a square root of $\Delta \pmod{N}$ for $\Delta \equiv 2, 3 \pmod{N}$, and $r \equiv (1 + \sqrt{\Delta})/2 \pmod{N}$ when $\Delta \equiv 1 \pmod{N}$, is revealed from k, l, N and E. Such additional information can be used to factor N, but we do not know how to do it. The algorithm presented in [7] has similar properties.

Remark 10. From the security point of view factorization of the curve order $|E(\mathbb{F}_p)|$ should be computationally infeasible. By Remark 9, a square root r of $\Delta \pmod{N}$, for $\Delta \equiv 2, 3 \pmod{N}$, and $r \equiv (1 + \sqrt{\Delta})/2 \pmod{N}$ when $\Delta \equiv 1 \pmod{N}$ is leaked in our construction. Note that, if one can choose $r' \not\equiv \pm r \pmod{N}$ such that $r'^2 \equiv r^2 \pmod{N}$, one could use r', r to factor N for $\Delta \equiv 2, 3 \pmod{N}$. We do not know how to find such a square root r' of Δ modulo N. Moreover, our construction computes $r \pmod{N}$ using $w_n \pmod{N}$, so this r does not leak extra information beyond that leaked by w_n (mod N). In [7], method for computing a square root of Δ (mod N) knowing just a nth root of unity modulo N was given. However, this method works only for $\Delta < 0$ such that $\sqrt{\Delta} \in \mathbb{Q}(e^{2\pi i/n})$, and takes at least $O(\varphi(\Delta))$ multiplication. For this reason, the algorithm may be impractical for large Δ.

Remark 11. The number $\rho = \log p / \log N$ is approximately 2. From implementation point of view ordinary elliptic curves of composite order should have embedding degrees and the ratio ρ chosen to minimize $\rho \cdot n$ [15].

5 An Illustrative Example

5.1 Case $\Delta \equiv 1$ (mod 4)

To demonstrate our ideas, we have implemented our algorithm. For this purpose, integers n and Δ are chosen randomly. Let $n = 119$ and $\Delta = -79$, so $K = \mathbb{Q}(\sqrt{-79})$, and $\mathcal{O}_K = \{a + b\frac{1+\sqrt{-79}}{2} : a, b \in \mathbb{Z}\}$. Let $f = 65$, $g = 73$, so $\gamma = 65 + 73\frac{1+\sqrt{-79}}{2}$. It is an elementary check $N(\gamma) = f^2 + fg + 20g^2 \equiv 1$ (mod 119). Procedure FINDPRIMEQ has generated $\alpha = a + b\frac{1+\sqrt{-79}}{2}$ such that $q = N(\alpha)$ is a 314-bits prime ,where

$q = 22890480958286002252536107573908112143186507397526423238972085990745876555823064438862876171491 \equiv 1$ (mod 119),

$a = 31748511241079110435916592268101932047369992571 \equiv 65$ (mod 119)

$b = 32293378804541847510319849609613288028925359950 \equiv 73$ (mod 119),

Let

$w_{119} = 2289048095828600225253610757390811214318650739752642323897208599074587655582306443886287617149$ (mod q),

be the primitive 119th root of unity modulo q. Procedure FINDPRIMEP has generated $k, l \in \mathbb{Z}$ and $\beta = c + d\frac{1+\sqrt{-79}}{2}$ such that $p = N(\beta)$ is a 641-bits prime, where

$p = 4805653650639284284086264833428955364688333489702571089660460107296704795640146325104198176059477307998026070656256961552071161793313249627545320452829855522330991593544900093669185131511295217 \equiv w_{119}$ (mod q),

$c = 5452598225146162905720793853270064334663037873688518930289066183729917985950211832789779079647 53 \equiv k$ (mod q),

$d = 4613454370357725769268451550203511549598816344407694400152159371775609799752684022993522876252 96 \equiv l$ (mod q),

$k = 18777876047403823876374891112711985417301411722574415853254864058583663781109070118513175602046 0$,

$l = 35358178700525318761230035421889120961514864902409752357742173626434488588071135220947641954 76$.

The ρ-value is 2.041. Moreover, for every $f|d$ there exists an elliptic curve E over $\mathbb{F}_p$ with complex multiplication by an order $\mathcal{O}_f = [1, f\omega] \subseteq K$ such that q divides $|E(\mathbb{F}_p)| = p + 1 - 2c - d$, and q divides $\Phi_{119}(p)$.

5.2   Case $\Delta \equiv 3 \pmod 4$

Let us fix $n = 339$ and $\Delta = -93$, so $K = \mathbb{Q}(\sqrt{-93})$, and $\mathcal{O}_K = \{a + b\sqrt{-93} : a, b \in \mathbb{Z}\}$. Let $f = 193$, $g = 203$, so $\gamma = 193 + 203\sqrt{-93}$. It is an elementary check $N(\gamma) = f^2 + 93g^2 \equiv 1 \pmod{339}$. Procedure FINDPRIMEQ has generated $\alpha = a + b\sqrt{-93}$ such that $q = N(\alpha)$ is a 320-bits prime ,where

$q = 18705285257870027473846006982562795616921295345270888843962983083$
$\quad 047950243653300497954389094497 37 \equiv 1 \pmod{339}$,

$a = 1413740367461424240364454757280283943958555531773 \equiv 193 \pmod{339}$

$b = 1410613344643814028182741488216190067909896 67584 \equiv 203 \pmod{339}$,

Let

$w_{339} = 18705285257870027473846006982562795616921295345270888843962 98308$
$\quad 3047950243653300497954389094497 37 \pmod{q}$,

be the primitive 339th root of unity modulo q. Procedure FINDPRIMEP has generated $k, l \in \mathbb{Z}$ and $\beta = c + d\sqrt{-93}$ such that $p = N(\beta)$ is a 653-bits prime, where

$p = 22534308956817616576212217488269644446047448212017544947775436167853$
$\quad 74348151690676311930801578494578918495357357542296134917219692870559$
$\quad 55634466521978032732804833266137752175189525605201222 62211521 \equiv w_{339} \pmod{q}$,

$c = 43628751191192986919664902152636273960644421694296447912422 2833993525$
$\quad 3894730637206279061650640129 8 \equiv k \pmod{q}$,

$d = 14894193508980357476557365911767295215747916392026811525344908609967$
$\quad 81008168253346792526973833263 \equiv l \pmod{q}$,

$k = 60659509809192372981908609274184404172544240017340357130742230834 2253$
$\quad 386903780917495521589057347$,

$l = 18004938284713382448635317033827725897298848975130589617604 0270286321$
$\quad 5837610942998224454607685104$.

The ρ-value is 2.040. Moreover, for every $f|d$ there exists an elliptic curve E over $\mathbb{F}_p$ with complex multiplication by an order $\mathcal{O}_f = [1, f\omega] \subseteq K$ such that q divides $|E(\mathbb{F}_p)| = p + 1 - 2c$, and q divides $\Phi_{339}(p)$.

Acknowledgements. The author thank Sorina Ionica, Steven Galbraith and anonymous reviewers of the conference for valuable suggestions and comments on the paper.

References

[1] Agrawal, M., Kayal, N., Saxena, N.: Primes is in P. Annals of Mathematics 160(2), 781–793 (2004)

[2] Atkin, A., Morain, F.: Elliptic curves and primality proving. Technical Report RR-1256, INRIA, Projet ICSLA (June 1990)

[3] Bach, E., Shallit, J.: Algorithmic Number Theory. Efficient Algorithms, vol. I. MIT Press (1996)

[4] Preneel, B., Tavares, S. (eds.): SAC 2005. LNCS, vol. 3897. Springer, Heidelberg (2006)

[5] Boneh, D., Franklin, M.K.: Identity-based encryption from the Weil pairing. SIAM J. Comput. 32(3), 586–615 (2003)

[6] Boneh, D., Lynn, B., Shacham, H.: Short signatures from the Weil pairing. Journal of Cryptology 17(4), 297–319 (2004)

[7] Boneh, D., Rubin, K., Silverberg, A.: Finding composite order ordinary elliptic curves using the Cocks-Pinch method. Journal of Number Theory 131, 832–841 (2011)

[8] Borevich, Z., Shafarevich, I.: Number Theory. Academic Press (1966)

[9] Brezing, F., Weng, A.: Elliptic curves suitable for pairing based cryptography. Designs, Codes and Cryptography 37(1), 133–141 (2005)

[10] Cha, J.C., Cheon, J.H.: An Identity-Based Signature from Gap Diffie-Hellman Groups. In: Desmedt, Y.G. (ed.) PKC 2003. LNCS, vol. 2567, pp. 18–30. Springer, Heidelberg (2002)

[11] Cocks, C., Pinch, R.: Identity-based cryptosystems based on the Weil pairing (2001) (unpublished manuscript)

[12] Cox, D.A.: Primes of the Form x + ny: Fermat, Class Field Theory, and Complex Multiplication. John Wiley & Sons, New York (1989)

[13] Dupont, R., Enge, A., Morain, F.: Building curves with arbitrary small MOV degree over finite prime fields. Journal of Cryptology 18(2), 79–89 (2005)

[14] Enge, A.: The complexity of class polynomial computation via floating point approximations. Math. Comput. 78(266), 1089–1107 (2009)

[15] Freeman, D., Scott, M., Teske, E.: A taxonomy of pairing-friendly elliptic curves. J. Cryptology 23(2), 224–280 (2010)

[16] Fröhlich, A., Taylor, M.: Algebraic number theory. Cambridge University Press (2000)

[17] Joux, A.: A one round protocol for tripartite Diffie-Hellman, J. Cryptology 17(4), 263–276 (2004)

[18] Lenstra, A.K.: Using cyclotomic polynomials to construct efficient discrete logarithm cryptosystems over finite fields. In: Boyd, C., Simpson, L. (eds.) ACISP. LNCS, vol. 7959, pp. 126–138. Springer, Heidelberg (2013)

[19] Miyaji, A., Nakabayashi, M., Takano, S.: New Explicit conditions of elliptic curve traces for FR-reduction. IEICE Transactions on Fundamentals of Electronics, Communications and Computer Sciences 84(5), 1234–1243 (2001)

[20] Narkiewicz, W.: Elementary and Analytic Theory of Algebraic Numbers. Springer (2004)

[21] Silverman, J.: The Arithmetic of Elliptic Curves. Springer (1985)

[22] Sutherland, A.V.: Computing Hilbert class polynomials with the chinese remainder theorem. Math. Comput. 80(273), 501–538 (2011)

[23] Watherhouse, W.C.: Abelian varietes over finite fields. Annales Scientifiques de l'É. N. S. 4e série 2(4), 521–560 (1969)

PandA: Pairings and Arithmetic

Chitchanok Chuengsatiansup[1], Michael Naehrig[2], Pance Ribarski[3], and Peter Schwabe[4,*]

[1] Technische Universiteit Eindhoven
c.chuengsatiansup@tue.nl
[2] Microsoft Research
michael@cryptosith.org
[3] Ss. Cyril and Methodius University in Skopje
pance.ribarski@finki.ukim.mk
[4] Radboud University Nijmegen
peter@cryptojedi.org

Abstract. This paper introduces PandA, a software framework for *Pairings and Arithmetic*. It is designed to bring together advances in the efficient computation of cryptographic pairings and the development and implementation of pairing-based protocols. The intention behind the PandA framework is to give protocol designers and implementors easy access to a toolbox of all functions needed for implementing pairing-based cryptographic protocols, while making it possible to use state-of-the-art algorithms for pairing computation and group arithmetic. PandA offers an API in the C programming language and all arithmetic operations run in constant time to protect against timing attacks. The framework also makes it easy to consistently test and benchmark the lower level functions used in pairing-based protocols.

As an example of how easy it is to implement pairing-based protocols with PandA, we use Boneh-Lynn-Shacham (BLS) signatures. Our PandA-based implementation of BLS needs only 434640 cycles for signature generation and 5832584 cycles for signature verification on one core of an Intel i5-3210M CPU. This includes full protection against timing attacks and compression of public keys and signatures.

Keywords: Cryptographic pairings, benchmarking, API design, BLS signatures.

1 Introduction

Since the late 1990s and early 2000s, when Ohgishi, Sakai, Kasahara[46,51,52] and Joux[39,40] presented the first constructive uses of cryptographic pairings, many pairing-based cryptographic protocols have been proposed. Early work

* This work was supported by the European Commission under ICT COST Action IC1204 TRUDEVICE and by the Netherlands Organisation for Scientific Research (NWO) under grant 639.073.005. Permanent ID of this document: 775a51985db9972bde7bd2acddf1d2a2. Date: November 3, 2013.

Z. Cao and F. Zhang (Eds.): Pairing 2013, LNCS 8365, pp. 229–250, 2014.

such as the identity-based encryption scheme by Boneh and Franklin[18] and the short signature scheme by Boneh, Lynn and Shacham[19], were followed by a flood of papers presenting more and more pairing-based schemes with exciting, new cryptographic functionalities. Examples include schemes for hierarchical identity-based encryption [38,29], attribute-based encryption [50], systems for non-interactive zero-knowledge proofs [35,34], and randomizable proofs and anonymous credentials [10].

In a highly related—but often somewhat independent—line of research, the performance of pairing computation was drastically improved. Milestones in this line of research were the construction of various families of pairing-friendly curves (for an overview, see [28]), many optimizations for the pairing algorithm including denominator elimination in the Miller loop [7], faster algorithms to compute the final exponentiation [56], and the introduction of loop-shortening techniques [36], that lead to the notion of *optimal pairings* [60]. Recently, several papers presented high-speed software that computes 128-bit secure pairings for various Intel and AMD processors [45,17,5,43], and for ARM processors with NEON support [53]. These efforts reduced the time required to compute a pairing at the 128-bit security level on current processors to below 0.5 ms.

Unfortunately, these advances in pairing performance do not immediately speed up pairing-based protocols. The reason is that protocols need much more than just fast pairings. They need fast arithmetic in all involved groups, fast hashing into elliptic-curve groups, fast multi-scalar multiplication (and multi-exponentiation), or specific optimizations for computing products of pairings. This means that, even if authors of speed-record papers for pairing computation make their software available, this software is typically not "complete" from a protocol designer's point of view, and does not necessarily include these other operations; and it is often not easy to use when it comes to prototyping a new pairing-based protocol to evaluate its practical performance. Also, once a protocol implementation has settled for one pairing library, it typically requires a significant effort to switch to another software or library.

Furthermore, as Scott points out in [54], which optimizations to the pairing computation or other arithmetic operations are most useful, strongly depends on the pairing-based protocol that is being implemented. Pairings are used in such protocols in different flavors, where in some scenarios pairing computation is the dominant cost in the overall protocol and in others the large number of non-pairing operations may be the bottleneck (see, for example, [48]). If the protocol contains many more group exponentiations than it has pairing computations, in some cases it might even make sense to choose different pairing-friendly curves to allow faster group operations at the cost of a slightly more expensive pairing (see the ratios of group exponentiation and pairing costs in [20]). In an implementation that has been tailored for high-speed pairings only, it is often difficult to account for such trade-offs.

This paper introduces PandA, a software framework that intends to address the above concerns by making improvements in pairing (and more generally group-arithmetic) performance easily usable for protocol designers. The project is inspired by the eBACS benchmarking project that defines APIs for various typical cryptographic primitives and protocols (such as hash functions, stream ciphers, public-key encryption, and cryptographic signatures). PandA can be seen as a generalization of eBACS to lower-level functions in the elliptic-curve and pairing setting. We are currently discussing a possible inclusion of PandA into eBACS with the editors of the eBACS project.

We encourage submissions of implementations of all the underlying functions to extend the implementation portfolio and to obtain consistent benchmarking as shown in the eBACS project. In particular, we hope that implementors of pairings will be motivated to submit more complete libraries that allow the implementation of full pairing-based protocols. We will make all software described in this paper available at http://panda.cryptojedi.org and place it in the public domain to maximize reusability of our results.

Type-1, Type-2 and Type-3 Pairings. Currently our reference implementation of the PandA API only implements a particular set of parameters for Type-3 pairings, but the API is designed to support arbitrary pairing-friendly curves. However, Section 2 explains how the API supports also Type-1 pairings. Until recently the standard approach to implementing high-security (e.g., 128-bit secure) Type-1 pairings was using supersingular curves over binary or ternary fields. However, advances on solving discrete-logarithm problems in multiplicative groups of small-characteristic fields by Joux in [41], by Göloğlu, Granger, McGuire, and Zumbrägel in [31], by Barbulescu, Gaudry, Joux, and Thomé in [6], and by Adj, Menezes, Oliveira, and Rodríguez-Henríquez in [1] have raised serious concerns about the security of such constructions. Granger commented that he does not "think the coffin has been firmly nailed shut just yet!" [1], and it is indeed not clear that all small-characteristic pairings are broken, but there is a strong consensus that pairings on curves over small-characteristic fields are not recommended anymore. We are therefore planning to include a reference implementation of Type-1 pairings that uses a 1536-bit supersingular curve with embedding degree 2 over a large-characteristic field. Even with serious optimization effort the resulting pairing computation (and also group arithmetic) will be very slow, but this simply reflects the cost of protocols that *need* Type-1 pairings.

We follow Chatterjee and Menezes stating in [24] that "Type 2 pairings are merely inefficient implementations of Type 3 pairings, and appear to offer no benefit for protocols based on asymmetric pairings from the point of view of functionality, security, and performance". Thus, we do not explicitly support Type-2 pairings, but it would be straight-forward to include Type-2 pairings in PandA (the only difference from an API perspective is missing hashing into the second group of pairing arguments).

The Type-3 pairing setting in this paper is as follows. The pairing is a nondegenerate, bilinear function $e : G_1 \times G_2 \to G_3$, where G_1 and G_2 are groups of prime order r consisting of rational points on an ordinary, pairing-friendly elliptic

---

[1] See http://ellipticnews.wordpress.com/2013/05/22/
joux-kills-pairings-in-characteristic-2/

curve E defined over a finite field $\mathbb{F}_p$ of prime characteristic p. The elliptic curve E has a small embedding degree k, which means that the group G_3 is the group of r-th roots of unity in the multiplicative group $\mathbb{F}_{p^k}^*$, i.e. all three groups have prime order r.

Arithmetic in Non-pairing Groups. PandA also has an API for arithmetic in groups that do not support efficient computation of pairings (like non-pairing-friendly elliptic curves). If protocols do not need efficient pairing computation they can choose from a much larger pool of groups in which the DLP is hard. When choosing from this larger pool one can typically pick groups with more efficient arithmetic. The group API supports all functions that are also supported for each of the three groups in the pairing setting. Our reference implementation of this API uses the group of the twisted Edwards curve that is also used for Ed25519 signatures [12,13]. However, this paper focuses on the description of the pairing setting in PandA.

The Importance of Constant-Time Algorithms. Aside from attacks against the hard problems that the security of modern cryptography is based on, major threats to cryptographic software are side-channel attacks. In particular timing attacks (that can even be carried out remotely in many cases) prove to be a very powerful attack tool. See [47,59], [22], [26], [61] for some examples of timing attacks against cryptographic software.

One could argue that a framework which is designed to evaluate the performance of cryptographic protocols should not pay attention to these issues, but rather keep the API simple, and add suitable timing-attack protection only for "real-world" software. We disagree for two reasons. First, once some pieces of unprotected cryptographic software have been written and publicized, it is almost impossible to ensure that it does not end up in some real-world software. Second, and more importantly, protecting software against timing-attacks does not add a constant overhead; the cost highly depends on protocol design, and algorithm and parameter choices made on a high level. For example, the completeness of the group law on Edwards curves [15,11] makes it easy to protect group addition against timing attacks. It is possible to protect Weierstrass-curve point addition against timing attacks (see Section 3) but it involves a significant overhead.

Optimizing performance of unprotected implementations of cryptographic protocols may thus lead to wrong decisions that are very hard to correct later. PandA acknowledges this fact by offering timing-attack protected (constant-time) versions of all arithmetic operations. For operations that do not involve any secret data (such as signature verification) there are possibly faster non-constant-time versions of all group-arithmetic operations. These unprotected versions of functions have to be chosen explicitly; the default is the constant-time versions.

Related Work. There exist various cryptographic *libraries* that expose low-level functionality such as group arithmetic and pairings through their API. However, the API that gives access to this low-level functionality is typically tailored to suit the specific needs of the higher-level primitives of the library. It is usually not designed for efficient implementation of arbitrary new protocols. Some libraries that use group arithmetic even decide to not expose the low-level functionality through the API, because this functionality was never written to be used outside the specific needs of the higher-level protocols. See, for example, the high-level API of NaCl [16]. Two notable examples of cryptographic libraries with a convenient API for pairings and group arithmetic are RELIC [4] and Miracl [23].

A library which has been explicitly designed for the use in arbitrary pairing-based protocols is the PBC library [42]. This careful design is the reason that it is still the preferred library for the implementation of various protocols; despite the fact that it does not offer state-of-the-art performance and (by default) no high-security curves. The PandA API is designed with the same usage profile as PBC in mind. However, the reference implementation of the PandA API presented in this paper offers state-of-the art performance with a curve choice that offers 128 bits of security. Furthermore, PandA is designed as a framework that supports (and encourages!) submissions by various designers to keep reflecting the state-of-the-art in group-arithmetic and pairing performance.

Another framework for easy implementation of cryptographic protocols is Charm [3]. Charm offers a high-level Python API and uses multiple crypto-graphic libraries to achieve good performance. For pairing-based cryptography it uses the PBC library. Charm is a higher-level framework than PandA; we see PandA not in competition to Charm but rather hope that Charm will eventually include some of PandA's high-performance pairing and group-arithmetic implementations to speed up protocols implemented in its high-level API.

Organization of the Paper. Section 2 explains the PandA API. Section 3 gives details of our reference implementation of this API and reports benchmark results of all arithmetic operations. Section 4 considers an example that shows how easy it is to implement pairing-based protocols that achieve state-of-the-art performance using the PandA API.

2   PandA API and Functionality

The API of PandA is inspired by the API of eBACS, which means in particular that the API is also for the C programming language. There are various advantages of using C. It is the language most commonly used for speed-record-setting cryptographic software (often combined with assembly), so a C API makes it easy to integrate fast software in PandA. Furthermore, protocols that need group arithmetic, pairings, and, for example, a hash function or a stream cipher, can easily combine software from PandA with software that is tested and benchmarked in eBACS.

In the eBACS API all functions are within the crypto namespace, i.e. all function names begin with crypto_. Similarly, all functions and data types related to arithmetic in groups that support efficient bilinear-pairing computation are in the bgroup namespace (for "bilinear group"); the API for group arithmetic without pairings uses the group namespace.

2.1   PandA Data Types

The functionality that is tested and benchmarked in PandA is on a lower level in the design of cryptographic protocols. In the eBACS project, complete cryptographic primitives and protocols are benchmarked, while PandA benchmarks arithmetic operations that are meant to be used to implement cryptographic protocols. This has consequences for the data type of inputs and outputs. In eBACS, all functions receive inputs as byte arrays (C data type `unsigned char`), the length of these arrays is specified in arguments of type `unsigned long long`. Outputs are again written to byte arrays. A typical implementation of a cryptographic protocol in eBACS first converts the input byte arrays to an internal representation for fast computation that depends on the architecture, then performs all computations in this representation, and then transforms the output to a unique representation as a byte array. These transformations typically contribute only little overhead to the cost of a cryptographic protocol if they are done only at the beginning and the end of the *protocol*. Protocols implemented using the PandA API typically need a sequence of functions from the PandA API and we clearly want to avoid transformations at the beginning and the end of each *function*. Implementations of the PandA API therefore define 4 data types—for elements of the three groups G_1, G_2 and G_3 and for scalars (modulo the group order)—in a file called `api.h`. These data types (`struct` in C) are called `bgroup_g1e`, `bgroup_g2e`, `bgroup_g3e`, and `bgroup_scalar`. The API provides two functions, one is used to convert an element of G_1, G_2, G_3, or a scalar to a unique byte array of fixed length (`pack`), the other one converts such a byte array back to a group element or scalar (`unpack`). Implementations of the PandA API furthermore specify the size of packed elements in `api.h`:

```
#define BGROUP_G1E_PACKEDBYTES 32
#define BGROUP_G2E_PACKEDBYTES 64
#define BGROUP_G3E_PACKEDBYTES 384
#define BGROUP_SCALAR_PACKEDBYTES 32
```

indicating that packed elements of G_1 need 32 bytes, packed elements of G_2 need 64 bytes, etc. From this file, PandA automatically generates the header file `panda_bgroup.h` that defines all functions of the API. Implementations of Type-1 pairings omit the implementation of G_2 and instead include a line

```
#define BGROUP_TYPE1
```

in the file `api.h`. For the group G_1, the `unpack` and `pack` functions are

```
int bgroup_g1e_unpack(bgroup_g1e *r, const unsigned char b[BGROUP_G1E_PACKEDBYTES]);

void bgroup_g1e_pack(unsigned char r[BGROUP_G1E_PACKEDBYTES], const bgroup_g1e *b);
```

Following eBACS convention, the `unpack` function returns an integer value, which is zero whenever a valid byte array is received that can be unpacked to a group element. On input of an invalid byte array that does not correspond to a packed group element, the function returns a non-zero integer. In the following, we mostly describe the API for arithmetic in G_1 as an example, Equivalent functions exist for G_2 and G_3.

2.2   PandA Constants

For each of the three groups, a PandA implementation has to define two constants: a generator and the neutral element. For the group G_1 these are called bgroup_g1e_base and bgroup_g1e_neutral. Each implementation needs to ensure that the pairing evaluated at bgroup_g1e_base and bgroup_g2e_base gives bgroup_g3e_base as result. Furthermore, each PandA implementation has to define two constants of type bgroup_scalar: namely bgroup_scalar_zero and bgroup_scalar_one for the element zero and the element one in the ring of integers modulo the order r of the groups G_1, G_2, and G_3.

2.3   Comparing Group Elements

One way to compare two group elements for equality is obviously to use the bgroup_g1e_pack function on both of them and compare the resulting byte arrays for equality. This is typically not the most efficient way to compare equality (except if packing of elements is required anyway). For example, consider two elliptic-curve points in projective coordinates. Conversion to a *unique* byte array requires transformation to affine coordinates, i.e., two inversions and several multiplications. Comparison for equality only needs a few multiplications. The API therefore has a comparison function

```
int bgroup_g1e_equals(const bgroup_g1e *a, const bgroup_g1e *b);
```

which returns 1 if the two elements are equal and 0 if they are not.

As explained in the introduction, this function must be guaranteed to not leak timing information about the two arguments. For cases where none of the two inputs is secret, there is a function

```
int bgroup_g1e_equals_publicinputs(const bgroup_g1e *a, const bgroup_g1e *b);
```

which behaves the same way but is not guaranteed to not leak timing information and may be faster than the constant-time version.

2.4   Addition and Doubling

In concrete implementations of pairings, the groups G_1 and G_2 are typically additive groups, while the group G_3 is a multiplicative group. Hence, the core operations for group arithmetic are additions and doublings in G_1 and G_2 and multiplications and squarings in G_3. It makes sense to treat all three groups as abstract abelian groups and therefore use a common notation for the group operation in all of them. Many papers that treat a pairing as a black box use multiplicative notation for G_1, G_2, and G_3. Instead, the PandA API uses additive notation following the crypto_scalarmult API of the SUPERCOP benchmarking framework used in eBACS.

Addition of two elements, doubling, and negation (computing the inverse of an element) are done through the functions:

```
void bgroup_g1e_add(bgroup_g1e *r, const bgroup_g1e *a, const bgroup_g1e *b);
void bgroup_g1e_double(bgroup_g1e *r, const bgroup_g1e *a);
void bgroup_g1e_negate(bgroup_g1e *r, const bgroup_g1e *a);
```

Note that the return value is always written to the first argument pointer (as in the eBACS API and also, for example, in the GMP API [30]). Note also that the implementation needs to ensure that the addition and doubling functions work for all elements of the group as inputs and that no timing information leaks about these inputs or the output. As before, there are also potentially faster non-constant-time versions of these functions:

```
void bgroup_g1e_add_publicinputs(bgroup_g1e *r, const bgroup_g1e *a,
                                 const bgroup_g1e *b);
void bgroup_g1e_double_publicinputs(bgroup_g1e *r, const bgroup_g1e *a);
void bgroup_g1e_negate_publicinputs(bgroup_g1e *r, const bgroup_g1e *a);
```

2.5   Scalar Multiplication

The default function for performing a scalar multiplication is simply

```
void bgroup_g1e_scalarmult(bgroup_g1e *r, const bgroup_g1e *a, const bgroup_scalar *s);
```

This function can be made much faster when multiplying a fixed base point that is known at compile time. This potentially faster version is supported for the generator bgroup_g1e_base through

```
void bgroup_g1e_scalarmult_base(bgroup_g1e *r, const bgroup_scalar *s);
```

Another improvement can be implemented for multi-scalar multiplication, i.e. whenever a sum $\sum_{i=0}^{m-1} s_i P_i$ of several scalar multiples needs to be computed for m scalars $s_0, \ldots, s_{m-1}$ and m group elements $P_0, \ldots, P_{m-1}$. Such computations are supported through the below function, in which the last (unsigned long long) argument specifies the number m of scalar multiplications to be performed in the sum.

```
void bgroup_g1e_multiscalarmult(bgroup_g1e *r, const bgroup_g1e *a,
                                const bgroup_scalar *s, unsigned long long alen);
```

Again, all group elements have to be supported as inputs, constant-time behavior has to be ensured by implementations, and the API also supports non-constant-time (publicinputs) versions of the functions. The input alen is considered public also for the constant-time version.

2.6   Hashing to G_1 and G_2

Many protocols require hashing of arbitrary bit strings to group elements in G_1 and G_2, which is also supported by the PandA API. The corresponding function for hashing into G_1 is:

```
void bgroup_g1e_hashfromstr(bgroup_g1e *r, const unsigned char *a,
                            unsigned long long alen);
```

As for the previous functions, there is also a non-constant-time (`publicinputs`) version of this function. Due to the different ways in which the constant-time and non-constant-time functions are computed, it can be the case that the hashed values obtained by evaluating each version on the same input bit string are different. It is not necessary to insist that both versions compute the same result, because we expect that throughout a protocol, the same input string to a hash function is always either public or private. Therefore, one can consistently select the right version of the function and thus take advantage of faster non-constant-time algorithms.

2.7 Arithmetic on Scalars

Various functions are supported for arithmetic on scalars modulo the group order, which are required in various protocols (for example for ECDSA signatures). Specifically these functions are the following:

```
void bgroup_scalar_setrandom(bgroup_scalar *r);
void bgroup_scalar_add(bgroup_scalar *r, const bgroup_scalar *s, const bgroup_scalar *t);
void bgroup_scalar_sub(bgroup_scalar *r, const bgroup_scalar *s, const bgroup_scalar *t);
void bgroup_scalar_negate(bgroup_scalar *r, const bgroup_scalar *s);
void bgroup_scalar_mul(bgroup_scalar *r, const bgroup_scalar *s, const bgroup_scalar *t);
void bgroup_scalar_square(bgroup_scalar *r, const bgroup_scalar *s);
void bgroup_scalar_invert(bgroup_scalar *r, const bgroup_scalar *s);
int  bgroup_scalar_equals(const bgroup_scalar *s, const bgroup_scalar *t);
```

Arithmetic on scalars is typically not the performance bottleneck in pairing-based protocols; furthermore we do not expect significant speedups for non-constant-time versions of scalar arithmetic. Therefore, the API does not include `publicinputs` versions of functions for arithmetic on scalars.

2.8 Pairings and Products of Pairings

Finally, the API function for computing a pairing is

```
void bgroup_pairing(bgroup_g3e *r, const bgroup_g1e *a, const bgroup_g2e *b);
```

Some protocols need—or can make use of—the product of several pairings (for an example see BLS signatures in Section 4). Computing the product of two pairings can be significantly faster than computing two independent pairings and then multiplying the results. One reason is that the final exponentiation has to be done only once, another reason is that squarings inside the Miller loop can be shared between the two pairings. To support these important speedups, the PandA API includes a function

```
void bgroup_pairing_product(bgroup_g3e *r, const bgroup_g1e *a, const bgroup_g2e *b,
    unsigned long long alen);
```

3 PandA Reference Implementation

This section describes our reference implementation of the API functions from Section 2. The implementation provides a 128-bit secure, Type-3 pairing framework.

3.1   Choice of Parameters

At the 128-bit security level, the most suitable choice of pairing-friendly curve is a Barreto-Naehrig curve [8] over a prime field of size roughly 256 bits. We use the 254-bit curve $E = E_{2,254}$ that has been proposed in [49] and has also been used in [5]. The curve parameter $u = -(2^{62} + 2^{55} + 1)$ yields 254-bit primes $p = p(u) = 36u^4 + 36u^3 + 24u^2 + 6u + 1$ and $r = r(u) = 36u^4 + 36u^3 + 18u^2 + 6u + 1$, and $E : y^2 = x^3 + 2$ over $\mathbb{F}_p$. Since the embedding degree is $k = 12$, the implementation needs to provide the field extension $\mathbb{F}_{p^{12}}$. This extension is implemented in the standard way as a tower $\mathbb{F}_p \subset \mathbb{F}_{p^2} \subset \mathbb{F}_{p^6} \subset \mathbb{F}_{p^{12}}$.

As usual, the elliptic-curve groups are $G_1 = E(\mathbb{F}_p)$ and G_2 is the p-eigenspace of the p-power Frobenius in the r-torsion group $E(\mathbb{F}_{p^{12}})[r]$, which is represented by an isomorphic group $G_2' = E'(\mathbb{F}_{p^2})[r]$ on a sextic twist E' of E over $\mathbb{F}_{p^{12}}$. Whenever we work with elements in G_2, we make use of their representation as elements in G_2', i.e. they are curve points with coefficients in $\mathbb{F}_{p^2}$ and arithmetic is actually arithmetic on E' over $\mathbb{F}_{p^2}$.

3.2   Algorithms

Packing and Unpacking. To pack elements of the groups G_1 and G_2, we use the usual way of point compression on elliptic curves. For elliptic-curve arithmetic, points are in Jacobian coordinates. To pack a point, it is first transformed to affine coordinates. The packed representation is the 32-byte array containing the point's 254-bit affine x-coordinate together with the least significant bit of its y-coordinate in one of the remaining two free bits. The other free bit is used to represent the point at infinity.

Given such a byte array, the unpacking algorithm recovers the x-coordinate and solves the curve equation for the y-coordinate, choosing the right square root according to the least significant bit given in the array. The core of this operation is a square root computation, for which we use different algorithms in G_1 and G_2. Since $p \equiv 3 \mod 4$, in G_1, we use $a^{(p+1)/4}$ to compute the square root of $a \in \mathbb{F}_p$. The unpack algorithm in G_2 uses [2, Algorithm 9] to compute the square root. After obtaining a point on the curve, it needs to be checked whether it has order r, i.e. whether it is in the correct subgroup.

The elements of G_3 are kept as elements of $\mathbb{F}_{p^{12}}^*$. The packing algorithm constructs a unique byte array composed of the twelve $\mathbb{F}_p$-coefficients of the unique $\mathbb{F}_{p^{12}}$-element in G_3. The unpack algorithm simply converts the byte array back to an $\mathbb{F}_{p^{12}}$-element and checks that the order of the element is r. At the time of writing this paper, the implementation does not compress pairing values. However, this will be changed. Pairing values can be compressed to one third the length of an $\mathbb{F}_{p^{12}}$-element by using the techniques described in [55,32,44,5].

Comparison. To compare elements of the groups G_1 and G_2, we need to compare points that are represented in (projective) Jacobian coordinates. The standard way of comparing these redundant representations is to multiply through by the respective powers of the Z-coordinate. This does not need inversions, in contrast to a conversion to affine coordinates. Comparison in the group G_3 can directly compare $\mathbb{F}_{p^{12}}$-elements or the respective compressed representations.

Hashing to G_1 and G_2. The standard non-constant-time algorithm to hash an arbitrary string to a point on an elliptic curve is the "try-and-increment" method introduced in [19]. The message is concatenated with a counter and hashed by a cryptographic hash function to an element of the underlying finite field. If this element is a valid x-coordinate, compute one of the corresponding y coordinates; otherwise increase the counter and repeat the procedure. We use this method for non-constant-time hashing to G_1 and G_2.

For constant-time hashing to G_1 and G_2 we use the algorithm described in [27] which is based on the algorithm by Shallue and van der Woestijne described in [57]. The conditional branches in the algorithm (in particular choosing between one out of three possible solutions) are implemented through constant-time conditional-copy operations.

We do not yet include the indistinguishable hashing described in [27]. This would require carrying out two independent hashing operations to the curve (e.g., by using two different cryptographic hash functions) and then adding the results.

Group Addition. We represent elements of G_1 and G_2 in Jacobian coordinates. For non-constant-time addition we use the addition formulas by Bernstein and Lange that take 11 multiplications and 5 squarings[2]. If the inputs happen to be one of the special cases that are not handled by the formulas we use conditional branches to switch to doubling or to returning the point at infinity. Doubling uses the formulas by Lange that take 5 squarings and 2 multiplications[3].

Constant-time complete addition on a Weierstrass curve is not easy to do efficiently. There exist no complete formulas [21, Theorem 1]. The unified formulas proposed in [37, 5.5.2] can handle doublings but they achieve this by moving the special cases to other points (specifically, addition of points of the form (x_1, y_1) and $(x_2, -y_1)$ with $x_1 \neq x_2$). Here, we evaluate two sets of formulas and use constant-time conditional copies to choose between the two outputs. We do that with the addition and doubling formulas described above. Note that protocols are typically not bottlenecked by additions but rather by scalar multiplications. Constant-time scalar-multiplication can use much faster dedicated addition as long as we can be sure that scalars are smaller than the group order. This is also compatible with the GLV/GLS decomposition described in the next paragraph.

Scalar Multiplication. For the scalar multiplication algorithms implemented in PandA for each of the three groups, we distinguish between constant-time algorithms and their more efficient counterparts public inputs. For each case, there are three algorithms: general scalar multiplication, scalar multiplication of a fixed base point, and multi-scalar multiplication.

---

[2] http://www.hyperelliptic.org/EFD/g1p/auto-shortw-jacobian-0.html
#addition-add-2007-bl

[3] http://www.hyperelliptic.org/EFD/g1p/auto-shortw-jacobian-0.html
#doubling-dbl-2009-l

Scalar multiplication of a fixed base point that is known at compile time is done by precomputing 512 multiples of that point in a table and then using these to compute the scalar multiple. The method we use is described in detail by Bernstein et al. [12,13, Section 4]. Since we do not expect a significant speed-up by moving from the constant-time to a variable-time version, we also use the constant-time algorithm in the function on public inputs.

The standard case of scalar multiplication uses efficient endomorphisms on the BN curve by splitting the scalars via 2-dimensional GLV in G_1 and 4-dimensional GLS decomposition in G_2 and G_3. See the work by Bos, Costello, and Naehrig [20] for details. In G_1, we slightly differ from the method in [20]. After the scalar decomposition in the constant-time function, we save a few additions by using a fixed signed window of size 5 and two additions per lookup, instead of the table with window size 2 and one addition. The function on public inputs uses a signed sliding window of size 5. The constant-time algorithms in G_2 and G_3 are as described in [20], the variable-time algorithms use signed sliding windows of size 4.

The variable-time algorithm for multi-scalar multiplication first applies the GLV/GLS scalar decomposition. For small batch sizes it then uses joint-signed-sliding-window scalar multiplication; for larger batch sizes (> 16 for G_1 and > 8 for G_2 and G_3) we use Bos-Coster scalar multiplication (described in [25, Section 4]). For the constant-time version, due to the slow complete addition routine, the function currently simply carries out each scalar multiplication separately and adds them together at the end.

For the group G_3, it seems worthwhile to implement exponentiations of compressed values using the methods of Stam and Lenstra [58]. We are planning to consider this optimization.

Pairing Computation. The pairing algorithm computes the optimal ate pairing on the same BN curve as [5]. Unlike [5] we do not use standard projective coordinates but Jacobian coordinates as in [45]. We use lazy reduction for arithmetic in the extension fields as described in [5]. The final exponentiation implements the same approach as [17], we use the cyclotomic squarings from [33, Section 3.1], but we do not use the compressed squarings described in [5, Section 5.2].

We are planning to continue optimizing pairing computation by experimenting with standard projective coordinates, a final exponentiation with compressed squarings [5], and faster low-level arithmetic.

Low-Level Arithmetic. The low-level arithmetic in $\mathbb{F}_p$ and arithmetic on scalars are implemented in AMD64 assembly. We use Montgomery representation for elements in $\mathbb{F}_p$; scalars are represented in "standard" form because in scalar multiplication we need access to the binary representation. Modular reduction of scalars uses Barrett reduction [9].

We have not yet implemented inlined arithmetic in $\mathbb{F}_{p^2}$ in assembly. We are planning to include this optimization and expect significant performance improvements for pairing computation and for arithmetic in G_2 and G_3.

We also have a compatible implementation of the field arithmetic entirely written in C to support other platforms. We will continue to optimize the software with assembly implementations for other platforms, in particular ARM processors with NEON support.

3.3 Performance

We benchmarked our software (with $\mathbb{F}_p$ arithmetic implemented in assembly) on one core of an Intel Core i5-3210M processor with Turbo Boost and Hyperthreading disabled. For each function we carried out 100 computations on random inputs. The median and quartiles of the cycle counts measured in these experiments are reported in Tables 1, 2, 3, and 4.

Table 1. Cycle counts for arithmetic operations in G_1 on Intel Core i5-3210M

API function	25% quartile	median	75% quartile
bgroup_g1e_unpack	39140	39184	39212
bgroup_g1e_pack	39512	39548	39568
bgroup_g1e_hashfromstr (59 bytes)	198780	198908	198964
bgroup_g1e_add	6052	6080	6100
bgroup_g1e_double	1204	1216	1224
bgroup_g1e_negate	36	36	40
bgroup_g1e_scalarmult	346852	347024	347180
bgroup_g1e_scalarmult_base	128468	128596	128696
bgroup_g1e_multiscalarmult			
$(n=2)$	705564	705820	706056
$(n=3)$	1058308	1058644	1059128
$(n=4)$	1411188	1411644	1411944
$(n=8)$	2822252	2823148	2826864
$(n=32)$	11294736	11296364	11298420
$(n=128)$	45181816	45186732	45193356
bgroup_g1e_equals	1124	1132	1140
bgroup_g1e_hashfromstr_publicinputs (59 bytes)	41752	83168	83696
bgroup_g1e_add_publicinputs	2456	2468	2476
bgroup_g1e_double_publicinputs	1180	1192	1200
bgroup_g1e_negate_publicinputs	36	36	40
bgroup_g1e_scalarmult_publicinputs	284228	288240	290788
bgroup_g1e_scalarmult_base_publicinputs	102184	104024	105772
bgroup_g1e_multiscalarmult_publicinputs			
$(n=2)$	415076	419860	423440
$(n=3)$	551124	556792	560712
$(n=4)$	710416	715396	722000
$(n=8)$	1229100	1238660	1246568
$(n=32)$	4727808	4741472	4752772
$(n=128)$	14590168	14605364	14635184
bgroup_g1e_equals_publicinputs	576	580	588

4 Implementing Protocols with PandA

In this section we consider BLS signatures [19] as a small example of a pairing-based protocol implemented in PandA. We choose this example, because it illustrates the use of most API functions of PandA and because cryptographic signatures (unlike more complex cryptographic protocols) are supported by the eBACS benchmarking project [14]. The software presented in this section implements the eBACS API for cryptographic signatures and we will submit our software to eBACS for public benchmarking.

4.1 The BLS Signature Scheme

We briefly describe the three algorithms — key generation, signing, and verification — of the BLS scheme for an asymmetric, Type-3 pairing. Let $Q \in G_2$ be a system-wide fixed base point for G_2.

Key Generation. Pick a random scalar $s \in \mathbb{Z}_r^*$. Compute the scalar multiple $R \leftarrow [s]Q$. Return R as the public key and s as the private key.

Signing. Hash the message m to an element M in G_1. Use the private key s to compute $S = [s]M$. Return the x-coordinate of the result S as the signature σ.

Verification. Upon receiving a signature σ, a message m, and the public key R, find an element $S \in G_1$ such that its x-coordinate corresponds to σ and it has order r. If no such point exists, reject the signature. Then calculate $t_1 \leftarrow e(S, Q)$. Compute the hash $M \in G_1$ of the message m, and compute $t_2 \leftarrow e(M, R)$. The signature is accepted if $t_1 = t_2$ or $t_1 = -t_2$ and rejected otherwise. Note that we use additive notation in G_3.

This scheme requires one scalar multiplication for key generation, one scalar multiplication for signature generation, and the comparison of two pairing values for signature verification. In our case the signature is the packed value of the elliptic-curve point, which includes the information on the sign of the correct y-coordinate. We therefore compute the unique point S corresponding to the signature σ, and to verify we only need to check whether $e(-S, Q) \cdot e(M, R) = 1$.

4.2 Implementation with PandA

Our example implementation follows the eBATS API which consists of three functions, namely, `crypto_sign_keypair`, `crypto_sign`, and `crypto_sign_open`. The details of each function are as follows.

The function `crypto_sign_keypair` generates the public and private key pair. It requires one fixed-basepoint scalar multiplication in G_2. The complete code for keypair generation is given in Listing 1. The macro `CRYPTO_BYTES` is required by the eBACS API and is set to `BGROUP_G1E_PACKEDBYTES` in a file called `api.h`.

The function `crypto_sign` computes the signature upon receiving the message. This function also requires hashing to G_1 (we assume that the message is public

Listing 1. Public and private key generation

```
int crypto_sign_keypair(
  unsigned char *pk,
  unsigned char *sk
)
{
  // private key //
  bgroup_scalar x;
  bgroup_scalar_setrandom(&x);
  bgroup_scalar_pack(sk, &x);

  // public key //
  bgroup_g2e r;
  bgroup_g2_scalarmult_base(&r, &x);
  bgroup_g2_pack(pk, &r);

  return 0;
}
```

Listing 2. Signature generation

```
int crypto_sign(
  unsigned char *sm,
  unsigned long long *smlen,
  const unsigned char *m,
  unsigned long long mlen,
  const unsigned char *sk)
{

  bgroup_g1e p, p1;
  bgroup_scalar x;
  int i,r;

  bgroup_g1e_hashfromstr_publicinputs(&p, m, mlen);
  r = bgroup_scalar_unpack(&x, sk);
  bgroup_g1e_scalarmult(&p1, &p, &x);
  bgroup_g1e_pack(sm, &p1);

  for (i = 0; i < mlen; i++)
  sm[i + CRYPTO_BYTES] = m[i];
  *smlen = mlen + CRYPTO_BYTES;

  return -r;
}
```

and use the publicinputs version) and one scalar multiplication in G_1. The complete code for signing is given in Listing 2.

The function crypto_sign_open verifies whether the signature belongs to the message. As described in the previous subsection, a naive method to compare whether two pairing values are equal is to first compute those two pairings, then compare the results. It is obvious that one can avoid the computation of two pairings. Instead, one computes a product of two pairings and checks whether it is equal to one. In this way, verification needs hashing to G_1 and one pairing-product computation. The code for signature verification is given in Listing 3.

4.3 Performance

We benchmarked the BLS implementation on the same Core i5-3210M running at 2.5 GHz that we also used for the detailed benchmarks of our reference

Listing 3. Signature verification

```
int crypto_sign_open(
  unsigned char *m,
  unsigned long long *mlen,
  const unsigned char *sm,
  unsigned long long smlen,
  const unsigned char *pk)
{
  bgroup_g1e p[2];
  bgroup_g2e q[2];
  bgroup_g3e r;
  unsigned long long i;
  int ok;

  ok  = !bgroup_g1e_unpack(p, sm);
  bgroup_g1e_negate_publicinputs(p, p);
  q[0] = bgroup_g2e_base;
  bgroup_g1e_hashfromstr_publicinputs(p+1, sm + CRYPTO_BYTES, smlen - CRYPTO_BYTES);
  ok &= !bgroup_g2e_unpack(q+1, pk);
  bgroup_pairing_product(&r, p, q, 2);

  ok &= bgroup_g3e_equals(&r, &bgroup_g3e_neutral);

  if (ok)
  {
    for (i = 0; i < smlen - CRYPTO_BYTES; i++)
      m[i] = sm[i + CRYPTO_BYTES];
    *mlen = smlen - CRYPTO_BYTES;
    return 0;
  }
  else
  {
    for (i = 0; i < smlen - CRYPTO_BYTES; i++)
      m[i] = 0;
    *mlen = (unsigned long long) (-1);
    return -1;
  }
}
```

implementation of the API. We will also submit the software to eBACS for public benchmarking. Key generation takes 378848 cycles. Signing (of a 59-byte message) takes 434640 cycles (this is a median of 10000 measurements, the quartiles are 428616 and 511764). Verification of a signature on a 59-byte message takes 5832584 cycles (again, this is a median, the quartiles are 5797640 and 5874292). To our knowledge these are the fastest reported speeds of a BLS signature implementation at the 128-bit security level. We would like to compare performance with the BLS implementation by Scott included in SUPERCOP. However, it seems that the software fails to build on 64-bit platforms; consequently eBACS does not contain benchmark results of the "bls" software on such platforms.

We ran the benchmark included in the RELIC framework (version 0.3.5) on the same machine that we used for benchmarking. The times reported by this RELIC benchmark are 609966 nanoseconds for BLS key generation, 510775 nanoseconds for signing and 6910615 nanoseconds for verification. At a clock speed of 2.5 GHz this corresponds to 1524915 cycles for key generation, 1276937 cycles for signing, and 17276537 cyles for verification; about three times slower than our implementation.

Table 2. Cycle counts for arithmetic operations in G_2 on Intel Core i5-3210M

API function	25% quartile	median	75% quartile
bgroup_g2e_unpack	1864580	1864884	1865396
bgroup_g2e_pack	42080	42124	42160
bgroup_g2e_hashfromstr (59 bytes)	2435116	2435564	2439536
bgroup_g2e_add	16048	16072	16096
bgroup_g2e_double	2924	2940	2948
bgroup_g2e_negate	60	60	64
bgroup_g2e_scalarmult	764628	764808	765088
bgroup_g2e_scalarmult_base	336788	336916	337060
bgroup_g2e_multiscalarmult			
$(n = 2)$	1563312	1563668	1564040
$(n = 3)$	2344964	2345496	2346704
$(n = 4)$	3126720	3127116	3131192
$(n = 8)$	6253984	6257528	6258700
$(n = 32)$	25024136	25027200	25031036
$(n = 128)$	100103176	100117420	100157284
bgroup_g2e_equals	3100	3112	3124
bgroup_g2e_hashfromstr_publicinputs (59 bytes)	298524	299884	894696
bgroup_g2e_add_publicinputs	6572	6596	6608
bgroup_g2e_double_publicinputs	2960	2972	2992
bgroup_g2e_negate_publicinputs	60	60	64
bgroup_g2e_scalarmult_publicinputs	612012	625636	635656
bgroup_g2e_scalarmult_base_publicinputs	273468	278372	283056
bgroup_g2e_multiscalarmult_publicinputs			
$(n = 2)$	1031736	1043332	1060796
$(n = 3)$	1477392	1492796	1510148
$(n = 4)$	1889684	1912744	1928124
$(n = 8)$	3443640	3467764	3489032
$(n = 32)$	10293932	10329088	10366420
$(n = 128)$	32941972	32991824	33061804
bgroup_g2e_equals_publicinputs	3104	3116	3120

Table 3. Cycle counts for arithmetic operations in G_3 on Intel Core i5-3210M

API function	25% quartile	median	75% quartile
bgroup_g3e_unpack	1832068	1832404	1833044
bgroup_g3e_pack	424	424	428
bgroup_g3e_add	8020	8032	8048
bgroup_g3e_double	5548	5560	5572
bgroup_g3e_negate	172	176	180
bgroup_g3e_scalarmult	1120300	1120552	1120936
bgroup_g3e_scalarmult_base	608964	609148	609320
bgroup_g3e_multiscalarmult			
$(n = 2)$	2255028	2255624	2258896
$(n = 3)$	3382628	3383284	3387392
$(n = 4)$	4510336	4511420	4515516
$(n = 8)$	9024924	9025736	9026820
$(n = 32)$	36100180	36103240	36109596
$(n = 128)$	144408660	144446076	144467856
bgroup_g3e_equals	8304	8324	8336
bgroup_g3e_add_publicinputs	8024	8044	8056
bgroup_g3e_double_publicinputs	5548	5556	5568
bgroup_g3e_negate_publicinputs	176	176	180
bgroup_g3e_scalarmult_publicinputs	852272	864136	877804
bgroup_g3e_scalarmult_base_publicinputs	609004	609188	609352
bgroup_g3e_multiscalarmult_publicinputs			
$(n = 2)$	2255104	2255424	2258836
$(n = 3)$	3382688	3383368	3387800
$(n = 4)$	4510680	4512684	4515652
$(n = 8)$	4272080	4297668	4330036
$(n = 32)$	12768868	12803832	12843124
$(n = 128)$	40764052	40825956	40876608
bgroup_g3e_equals_publicinputs	8304	8320	8332

Table 4. Cycle counts for pairing computation on Intel Core i5-3210M

API function	25% quartile	median	75% quartile
bgroup_pairing	2566580	2567116	2572096
bgroup_pairing_product			
$(n = 2)$	3831724	3832644	3837688
$(n = 3)$	5089192	5093724	5094728
$(n = 4)$	6347328	6351260	6352588
$(n = 8)$	11380604	11381384	11383420
$(n = 32)$	41565448	41569424	41588976
$(n = 128)$	162321836	162364916	162387468

References

1. Adj, G., Menezes, A., Oliveira, T., Rodríguez-Henríquez, F.: Weakness of $\mathbb{F}_{3^{6 \cdot 509}}$ for discrete logarithm cryptography (2013), http://eprint.iacr.org/2013/446/
2. Adj, G., Rodríguez-Henríquez, F.: Square root computation over even extension fields (2012), http://eprint.iacr.org/
3. Akinyele, J.A., Garman, C., Miers, I., Pagano, M.W., Rushanan, M., Green, M., Rubin, A.D.: Charm: a framework for rapidly prototyping cryptosystems. Journal of Cryptographic Engineering, 3(2):111–128 (2013), http://eprint.iacr.org/2011/617/
4. Aranha, D.F., Gouvêa, C.P.L.: RELIC is an Efficient LIbrary for Cryptography, http://code.google.com/p/relic-toolkit/ (accessed November 5, 2013).
5. Aranha, D.F., Karabina, K., Longa, P., Gebotys, C.H., López, J.: Faster explicit formulas for computing pairings over ordinary curves. In: Paterson, K.G. (ed.) EUROCRYPT 2011. LNCS, vol. 6632, pp. 48–68. Springer, Heidelberg (2011), http://eprint.iacr.org/2010/526/
6. Barbulescu, R., Gaudry, P., Joux, A., Thomé, E.: A quasi-polynomial algorithm for discrete logarithm in finite fields of small characteristic (2013), http://eprint.iacr.org/2013/400/
7. Barreto, P.S.L.M., Kim, H.Y., Lynn, B., Scott, M.: Efficient Algorithms for Pairing-Based Cryptosystems. In: Yung, M. (ed.) CRYPTO 2002. LNCS, vol. 2442, pp. 354–368. Springer, Heidelberg (2002), http://eprint.iacr.org/2002/008
8. Barreto, P.S.L.M., Naehrig, M.: Pairing-Friendly Elliptic Curves of Prime Order. In: Preneel, B., Tavares, S. (eds.) SAC 2005. LNCS, vol. 3897, pp. 319–331. Springer, Heidelberg (2006), http://cryptosith.org/papers/#bn
9. Barrett, P.: Implementing the Rivest Shamir and Adleman Public Key Encryption Algorithm on a Standard Digital Signal Processor. In: Odlyzko, A.M. (ed.) CRYPTO 1986. LNCS, vol. 263, pp. 311–323. Springer, Heidelberg (1987)
10. Belenkiy, M., Camenisch, J., Chase, M., Kohlweiss, M., Lysyanskaya, A., Shacham, H.: Randomizable Proofs and Delegatable Anonymous Credentials. In: Halevi, S. (ed.) CRYPTO 2009. LNCS, vol. 5677, pp. 108–125. Springer, Heidelberg (2009), http://research.microsoft.com/pubs/122759/anoncred.pdf
11. Bernstein, D.J., Birkner, P., Joye, M., Lange, T., Peters, C.: Twisted Edwards Curves. In: Vaudenay, S. (ed.) AFRICACRYPT 2008. LNCS, vol. 5023, pp. 389–405. Springer, Heidelberg (2008), http://cr.yp.to/papers.html#twisted
12. Bernstein, D.J., Duif, N., Lange, T., Schwabe, P., Yang, B.-Y.: High-Speed High-Security Signatures. In: Preneel, B., Takagi, T. (eds.) CHES 2011. LNCS, vol. 6917, pp. 124–142. Springer, Heidelberg (2011) see also full version [13]
13. Bernstein, D.J., Duif, N., Lange, T., Schwabe, P., Yang, B.-Y.: High-speed high-security signatures. Journal of Cryptographic Engineering 2(2), 77–89 (2012), http://cryptojedi.org/papers/#ed25519, see also short version [12]
14. Bernstein, D.J., Lange, T.: eBACS: ECRYPT benchmarking of cryptographic systems, http://bench.cr.yp.to (accessed August 15, 2013)
15. Bernstein, D.J., Lange, T.: Faster Addition and Doubling on Elliptic Curves. In: Kurosawa, K. (ed.) ASIACRYPT 2007. LNCS, vol. 4833, pp. 29–50. Springer, Heidelberg (2007), http://cr.yp.to/papers.html#newelliptic
16. Bernstein, D.J., Lange, T., Schwabe, P.: The Security Impact of a New Cryptographic Library. In: Hevia, A., Neven, G. (eds.) LatinCrypt 2012. LNCS, vol. 7533, pp. 159–176. Springer, Heidelberg (2012), http://cryptojedi.org/papers/#coolnacl

17. Beuchat, J.-L., Díaz, J.E.G., Mitsunari, S., Okamoto, E., Rodríguez-Henríquez, F., Teruya, T.: High-speed software implementation of the optimal ate pairing over Barreto-Naehrig curves (2010), http://eprint.iacr.org/2010/354/

18. Boneh, D., Franklin, M.: Identity-Based Encryption from the Weil Pairing. In: Kilian, J. (ed.) CRYPTO 2001. LNCS, vol. 2139, pp. 213–229. Springer, Heidelberg (2001), http://www.iacr.org/archive/crypto2001/21390212.pdf

19. Boneh, D., Lynn, B., Shacham, H.: Short signatures from the Weil pairing. Journal of Cryptology 17(4), 297–319 (2004),
http://crypto.stanford.edu/~dabo/pubs/papers/weilsigs.ps

20. Bos, J.W., Costello, C., Naehrig, M.: Exponentiating in pairing groups. In: Selected Areas in Cryptography – SAC 2013. LNCS (to appear, 2013),
http://cryptosith.org/papers/#exppair

21. Bosma, W., Lenstra, H.W.: Complete systems of two addition laws for elliptic curves. Journal of Number Theory 53, 229–240 (1995),
http://www.math.ru.nl/~bosma/pubs/JNT1995.pdf

22. Brumley, B.B., Tuveri, N.: Remote timing attacks are still practical. In: Atluri, V., Diaz, C. (eds.) ESORICS 2011. LNCS, vol. 6879, pp. 355–371. Springer, Heidelberg (2011), http://eprint.iacr.org/2011/232/

23. Certivox. MIRACL Cryptographic SDK, http://www.certivox.com/miracl

24. Chatterjee, S., Menezes, A.: On cryptographic protocols employing asymmetric pairings – the role of ψ revisited. Discrete Applied Mathematics 159, 1311–1322 (2011), http://eprint.iacr.org/2009/480/

25. de Rooij, P.: Efficient exponentiation using precomputation and vector addition chains. In: De Santis, A. (ed.) EUROCRYPT 1994. LNCS, vol. 950, pp. 389–399. Springer, Heidelberg (1995)

26. Fardan, N.J.A., Paterson, K.G.: Lucky thirteen: Breaking the TLS and DTLS record protocols. In: 2013 IEEE Symposium on Security and Privacy, pp. 526–540. IEEE Computer Society (2013), www.isg.rhul.ac.uk/tls/TLStiming.pdf

27. Fouque, P.-A., Tibouchi, M.: Indifferentiable hashing to barreto–naehrig curves. In: Hevia, A., Neven, G. (eds.) LatinCrypt 2012. LNCS, vol. 7533, pp. 1–17. Springer, Heidelberg (2012), www.di.ens.fr/~fouque/pub/latincrypt12.pdf

28. Freeman, D., Scott, M., Teske, E.: A taxonomy of pairing-friendly elliptic curves. Journal of Cryptology 23(2), 224–280 (2010), http://eprint.iacr.org/2006/372/

29. Gentry, C., Silverberg, A.: Hierarchical ID-Based Cryptography. In: Zheng, Y. (ed.) ASIACRYPT 2002. LNCS, vol. 2501, pp. 548–566. Springer, Heidelberg (2002), http://www.cs.ucdavis.edu/~franklin/ecs228/pubs/extra_pubs/hibe.pdf

30. The GNU MP library, http://gmplib.org/ (accessed November 02, 2013)

31. Göloğlu, F., Granger, R., McGuire, G., Zumbrägel, J.: Solving a 6120-bit DLP on a desktop computer. In: Selected Areas in Cryptography. LNCS. Springer (to appear, 2013), http://eprint.iacr.org/2013/306

32. Granger, R., Page, D., Stam, M.: On small characteristic algebraic tori in pairing-based cryptography, p. 132 (2004), http://eprint.iacr.org/2004/132

33. Granger, R., Scott, M.: Faster Squaring in the Cyclotomic Subgroup of Sixth Degree Extensions. In: Nguyen, P.Q., Pointcheval, D. (eds.) PKC 2010. LNCS, vol. 6056, pp. 209–223. Springer, Heidelberg (2010)

34. Groth, J.: Short Pairing-Based Non-interactive Zero-Knowledge Arguments. In: Abe, M. (ed.) ASIACRYPT 2010. LNCS, vol. 6477, pp. 321–340. Springer, Heidelberg (2010), http://www.cs.ucl.ac.uk/staff/J.Groth/ShortNIZK.pdf

35. Groth, J., Sahai, A.: Efficient noninteractive proof systems for bilinear groups. SIAM J. Comput. 41(5), 1193–1232 (2012),
http://www0.cs.ucl.ac.uk/staff/J.Groth/WImoduleFull.pdf

36. Hess, F., Smart, N.P., Vercauteren, F.: The eta pairing revisited. IEEE Transactions on Information Theory 52(10), 4595–4602 (2006),
http://eprint.iacr.org/2006/110
37. Hışıl, H.: Elliptic Curves, Group Law, and Efficient Computation. PhD thesis, Queensland University of Technology (2010), http://eprints.qut.edu.au/33233/
38. Horwitz, J., Lynn, B.: Toward Hierarchical Identity-Based Encryption. In: Knudsen, L.R. (ed.) EUROCRYPT 2002. LNCS, vol. 2332, pp. 466–481. Springer, Heidelberg (2002), http://theory.stanford.edu/~horwitz/pubs/hibe.pdf
39. Joux, A.: A one round protocol for tripartite Diffie-Hellman. In: Bosma, W. (ed.) ANTS 2000. LNCS, vol. 1838, pp. 385–393. Springer, Heidelberg (2000), cgi.di.uoa.gr/~aggelos/crypto/page4/assets/joux-tripartite.pdf
40. Joux, A.: A one round protocol for tripartite Diffie-Hellman. Journal of Cryptology, 17(4):263–276 (2004)
41. Joux, A.: A new index calculus algorithm with complexity $L(1/4 + o(1))$ in very small characteristic. In: SAC 2013. LNCS. Springer (invited paper) (to appear, 2013), http://eprint.iacr.org/2013/095/
42. Lynn, B.: PBC library – the pairing-based cryptography library, http://crypto.stanford.edu/pbc/ (accessed November 05, 2013).
43. Mitsunari, S.: A fast implementation of the optimal ate pairing over BN curve on Intel Haswell processor (2013), http://eprint.iacr.org/2013/362/
44. Naehrig, M., Barreto, P.S.L.M., Schwabe, P.: On Compressible Pairings and Their Computation. In: Vaudenay, S. (ed.) AFRICACRYPT 2008. LNCS, vol. 5023, pp. 371–388. Springer, Heidelberg (2008), http://eprint.iacr.org/2007/429/
45. Naehrig, M., Niederhagen, R., Schwabe, P.: New Software Speed Records for Cryptographic Pairings. In: Abdalla, M., Barreto, P.S.L.M. (eds.) LATINCRYPT 2010. LNCS, vol. 6212, pp. 109–123. Springer, Heidelberg (2010), http://cryptojedi.org/users/peter/#dclxvi
46. Ohgishi, K., Sakai, R., Kasahara, M.: Notes on ID-based key sharing systems over elliptic curve (in Japanese). Technical Report ISEC99-57, IEICE (1999)
47. Osvik, D.A., Shamir, A., Tromer, E.: Cache attacks and countermeasures: the case of AES. In: Pointcheval, D. (ed.) CT-RSA 2006. LNCS, vol. 3860, pp. 1–20. Springer, Heidelberg (2006), http://eprint.iacr.org/2005/271/
48. Parno, B., Gentry, C., Howell, J., Raykova, M.: Pinocchio: Nearly practical verifiable computation. In: Proceedings of the IEEE Symposium on Security and Privacy. IEEE (2013), http://eprint.iacr.org/2013/279
49. Pereira, G.C.C.F., Simplício Jr., M.A., Naehrig, M., Barreto, P.S.L.M.: A family of implementation-friendly BN elliptic curves. Journal of Systems and Software 84(8), 1319–1326 (2011), http://cryptojedi.org/papers/#fast-bn
50. Sahai, A., Waters, B.: Fuzzy Identity-Based Encryption. In: Cramer, R. (ed.) EUROCRYPT 2005. LNCS, vol. 3494, pp. 457–473. Springer, Heidelberg (2005), http://eprint.iacr.org/2004/086/
51. Sakai, R., Ohgishi, K., Kasahara, M.: Cryptosystems based on pairing. In: The 2000 Symposium on Cryptography and Information Security, Okinawa, Japan, pp. 135–148 (2000)
52. Sakai, R., Ohgishi, K., Kasahara, M.: Cryptosystems based on pairing over elliptic curve (in Japanese). In: The 2001 Symposium on Cryptography and Information Security, Oiso, Japan, pp. 23–26 (2001)
53. Sánchez, A.H., Rodríguez-Henríquez, F.: NEON Implementation of an Attribute-Based Encryption Scheme. In: Jacobson, M., Locasto, M., Mohassel, P., Safavi-Naini, R. (eds.) ACNS 2013. LNCS, vol. 7954, pp. 322–338. Springer, Heidelberg (2013), http://cacr.uwaterloo.ca/techreports/2013/cacr2013-07.pdf

54. Scott, M.: On the efficient implementation of pairing-based protocols. In: Chen, L. (ed.) IMACC 2011. LNCS, vol. 7089, pp. 296–308. Springer, Heidelberg (2011), http://eprint.iacr.org/2011/334/

55. Scott, M., Barreto, P.S.L.M.: Compressed Pairings. In: Franklin, M. (ed.) CRYPTO 2004. LNCS, vol. 3152, pp. 140–156. Springer, Heidelberg (2004)

56. Scott, M., Benger, N., Charlemagne, M., Dominguez Perez, L.J., Kachisa, E.J.: On the Final Exponentiation for Calculating Pairings on Ordinary Elliptic Curves. In: Shacham, H., Waters, B. (eds.) Pairing 2009. LNCS, vol. 5671, pp. 78–88. Springer, Heidelberg (2009), eprint.iacr.org/2008/490/

57. Shallue, A., van de Woestijne, C.E.: Construction of Rational Points on Elliptic Curves over Finite Fields. In: Hess, F., Pauli, S., Pohst, M. (eds.) ANTS 2006. LNCS, vol. 4076, pp. 510–524. Springer, Heidelberg (2006)

58. Stam, M., Lenstra, A.K.: Efficient subgroup exponentiation in quadratic and sixth degree extensions. In: Kaliski Jr., B.S., Koç, Ç.K., Paar, C. (eds.) CHES 2002. LNCS, vol. 2523, pp. 318–332. Springer, Heidelberg (2003)

59. Tromer, E., Osvik, D.A., Shamir, A.: Efficient cache attacks on AES, and countermeasures. Journal of Cryptology 23(1), 37–71 (2010), http://people.csail.mit.edu/tromer/papers/cache-joc-official.pdf

60. Vercauteren, F.: Optimal pairings. IEEE Transactions on Information Theory 56(1) (2010), http://www.cosic.esat.kuleuven.be/publications/article-1039.pdf

61. Yarom, Y., Falkner, K.: Flush+reload: a high resolution, low noise, L3 cache side-channel attack (2013), http://eprint.iacr.org/2013/448/

Author Index